CENTURY PSYCHOLOGY SERIES

Kenneth MacCorquodale
Gardner Lindzey
Kenneth E. Clark
Editors

ESSAYS IN NEOBEHAVIORISM

Kenneth W. Spence: 1907-1967

ESSAYS IN NEOBEHAVIORISM

a memorial volume to KENNETH W. SPENCE

edited by

Howard H. Kendler

University of California, Santa Barbara

Janet T. Spence

University of Texas at Austin

New York

APPLETON-CENTURY-CROFTS
educational division
MEREDITH CORPORATION

71 72 73 74 75/10 9 8 7 6 5 4 3 2 1
Library of Congress Card Number: 79–163704

PRINTED IN THE UNITED STATES OF AMERICA
390–50340–1

ACKNOWLEDGMENTS

Pp. 1–8: "Kenneth W. Spence: 1907–1967." Reprinted from *Psychological Review*, 1967, *74*, 335–341. By permission of the American Psychological Association.

Figure 5, p. 105: Reprinted from Irving Maltzman, "Theoretical Conceptions of Semantic Conditioning and Generalization," in Theodore R. Dixon and David L. Horton, Eds., *Verbal Behavior and General Behavior Theory*, © 1968. By permission of Prentice-Hall, Englewood Cliffs, N.J.

Figures 1 and 2, pp. 122, 123: From Dennis McLaughlin, "Some Necessary Conditions for the Acquisition of Observing Responses." Unpublished doctoral dissertation, Emory University, 1968. By permission of the author.

Figure 4, p. 130: Reprinted from Charles Perkins, "Proportion of large-reward trials and within-subject reward magnitude effects," *Journal of Comparative and Physiological Psychology*, 1970, *70*, 170–172. By permission of the American Psychological Association.

Figure 1, p. 223: Reprinted from K. W. Spence and J. T. Spence (eds.), *Psychology of Learning and Motivation.* Vol. I, p. 33. New York, Academic Press, 1967. By permission of the publisher.

Figure 2, p. 224: Reprinted from John R. MacKinnon, *Interactive Effects of Two Rewards in a Differential Magnitude of Reward Discrimination.* Washington, D.C., American Psychological Association, 1967. By permission of the American Psychological Association.

Figures 4 and 5, pp. 227, 228: Adapted from Karen J. Galbraith, "Mediation in Animal Discrimination Learning." Unpublished doctoral dissertation, University of Toronto, 1969. By permission of the author.

Figure 6, p. 232: Reprinted from J. Scull, K. Davies, and A. Amsel, *Behavioral Contrast and Frustration Effect in Multiple and Mixed Fixed-Interval Schedules in the Rat.* Washington, D.C., American Psychological Association, 1970. By permission of the American Psychological Association.

Figure 1, Tables 2, 3, 5, pp. 245, 251, 257: Reprinted from T. S. Kendler, B. H. Basden, and J. B. Bruckner, "Dimensional dominance and continuity theory," *Journal of Experimental Psychology,* 1970, *83,* 309–318. By permission of the American Psychological Association.

Table 4, p. 253: From B. H. Basden, "Dimensional Dominance: Its Assessment, Interpretation, and Application as a Variable Influencing Discrimination Learning in Rats." Unpublished doctoral dissertation, University of California, Santa Barbara, 1969. By permission of the author.

Table 6, p. 260: Reprinted from T. J. Tighe and L. S. Tighe, "Overtraining and optional shift behavior in rats and children," *Journal of Comparative and Physiological Psychology,* 1966, *62,* 49–52. By permission of the authors and the American Psychological Association.

Contributors

ABRAM AMSEL	University of Texas at Austin
M. RAY DENNY	Michigan State University
G. ROBERT GRICE	University of New Mexico
HOWARD H. KENDLER	University of California, Santa Barbara
TRACY S. KENDLER	University of California, Santa Barbara
GREGORY A. KIMBLE	University of Colorado
FRANK A. LOGAN	University of New Mexico
IRVING MALTZMAN	University of California, Los Angeles
CHARLES C. PERKINS, JR.	Kansas State University
JOHN R. PLATT	McMaster University
LEONARD E. ROSS	University of Wisconsin
JANET T. SPENCE	University of Texas at Austin
BENTON J. UNDERWOOD	Northwestern University
ALLAN R. WAGNER	Yale University

Preface

This volume was prepared to honor the memory of Kenneth W. Spence as well as to acknowledge his intellectual influence.

The plans for this memorial volume were developed at an informal meeting of several of Spence's earlier doctoral students in the spring of 1968. It was recognized at that time that the number of potential contributors far exceeded the number of essays that could fit comfortably into a reasonable-sized book, and the decision was made to restrict the memorial volume to essays prepared by former doctoral students. We regret that all of Spence's students who would have liked to express their indebtedness to his ideas and ideals could not have the opportunity to contribute to this volume. This book could have profited from their contributions.

We are indebted to the American Psychological Association for permission to include the necrology of Kenneth W. Spence which originally appeared in the *Psychological Review*. The photograph of Kenneth W. Spence which appears in this volume was kindly provided by The University of Iowa Photographic Service. The royalties from this volume will be donated to the Spence Memorial Library in the Department of Psychology at the University of Iowa.

During the time that this volume was being prepared, one of the editors (H.H.K.) was a Fellow at the Center for Advanced Study in the Behavioral Sciences, and was assisted immeasurably, both in his editorial efforts and in his task of coauthoring one of the essays, by his year there.

H.H.K.
J.T.S.

Contents

ESSAYS IN NEOBEHAVIORISM

Kenneth W. Spence: 1907–1967

To the shock and despair of his friends and admirers, Kenneth W. Spence died on January 12, 1967, at the age of 59. It seemed incongruous that a man of such strength and vitality could succumb to any illness before reaching an advanced old age.

The raw facts of Kenneth Spence's life are that he was born in Chicago, Illinois, but moved, when four, to Montreal, Canada, where his father, an electrical engineer, had been transferred by Western Electric. He went to West Hill High School in Montreal and attended McGill University where he received a BA in 1929 and MA in 1930. He received his PhD in 1933 from Yale University, his doctoral thesis being sponsored by Robert M. Yerkes. From 1933 to 1937 he was a National Research Council Fellow at the Yale Laboratories of Primate Biology in Orange Park, Florida. He served as an Assistant Professor of Psychology at the University of Virginia during the 1937–38 academic year. In 1938 he was appointed Associate Professor of Psychology at the University of Iowa, where in 1942 he became Professor and Head of the Department of Psychology, a position he occupied until 1964, when he moved to the University of Texas.

Kenneth Spence was a recipient of many honors in recognition of his scientific talent and achievements including the Wales Gold Medal in Mental Sciences in 1929, the Governor-General's Medal for Research in 1930 from McGill University, the Howard Crosby Warren Medal of the Society of Experimental Psychologists in 1953, and the invitation to deliver the Silliman Lectures at Yale University in 1955. He received the APA Distinguished Scientific Contribution Award in 1956, the first year that it was presented. He was a mem-

Reprinted from *Psychological Review*, 1967, *74*, 335–341.

ber of the National Academy of Sciences and the Society of Experimental Psychologists.

For more than three decades Spence played a major role in psychology as an experimentalist, theorist, methodologist, and teacher. These different activities were carried on in an integrated manner, cemented together by an overriding concern with experimental facts. Theory, methodology, and teaching justified themselves only in the manner they contributed to the gathering and ordering of empirical data. His concern with theory, strong and persistent, was only with postulates that had apparent experimental implications. In spite of an obvious enchantment with the philosophy of science, he avoided getting entangled with subtle issues that had no bearing on his experimental and theoretical efforts. Finally, as a teacher, he judged his success by the scientific productivity of his students.

Throughout his career Kenneth W. Spence's name was associated with that of Clark L. Hull. This is understandable because Spence's efforts can be viewed as a continuation and extension of Hull's work. Their styles and contributions, however, differed in several significant ways which can best be explicated along with the description of their similarities.

Both Hull and Spence were committed objectivists, lineal descendents of Watsonian methodological behaviorism. It may seem redundant to characterize a scientist as an objectivist, but with the renewed interests in mentalistic concepts, the advent of existential psychology, and the concern in all sections of society with subjective experience, it is helpful to identify a psychologist's position along the subjective-objective continuum. Hull's objectivism was self-conscious and idealistic, expressing itself in ingenious conditioning explanations of complex behavior and in formulation of theoretical systems that emulated the structure of conceptual systems from the physical sciences. Spence's objectivism, on the other hand, was more pragmatic and realistic. Rather than merely accepting and praising objectivism, Spence searched for its fundamental tenets in the philosophy of science which were relevant to his own efforts as an empirical scientist. This led him to adopt logical empiricism as a working methodological orientation. In this facet of his career he was greatly helped by his close and productive relationship with Gustav Bergmann, the philosopher. He never believed, as some of his critics suggested, that logical empiricism could serve as a working plan for constructing fruitful concepts or viable theories. For example, he was one of the first psychologists to view operationism in its appropriate perspective. Precise operational definitions by themselves had no value. They paid off only when they were embedded in significant empirical relationships. And he noted that no recipe existed for formulating fruitful operational definitions, or theories. Logical positivism, in essence, provided Spence with a frame of reference that enabled him to gain penetrating insights into various theoretical formulations, including his own, and to make sophisticated judgments about their virtues and limitations. He regarded logical empiricism as a useful tool in the scientific enterprise but recognized originality, ingenuity, and persistence as imperatives for creative scientific efforts. In the final analysis, Spence was an objectivist who would accept anything that would both work and lead to collective understanding. In this sense, Spence, as a methodologist, was closer to the pragmatic position of Tolman than he was to the idealized attitudes of Hull.

Like Hull, and certainly through his influence, Spence approached the task of formulating a general theory of behavior through an analysis of learning. He accepted and adopted Hull's strategy of investigating what they both considered to be the basic and most elementary form of learning, classical conditioning. They both shared the view that the relationships observed in conditioning could provide the conceptual properties of some of the basic theoretical concepts used in general behavior theory with the full realization that additional constructs and principles would be needed. They were both committed to the ultimate goal that a theory of behavior must be expressed mathematically. Hull, perhaps because he began his work in learning theory rather late in his career, was impatient and impulsive, not hesitating to formulate theoretical principles when the available evidence was slight, or to engage in ambitious, but unsophisticated, mathematical theorizing. Hull was immersed in his own efforts, constantly attempting to push his formulations forward, disregarding, for the most part, competing theories and ideas. Whereas Hull often shot from the hip to score a theoretical point or suffer a miss, Spence took careful aim when engaging in conceptual tasks. Although primarily concerned with his own theoretical efforts, Spence patiently reviewed the literature and theorizing of others whose methodological commitments allowed for a fruitful comparison. He delved below the surface of what other learning theorists wrote and extracted, by creative scholarship, a frame of reference to make significant comparisons among various theorists, most notably Tolman, Guthrie, and Hull. Spence's relative cautiousness also sprang from his talent to generate several competing theoretical explanations of a single set of data. He required some empirical evidence before committing himself to one alternative. Constantly being aware of numerous theoretical possibilities curbed any temptation to premature commitments.

Like most psychologists of his generation, Spence was not well prepared in mathematics. After finishing his graduate work, Spence applied for a postdoctoral fellowship to study mathematics, but his application was rejected by a biologist who believed that psychology would never be sufficiently precise to require any sophisticated mathematical know-how. Spence nevertheless tried to improve his mathematical skills and continuously sought to represent his theoretical notions into some mathematical form, typically provisional in nature and modest in scope; but always organizing available data and providing direction for future research.

Never able to ignore the facts of the laboratory and the incompleteness of available knowledge, he looked upon applications of mathematical models to learning phenomena with some reservations. While impressed with the achievements of some mathematical models, Spence thought many to be insignificant because their empirical base was too narrow to support a general theory of learning, much less a theory of behavior. He also believed that the concern with mathematical models would divert attention away from the essential task of gathering facts on which a sound mathematical theory could be constructed. But he was reluctant to criticize mathematical models for fear that his comments would be interpreted to be opposed to their goals rather than their achievements. He was as strongly committed to the ideal of a mathematical theory of learning as the most romantic mathematical modeler.

Kenneth W. Spence's efforts in theoretical psychology are characterized by a consistent direction and a persistence that is unusual for a career that spanned almost four decades. His goals were set very early in his career, partly through the inspiration of Clark L. Hull. His style of handling problems, both empirical and theoretical, was also revealed early, changing gradually over the years only in breadth and depth.

This style is seen in a paper (Spence, 1932) on the order of elimination of blind alleys that was prepared when he was a graduate student in Hull's seminar. This effort is characterized by (*a*) a lucid prose, which was a joint product of clear thinking and hard work, (*b*) a clear and organized analysis of available data, (*c*) a proposed theoretical integration based upon the interaction among different theoretical processes, and (*d*) a simple mathematical analysis to buttress the theoretical formulation. The fundamental contribution of this paper was a conceptual analysis that structured an empirical problem so that further theoretical clarification and empirical development could take place.

One of the finest examples of Spence's style of theoretical and empirical structuring is seen in the still widely quoted analysis of discrimination learning (Spence, 1936) which appeared only three years after he received his doctorate. This theory has been criticized as being both too narrow and too general. Both criticisms are valid, but, nevertheless, inappropriate if one understands Spence's goal. He tried to identify the fundamental learning principles that operated in discrimination learning but he had no illusions that he was offering a complete picture of the discrimination process. Failing to deal with motivational or perceptual variables did not deny their existence but instead reflected a realistic conviction that the problem must be simplified if it is to be investigated fruitfully. On the other hand, Spence was aware that his theory could be made more exact but was not willing to sacrifice his goal of structuring the problem of discrimination learning for detailed treatment that would lack general implications. Imprecision or incompleteness did not bother him as long as his conceptions would generate empirical predictions, and they always did.

His discrimination theory had many ramifications including setting "lines of battle" for the continuity versus noncontinuity interpretations of discrimination learning and the creation of an ingenious analysis of the transposition phenomenon (Spence, 1937), both of which led to much productive research and theorizing.

In 1938, at the time Spence arrived at the University of Iowa, his dominant interest was in the theory of discrimination learning. As a result of certain pressures, some coming from himself, Spence's interests broadened. One such pressure resulted from Hull's manuscript of the *Principles of Behavior*. Hull and Spence had enjoyed a mutually stimulating correspondence in which they exchanged ideas and formulated new ones. This correspondence continued throughout the preparation of *Principles of Behavior*, with Spence assuming the combined role of a critic and contributor with devoted unselfishness. Hull acknowledged his efforts when he wrote in the preface ". . . Spence contributed generously and effectively with suggestions and criticisms, large numbers of which have been used without indication of their origin." Spence's efforts, although not always successful, were in general directed at broadening the empirical foundation of the theory, relating Hull's conceptions to the formulations of other theorists, including alternative "Hullian" explanations, and eliminating unnecessary material, such as the physiologizing, which tended to confuse the theoretical issues.

As already noted, Gustav Bergmann had a catalytic effect on the development of Spence's talents as a methodologist. Spence served as an able interpreter of the philosophy of science to the psychological community. His methodological talents, welded with his own activities as a learning theorist, made him a penetrating observer of the theoretical scene in the field of learning. On several occasions during his career he wrote articles and chapters comparing and contrasting the leading contemporary learning theories in a systematic fashion. He was particularly adept at penetrating the verbiage and abstracting similarities and differences that were not apparent to others.

Tolman, of all the competing theorists, interested him most. Spence designed a series of simple, clever experiments that sought to test the implications of the sign-gestalt theory of learning. Although conceived primarily as a test of Tolman's views these studies posed problems for Hullian formulations as well and revealed the inadequacies and limitations of all the general learning theories of those days. These irrelevant-incentive studies influenced Spence's ideas in three major ways. First, they made him more conscious of boundary conditions of theoretical formulations. Second, they dissuaded him from pursuing the problem of the fundamental nature of the reinforcement process. Third, and most important, these studies encouraged Spence to make wider use of the concept of the fractional anticipatory goal response which was originally proposed by Hull. He recognized that by using this concept some of the apparent theoretical differences between Tolman and himself disappeared. But he maintained that the r_g-s_g mechanism had the advantage over the expectancy concept because it was derivable from the empirical facts of conditioning and in turn could generate deductions about the conditions under which rats could form "expectations."

Because of the important role he assigned to classical conditioning where the acquisition and extinction of a response could be studied in relative isolation from the simultaneous acquisition or extinction of other responses, Spence could not avoid engaging in this research area. He developed an eyelid-conditioning laboratory and began publishing conditioning studies in 1950 and continued to do so for the remainder of his career. Whereas eyelid-conditioning studies had been used primarily to investigate associative processes, Spence saw it as a powerful tool to observe how motivation influenced the conditioning process. The research on eyelid conditioning led to a broadening of the motivational concept in Spence's thinking not only in terms of its conceptual properties but also in the range of data to which it was applied.

In 1955 Spence was invited to deliver the Silliman Lectures at Yale, a prestigious series which up to that time had been given by distinguished physical and biological scientists of the likes of Ernest Rutherford, Enrico Fermi, and Charles Sherrington. To Spence this was not only a personal honor but also a recognition of the maturity of the science he represented. He felt responsible to do justice to psychology as well as to himself. The lectures, later published as *Behavior Theory and Conditioning* (1956), reveal the intimate and fruitful reciprocal relationship between Spence's theorizing and experimentation. The entire book, much less formal than Hull's *Principles of Behavior,* is obviously in the same theoretical tradition. In both books learning and motivation are the dominant theoretical processes and they are assumed to interact multiplicatively to determine response strength. But the experimental variables that defined each of these two intervening variables changed markedly. Hull, in *Principles of Behavior,* defined learning (*habit*) broadly, in terms of widely different experimental operations, and motivation (*drive*) narrowly, in terms of a few independent variables. Spence reversed this relationship, motivation (*drive* + *incentive motivation*) was complexly determined by several different interacting experimental variables while *habit strength* was solely a function of the number of stimulus-response pairings. This greater emphasis on the motivational concept did not represent a radical change of opinion. During the time that *Principles of Behavior* was being prepared, Spence, because of his first-hand knowledge of the studies with chimpanzees that varied the magnitude of goal objects, tried to persuade Hull to assign motivational properties to this variable instead of purely associationistic properties. The Iowa irrelevant-incentive studies further suggested to Spence that the goal object could effect motivation through the mechanism of the fractional anticipatory goal response, the assumption being that the r_g-s_g mechanism has motivational properties that vary with the vigor with which it occurs. Spence also postulated that the basic mechanism determining the amount of motivation in aversive forms of stimulation is an internal emotional response. In addition, the influence of the delay of reinforcement which Hull thought to be primarily a function of time, Spence believed to be largely determined by what the animal did during the delay period. In essence then, Spence's formulation, as compared to Hull's, shifted in the direction of paying more attention to the behavior of the animal in interpreting the theoretical consequence of a given experimental variable. This difference seems inevitable if it is remembered that Hull was resolute in his determination to present his theory in a formal manner. No doubt this methodological commitment encouraged him to select postulates that could be stated simply and neatly. Spence, in contrast, more sensitive to the fine nuances of experimental data and more aware of the provisional nature of psychological theorizing, did not feel any compulsion to offer anything resembling a final solution. His aspirations were in touch with the realities of his subject matter and within these constraints he worked to interpret available data and predict new findings. His pragmatic approach to theorizing is brilliantly revealed in the concluding chapter of *Behavior Theory and Conditioning* in which he demonstrates how fundamental principles of conditioning can be applied profitably to the analysis of complex learning tasks.

In the last decade of life, Spence, in his single-minded fashion, pursued the implications of his theory while attempting to clarify and modify his formulation in light of new data. In one of his last published articles (Spence, 1966) he successfully unravelled, both theoretically and experimentally, the puzzle of the difference in the extinction rates of the conditioned eye blink in animals and men. With an ingenious technique that masked the transition from acquisition to extinction trials, Spence was able to demonstrate how the human eyelid response could proceed at the same slow rate as it does with animals. By demonstrating the independent influence of human cognitive and drive factors, Spence showed the similarities and differences between human and animal conditioning behavior and illustrated how they both could be interpreted within a common conceptual system, a goal that he believed was not only desirable but also feasible.

Although recognizing that the psychology of language required new theoretical postulates, he denied the existence of a sharp and complete discontinuity between human language behavior and the conditioning behavior of animals. Similarities and differences existed and it was the task of the experimentalist to discover both and the job of the theorist to fit them into a general theory of behavior.

Kenneth W. Spence would have preferred his necrology to be completely impersonal. If it were it would be incomplete. His empirical and theoretical contributions cannot be limited to the publications which bear his name but must also include the efforts of his 74 doctoral students, the last two from the University of Texas. Spence's impact on students was enormous, and, to understand why, it becomes necessary to describe Spence as the scholar and man.

His personality was drawn in bold lines; strong attitudes, powerful opinions, prodigious worker. He was very demanding of others, sometimes too demanding. But this was understandable, even excusable, because he was much more demanding of himself. Everything he published went through numerous drafts, and what seemed acceptable to others often failed to meet his own high standards. He prepared his lecture notes with the thoroughness that he prepared his papers. He loved to talk about psychology and once he honed in on a problem his powers of concentration were awesome. Nothing could distract him from pursuing his line of thought.

By example and dedication, and by a quaint and charming mixture of childish enthusiasm and stern paternal demands, he was able to transmit to students the excitement of theoretical psychology and the essential role that experimentation played. All of his doctoral students carry with them some of Spence's ideas and commitments and a desire to achieve a level of quality in their own work that would be acceptable to their Professor.

It is difficult to penetrate the haze of the future and locate Kenneth W. Spence's position in the history of psychology. So much depends on the direction psychology will take as well as whether it will be able to retain its integrity as a single discipline. But if we look back to help us get a peek at the future we may note that psychology, with its penchant for the novel and its rapidly shifting allegiances, has progressed forward in a spiral manner, reducing its commitment to a problem or an orientation only to return to it later better equipped. No matter what the future brings, psychology, if it is to fulfill its destiny, will have to offer a broad conception of discrimination learning, and an analysis of conditioning and learning that includes an interpretation of the interaction between motivational and learning variables, and this future formulation, in terms of its conceptual structure and empirical foundation, will bear the imprint of Kenneth W. Spence.

Howard H. Kendler

REFERENCES

Spence, K. W. The order of eliminating blinds in maze learning by the rat. *Journal of Comparative Psychology*, 1932, *14*, 9–27.

Spence, K. W. The nature of discrimination learning in animals. *Psychological Review*, 1936, *43*, 427–449.

Spence, K. W. The differential response in animals to stimuli varying within a single dimension. *Psychological Review*, 1937, *44*, 430–444.

Spence, K. W. *Behavior theory and conditioning*. New Haven: Yale University Press, 1956.

Spence, K. W. Cognitive and drive factors in the extinction of the conditioned eye blink in human subjects. *Psychological Review*, 1966, *73*, 445–451.

METHODOLOGY

Tenets of Neobehaviorism

HOWARD H. KENDLER
JANET T. SPENCE

Revolutionaries are more in agreement about what they reject than what they accept. This maxim is as true for science as it is for politics. In the history of psychology, for example, the early behaviorists unequivocally repudiated the notion that psychology is the science of the mind with introspection as its major method of investigation. Although they appeared to be united by a common goal—an objective science of psychology in which the investigator was completely detached from the behavior he was observing—it soon became apparent that the meaning of objectivity was debatable, particularly when considered in relation to *theory* and *explanation*. As a result the unity of behaviorism was replaced by a variety of behaviorisms, each with its own methodological prescriptions and commitments. One such variant is neobehaviorism, a general methodological and theoretical approach that was initiated by Clark L. Hull, but revised and extended by his many followers, most notably Kenneth W. Spence and Neal E. Miller.

Neobehaviorism, like other coherent scientific traditions, represents a network of commitments about methodological, conceptual, theoretical, and empirical matters which a particular scientific community shares—what Kuhn (1962), in short, has identified as a "paradigm." The goal of this essay is to describe the methodological commitments of neobehaviorism—its epistemological underpinnings and the strategic decisions involved in its theoretical effort. It is important to understand that these commitments do not represent a set of logically intertwined premises, each requiring support from the others. Instead they are a cluster of autonomous presuppositions which when joined together confer a distinctive character to a systematic orientation, such as neobehaviorism. Each commitment, it must be emphasized, possesses an independent existence capable of being linked to a set of entirely different preconceptions. Further, as we move from broad epistemological issues toward more empirically oriented questions of the appropriate tactics of research, we find differences of opinion appearing among those who call themselves neobehaviorists, as a number of essays in this volume will amply illustrate.

These individual independent commitments exist because systematic orientations are outgrowths of many historical trends and the personal experiences of their intellectual leaders. Some methodological decisions are carefully enunciated and adopted only after lengthy debate, while others creep into the orientation with little examination. At the time the orientation gains the allegiance of a sizable number of followers, its tenets are not explicated in detail because some are not fully understood while others are not completely recognized. Only within an historical perspective does it become possible to extract those epistemological assumptions and strategic decisions that guided the development of a particular paradigm.

In our attempt to describe the tenets of neobehavorism, we cannot help being indebted to and influenced by the writings of Kenneth W. Spence, who, because of his persistent interest in the epistemological foundations of psychology, became the most influential methodologist of the neobehaviorists.

EPISTEMOLOGY AND STRATEGY

In discussing the methodological commitments of neobehaviorism, we must first recognize that the primary concern of neobehaviorists has always been the gathering and ordering of experimental data. Concern with the philosophy of science has never been considered an end in itself, but only the means of improving empirical and theoretical efforts. Consequently the epistemological decisions of the neobehaviorists cannot be understood if limited to their philosophical implications. In fact one can argue, as we shall, that their epistemological decisions have been more an outgrowth of pragmatic than of philosophical considerations. Our discussion of the neobehavioristic epistemological orientation will therefore involve matters of experimental and theoretical strategy as well as philosophical doctrines.

Two epistemological decisions have played central roles in the history of neobehaviorism. These are that *sensory experience of the observing scientist is the basic datum of psychology*, and *explanation is equated with theoretical deduction*. The first is a direct outgrowth of behaviorism's rejection of the structuralist's view that psychology is the science of consciousness, while the second decision represents a confluence between an epistemological choice and a value judgment about the intellectual goal of the scientific enterprise. The combined impact of these two decisions, along with related strategic actions, gives neobehaviorism its distinctive character.

THE BASIC DATUM OF PSYCHOLOGY

Behaviorism can be more clearly understood when it is viewed within its historical context. When so perceived it becomes apparent that behaviorism's success has been due in part to structuralism's failures. Within the pragmatic framework of American culture, structuralism offered an unappealing conception of psychology: a subjective science that was not only restricted to a narrow set of phenomena but also incapable of resolving its own theoretical disputes by empirical methods. By accepting the assumption that psychology was in principle similar to the biological and natural sciences, behaviorism offered an attractive alternative: an objective science that would investigate a wide range of behavioral phenomena, resolve theoretical differences by experimental tests, and contribute solutions to practical social problems.

John B. Watson, who styled himself as "the behaviorist," was successful in persuading his contemporaries, and even more, following generations of psychologists, that behavior rather than consciousness should be studied. But history shows that Watson's polemics were more effective in converting psychologists to behaviorism than in providing solid epistemological underpinnings for his general methodological position. Polemics and subtle methodological analyses do not mix, and as a result most behaviorists adopted a methodological position which simply placed a premium on objectivity while simultaneously ignoring or avoiding the complex issues associated with defining or analyzing what they valued. Consequently, the epistemological justification of behaviorism had to await the efforts of second- and third-generation behaviorists.

When Watson initially rejected conscious experience as the subject matter of psychology, he limited his conclusions to pragmatic considerations; psychology, he wrote, "needs introspection as little as do the sciences of chemistry and physics [Watson, 1913, p. 176]." Although denying that analyzing consciousness was the task of psychology, he did not in his early writings deny the existence of conscious experience per se.

> If you will grant the behaviorist the right to use consciousness in the same way that other natural scientists employ it—that is, without making consciousness a special object of observation—you have granted all that my thesis requires. . . . In this sense consciousness may be said to be the instrument or tool with which all scientists work [Watson, 1913, pp. 175–176].

But in the wake of intense controversy between behaviorism and its opponents Watson later adopted such extreme positions as the exclusion of mentalistic terms from psychology and the explicit denial of the existence of consciousness. This change in position can be described as a shift from *methodological behaviorism,* which asserts that behavior can be investigated and explained without direct examination of mental states, to *metaphysical behaviorism,* which denies existence of mental states (Bergmann, 1956).

The fundamental problem with which Watson was wrestling but was unable to pin down was to describe the basic datum of psychology. This question has received much attention from the logical empiricists and their conclusions concerning the unity of all sciences seemed to provide the epistemological rationale for Watson's insistence that fundamentally psychology was no different from the physical and biological sciences. All sciences, according to this view, were public enterprises involved with describing and explaining empirical events observable to all with the requisite sensory equipment. Behavior, not consciousness, meets this requirement and the pragmatic challenge is to specify a language system that permits psychologists to communicate among themselves the descriptions as well as the explanations of publicly observable data. The proposed solution, accepted by the neobehaviorists, has been to use a vocabulary that is reducible to external objects and events. The essence of this position as it was interpreted for psychology by Spence is as follows:

> Empirical science, aiming as it does at general principles that will provide for the explanation and integration of particular events, has evolved comprehensive systems of terms (concepts) and sentences that may be arranged in a hierarchy. Highest in the hierarchy of the language of any science are the abstract terms and statements that provide for theories of wide scope and great precision. These theoretical concepts, if they are to serve this function, must be connected . . . to the terms lower in the hierarchy, and ultimately to a class of elementary, undefined terms and sentences that have direct experiential reference. Another manner of stating this is to say that all abstract, defined terms . . . must be traceable to a basic set of descriptive or observational terms [Spence, 1957, p. 98].

This statement touches upon two related problems that have proved to be a source of controversy among behaviorists. The first relates to theory and for the present it need only be noted that Spence found it acceptable to admit into the vocabulary of science abstract, theoretical concepts provided that they were connected in some fashion to the observations of the scientist. By implication, the exact terms used would be unimportant, whether mentalistic, physiological, mathematical, or purely imaginary, as long as the observational requirement was met. The second problem, to which our attention is currently directed, is the meanings that can be assigned to the phrase *direct experiential reference* and such synonymous terms as *observational terms, sense data, experiential data, descriptive terms,* and *basic observation.*

The first point is that whatever specific empirical events may constitute his basic observation, a suitable vocabulary must be developed to permit a scientist to communicate to other members of the scientific community what he has observed. For the most part psychologists with a behavioristic bent have either ignored or been unaware of the existence of a choice in vocabulary—

either phenomenalistic or physicalistic—in describing the *direct experiential reference* of the observing scientist. During the early stages of logical empiricism Carnap (1928) suggested that a phenomenalistic vocabulary (e.g., *perceiving red, feeling anger*) was appropriate for reporting the observations of the scientist. Later on he shifted his position (1934, 1936) in favor of a physicalistic vocabulary (e.g., *a spectral homogeneous light of a wave length of 660 nanometers, Johnny strikes Jimmy*). Spence's reaction to this historical development is of great significance for our understanding of neobehaviorism:

> I should prefer, *as a scientist,* to keep as far away as possible from metaphysical issues. Leaving aside all epistemological considerations, then, I would propose to accept as the criterion for the selection of this basic vocabulary of psychology the methodological requirement that its terms designate a class of observations (items or aspects of experiential data) that display the highest possible degree of intersubjective consistency. By the degree of intersubjective consistency is meant the extent to which there is agreement among observers concerning a particular observable datum [Spence, 1957, p. 99].

Thus we see in Spence's position a very explicit rejection of metaphysical consideration in favor of a simple, pragmatic rule to favor a vocabulary that generates the greatest amount of agreement among observers. This rule leads to the selection of a physicalistic, in preference to a phenomenalistic, vocabulary. It is important to recognize that this choice does not imply any metaphysical distinction. It carries no implication that a person's private conscious experience—for example, experiencing an image of a lake—is in any way less real than experiencing an external event—the lake itself. In order to guard against such an interpretation the common language distinction between *subjective* and *objective*, a distinction that implies that reality can be objectively experienced independently of the experiencing observer, has been dropped in favor of the distinction between *intrasubjective* and *intersubjective*, which acknowledges that personal conscious experience is involved in observations of both private and public events. It is not the experience itself that distinguishes private from public observations but instead the availability of the event that is being observed to the personal scrutiny of other observers. When an event can, in principle, be observed by more than one person, socially agreed-upon criteria, such as the results of physical measurement, can be adopted to encourage agreement as to what is being observed. If a person reports that a lake is green and not blue, other observers can check on the accuracy of his observations, and if necessary make appropriate physical measurements. This type of verification is not the case if the same person reports that the color of his imagined lake is green.

In sum, then, the methodological assumptions of neobehaviorism acknowledge personal observations as the foundation of scientific knowledge. The nature of man and the world makes it easier to achieve intersubjective agreement with a physicalistic language with public definitions than through a phenomenalistic language with private criteria; for these reasons, physicalistic terms are to be preferred, but phenomenalistic ones need not be barred assuming that satisfactory intersubjective reliability can be reached. The choice of a physicalistic language, then, neither denies the existence of conscious experience nor bars it from scientific investigation.

Operationism

One consequence of accepting the sensory experience of the observing scientist as the basic datum of psychology was to identify the meaning of a concept, at least partially, with its operational definition. The meaning of a term, such as *habit, intelligence,* or *closure,* is revealed in the observations of the operations or manipulations made by the scientist when his work involves that term. For example, the operational definition of length is given in the specifications of the procedure used in measurement: the successive superimposing of the ruler on the thing to be measured. Or, to use an example from psychology, the operational definition of intelligence is given in the description of the technique of intelligence testing.

The proposal that the meaning of terms should be equated with operational definitions met with a degree of enthusiasm that seems odd in retrospect. However, if we remember that structuralism and other methodological orientations that accepted the mind as the subject matter of psychology were plagued with imprecision and unresolvable theoretical disputes, it becomes understandable why a prescription that seemed to promise definitional agreement would generate overly optimistic expectations among certain segments of the psychological community.

The hope was to a large extent misplaced. Instead of accepting operationism's limited value, some psychologists overestimated its importance. Rather than perceiving it as a means towards an end, some considered it almost an end in itself (e.g., McGeoch, 1936; Seashore & Katz, 1937). By offering, or demanding from others, operational definitions, a faith was generated that conceptual ambiguities would dissipate, theoretical differences would disappear, and progress would be ensured. In reacting to such attitudes Spence was particularly helpful in clarifying the role operationism played in science.

The role of operational definitions was simply to further meaningful discourse. Misunderstanding could be reduced and, it was hoped, eliminated by tracing the meaning of an abstract term back to its observational base. But operationism did not offer a recipe that if properly followed would automatically produce fruitful concepts. *Cephalic index,* the ratio multiplied by 100 of the maximum breadth of the head to its maximum length, is operationally defined when the techniques of measuring maximum breadth and length are clearly stated. Nevertheless its elegant clarity has failed to give psychology a concept of any theoretical significance for the simple reason that no one has been able to relate cephalic index to behavior.

Because operationism was overvalued by some it was denigrated by others. A common complaint was that it tended to freeze the meaning of a concept before it could be developed into a fruitful construct. Such a criticism is inappropriate if the proper scope of operationism is realized. An operational definition is not permanent. Its meaning can be modified by the addition of new, or the elimination or modification of old, operations. Bergmann and Spence (1941) note that

> A statement such as . . . Operationism requires that all the conditions be taken into account, can be quite misleading. For a construct which unwittingly leaves out a relevant factor (or determining condition) just leads to a different formulation of the empirical laws. For example, by telling us what manipulations he performs, what pointers he reads, . . . and what computations he carries out with the numbers thus obtained . . . , a primitive physicist would give us a methodologically correct definition of his *empirical construct* "density of a liquid." And this in spite of the fact that he might not have given any attention to the temperature in his laboratory, one of the conditions upon which, as we know, and as he might not know at that state of his investigation, the results of his manipulations and computation depends. The point is that we are able to trace back the terms of his language to the immediately observable. He has laid down all the conditions under which he is going to say: "This liquid has the density 1.3." Therefore, we know what he means, and that is all general methodology can insist upon at this level of the so-called *operational definition of empirical constructs* [p. 3].

Another criticism frequently heard is that operationism places an unnecessarily heavy demand on the creative scientist. Demanding a set of operations while one is vaguely forming an idea of a concept may be too much of a burden for the creative process. Again we find a criticism that is not aimed at the proper target. Operationism does not offer a prescription for productive thinking. A scientist may have only a vague, imprecise notion of a concept when first thinking about it. When he is "thinking through" the concept, indulging in *intra*subjective communication, the requirements of operational definitions need not be considered, and certainly not met. When the realm of *inter*subjective communication is entered, which depends on the researcher's own decision, the need for operational definitions becomes compelling. But this need is not as difficult to meet as is frequently thought. If the concept during its early stages of conception has been experimentally treated, or even considered within some planned research design, then the basic ingredients for an operational definition are available. If the scientist is not willing to offer a tentative operational definition, it might be suggested that he keep the concept to himself until he is ready to meet the demands of intersubjective communication.

The turning aside of criticisms directed at operational definitions does not mean that such definitions are trouble-free. Two fundamental questions have been raised about the purity and precision of operational definitions. The first problem is whether perceptions can be immaculate. Is the observational base of operational definitions free of the preconceptions of the observing scientist? The second problem concerns the isolation of an operational definition from surplus meaning, meanings other than the denotative ones expressed by the description of the observable events.

The fundamental assumption underlying operationism is that observations can be reported neutrally; they can be perceived independently of the preconceptions and theoretical biases of the observer. Although scientists will differ about hypotheses and theories they can agree about what they are talking about —the meaning of a concept as it is used in a specific system, when the concepts are properly moored to sense data.

This conception has been attacked as an illusion, dictated more by desire than by reality. The relationship between sensing and knowledge is not simple; the scientist's observations do not purely reflect the "raw data" but instead are influenced by the observer's experiences and expectations. In short, the raw data of science are contaminated: "Observer and observed are not separable [Kessel, 1969, p. 1002]."

The results of psychological experiments have been offered to support the argument that the observational base of science is impure (e.g., Hanson, 1958; Kuhn, 1962). Kuhn, for example, cites an experiment of Bruner and Postman (1949) which indicated that when an incongruous playing card such as a black four of hearts is briefly exposed to college students, most of them identify it as a red four of hearts or a black four of spades. That is, their perceptions are not determined *exclusively* by physical characteristics of the cards but also by the conceptual categories that they previously learned, black spades and red hearts.

In evaluating the purity of sense data one must distinguish among several issues. The statement that a person's perceptions can be influenced by his past training and present set is beyond debate. Numerous experimental results support this principle. Nor is the use of psychological evidence in an epistemological analysis controversial. After all, scientific knowledge is an end product of human behavior and consequently psychological principles are relevant to epistemological analyses. Nor do we deny that a scientist's observations can be contaminated by his preconceptions. We are also not disputing the notion that theoretical commitments direct observers to attend to certain events while ignoring others. Finally, we agree that a scientist's conceptual framework will determine what observations are considered significant.

The fundamental point at issue is whether studies such as Bruner and Postman's (1949) that show that a person's preconceptions can influence his perceptions are appropriate models of scientific observations. Must observations of a given event inevitably be contaminated by an observer's theoretical bias? We believe it is possible for observations to remain independent of theoretical affiliations. And in light of this conclusion it should be noted that in the Bruner and Postman study, longer exposure times helped most *S*s correctly identify the anomalous card without difficulty. One can speculate what would have been the results of the experiment if it had been designed to reflect actual research practices. Presumably efforts would have been made to observe the significant event, the red four of spades, under optimal conditions which would have encouraged accurate identification. And if an error were made, and no doubt errors are more likely to occur when events are at odds with prevailing conceptions, then the self-correcting practice of using several observers or replicating the study would most likely have uncovered the observational error. In sum, although preconceptions may influence observations they do not necessarily have to, especially when one guards against them.

Intuitive, operational, and theoretical meanings. Our analysis of operationism has been concerned with the meaning of concepts when they are considered in isolation rather than when they are related to other concepts in an empirical proposition or in a theoretical network. The question, however, can be raised as to whether an operational definition of a construct can be completely isolated from the conceptual network in which it is embedded. Consider the meaning of the term *intelligence,* a term that is perennially involved in controversy. Operationally *intelligence* is *what the intelligence test measures.* Although such a definition is completely unsatisfying to the person who wants to know the origins as well as the structure of intelligence, the definition, in its circular manner, does contain the essential information to trace back to the sense level the operations that are used to measure intelligence. The task of describing all the operations is, of course, much more complex than is implied by the simplicity of the definition. But the fact is that a person who is knowledgeable about psychological testing understands another's usage of the term *intelligence* whether or not he believes that the particular test or set of operations on which the definition is based is useful or valid.

As has already been noted, an operational definition by itself does not guarantee the fruitfulness of a concept. Continuing with our example, there is in the case of intelligence, as measured by specific tests such as the Stanford-Binet or Wechsler-Bellevue, sufficient evidence to demonstrate the empirical utility of the concept. Yet in spite of this, the concept with its operational definition generates much confusion, not only among laymen but in scientific circles as well. The confusion is primarily generated by the failure to distinguish between operational definitions and theoretical meaning. This distinction can be exemplified by the relationship in Hull-Spence theory between the concepts of *habit* and *drive.* In a particular experimental situation *habit* might be operationally defined by the number of reinforced instrumental responses while *drive* might be operationally defined by the hours of food deprivation. Although these definitions denote the observations that define the concepts, they contribute no information as to how the two interact with each other (e.g., multiplicatively, additively, etc.) or with other constructs in the theoretical system. No information can be extracted from an operational definition that will suggest an appropriate interaction hypothesis for the simple reason that theoretical notions do not reside in operational definitions but instead in the ingenuity of the theorist.

Historical pressures in the area of intelligence testing perhaps have created conflicts between the development of operational definitions and the development of a theory of intelligence. Although Binet was interested in theoretical problems concerning intellectual functioning he ignored them in order to develop a psychological test capable of predicting school success. This pragmatic concern was shared by others who constructed intelligence tests. A psychologist interested in a theory of intelligence—its development, conceptual properties, influence on behavior—may be unwise to tie his theoretical construct to test scores. An operationally defined test may effectively serve the needs of prediction but nevertheless prove barren for the development of a theory. This point is not offered as an historical truism but instead to underline the point that theoretical structures are manifestations of the creative process and not some mechanical ordering of a set of operationally defined concepts.

The implication of our discussion is that a concept typically possesses more meaning than its operational definition. It may possess a rich intuitive meaning which the scientist strives to transform into a theoretical system with determinate empirical consequences. A concept can also possess theoretical meaning associated with hypothetical properties that specify its interaction with other constructs. The energizing (multiplicative) function of drive is an example of this kind of meaning and, as has been noted, such hypothetical properties are independent of the operational definitions.

The fundamental issue is whether the various kinds of meaning a concept possesses—the intuitive model, the theoretical properties, and operational definition—can be segregated. The implication of our analysis is that such separation is possible. Admittedly, however, the separation is easier in principle than in practice because scientists rarely isolate the three meanings in their thought processes or in their writings. But we contend that it is beneficial to recognize the distinctions that have been made, especially between a concept's operational definition and theoretical properties. Not only does the recognition of this difference contribute to a better understanding of a formulation, but it may also suggest ideas for future theoretical developments.

Thus our analysis of the neobehavioristic decision to accept sense data as the basic data of psychology and the decision which it entails to define concepts in terms of their operations leads us to conclude that these decisions are both valuable and useful for the researcher, theorist, and student. They reduce ambiguity and encourage precision of meaning. Admittedly the problem of observational contamination by theoretical commitments was not fully appreciated when the operational approach was self-consciously adopted approximately three decades ago. But once we recognize such dangers, the best safeguard against observational errors appears to be the decision to accept sensory experience as the basic data of psychology.

EXPLANATION IN PSYCHOLOGY

Contemporary psychology is confronted with an explanatory crisis. Conflicting interpretations of explanation accepted by different segments of the psychological community are at the roots of many of the significant controversies that rage within the discipline of psychology, and different conceptions of the nature of explanation appear to mold psychological knowledge into strikingly different forms.

The neobehavioristic tradition on the nature of scientific explanation clearly is at odds both with that segment of the behavioristic community (Skinner, 1950) that assumes a radical positivist position, denying any need for theories, and with varieties of phenomenology (e.g., Allport, 1955; Smedslund, 1969) which in one way or another seek the explanation of human conduct in terms of the phenomenology of the experiencing individual. After describing briefly the explanatory position of the neobehaviorists and contrasting it with competing conceptions, we will direct our main effort to clarification of the fundamental causes of the existing differences in explanatory goals and their implications for the future.

The neobehavioristic decision concerning the nature of explanation is, in principle, both clear and simple. Explanation is equated with theoretical deduction: an event is explained by deducing it from one or more general propositions. The deductive process is analogous to mathematical proof although its precision can vary from mathematical verification to the logical use of ordinary language. The constructs used in the theoretical propositions must in some manner be representative of the concepts involved in the events to be explained. In other words the theoretical constructs must be coordinated with the empirical events.

Accepting the deductive model of explanation does not imply any preference for a particular strategy, such as an axiomatic system, inductive generalizations, formulating intervening variables, reductionistic hypotheses, etc. The deductive model sets the goal for explanation but not the means by which it is to be attained.

The role of theory in science

In opposition to the deductive model of explanation is the radical positivistic position, at times enunciated by Skinner (1950), that theories are unnecessary. The scientist's task is to manipulate experimentally events that are directly observable in order to discover the facts as they are, and nothing more. One historical factor encouraging this atheoretical position was the desire of the early behaviorists to rid psychology of vague subjective concepts. A suspicion developed that the ambiguity of mentalism would reenter psychology in the form of theoretical constructs.

Skinner's atheoretical position has generated much confusion simply because it is itself unclear. It is one thing to state that at a particular time in the history of psychology the systematic collection of data without any theoretical preconceptions, but with a desire to control phenomena, may be more productive than self-conscious efforts to erect theoretical structures that cannot be supported by available empirical evidence. It is quite another thing to state that theories are unnecessary and should be ignored as a scientific goal. Skinner seems to maintain both of these positions, frequently arguing in favor of the latter, but defending it in terms of the former (see Scriven, 1956).

In truth, the denial of the significance of the theoretical goal in psychology has been more of a debator's point than a controversy that reflects in actual practice two forms of scientific effort. Skinner himself has theorized extensively, in his efforts both to systematize the variables that determine behavior and to generalize from the operant-conditioning situation to all aspects of life. But his theorizing has been covert and thus he has felt no need to defend his speculations. In addition, many of his students have discovered that scientists cannot live by facts alone and have self-consciously entered the theoretical arena (e.g., Terrace, 1968). Thus we are forced to conclude that a fundamental disagreement about one of the most central issues in science, the role of theory, does not prove to exert as great an impact as would be expected from the extent of the divergence of the competing views.

Deductive explanation vs. intuitive understanding

The issue of understanding behavior within a phenomenologically oriented psychology raises a difference that is fundamental not only in conception but also in practice. Whereas behavioristic psychology views behavior, whether of animals or men, from the "outside," just as a natural scientist observes the phenomena which he investigates, the phenomenological psychologist desires to understand behavior from the "inside" in terms of what the action means to the person who is behaving. Whereas a neobehaviorist explains behavior by deducing consequences through propositions formulated from previously observed regularities, the phenomenological psychologist explains behavior by "crawling into a person's mind" and showing how his resulting behavior was inevitable.

Implicit in this "outside-inside" difference are several independent problems that should be identified before this discussion continues. The first is the existence of phenomenal experience in man. Reference to this problem has been made previously and it was concluded that the observations of *both* private and public events involve personal conscious experience. Thus if we limit our interest to humans, who are capable of reporting subjective events, then we must conclude that the problem of accepting conscious experience as a valid event is not a source of dispute between the neobehaviorist and the phenomenologist. Two related questions are at issue. The first is whether phenomenal experience should be investigated. Assuming a positive response, the second is, How should it be done?

The decision to investigate phenomenal experience will depend upon the place one assigns to it in psychology. If phenomenal experience is considered, by definition, to be the major object of investigation, as the structuralist decided, then the only choice is to investigate it. But this justification does not entail a specific method of procedure. One possibility is to investigate phenomenological experience within a conception of science that demands intersubjective agreement and deductive explanation, the same framework that guides the work of neobehaviorists. Whether phenomenological research can meet such demands is an open question. Some psychologists either forget or ignore the point that the methods of structuralism are not the only ones that can be applied to the investigation of phenomenal experience. It can be argued that the failure of structuralism should not be interpreted as a general indictment of the pursuit of phenomenological experience, but instead as a condemnation of a particular method.

Another possibility is that phenomenological research can adopt a different epistemological framework. To pursue this alternative the distinction between *deductive explanation* and *intuitive understanding* should be made. The clearest example of deductive explanation is a successful mathematical model capable of generating deductions in agreement with empirical data. Yet models that provide only a mathematical description in the absence of any conceptual interpretation fail to generate in some psychologists an intuitive understanding of the causal foundations of a set of facts. Consider conditioning. One can represent the conditioning process exclusively in terms of mathematical changes as a function of practice or one can inject, as Estes (1959) did, a conceptual analysis (stimulus sampling) of the conditioning process. From the explanatory point of view these two conceptions, assuming the mathematical properties are the same, are not fundamentally different. However, from the viewpoint of intuitive understanding the conceptions differ in the phenomenal experience they evoke, at least for some persons.

Intuitive understanding, however, does not depend upon deductive explanation. One can obtain a sense of deep understanding of behavior from the writings of a perceptive novelist, such as Dostoevsky or Camus. One can speculate that this intuitive understanding stems from the ability of the literary work to generate empathic reactions which create in the reader an intuitive understanding of the character's, and perhaps even the reader's own, behavior. These literary descriptions possess no deductive consequences as does a logically constructed theory and therefore do not qualify as deductive explanations, even though they do generate intuitive understanding. Our aim, it should be noted, has not been to characterize all aspects of intuitive understanding, a task more appropriate for phenomenologists than for neobehaviorists, but instead to emphasize the distinction between two forms of understanding, the deductive and the intuitive.

This analysis suggests that two kinds of data, objective responses and personal phenomenal experience, and two types of interpretations, deductive explanation and intuitive understanding, are available to psychologists. Neobehaviorism has clearly opted for objective responses as the dependent variable in psychology and for deductive explanation as the method of interpretation. In opposition are varieties of phenomenological psychology which recently have become popular as a consequence of the interior immigration within all segments of society from the objective to the subjective world. These phenomenological orientations assign a central role to phenomenal experience in psychology and accept as an explanation some criterion of shared experience between an observer and the person whose behavior he seeks to understand. The objection of neobehaviorism to phenomenological psychology is not in the recognition of phenomenal experiences as an observable event, or even in acknowledging their special importance, but instead in the failure of the conceptualization and explanation of phenomenal experience to meet the requirements of their epistemological principles.

The adoption by the neobehaviorists, as well as most other experimental psychologists, of a deductive model of explanation frequently has been attributed to their frank desire to emulate physics. Assigning motivations to actions, particularly those involved in intellectual pursuits, is a tricky business and perhaps should be avoided, or at least expressed in less confident terms. Brodbeck (1962) argues that accepting the deductive model does not mean that physics is being imitated but instead that physics is being admired. The most compelling point about the deductive model is its conclusiveness. Proof is in the explanatory statements available to all, rather than in the mind of the person asserting them. In any case it may be best to consider the intrinsic worth of the deductive model instead of trying to discover the psychological reasons for its adoption. Nobody should be surprised, however, that a systematic position that values intersubjective agreement should embrace the deductive model of explanation.

THE STRATEGY OF NEOBEHAVIORISM

Epistemological decisions must be distinguished from the strategy with which any scientific discipline implements them in an attempt to develop an empirical body of knowledge. The decisions themselves, such as adopting the deductive model of explanation, do not imply any strategy by which the intent of the decision can be accomplished. The decision establishes the objectives; the strategy describes the intellectual methods used to achieve them. But since any particular strategy is not demanded by any given decision, that is, others are possible, the strategy itself is not as central to a particular orientation, such as neobehaviorism, as is an epistemological decision. Nevertheless, the strategies are important in characterizing a given systematic position because they differentiate it from other approaches that share the same epistemological commitments. Several schools of psychology considered the mind to be the subject matter of psychology but it was the strategy of observing the mind by introspection and analyzing it into its basic elements that distinguished structuralism from other mentalistic approaches. Similarly Tolman (1932) shared with neobehaviorism the epistemological decision to regard behavior as the object of study but differed in terms of the strategy he advocated in developing a theory of behavior.

Strategy of theoretical development

Neobehaviorism, in its early stages of development, chose to pursue the task of theoretical development by using classical conditioning phenomena as a source for primary theoretical assumptions. This approach was seen to possess two advantages. Principles of conditioning, considered the simplest form of learning, presumably would also enter in more complex forms of learning. Classical conditioning also was a highly controlled and flexible experimental technique that could generate additional information that would be needed to refine and expand the theoretical structure.

However, if we look upon the choice of an experimental paradigm to reflect theoretical principles in a somewhat more detached manner, other alternatives to classical conditioning in the field of learning were available. Tolman preferred T-maze learning because he believed that choice behavior was fundamental to all behavior, while Skinner chose free-operant conditioning because he felt that the probability of a response was the basic measure of behavior and that the schedule of reinforcement was the most important psychological variable. How are these discrepancies in choice of a fundamental experimental situation to be explained? Do they result from information which, if properly understood, would lead to the unanimous selection of one particular situation? Or is the choice determined by some pretheoretical model of behavior which expresses an intuitive a priori judgment about the nature of the process which is being investigated?

Neobehaviorists, particularly Hull and Spence, have argued that the classical conditioning situation is simpler than other laboratory paradigms, or at least can and typically has been arranged to be. In single and multiple T-mazes, puzzle boxes, and other trial-and-error situations popular during the initial development of neobehaviorism, performance was said to reflect the simultaneous *acquisition* of one response or response chain and *extinction* of a number of competing responses. In contrast, the relative simplicity that could be built into the classical conditioning arrangement—that is, the limited number of stimulus variables assumed to determine performance and the possibility of strict control in such matters as stimulus reception, made it the paradigm of choice for discovering many basic phenomena. Thus, not only could the acquisition and extinction of a single S-R association be studied in isolation, but other processes such as motivational and inhibitory ones could be as well. Skinner's lever-pressing paradigm—whether free-operant or discrete-trial—was characterized by Spence as "limiting cases of selective learning [1956, p. 39]," a situation in which competing response tendencies were minimized and the organism under greater external control and thus more closely approximating the classical conditioning situation.

Too little work had been done with the operant technique, in any event, to be of much assistance to the early neobehaviorists. Thus when Hull was developing his systematic behavior theory, he leaned heavily on Pavlovian concepts as well as classical conditioning phenomena in attempting to describe the basic laws of learning. Hull himself did very little research in classical conditioning. Spence, whose major early work was with discrimination learning, used phenomena discovered in the context of classical conditioning as a source of his theoretical hypotheses but did not engage in classical conditioning research until the late 1940s, his first empirical investigation being published in 1950 (Spence & Norris, 1950). His purpose in turning to classical conditioning is described in the following statements, which were intended as a broader justification of the predilection of objective psychologists to confine their research to simple laboratory situations:

> The primary criterion that has guided us in any priorities that we have given to various areas of psychological study has been our estimate of the likelihood of successful accomplishment of our aim of discovering scientific laws about the phenomena. Being guided by such purely scientific objectives, and not having any special interests, humanitarian, religious, social betterment or otherwise, no particular area of human or animal behavior is seen as more important than another. We have chosen to investigate simpler phenomena first because we are of the belief that progress in the formulation of psychological laws and theories will be more rapid in this area than in the case of more complex behavior. We also believe that many of the variables and laws isolated in the study of simpler forms of behavior will be operative in more complex instances, interacting presumably with the additional factors introduced into these more complex situations. If such is the case it would appear to be more efficient in the long run to investigate the simpler phenomena first [Spence, 1957, p. 103].

It is critical to note Spence's assumption that there are basic transsituational laws. The experimental operations defining classical conditioning are obviously not identical to those defining instrumental conditioning, yet, in theoretical terms, the growth of the learning construct, habit (H), for example, was assumed to have the same functional relationship to the number of reinforced trials (N), in both instances. His remarks further assume that experimental paradigms in which learning is being investigated can be roughly arranged on a simplicity-complexity continuum, with classical conditioning being at one extreme.

Although these arguments are reasonable they are not compelling. Justifying any given experimental situation as being more fundamental or simple than any other involves circular reasoning. The pretheoretical model demands a particular basic experimental design which in turn is justified by the same pretheoretical model. But it must be remembered that the pretheoretical model is justified not by a validated theory but only by an unproven judgment. When viewed in this light other pretheoretical models are possible, and if persuasively rationalized, equally defensible.

The analysis of the rational underpinnings of a choice of a primary source of theoretical principles is not offered as a criticism of the decision to afford classical conditioning a central role in the development of a theory of learning. No other method exists for selecting a basic experimental paradigm. Prejudgments must be made without guarantees of their eventual value. A theorist must gamble. But it must not be forgotten that the final test of a basic experimental paradigm is not the rationalization offered in its support; it is its ultimate fruitfulness.

A problem for contemporary neobehaviorists who are interested in extending their formulations to complex behavior is to judge the potential of classical and other forms of conditioning, single-trial instrumental and operant, to continue as primary sources of theoretical assumptions as well as of productive experimental procedures.

Although Spence never wavered in his belief that classical conditioning was both a fertile source of theoretical hypotheses and an invaluable experimental technique, he was always alert to the problems of boundary conditions of his theoretical formulations, particularly when verbal processes were involved. Early in his career, when discussing his discrimination-learning theory (1936), he hinted at the limitations of conditioning postulates, "It is possible only with the advent of verbal processes that the simple mechanism of learning discrimination problems we have proposed, is transcended [Spence, 1937, p. 99]." Accepting this suggestion, his student Margaret Kuenne investigated transposition in young children, and concluded that

> there are at least two developmental stages so far as the relation of verbal responses to overt choice behavior is concerned. In the first, the child is able to make differential verbal responses to appropriate aspects of the situation, but this verbalization does not control or influence his overt choice behavior. Later, such verbalizations gain control and dominate choice behavior [Kuenne, 1946, p. 488].

The acknowledgment of a theoretical distinction between single-unit behavior, which involves a response directly controlled by a stimulus (as was postulated in Spence's [1936] original discrimination theory), and mediated behavior, in which implicit symbolic responses exert control over behavior, raises the issue of whether a strategy that uses conditioning principles and heavily emphasizes conditioning as a research tool is appropriate for the analysis of verbal behavior. This issue is to some extent central to a current debate raging over the relationship between learning theory and language behavior. At one extreme is the attempt to analyze verbal behavior in terms of principles of operant conditioning (Skinner, 1957). At the other extreme is an unqualified denial that this is possible (Chomsky, 1959), or that any associative-learning theory can properly interpret the more significant aspects of verbal behavior such as language acquisition (Bever, Fodor, & Garrett, 1968). In regard to neobehaviorism, these latter arguments lose sight (a) of the skimpiness of the empirical information concerning language acquisition, (b) of the fact that most associative-learning theories, most notably neobehavioristic theory, are neither closed systems nor exclude nonassociative theoretical mechanisms including genetic ones, and (c) of the possibility that maturational factors can be considered to complement rather than conflict with learning processes.

A more reasonable position, in our view, is to consider the relevance of conditioning principles and procedures to verbal behavior as an open issue to be resolved by future achievements instead of current prejudgments. However, this strategy should not conceal the impact of certain neobehavioristic preconceptions on empirical and theoretical efforts, and thus prevent their possible reexamination. The fact that classical and other forms of conditioning have provided interesting data in the field of verbal behavior (e.g., Cerewicki, Grant, & Porter, 1968; Razran, 1961) should not encourage one to ignore the question of whether other experimental procedures might better reveal the basic phenomena of verbal behavior. And in regard to conditioning principles, a similar consideration of alternatives should be in order. When interpreting behavior, neobehaviorists tend to invoke theoretical principles that represent the influence of motivation, past training, and the present situation, to the exclusion of other possible processes, such as the behavioral capabilities of the organism. Nothing inherent in the neobehavioristic model prevents incorporation of principles based on differences in behavioral capacities whether they result from phylogenetic, ontogenetic, or individual sources. Spence was addressing himself to this kind of difference in capacity when he suggested limits on the generality of his discrimination-learning theory. He also investigated such differences when investigating the influence of emotional responsiveness on classical conditioning (Spence, 1958). And within the neobehavioristic tradition, a coordinated single-unit and mediational formulation has been proposed (Kendler & Kendler, 1968, 1970) which postulates that the ontogeny of discrimination learning is characterized by an initial stage in which the behavioral capability is limited to instrumental responses, but that with development, the child acquires the capacity to generate internal modes of representation. This mediated representational stage presumably has its own course of development with successively more abstract symbolic representations becoming available to the child as he matures.

The implication of our remarks is that conditioning may have been and perhaps will continue to be a fruitful source of empirical data and theoretical postulates, but as neobehaviorism enlarges its empirical domain, other standard experimental paradigms and theoretical processes should be considered. No recipe can be offered for successfully implementing this advice, except that actively considering new empirical and theoretical alternatives is the first step.

The role of mathematics in psychological theory

At its inception neobehaviorism explicitly and enthusiastically adopted mathematical representation of theory as a goal for psychology as it has been for physics. This decision was a natural consequence of adopting a deductive model of scientific explanation. Mathematical theorizing was not to be postponed to some future date when some signs would indicate that psychology had achieved an appropriate level of maturity. The attitude was to proceed with mathematical representation and then judge its value. The early attempts at mathematical theorizing about the goal-gradient hypothesis (Hull, 1932) and discrimination learning (Spence, 1936) succeeded in explaining certain facts and in stimulating new research and theorizing. But the mathematics used was rather simple as compared to the streamlined probabilistic models that began to appear later (Bush & Mosteller, 1951; Estes, 1950).

Perhaps the most ambitious mathematical theorizing about a broad range of phenomena in the history of neobehaviorism was Hull's *Principles of Behavior* (1943). As a mathematical formulation it was largely unsuccessful, although it did encourage the development of later mathematical theories. In certain respects, aside from its relatively primitive mathematical base, it was different from contemporary models. Hull aspired to formulate a set of theoretical postulates that would be relevant to all forms of behavior. Although this expressed a self-conscious romantic ideal it nevertheless shaped the subsequent development of neobehaviorism. It led, among other things, to the tactic of selecting intervening variables which presumably possessed broad theoretical implications.

The aspiration to formulate a general behavior theory was shared by some of the early mathematical modelers; Estes (1950), for example, conceptualized the learning process in terms of stimulus sampling, an interpretation that also possessed general implications for a wide range of learning and motivational phenomena. But interest in mathematical models with broad implications seemed to dissipate in proportion to the increased concern with the fine-grain analysis of various properties of the learning process. Over the years mathematical models have moved toward more circumscribed representations of empirical events. Within a historical context, the more modest aspiration of the mathematical modelers in regard to a general behavior theory can be viewed as an appropriate reaction to the lack of success of such general theorists as Hull, Lewin, Tolman, and Koffka. Even within the neobehavioristic tradition one can observe a definite backtracking from the goal of general behavior theory to the development of more specific formulations. Whereas Hull (1943) regarded his *Principles of Behavior* "as a general introduction to the theory of all the behavioral (social) sciences [p. v]," Spence (1956) more cautiously described his *Behavior Theory and Conditioning,* which actually covers a wider range of empirical phenomena, as having "as its primary purpose the integration (derivation) of [data from a number of simple conditioning situations and] . . . to show how the theory . . . may be extended to more complex types of behavior phenomena such as selective and paired-associate learning [p. vi]." And as the following essays suggest, most of the current theoretical attempts within the neobehavioristic tradition have been concerned with an even more restricted range of phenomena.

Perhaps general theories that cover an entire scientific discipline or even a large area within it are unrealizable dreams, especially in psychology. But the neobehavioristic tradition of pointing one's formulations in the direction of general theory will no doubt persist. It will be expressed by theoretical constructs with conceptual properties that extend beyond the empirical confines of a specific experimental paradigm. The success of such efforts will depend on the standards set for the theoretical deductions both in regard to their level of precision and the range of data involved. Precision and generality can be countervailing forces in the development of psychological theories and any orientation that simultaneously seeks to achieve both, as did neobehaviorism, is perhaps bound to suffer failures in each.

Stimulus-response language

Of all the strategies that the neobehaviorists have adopted, the choice of stimulus-response associationism as a theoretical framework has generated the greatest opposition and the most controversy. To some extent the source of the dispute lies in the fact that the concept of S-R associationism has several facets. Mistaken interpretations added to these multiple meanings have generated needless disputes and confusion. To make a proper assessment of S-R associationism, it is imperative to treat the various components separately.

One of us (Kendler, 1965) has suggested that the S-R concept can be divided into four components: (a) a technical language that analyzes psychological events into three major categories: stimuli, responses, and the associations between them, (b) a methodological orientation that can be succinctly characterized as physicalistic, operational, and experimental (Estes, 1959), (c) a pretheoretical model that is used as an informal conception of behavior and operates as an analogy (e.g., concept formation is conceived as analogous to discrimination learning), and (d) a group of theories with different, and frequently conflicting, theoretical assumptions.

Of these four components only the first and third qualify as strategic decisions. Since the third has already been discussed when we evaluated classical conditioning as a paradigm for other forms of behavior, we will now examine the first category—the implication of using S-R language.

Stimulus-response language, as we have said, is used to represent psychological phenomena in terms of three important sets of variables: stimuli, responses, and the association—the hyphen—between them. This language can be applied to both empirical events and theoretical constructs. On the empirical level, an auditory conditioned stimulus in classical conditioning could be defined by the frequency of the sound waves and the response by the frequencey of the conditioned eyeblink. The association between them, on the purely empirical level, is represented by the functional relationship between the two. But these three constructs can be conceptualized as possessing abstract properties above and beyond their specific empirical referents. A sound wave belongs to a class of physically or socially defined events (e.g., a light wave of 660 nanometers, an American flag) that possess a tendency to evoke a response. Similarly, an eyeblink response belongs to a set of events that characterize physical or social attributes of an organism's behavior (e.g., leg flexion, a hostile remark) which are functionally related to stimulus events. Stimuli and responses can also be inferred; a child of a certain mental age who is discriminating between sets of pictures of animals and fruits can be assumed to be making implicit conceptual responses appropriate to each picture and these inferred responses can be assumed to produce cues that control his discriminative behavior. The justification of such inferences obviously depends on their value for interpreting data.

Stimulus-response language, either when used to refer to empirical events or to characterize theoretical processes, is not demanded by the nature of psychology. Its justification is purely pragmatic, and the verdict of neobehaviorism is that S-R language can play a useful role both in collecting data and in constructing a theory. The exact influence of S-R language on neobehaviorism is difficult to assess because no historical comparison is available between neobehaviorism and a similar orientation with a different language system. In isolating the influence of S-R language, it therefore becomes necessary to identify those special characteristics of neobehaviorism that seem to emanate from its adopted language.

Probably the greatest impact of S-R language on neobehaviorism and other systematic positions that use this language is that it forces psychologists to think in terms of manipulable environmental variables and measures of objective behavior. To use the language properly one must specify characteristics of both the environment and behavior. Identifying these two sets of variables stimulates research directed at relating them and simultaneously forces the theorist to specify the dependent variables he seeks to predict. In sum, S-R language clarifies the experimental and theoretical task of the psychologist by focusing attention on the empirical relationships to be investigated and explained.

Neobehaviorists adopted stimulus-response language because it represented important traditions from which their orientation emerged: British associationism, classical conditioning methodology, and a methodological commitment to objectivity. Because of this background, the use of S-R language encouraged learning research while it simultaneously slighted perception and many nonassociative processes. The significant question is whether some intrinsic characteristic of S-R language makes it difficult or impossible to incorporate other than learning processes within its representational system. We think not; neobehaviorism from its inception has shown a concern for motivational processes and more recently has attempted to deal with problems of perception and representational responses (as several essays in this volume illustrate). Constructs other than stimulus, response, and association can and have been incorporated into an S-R theoretical representation.

Stimulus-response language has no doubt encouraged neobehaviorists to investigate how behavior changes (e.g., lever pressing, an approach response to black) as a function of practice in a relatively unchanging environment. This interest reflects the concern with the theoretical construct of habit which conceptually characterizes the change in the tendency of a particular stimulus to evoke a particular response. The concept of habit works well in explaining facts from situations in which the response measure remains unchanged throughout the experiment. But in transfer of training designs where the organism is required to exhibit new responses, neobehaviorists, as well as other S-R psychologists, are confronted with the task of postulating theoretical mechanisms that will permit one particular response to be transformed into another. It is an open question whether this can be accomplished most effectively by (a) formulating principles that govern relationships among different response systems via some mechanism of response generalization or by (b) postulating response systems that are organized into some hierarchical system in which the acquisition of a superordinate response will enable an organism to respond appropriately to a range of situations. S-R language itself does not imply any universal principle about the specificity of the learning process. Instead it encourages theoretical response-estimates, thus avoiding the embarrassment, as Guthrie (1952) once remarked in discussing Tolman's cognitive theory, of leaving the organism "buried in thought [p. 143]."

All theories that accept behavior as the dependent variable in psychology must be response theories in the sense of yielding theoretical estimates of behavior; and the nature of the S-R language, as noted, helps to ensure that this demand will be met. Nevertheless it must be recognized that it is most difficult to meet this demand, and probably elaborate modifications of the theoretical structure will be required when problems of transfer of training, particularly in human intellectual tasks, are analyzed.

Physiology and psychology

Discussions about the relationship between behavior and physiology frequently have been marked by extreme positions, such as assumptions that behavior *must* be explained in terms of physiological events, or that it *cannot* be so explained. For the most part, neobehaviorists have been free from such prejudices, although they have tended to take an aphysiological position. Spence in particular shared Tolman's early view that "psychological facts and laws have . . . to be gathered in their own right. A psychology cannot be explained by physiology until one has a psychology to explain [1936, p. 92]." This strategy served both as a justification and an impetus for purely behavioral research. But the strategy that has been followed through the years neither prejudges nor prescribes the nature of the relationship between the two disciplines, but instead permits the state of knowledge to dictate whether the development of a theory of behavior can be assisted by physiological procedures and information. Within such a framework the empirical problem determines the relevance of physiology to psychology. Rarely do sensory psychologists ignore physiology, while only a small minority of social psychologists consider physiological processes.

The relevance of the neurophysiology of the time to the major concern of most neobehaviorists, the psychology of learning, has always been difficult to gauge. Hence the wisdom of interpreting learning within a physiological framework has been a source of disagreement, even among neobehaviorists. Hull felt compelled to offer some highly problematical physiological analogue to his theoretical constructs while Spence expressed a fear that such speculations would produce confusion and avoided any physiological interpretations of his theories. However, in 1956 he wrote,

> With the advent of the functional and behavioristic viewpoints interest in physiological research declined markedly until it now represents a relatively small proportion of the current research activity of psychologists. Presumably, as psychology attains a fairly well-developed body of environmento-behavioral laws, more and more attention will once again be directed to these physiological variables [Spence, 1956, p. 17].

Soon after he wrote this Spence's prediction was borne out by a rapid increase in physiologically oriented research among psychologists, although the increase resulted more from the impact of the development of new electrical brain stimulation techniques than from the advances in behavior theory. The greater knowledge of behavioral laws served as a framework to judge the influence of specific physiological variables. Within the neobehavioristic tradition, the efforts of Neal Miller exemplify how physiological techniques can be combined with behavioral research to illuminate psychological theory.

The fundamental epistemological relationship between behavior and physiology has for the most part been ignored. This is understandable because at present our knowledge of both is so incomplete that questions about their ultimate relationship seem almost irrelevant. But perhaps something can be gained from considering the meaning of reductionism, so that strategies which demand or reject it as an achievable goal can be evaluated.

To assume that behavior can be reduced to neurophysiology depends not only upon formalizing a behavior theory, as Tolman (1936) suggested, but also a neurophysiological theory. If the primary assumptions of the behavior theory can be deduced from the neurophysiological theory, then it can properly be stated that behavior has been reduced to neurophysiology. Expressed in this fashion reductionism is a much more demanding task than is usually realized when one casually assumes that behavior can be reduced to neurophysiology.

Problems of reductionism have contemporary significance for only those areas of sensory physiology in which certain perceptual phenomena can be predicted from our knowledge of patterns of neural impulses (e.g., Ratliff, 1965). For the rest of psychology the closest approach to reductive success has been in the *interpretation* of behavior in terms of neurophysiological processes. Examples are the interpretation of reinforcement in terms of electrical changes in the brain (Olds & Olds, 1965) or the interpretation of motivation in terms of hypothalamic functioning (Stellar, 1954).

Although these interpretations are in the direction of reducing behavior to physiology, two points must be recognized. First, such interpretations are far removed from formal reduction, and second, the reduction of behavior to neurophysiology is not inevitable. Kaplan's (1964) reaction to the question of whether laws of behavior are reducible to laws of neurophysiology (or chemistry or physics) summarizes rather well a position that would be consistent with the pragmatic orientation of neobehaviorism:

> An affirmative answer . . . as a matter of doctrine, seems to be . . . both unwarranted and useless. . . . As a methodological presupposition . . . it provides a valuable perspective in which the behavioral scientist can see continuing possibilities for turning to his own use the findings of other sciences. But the significance of such possibilities appears only as they are actualized; otherwise their affirmation expresses only a hope. It may well be that the psychologist can derive the whole of his discipline from neurology, biochemistry and the rest: it is not destructive skepticism but productive pragmatism to say, "I'd like to see him do it!" [Pps. 124–125]

Phenomenology and behavior

Reference has already been made to the distinction between *metaphysical behaviorism* and *methodological behaviorism* (Bergmann, 1956), the former denying the existence of mental states, the latter asserting that behavior rather than mental states is the primary datum of psychology. Watson ultimately adopted the extreme position of metaphysical behaviorism in his polemics against structuralism but neobehaviorism, as has been noted, had to reject such a position if only to be consistent with its assumption about the fundamental role of experiential data in scientific knowledge and the importance of achieving intersubjective agreement in scientific communication. The doctrine of *methodological behaviorism,* adopted by neobehaviorism, demands that the dependent and independent variables, as well as the theoretical constructs, be defined in terms of intersubjectively agreed-upon events.

What, if any, role can phenomenal experience play in neobehaviorism? A person's behavior cannot be explained by his state of mind, certainly, because his private experience is unavailable to the inspection of other observers. But a person's report of his inner state, expressed as a verbal description or as a pattern of responses to a series of questions in a personality inventory, is a public event. Observers can agree on what the person said or what his inventory responses were; in principle, these self-reports are no different than any other type of behavior, and may therefore enter into an explanatory system. This epistemological position is succinctly expressed in Max Meyer's (1921) informative title of his book, *The Psychology of the Other One.* Thus personal phenomenal experience is excluded from any formal explanation of behavior, but reports of such events are not if they are used within a theoretical network that meets both the demands of intersubjective agreement of meaning and the demands of the deductive model of explanation. The methodological disagreement between the phenomenologist and the neobehaviorist, then, is that while the former tends to regard self-report as having a high degree of correspondence with private experience and thus acts as though these experiences were raw data, the neobehaviorist makes no further assumptions and gives verbal reports no special status.

Whether or not phenomenological data (i.e., self-reports) should be incorporated into a neobehavioristic system is another issue. Three possible strategies suggest themselves. (a) The first is to ignore such data, the argument being they cannot help, and possibly can harm by sowing confusion and directing attention from significant variables. Using arguments of this sort, behaviorists such as Skinner, to give only a contemporary example, have spurned the introduction of phenomenological experience into their system. Neobehaviorists have been less militant although they have never used introspective data extensively, in part because of their historical identification with the early behavioristic struggle to reject mind as the subject matter of psychology, but also because of their preoccupation with relatively simple experimental situations. Much of their research has involved animal *S*s, and more recently young children, thus precluding the use of phenomenal data. In instances where adult human *S*s were used, the theoretical model implicitly suggested that phenomenal data would not be particularly useful, a position that has been challenged with increasing frequency in recent years. (b) The second possibility is to use phenomenal reports as a source of theoretical hypotheses. For example, in the study of memory, where encoding processes are beginning to assume a central theoretical role, introspective reports can serve as a rich source for stimulating, interesting conjectures. (c) The third alternative is to develop a theoretical structure to represent conscious experience. The rationale for such an effort, a model of the mind, is that in many situations the most useful information for predicting behavior would be introspective evidence. If this is so, a theoretical representation of inner states could prove to be a fruitful model in interpreting behavior.

It may very well prove that a uniform strategy for relating phenomenology to behavior will not be the most effective method because each strategy might have special advantages for particular forms of behavior. The key methodological issue in treating phenomenal experience within neobehaviorism is to recognize that the *S*'s phenomenal data, unlike those of the experimenter, are inferred, and not directly observed. Since phenomenal experience is inferred, and not directly observed, its epistemological status is that of a theoretical construct instead of a raw datum.

The key pragmatic issue, and one that can be easily overlooked, is that the *S*'s observation of his own phenomenal experience is not a simple task devoid of all subtleties and complexities. The history of structuralism and other mind-oriented psychologies testifies to this point. Perceptions of external events are influenced not only by what the *S* observes, but by how he observes it. The same principle no doubt operates with self-observation (see Natsoulas, 1970). The potential contributions of phenomenal experience to behavior theory will no doubt vary with the methods used by *S*s to observe and report phenomenological events.

CONCLUDING REMARKS

Almost a hundred years have passed since the establishment of the first psychological laboratories; psychology is beginning to have a history as well as a past. Although the goal of this essay has been to describe the epistemological bases and strategic decisions of neobehaviorism, an appreciation of even these purely methodological commitments requires that neobehaviorism be placed in historical context.

By the turn of the century functionalists such as Dewey and Angell had broadened the limited view of the structuralists that psychology had consciousness as its subject matter, to include as well the study of behavior. But it was not until the 1910s that Watson carried the functionalist movement to its logical extreme by proposing that psychology be solely the science of behavior. Spirited intellectual battles over what kind of a science psychology was to be ensued, and it was not until the early 1930s that it could safely be said that experimental psychology in this country had cast its methodological lot with behaviorism.

The struggle over, the period of the 1930s and early 1940s was highly creative, as behaviorism sought to find a solid methodological base, as well as to get on with the business of developing a science of psychology. The intervening variable approach to theorizing was introduced by Tolman (1936), while Hull became intrigued with the method of formal postulates which he used most formidably in his *Mathematico-Deductive Theory of Rote Learning* (1940). Stimulated by the contributions of logical empiricists such as Carnap (1934), the epistemology of behaviorism was developed, most notably by Spence, often in collaboration with the philosopher Gustav Bergmann.

During this same period, there appeared three remarkable books, all behavioristic in orientation, whose influence dominated experimental psychology for the next several decades: Tolman's *Purposive Behavior in Animals and Men* (1932), Skinner's *The Behavior of Organisms* (1938), and Hull's *Principles of Behavior* (1943). Tolman's intellectual ancestry was closer to European phenomenology, with its emphasis on perception and organization, than to British associationism, but he shared with Hull and Skinner the methodological tradition of behaviorism and a commitment to a deductive theoretical model. Of the three attempts to develop a general behavior theory (Skinner's rejection of theory for the ultrapositivistic approach came later), Hull's was the most ambitious in its detail and theoretical formality and proved to be the most immediately and directly influential.

The early neobehaviorists were infected by a heady optimism. Having found the proper direction in which to go and the methodological vehicles to take them, they believed not only that a general behavior theory was possible to construct but that its development would be relatively rapid. Scientific progress would be further facilitated, they believed, if instead of complex learning and cognitive processes, "simple" phenomena such as classical and instrumental conditioning were studied first. The lack of success of their predecessors and contemporaries in advancing scientific understanding of "complex" phenomena gave impetus to the tactic of using conditioning as a source of deductive principles.

The easy optimism of the early years has not been justified, even "simple" situations proving to be unexpectantly recalcitrant to both empirical and theoretical analysis. Neobehaviorists have largely abandoned their attempts to erect a theoretical structure with broad implications, and along with others with whom they share the behavioristic tradition, including most of the builders of mathematical models, attack limited problem areas about which they develop "miniature systems."

Emboldened perhaps by the successes of neobehaviorism as well as by its failures, and often guided by theoretical models of quite different origins, many contemporary psychologists have redirected their interests to cognitive-perceptual problems which neobehaviorism historically has tended to slight, either because of its preoccupation with learning or of its tactical decision to concentrate on the investigation of relatively simple phenomena. At least the more enthusiastic proponents of these new theoretical developments claim for them the same broad, all-encompassing implications that were the original goal of neobehaviorism. Whether these or any general theoretical efforts will succeed, or whether problem areas rather than general theories will prove to be the cohesive force of the future cannot yet be foretold.

With the death of Clark L. Hull and Kenneth W. Spence, the two most eminent of the neobehavioristic theorists and the driving forces in erecting a theoretical structure with broad implications, perhaps the neobehavioristic tradition will merge with other less ambitious behavioristic orientations. Hull aspired to be a Newton, while Spence would have been pleased to be a Galileo. In fact their influence may prove to be more like that of Darwin: providing a conception that structured a field and led to subsequent discoveries and theoretical developments. This comment does not suggest that a neobehavioristic theoretical model has achieved a level of integrating facts resembling that of Darwin's theory of evolution—no psychological theory has. But it does imply that both conceptions share a common quality of relative imprecision by the standards of physical sciences but nevertheless offer integrative power and heuristic value.

Only the future can tell whether the boundaries between neobehaviorism and other objectively oriented psychologies will continue to become fainter and finally disappear or whether neobehaviorism will, among future generations of psychologists, retain and sustain some of its original character.

REFERENCES

Allport, G. *Becoming: Basic considerations for a psychology of personality.* New Haven: Yale University Press, 1955.

Bergmann, G. The contributions of John B. Watson. *Psychological Review,* 1956, *63,* 265–276.

Bergmann, G., & Spence, K. W. Operationism and theory construction. *Psychological Review,* 1941, *48,* 1–14.

Bever, T. G., Fodor, J. A., & Garrett, M. A formal limit of associationism. In T. R. Dixon & D. L. Horton (Eds.), *Verbal behavior and general behavior theory.* Englewood Cliffs, N.J.: Prentice-Hall, 1968. Pp. 582–585.

Brodbeck, M. Explanation, prediction, and "imperfect" knowledge. In H. Feigl & G. Maxwell (Eds.), *Minnesota studies in the philosophy of science.* Vol. III. Minneapolis: University of Minnesota Press, 1962. Pp. 231–272.

Bruner, J. S., & Postman, L. On the perception of incongruity: A paradigm. *Journal of Personality,* 1949, *18,* 206–223.

Bush, R. R., & Mosteller, F. A. A mathematical model for simple learning. *Psychological Review,* 1951, *58,* 313–323.

Carnap, R. *Der logische Aufbau der Welt.* Leipsig: F. Meiner, 1928.

Carnap, R. *The unity of science.* London: Kegan Paul, Trench, Trubner, 1934.

Carnap, R. Testability and meaning. *Philosophy of Science,* 1936, *3,* 419–471; 1937, *4,* 1–40.

Cerewicki, L. E., Grant, D. A., & Porter, E. C. The effect of number and relatedness of verbal discriminanda upon differential eyelid conditioning. *Journal of Verbal Learning and Verbal Behavior*, 1968, *7*, 847–853.

Chomsky, N. A review of B. F. Skinner's "Verbal Behavior." *Language*, 1959, *35*, 26–58.

Estes, W. K. Toward a statistical theory of learning. *Psychological Review*, 1950, *57*, 94–107.

Estes, W. K. The statistical approach to learning theory. In S. Koch (Ed.), *Psychology: A study of a science*. Vol. 2. New York: McGraw-Hill, 1959. Pp. 380–491.

Guthrie, E. R. *The psychology of learning*. (Rev. ed.) New York: Harper & Row, 1952.

Hanson, N. R. *Patterns of discovery*. Cambridge: Cambridge University Press, 1958.

Hull, C. L. The goal gradient hypothesis and maze learning. *Psychological Review*, 1932, *39*, 25–43.

Hull, C. L. *Principles of behavior*. New York: Appleton-Century, 1943.

Hull, C. L., Hovland, C. I., Ross, R. T., Hall, M., Perkins, D. T., & Fitch, F. B. *Mathematico-deductive theory of rote learning*. New Haven: Yale University Press, 1940.

Kaplan, A. *The conduct of inquiry*. San Francisco: Chandler, 1964.

Kendler, H. H. Motivation and behavior. In D. Levine (Ed.), *Nebraska symposium on motivation*, 1965. Lincoln: University of Nebraska Press, 1965. Pp. 1–23.

Kendler, H. H., & Kendler, T. S. Mediation and conceptual behavior. In K. W. Spence & J. T. Spence (Eds.), *Psychology of learning and motivation*. Vol. 2. New York: Academic Press, 1968. Pp. 197–243.

Kendler, H. H., & Kendler, T. S. Developmental processes in discrimination learning. *Human Development*, 1970, *13*, 65–89.

Kessel, F. S. The philosophy of science as proclaimed and science as practiced: "Identity" or "dualism"? *American Psychologist*, 1969, *24*, 999–1005.

Kuenne, M. R. Experimental investigation of the relation of language to transposition behavior in young children. *Journal of Experimental Psychology*, 1946, *36*, 471–490.

Kuhn, T. S. *The structure of scientific revolutions*. Chicago: University of Chicago Press, 1962.

McGeoch, J. A. The vertical dimensions of mind. *Psychological Review*, 1936, *43*, 107.

Meyer, M. F. *Psychology of the other one*. Columbia, Missouri: Missouri Book, 1921.

Natsoulas, T. Concerning introspective "knowledge." *Psychological Bulletin*, 1970, *73*, 89–111.

Olds, J., & Olds, M. Drives, rewards, and the brain. In *New directions in psychology*. New York: Holt, Rinehart and Winston, 1965. Pp. 329–410.

Ratliff, F. *Mach bands*. San Francisco: Holden-Day, 1965.

Razran, G. The observable unconscious and the inferable conscious in current Soviet psychophysiology: Interoceptive conditioning, semantic conditioning, and the orienting reflex. *Psychological Review*, 1961, *68*, 81–147.

Scriven, M. A study of radical behaviorism. In H. Feigl & M. Scriven (Eds.),

Minnesota studies in the philosophy of science. Vol. 1. Minneapolis: University of Minnesota Press, 1956. Pp. 88–130.

Seashore, R. H., & Katz, R. H. An operational definition and classification of mental mechanism. *Psychological Record,* 1937, *1,* 3–24.

Skinner, B. F. *The behavior of organisms.* New York: Appleton-Century, 1938.

Skinner, B. F. Are theories of learning necessary? *Psychological Review,* 1950, *57,* 193–216.

Skinner, B. F. *Verbal behavior.* New York: Appleton-Century-Crofts, 1957.

Smedslund, J. Meanings, implications and universals: Towards a psychology of man. *Scandinavian Journal of Psychology,* 1969, *10,* 1–15.

Spence, K. W. The nature of discrimination learning in animals. *Psychological Review,* 1936, *43,* 427–449.

Spence, K. W. Analysis of the formation of visual discrimination habits in chimpanzee. *Journal of Comparative Psychology,* 1937, *23,* 72–100.

Spence, K. W. *Behavior theory and conditioning.* New Haven: Yale University Press, 1956.

Spence, K. W. The empirical basis and theoretical structure of psychology. *Philosophy of Science,* 1957, *24,* 97–108.

Spence, K. W. A theory of emotionally based drive (D) and its relation to performance in simple learning situations. *American Psychologist,* 1958, *13,* 131–141.

Spence, K. W., & Norris, E. Eyelid conditioning as a function of the intertrial interval. *Journal of Experimental Psychology,* 1950, *40,* 716–720.

Stellar, E. The physiology of motivation. *Psychological Review,* 1954, *61,* 5–22.

Terrace, H. S. Discrimination learning, the peak shift, and behavioral contrast. *Journal of Experimental Analysis of Behavior,* 1968, *11,* 727–741.

Tolman, E. C. *Purposive behavior in animals and men.* New York: Appleton-Century, 1932.

Tolman, E. C. Operational behaviorism and current trends in psychology. In H. W. Hill (Ed.), *Proceedings, 25th American celebration of the inauguration of graduate studies, The University of Southern California.* Los Angeles: The University of Southern California Press, 1936. Pp. 89–103.

Watson, J. B. Psychology as the behaviorists view it. *Psychological Review,* 1913, *20,* 158–177.

CONDITIONING

A Theory of Experimental Extinction and Its Relation to a General Theory

M. RAY DENNY

INTRODUCTION

Back in the middle and late 1940s, at least for Iowa students, there were two main conceptions of inhibition (extinction)—Hull's theory of response-generated inhibition (Hull, 1943) and some sort of frustration notion, including the earliest ideas of Rohrer (1949). At Iowa the climate for theorizing about frustration and extinction was excellent: Spence was consistently critical of Hull's concept of reactive inhibition (I_R) as applied to the extinction of molar behavior and quite leniently disposed toward frustration as a mechanism to mediate the effects of nonreward (Spence, 1936). In this context he pointed out that Hull had, in fact, previously invoked frustration to account for extinction effects (Hull, 1934).

In doctoral research under Spence (Denny, 1946) I was therefore alert to what the rat did on those occasions when it was nonreinforced, and I was impressed with what I saw. In three different situations involving nonreinforcement, numerous rats exhibited similar, characteristic behaviors. In the first of these, the circumstances were as follows: during pretraining in a runway some *S*s received limited discriminative training designed to facilitate the development of secondary reinforcement, say, to a positive white chamber as opposed to a negative black chamber. Sudden halts, rapid recoiling, retracing, and attempts to escape the alley were often observed when the negative chamber was at the end of the alley, especially in the later stages of this training. The same sort of behavior occurred in the intermediate and later stages of T-maze training on those occasions when *S* received forced trials to the incorrect arm of the T. Once *S* had learned the correct response fairly well and was responding correctly on the two initial free trials of each day, the forced trials were being rather consistently nonreinforced, with the result that frustration-instigated behaviors could be observed on these trials. Typically, but just for a trial or two, withdrawal responding was first noted when *S* looked into the distinctive negative end box; then withdrawal occurred most frequently just after *S* had entered the arm on the nonreinforced side; finally *S* refused to enter the negative arm and stayed in the stem, where it was removed after 90 sec. The initial extinction trials constituted the third situation in which I observed these same behaviors occurring. Here attempts to escape the original goal box, which I had heretofore not observed in this experiment, were especially noted. I will never forget one rat's behavior on its very first extinction trial. The rat leaped so hard and high that it knocked the top off the foot-high goal box and landed on the upper edge of the box, and when I picked it up from the ledge it jumped from my hand onto the floor. These observations and countless others like them (e.g., Spence, 1960, p. 97), combined with other considerations, have made it difficult for me to accept the suggestion of some theorists (Capaldi, 1967; Skinner, 1938) that it is unnecessary to posit active inhibitory effects in our explanations of discrimination learning and experimental extinction.

So it is not surprising that in 1945–46 in my first post-PhD study using rats I attempted to pit sheer response against frustration to determine the relative role each played in producing extinction effects. About all that was accomplished at this time was working out a procedure that looked promising. This idea lay dormant until 1950 when Jack Maatsch, under my sponsorship, did his MA research on the problem (Maatsch, 1951).

Maatsch's study as the origin of elicitation theory

The rationale for Maatsch's experiments flowed directly from a two-factor approach to inhibition. In such a theory one factor is intrinsic inhibition (I) or a negative drive state whose effects dissipate with the passage of time; the second factor is an interfering response which is learned on the basis of the reduction of this negative drive. According to Hull, the negative drive (I_R) is a function of responding per se and thus independent of nonreward. I_R inhibits the response that generated this state. According to one common interpretation of Hull, when this drive is reduced by the nonoccurrence of the original response (R_o) this event reinforces some kind of interfering response, such as a resting response. This hypothetical process of the development of a response which competes with R_o Hull labeled conditioned inhibition (${}_SI_R$). Rohrer's treatment of frustration through nonreward was a straight translation of the Hullian model: thus the frustration drive (FD), generated by nonreinforcement, is a negative drive state (I); and reduction of frustration mediates the learning of relevant competing responses (presumably responses that reduce FD by removing the stimuli associated with FD).

Maatsch's experiments were specifically designed as if the operation of either I_R or *FD* or some combination thereof represented the way things were. Thus it was assumed that it would be possible to measure the amount of *I* generated by a single occurrence of the instrumental response or by a single occurrence of frustration and to compare the two effects. Even twenty years ago this approach seemed a bit idealistic, but such measurable effects seemed to be implied by two-factor theories of inhibition. That is, immediately after a response (in Hull's system), or immediately after a response had led to frustration (in Rohrer's), there should be a finite amount of *I* present that is detectable as a response decrement. Presumably, the *I* that had been produced would be sufficient in amount to mediate the learning of the relatively permanent interference factor. Since *I* is assumed to dissipate rapidly with the passage of time, how else could discrimination learning and experimental extinction take place with well-spaced trials? How else could an alternative response be "motivated" and, through its occurrence, begin the reduction of I_R or *FD* and thereby produce the extinction of well-spaced responses?

At that time we assumed that the learning of the interfering response would take place primarily on the trial which followed the trial(s) which produced the *I*. Residual *I* would occasion the alternative response and its learning. For highly spaced trials, however, it seemed necessary to assume that the learning of the interfering response could start near the end of the very same trial on which *I* developed (e.g., as soon as the empty food tray had been examined and *FD* activated). Such an interfering response, we assumed, would start the reduction of *I* and would be conditioned first to the cues of the goal box, and then by chaining or generalizing to the cues of the start box, thus mediating inhibition there. Such learning would not depend on residual *I* and could occur on successive trials regardless of the degree of spacing.

If, instead of being given spaced trials, *S* were removed from the goal box as soon as the food tray had been examined and immediately given another trial, then the amount of *I* present at the beginning of the second trial should be no less than the amount of *I* that is assumed to mediate learned inhibition with spaced trials and should therefore be detectable on this succeeding trial. If no inhibition is detected two-factor theory is suspect. It makes no sense here to suggest that *I* might accumulate with repeated, spaced trials. The length of an intertrial interval that permits extinction can greatly exceed the length of a rest interval that yields complete recovery (reminiscence) from the cumulative inhibitory effects of many massed trials (Ammons, 1947; Kimble & Horenstein, 1948).

In the Maatsch study, *I* was measured on individual test trials which immediately or quickly followed the presumed inhibition-producing condition (inhibition trial). Any increase in running time on this "massed" test trial over the running time present on directly preceding spaced trials represented the measure of *I*. I_R was measured after a reinforced response and *FD* after a nonreinforced response. To be brief, the study involved running a number of independent groups in a straight runway in which the goal box differed in width, height, color, and flooring from the remainder of the alley and was not visible until *S* pushed through the one-way door of the goal box. The experimental treatments began after 21 regularly reinforced trials, with 6 trials given daily for at least 9 days. For the same *S* but in different combinations for different groups, some trials each day were spaced, some were massed, some were reinforced, and some nonreinforced. The results of this study suggested certain conclusions which were reinvestigated and later confirmed in Maatsch's doctoral research (Maatsch, 1955):

1. When a set of two trials is highly massed and both trials are reinforced, rats run just as fast on the second trial as when the set of two reinforced trials is spaced. Once performance has become asymptotic there is no detectable increment in inhibition that comes strictly from an immediately prior runway response (see the left half of Figure 1).
2. After a nonreinforced trial the immediately following running response is just as fast as a running response which is immediately preceded by a reinforced trial.*
3. Over days, inhibition (increased running time) only builds up gradually on those trials which are consistently nonreinforced and which possess a common cue at the beginning. This phenomenon is seen in the curve of Figure 1. Only one group that Maatsch ran is shown, a group which shows points 1 and 3 in an unencumbered, straightforward fashion.

In Maatsch's research, the cue for mediating the learned inhibition (an increase in running time of about 30 sec.) was found to be the massing procedure used. Typically the third and sixth trials of a day (test trials) immediately followed the second and fifth trials, respectively, while all other trials came at least five minutes after the preceding one. The evidence for massing functioning as the cue was clear-cut: (a) When inhibition had developed fully on the third and sixth trials because these massed trials were nonreinforced, this inhibition transferred completely to other trials of the same day when, for test purposes, those trials immediately followed the preceding trial. (b) No evidence of inhibition appeared on Trials 3 and 6 when, for test purposes, they were spaced with respect to the preceding trial. (c) No inhibition developed on Trials 3 and 6 when they were nonreinforced and all trials of a day were spaced

* Even though *S* was handled and manually transported in Maatsch's procedure, his attempt to measure *FD* was quite similar to the well-known double alley measure first used by Amsel and Roussel (1952) to study the energizing effects of frustration (frustration effect or *FE*). Results of the many double alley experiments are quite compatible with Maatsch's conclusion about *FD* since frustration in the first alley facilities rather than inhibits performance in the second alley. Probably Maatsch's failure to find a facilitating effect after a frustration event was due to nonreinforcing intentionally every test trial that followed a frustration trial throughout the series of such trials (the running response in the second alley, G_2, is always reinforced in the double alley experiments).

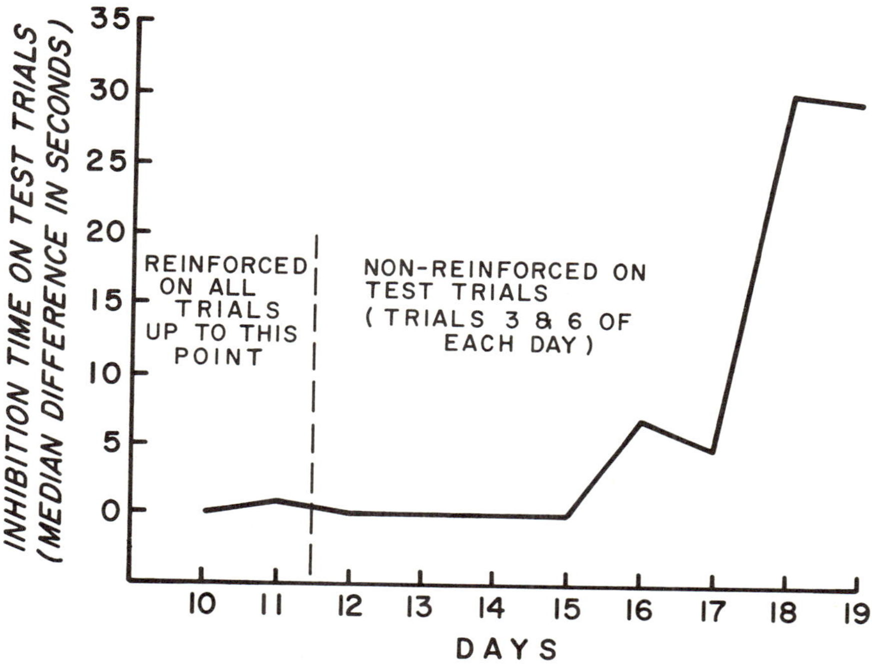

FIGURE 1. A plot of the median difference between the running time on test trials and the running time on prior ("inhibition") trials. All trials were reinforced until Day 12 and on all trials except the test trials after Day 12.

throughout the experiment; that is, the results were similar to what commonly occurs with a partial reinforcement schedule.

The critical aspect of these findings is that the development of inhibition on the test trial was independent of whether the *previous* trial had been reinforced or nonreinforced. The growth of inhibition depended on a cue (massing) being present at the start of a to-be-nonreinforced trial and being absent on reinforced trials. Such a finding simply reflected the presence of a discrimination learning paradigm, which we promptly recognized. But, again, the important point was that the results, literally interpreted, contradicted prevailing two-factor theories of inhibition. Interfering responses (reflected in increased running times) could be readily learned without there being the slightest evidence in measurable behavior of the existence of a negative drive state (I_R or FD) which, when subsequently reduced, could mediate the learning of the interfering response (e.g., ${}_SI_R$). The intrinsic, or negative drive, component of two-factor inhibition theory appeared to be excess baggage. It seems clear that most current theories of extinction reflect a similar conclusion (Amsel, 1958; Capaldi, 1967; Spence, 1960).

A brief description of a theory of extinction

Largely from Maatsch's data and our interpretation of them an interference theory of extinction evolved, and close on its heels a monistic conception of learning (elicitation theory) began to emerge. The interference theory, as originally formulated, was as follows: the animal immediately upon being nonreinforced on a test trial makes a withdrawal response (Denny, 1946). This characteristic class of competing responses (R_c) has the character of an UR, and it is postulated that the *removal* of the reinforcer from the established behavior sequence is the US for R_c. Since any basis for assuming the operation of a negative drive and its reduction has been ruled out as an explanation of learned inhibition, R_c is assumed to be classically conditioned to the concurrent stimuli solely on the basis of contiguity. Theoretically, such learning can proceed equally well during spaced or massed trials. Extinction results because R_c as a response tendency is pitted against the original response tendency (S-R_o) and effectively competes with it. That is, no weakening of S-R_o or unhooking of R_o is assumed. The R_c can be a simple response class or a family of different responses which can have varying degrees of incompatibility with R_o. The resultant response tendency, in the flavor of Spence and Hull, is assumed to be some algebraic, vector summation of S-R_c and S-R_o. The suggestion that degree of incompatibility of R_o and R_c is an important variable has served primarily as a guideline for future research, although in the broad sense the study by Adelman and Maatsch (1955) was directed at this issue, and again in the broad sense, their results which showed that type of R_c was critical to extinction were confirmatory.

In an instrumental approach situation, the theory obviously says that R_c originates in the goal region at the end of the behavior sequence and gets progressively conditioned in a backward order in much the same way as R_o does. The "backchaining" assumption in extinction is essentially the same conception as the one shared by Amsel (1958) and Spence (1960) in their treatments of extinction, except that r_f rather than an overt R_c is being classically conditioned in their case. The fact that extinction of a response sequence often seems to occur in an all-over-at-once fashion does not necessarily contradict the backchaining hypothesis. R_c is typically a response class that is nonspecific so that it can occur anywhere in the behavior sequence, and the typical learning situation (straight runway) is usually homogeneous in structure, shape, and color throughout. Thus stimulus generalization can mediate the generalized extinction effect.

This series of notions promptly suggested that the main theoretical reason typically given for positing a factor of intrinsic inhibition, namely, to explain spontaneous recovery, was quite irrelevant. Generalization decrement also accounts in part for many inhibitory effects; and, when used in conjunction with a principle of stimulus reinstatement, it can readily handle the phenomenon of spontaneous recovery as well as other extinction effects (Denny & Adelman, 1955; Maatsch, 1954). In the theory we assert, for example, that R_c is nearly always conditioned to a stimulus situation (extinction) which to some extent is different from the acquisition situation to which R_o has been conditioned. There are two major implications of this view: (a) The greater the stimulus difference between acquisition and extinction the faster the extinction of R_o, with PRE reflecting the converse—the less the stimulus difference the slower the extinction; and (b) any reinstatement of the stimulus elements of acquisition strengthens S-R_o, and any change in the elements of extinction weakens S-R_c so that the resultant tendency, depending on the situation at hand, yields spontaneous recovery or disinhibition effects. Similar points in regard to the explanation of spontaneous recovery have been independently made by Skinner (1950) when he emphasized that extinction typically takes place in the latter part of an operant extinction session rather than in the early part; by Estes (1955) in his stimulus sampling or stimulus fluctuation theory; and more recently by Capaldi (1967) in a fashion similar to our own. The analysis of extinction phenomena in the elicitation framework will be elaborated later.

CERTAIN CHARACTERISTICS OF THE GENERAL THEORY

The next step in our thinking was to assume that if extinction-producing responses get learned through the consistent elicitation of these responses in close contiguity with S, then perhaps all learning proceeds in the same way. Our focus then was on the analysis of instrumental approach learning, and I held to the Hull-Spence view that the incentive-elicited response that was classically conditioned to the contiguous stimuli was the fractional consummatory response (r_g). The r_g-s_g sequence, per Hull's analysis (1931), would then mediate approach because approach was conditioned to s_g; tentatively, the reinforcement for this learning was the increased elicitation of r_g further along in the behavior sequence.

Maatsch suggested that while something like r_g-s_g was probably being conditioned, this part of the analysis might be relatively unimportant and misleadingly roundabout. His point was that direct approach was being consistently elicited by the visual and olfactory attributes of the incentive (reinforcer) and thereby being conditioned to the stimuli in the vicinity of the food tray (water dipper). Approach must invariably or consistently occur, for before the animal can eat the food or drink the water it must first approach it.

For two main reasons I soon went along with Maatsch's simplifying assumption: (a) Martindale in his MA research (Denny & Martindale, 1956; Martindale, 1950) had found that a significant increment to the approach response tendency in a T-maze occurred on the very first reinforced trial (i.e., prior to any possible establishment of r_g-s_g to one side of the maze). This increment occurred as much in naive rats that had never been fed in a maze-like situation as in those pretrained rats that had been fed earlier in a maze-like situation (exposed to general r_g-s_g conditioning). This occurred even though the naive rats initially took at least a minute to begin eating the familiar checkers of food strewn all over the goal box floor. These rats, however, did appear to make direct approach (investigatory) responses to the food on the floor as soon as they arrived in the goal box on the first reinforced trial. One could interpret the reinforcement here as a case of secondary reinforcement via perception of familiar food (i.e., in the same way that Schlosberg and Pratt [1956] did when their rats learned without eating). However, it seemed more cogent to us to turn the proposition around and say that all reinforcement is like secondary reinforcement, namely, a matter of consistently eliciting a response, in this case, approach. Otherwise, just what is it that makes a secondary reinforcer reinforcing? In any case, because learning occurred with the very first reinforcement, the increased elicitation of r_g further along in the sequence was a very poor candidate for the explanation of reinforcement, secondary or otherwise. (b) When Maatsch's assumption is made, all learning, human and otherwise, is basically the same. One does not need to invoke contiguity principles arbitrarily at one point in the behavior sequence and a modified law of effect at another point. A monistic view of learning obtains throughout.

An analysis of operant or instrumental learning using classical conditioning principles

In the elicitation framework, the critical UR in instrumental reward learning (multiple-choice devices, runways, operant-conditioning apparatus, etc.) is the rather broad response class of approach to the relevant incentive. And the learning of instrumental responses is based on continued, or higher-order, conditioning (backchaining) of the particular members of the long-lasting approach class that can come forward in the behavior sequence. *Such backchaining continues as long as stimuli in the chain remain discriminative and the terminal member of the approach sequence overlaps the US (incentive).* For example, when *E* puts the key noisily into the lock of the door of the colony room and the rats leap toward their cage door, even this may represent the beginning of an extended approach sequence that is eventually reinforced by food in the food tray of whatever device the rats are being trained in.

The gist of the argument for deriving operant conditioning from contiguity principles is that an operant situation does not permit direct approach to the goal; that is, the learned operant represents an indirect or detour route to the goal in which approach is differentially conditioned to the chain of response-produced cues (CSs) that are consistently present when *S* ends up at the goal. Such an analysis implies that the simplest operant learning situation involves a good deal of discrimination learning. Let us illustrate by describing how, in elicitation terms, a rat learns to press the bar in a Skinner box. The first response that *S* learns is to make a clear-cut approach response to the food tray or water dipper. With the strengthening of this approach response, *S* learns to be a goal-sticker, making strong approaches to the food tray (dipper) without first pressing the bar. But such behavior means that *S* will not continue to be reinforced, and at this point the absence of the incentive in the tray (dipper) is itself a US which elicits antagonistic responses, responses that remove the animal from the vicinity of the tray. Fairly often, these antagonistic responses include aggressive or tangential responses that involve banging away at the bar, so that the rat typically finds food in the tray at its next visit. A type of discrimination learning then proceeds in which the rat learns to press the bar *before* visiting the food tray. That is, the rat learns to inhibit direct approaches to the food tray and to approach it by way of the detour route of first going to the bar, pressing it, and then going to the tray. Theoretically this chain is constructed in the following chronological order. The cues attendant upon bar pressing, which usually include the "click" of the reward mechanism, are conditioned to the response of approaching the incentive. With further conditioning the stimuli produced by the response of approaching the bar become conditioned to pressing the bar; and finally the response-produced cues of ingesting the food (water) become the main CS (S^D) for approaching the bar. The chain is complete. A similar detailed analysis of instrumental T-maze learning can be found elsewhere (Denny, 1967, 1971; Denny & Adelman, 1955), as well as a similar backchaining analysis of escape-avoidance learning (Denny, 1971).

Some implications of the theory

In this theory, learning is the process in which one response tendency (S-R) becomes predominant over alternative response tendencies because the to-be-learned R is consistently elicted in the presence of S. When it is assumed that contiguity of S and R primarily determines what is learned, it follows, in much the way that Guthrie (1952) put it, that learning requires the consistent elicitation of R in close temporal contiguity with S (this means that alternative responses are excluded or minimized). In contrast to elicitation theory, however, Guthrie did not exploit the idea that traditional reinforcers are consistent elicitors of the to-be-learned response, nor did he view the absence of a reinforcer as the consistent elicitor of R_c (in extinction or in contiguity with the negative cue of a discrimination experiment).

One important implication of this view of learning is that the many variables that facilitate learning across trials do so mainly through ensuring the consistent elicitation of the to-be-learned response and through minimizing the occurrence of alternative Rs in the presence of S. A bit of reflection suggests that the variables traditionally manipulated—motivational (including verbal instructions), temporal, reinforcement, stimulus, and habituation—all readily fit this formula. For example: (a) spacing of trials in classical conditioning can be viewed as a method that prevents the US from habituating, i.e., from losing its consistent eliciting property. (b) It is important to let *S* ingest the incentive at the end of behavior chain, not because it is satisfying à la the law of effect, but because an alternative, frustration-elicited response will supplant approach if *S* is not permitted to do so. (c) When cues, in a discrimination-learning task, are relevant (+ or −) or irrelevant in terms of reinforcement contingencies, then it becomes possible to coordinate them to either an approach or withdrawal response. A relevant cue is one that *consistently* precedes a given R and fails to accompany alternative Rs, that is, the definitions of a relevant cue and of learning are one and the same. When two different Rs are elicited equally often, either in the presence or absence of a cue, neither response wins out and the cue is irrelevant; that is, no learning has occurred. (d) The traditional delay of reinforcement variable becomes an ordinary CS-US interval for the establishment of the CR of approach (the "click," let us say, is the CS, and food in the tray is the US). Reinforcement, if the term is used, is never delayed; it occurs simultaneously with the elicitation of R in contiguity with whatever stimuli prevail.

An important implication of this formulation is that almost any stimulus can be used as a reinforcer in an instrumental learning situation (i.e., if the situation is appropriately arranged). Following are two examples: (a) a satiated stimulus complex, the arm of an enclosed T-maze that *S* is more frequently forced to visit, seems to elicit avoidance of this arm, while a relatively unsatiated stimulus complex (less often visited arm) elicits approach or exploration. When *S* is so exposed to stimuli, such an arrangement mediates a learned preference for selecting the less often visited arm whenever *S* has the opportunity to choose between them (free choice trials). This preference develops in the face of food reinforcement that is given *only* on the more frequently visited side and is almost as stable as a traditional, food-reinforced response in a T-maze when extinction, or repeated free choice, trials are administered one per day (Denny, 1957; Denny & Leckart, 1965). (b) When a wheel-turning tendency is stronger than the tendency of water-satiated *S*s to drink and availability of the wheel is contingent on drinking, it has been found that *S* learns an instrumental drinking response (Premack, Schaeffer, & Hundt, 1964). Since I am not the first to say it, at least in print (Bolles, 1967), I can comfortably agree that Premack's reinforcement principle (Premack, 1959) represents a special case of elicitation theory.

Another implication relates to comparative psychology. Since learning is assumed to occur through responding and therefore only involves responses that are already in an organism's repertoire, it is obvious that species affiliation, critical periods, and genetic factors in behavior can be critical variables in the theoretical analysis of learned behavior. Whether a response can be learned, how rapidly, and when, in the maturational development of the organism, are all determined by such variables. The extensive implications of this point are covered in book form (Denny & Ratner, 1970).

Evidence pertaining to the theory of extinction

Since this essay deals mainly with an analysis of experimental extinction, the evidence to be discussed here relates to extinction rather than to the theory as a whole. Our first research effort after formulating the present interference theory was to obtain evidence that effort was essentially irrelevant in the extinction of a free operant when *S* was extinguished on the same effort level used in training (Maatsch, Adelman, & Denny, 1954). The next set of experiments relative to the theory was conducted by Adelman and Maatsch (1955, 1956), and the results of these rather well-known studies probably provide the best published support for the theory.

The Adelman-Maatsch (A-M) studies. Adelman and Maatsch proposed that extinction is a direct function of the type of R that is elicited by frustration and permitted to occur. If this R is directly incompatible with R_o, extinction is facilitated. If this R is allied with R_o, extinction is prolonged or prevented. Other, tangential, Rs have an intermediate effect. In the main study, rats were given 37 reinforcements in a runway which included a start box and goal box, each of the same size. The runway was natural wood, the start box grey, and goal box black; a screen above the goal box entrance prevented *S* from seeing the alley when it was perched on the goal box ledge. Three separate groups were then extinguished under one of the following conditions: (a) allowed to jump out of the goal box onto a 2-in. ledge for 20 sec.; (b) allowed to recoil from the goal box for a period of 20 sec. and retrace; (c) stayed in goal box for 20 sec.—regular extinction. As predicted, the results indicated that extinction occurs most rapidly when the response elicited by frustration (R_c) is directly incompatible with R_o: the recoil group extinguished fastest and the jumpout slowest. The latter, in fact, extinguished hardly at all within 30 spaced, or even 100 additional massed, extinction trials.

In the jumpout group the latencies of jumping from the goal box declined progressively with successive extinction trials (Adelman & Maatsch, 1956), indicating that the jumping associated with frustration is learned. Typically this learning has been interpreted as being mediated by frustration reduction (escape from the goal box), as has the maintenance and acquisition of hurdle-jumping in similar frustration situations (Daly, 1969a; Wagner, 1963). This is a dubious interpretation. For instance, Adelman and Maatsch (1956) found that the jump response of extinction was learned more rapidly than a food-reinforced jump and interpreted the faster learning in terms of the jump response of extinction being consistently elicited by frustration. All of the data that are usually adduced in support of frustration reduction (Amsel, Ernhart, & Galbrecht, 1961; Amsel & Prouty, 1959; Amsel & Ward, 1954; Daly, 1969a; Wagner, 1963) can be reinterpreted in terms of the consistent occurrence of a frustration-elicited response. Even if it were critical that *S* escapes the cues associated with frustration when, for example, it jumps out of a box, this fact may simply mean, à la Guthrie, that escaping prevents the occurrence of alternative responses when *S* is in the box. There appear to be no data that favor frustration reduction over the eliciting effects of frustration, but there is some experimental evidence that favors the elicitation position:

1. The fact that the jump response in the A-M study was learned faster when elicited by frustration than when reinforced with familiar food on the goal box ledge is consistent with the assumption of elicitation theory that the instrumental response which is reinforced by food must chain from the ledge of the goal box back to the floor of the goal box. Jumping via frustration, on the other hand, is directly elicited inside the goal box and directly conditioned to these cues; thus, such jumping is learned rapidly. To argue that the particular food reinforcer used might have been inferior to this presumed instance of frustration reduction, when there is considerable evidence to indicate that the rate of learning a simple instrumental response is relatively independent of incentive magnitude, hardly seems to be a reasonable alternative.
2. During extinction, if the R_c elicited in the goal box were reinforced by removal of *S* from the empty goal box, then one would expect that a fairly prompt removal of *S* (minimum delay of reinforcement via frustration reduction) would facilitate extinction. But the opposite is true; the longer *S* stays in the empty goal box, or the more R_c that is elicited, the faster *S* extinguishes (Campbell, 1969; Capaldi & Poynor, 1965; Tombaugh, 1966; Wike, Mellgren, & Wike, 1968).
3. It would seem that a rigorous, unequivocal way to show that the removal of frustration has reinforcing value is to pair a neutral stimulus with the period that immediately follows the removal of frustration. Do this for many trials and then test this stimulus for the acquisition of possible "secondary" reinforcing properties. Such attempts in our laboratory, like that of Sutey (1967), have been remarkably unsuccessful in demonstrating the presence of any such reinforcing property.
4. At least temporarily in a key-pecking situation, a pigeon maintains an alternative, presumably frustration-instigated, response even though the response does not lead to escape from the S— of an established discrimination (Rilling, Askew, Ahlskog, & Kramer, 1970). In the presence of S— (e.g., red light) such pigeons (controls) pecked the alternative key (white light) at the rate of 1.25 pecks/min. during the first two 40-min. discrimination sessions in which white light was first made available, and just as frequently as a group for which each peck of this key produced a 30-sec. timeout (removal of S— and all other lights). For comparison, the white light was also present during S+. Subsequently, the pecking rate of the control group dropped below the rate of those for which timeouts were contingent on pecking the white

key. This drop can be explained by invoking frustration reduction in the contingent *S*s or by reference to the extended opportunity for the controls to make additional alternative responses in the continued presence of S— and white light. But what explains the early and relatively high level of responding to the white light in the controls, if it is not just frustration-elicited pecking?

Partial replications of the A-M studies. Few experiments test an interference theory of extinction, and at least as many have obtained results that do not appear to support an interference theory as those that do. Here it should be emphasized, because so little has been published on the elicitation position, that the investigators who tested interference theory could hardly have anticipated many of the points that I will raise. Let us begin by focusing on some partial replications of the A-M study. Chronologically, the first was a study by Haggard (1959) in which he found no evidence for the jump response to prolong extinction. The physical setup in his experiment was quite different from the one used by Adelman and Maatsch, but the only point necessary to stress is that there was a *corrugated* rim around the upper edge of the goal box which, by Haggard's admission, had clear-cut *aversive* properties. By contrast, the rat in the A-M study when perched on the *flat* 2-in. ledge of the goal box reacted in a relaxed exploratory, rather than fearful, manner. It seems obvious that, in order for the jumpout response to be compatible with runway locomotion (approach) and thereby retard extinction, it must represent a definite continuation of an approach response. Whatever the reason *S*s in Haggard's experiment were reluctant to jump to the corrugated rim, his experiment does not represent a test of the original hypothesis, especially in a framework which posits that jumping is learned (reinforced) through being consistently elicited.

When the Haggard study appeared in print I immediately went to the laboratory and repeated the jumpout portion of the A-M study with about eight rats in a stimulus situation which was more similar to Haggard's than A-M's: homogeneous alley 8 in. high, homogeneous extra-alley cues, a relatively long alley, and a relatively large number of acquisition trials. Although the research was purely exploratory, it is relevant to mention that several of the jumpout *S*s were running just as fast after 200 extinction trials as they were at the end of acquisition.

Another reported disconfirmation of the jumpout portion of the A-M study is by Theios and Bower (1964), which they describe as their third failure in an attempt to replicate the finding that jumping from the goal box prolongs extinction. However, there are at least three published confirmations of this result (Bacon, 1967; Cotton, Lewis, & Metzger, 1958; Gray, 1969). The study by Gray shows that frustration both mediates the learning of a jump response (Adelman & Maatsch, 1956; Daly, 1969a, 1969b) and increases resistance to extinction (Adelman & Maatsch, 1955).

When all of these experiments are considered in conjunction with the results of an unpublished portion of the original A-M study (Adelman, 1954), it may be possible to identify the reason for Theios and Bower's negative findings. Theios and Bower used an alley, minus end boxes, that was 72 in. long, while giving *S* only 30 reinforced trials. In Adelman's research the alley was only 18 in. long, and three different groups received 36, 24, or 12 reinforcements during acquisition. After 12 reinforcements, *S*s learned to jump from the goal box, although somewhat more gradually than the other two groups, but, in marked contrast to the 24 and 36 reinforcement groups, they completely extinguished within 15 extinction trials. That is, they were much like the jump-out groups of Theios and Bower which learned to jump but still extinguished rapidly. Adelman's original interpretation of this finding for the 12-reinforcement group still seems appropriate. The reason the jump response did not prevent the extinction of the running response in the 12-reinforcement group, Adelman suggested, is that the weak runway tendency underwent extinction from the many other elicited components of R_c before the anticipatory components of jumping (running) could chain to the start box. The assumption here is that in the groups with 24 or 36 prior reinforcements, anticipatory running became conditioned the length of the chain by virtue of the fact that running (R_o) was there in strength throughout the conditioning period (early extinction trials).

According to Adelman's analysis, the original runway response is "really extinguished" even though *S* continues to run rapidly down the alley: the original response has been replaced by a completely compatible response of traversing the alley in order to jump out of the goal box. This interpretation fits the fact that during extinction *S* soon ignores the empty food dish. Thus for the 12-reinforcement group, if the approach response of running has already extinguished, the act of jumping from the goal box cannot by itself mediate the learning of an alley-running response. After all, *S* is attempting to leave the goal box, not approach it.

It follows that the effectiveness of a jump response in increasing resistance to extinction depends jointly on the length of the alley and the number of original acquisition trials: during extinction the establishment of the chain of anticipatory jumping (running) requires more trials the longer the alley; thus, the longer the alley the stronger R_o must be in order not to extinguish before the new running response is established.

It seems that the conditions of long alley and 30 reinforcements in the Theios and Bower study are most comparable to the A-M group that only received 12 reinforcements in a very short alley. This view fits the fact that the jump response has prolonged extinction in two studies that used long runways but a relatively large number of reinforcements during acquisition. Bacon (1967) gave his rats 60 reinforcements in a 55-in. alley (minus end boxes) using 30-sec. access to water as the incentive; the effects for the jumpout group, though clear, were not as pronounced as those found by Adelman and Maatsch. Gray (1969) gave his rats 88 reinforcements in a 64-in. alley, using virtually the same size food pellet as used in the A-M study. Gray's results resemble a carbon copy of the jumpout results of the A-M study. The related study by Cotton et al. (1958), using 40 reinforcements in a 48-in. runway, obtained results that were intermediate to the Gray-Bacon results and those of Theios and Bower.

Other partial replications of the A-M study have been directed at testing the hypothesis that the repeated occurrence of an incompatible response facilitates extinction. Marx (1967a, 1967b) has investigated this problem in a runway, with retracing from the goal box as the incompatible response; the thrust of his findings has been negative. Let us see how this might be so and still be compatible with the findings and conclusions of Adelman and Maatsch.

The crux of the analysis in the studies of Marx is probably a cue variable. His alley has either been all gray or all gray expect for vertical black-white 1-in. stripes in the goal box, with presumably a homogeneous extra-maze environment. Not only were the three sections of the short A-M runway differentiated as to interior cues, but the extra-maze environment was probably as heterogeneous as one could arrange it, with the added factor that the large black screen above the goal box clearly specified the location of the goal as opposed to the start.

All of this means that retracing the alley is not going to be truly incompatible with the original running response unless both R_o and R_c are each clearly oriented as to direction (*opposite* directions). A recoil-running response which is *not* conditioned discriminatively to the cues of the alley might well prolong extinction rather than facilitate it: *S* simply learns to run, period. Even in the differentiated alley of the A-M study the jump response definitely tended to generalize from goal box to start box so that a glass cover had to be put over the start box during extinction trials.

Such an interpretation of Marx's results is at least consistent with the following: (a) *S*s that were permitted to retrace in Marx's studies actually showed significantly greater resistance to extinction than *S*s that were not permitted to retrace. (b) In the study by Barrett and Carlson (1966) in which running was an escape response in the same direction as the original approach response (i.e., out the food end of the goal box), the effect of this allied response in prolonging extinction, per the jump response in the A-M study, was enhanced by differentiating the sections of the runway so that running, according to the present interpretation, was correlated with a specific sequence of stimulation and could therefore be oriented for direction. (In this case generalization decreases rather than increases resistance to extinction because any reduction in directionality means that running tends to become a competing response.) (c) In the Marx studies, reentries to the goal area after *S* had left it occurred rather frequently during extinction, while such responding was not permitted nor were such attempts generally observed in the A-M study. The main point in (c) is that the frequent occurrence of reentries to the goal box definitely implies that *S* was running irrespective of direction of running.

Other tests of the interference position. Using a runway, Longstreth (1964a) found no relationship between a count of observed goal-box behavior (backing and turning around in the goal box) and resistance to extinction; but he did report that *S*s that showed the greatest avoidance of the goal box (traversing alley but failing to enter the goal box) extinguished the fastest. That is, when R_c has presumably chained beyond the goal box where it can effectively mediate extinction, the relationship is as predicted by interference theory. How soon R_c behavior occurs in the goal box after the start of extinction would seem to be a more crucial measure than total amount of R_c, but this was not evaluated in Longstreth's report.

Longstreth interpreted the facilitation of extinction by goal-box avoidance in terms of frustration reduction that obtains when *S* stays away from the cues associated with frustration. In another experiment, Longstreth (1964b) tested this reinforcement hypothesis of interference learning by removing *S* immediately from the goal box whenever it made an R_c (climbed the side of the goal box or turned around). As is consistent with the elicitation position there was virtually no difference between these *S*s and yoked controls removed after equal time in the goal box; R_c is elicited by frustration and not necessarily reinforced by its removal, a point which Capaldi and Poynor (1965) also make.

Longstreth interpreted the findings of his second study as failing to support interference theory rather than failing to support a traditional version of reinforcement—even though this interpretation directly contradicted the earlier interpretation (Longstreth, 1964a). His two sets of data, however, are quite compatible in the elicitation framework: in both experiments R_c is simply learned by means of frustration-elicitation.

Another study by Marx (1968) is relevant to this last point. His study tested interference theory in a bar-pressing situation in which *S* was allowed to make an interfering response by pressing a second bar. Opportunity to press this secondary bar did not reduce resistance to extinction and thus the results were interpreted as failing to support interference theory. However, such a result can be viewed as compatible with the elicitation point of view. The learning of R_c during extinction requires the consistent elicitation of R_c just as the learning of R_o requires the consistent elicitation of R_o. One cannot define arbitrarily the specific R_c that the rat will learn. In such situations, R_c is consistently elicited by frustration, and the components of R_c which are most consistently elicited are the main ones acquired. These components are expected to vary across *S*s but in general to fall into the broad class of withdrawal response. In the case of bar pressing, then, R_c is most likely to involve withdrawal from any region of the apparatus which contains a bar. Thus one would expect the number of bars present during extinction to be largely irrelevant or, if anything, to increase slightly resistance to extinction. For with two bars, R_c (withdrawal) would not be exclusively conditioned to the region of the original bar.

Other studies, for instance, those of Estes (1950) and Deutsch and Wiener (1969), provide good empirical support for an interference position.

APPLICATION OF THE THEORY TO EXTINCTION PHENOMENA

Theorizing about extinction has centered on PRE and has occupied the attention of several theorists (Amsel, 1958; Capaldi, 1967, 1970; McCain, 1966; Spence, 1960; Weinstock, 1958). The elicitation position could probably be characterized as a conglomerate of these analyses and thus has little to add except possibly for the analysis of PRE in a free-operant, as opposed to a discrete-trial, situation (Denny, Wells, & Maatsch, 1957). The relatively neglected phenomena of extinction are also important and as much in need of explanation as PRE. This section is therefore devoted to analyzing spontaneous recovery and disinhibition.

An explanation of spontaneous recovery

This analysis is straightforward and bears strong resemblance to Capaldi's analysis of PRE. During acquisition the original response (R_o) is conditioned in part to the internal stimuli that prevail, including aftereffects of the US (reinforcer) from the previous trial, at least when the trials are not widely spaced (a nonemotional state). With the introduction of extinction, the aftereffects of nonreinforcement replace many of the internal cues that were present during acquisition, and R_c is conditioned to a stimulus complex which contains these new cues. As internal cues, the aftereffects of frustration are especially relevant; this is because R_c is elicited in their presence on every extinction trial except the first trial of a day. In other words, the stimuli present during extinction (S_E) differ from the stimuli present during acquisition (S_A); and to the extent these two stimulus complexes differ, extinction is facilitated. Extinction, in the theory, is pitting S_E-R_c against S_E-R_o so that the weaker S_E-R_o is through generalization decrement, the less S_E-R_c must be to counteract S_E-R_o.*

* A common elements theory of stimulus generalization is an integral part of the theory and is applied extensively in this section of the essay: stimulus generalization is the transfer of response tendency from one stimulus complex to another. The magnitude of the generalization is a direct function of the proportion of relevant stimulus elements common to the situations under consideration (where *element* is defined as any unanalyzable part of a stimulus complex and *relevant* elements are those that are exclusively conditioned to the response in question). Thus prior to differential training, when only one or only a limited number of relevant elements have been changed when switching from one stimulus complex to another,

When a rest period is introduced after extinction has occurred, it follows that the cues unique to extinction (aftereffects of frustration) will dissipate or change with the passage of time. A change in these emotion-produced cues means a weakening of the R_c tendency and probably a strengthening of the R_o tendency as the result of a partial reinstatement of the internal cues of acquisition. The net effect is spontaneous recovery, as represented in Figure 2 and described in the caption. That is, the stimulus situation resulting from the introduction of a rest period contains all of the cues that are common to acquisition and extinction but contains neither set of cues (aftereffects) that are unique to ac-

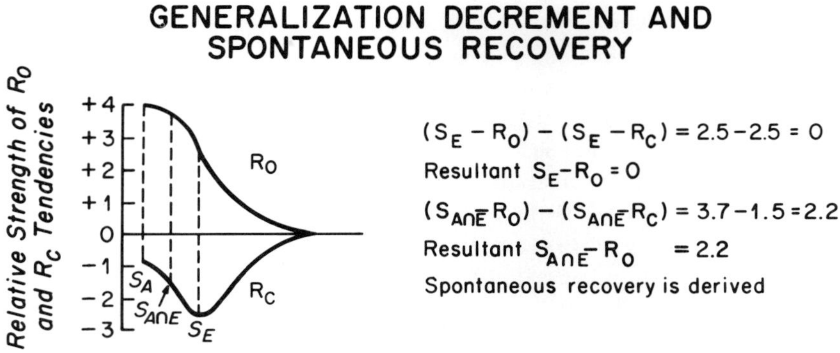

FIGURE 2. Hypothetical stimulus generalization gradients for R_o and R_c. S_A and S_E designate the stimulus conditions that prevail for acquisition and extinction, respectively. $S_{A\cap E}$ represents the stimulus complex that exists when extinction is followed by a rest period—a stimulus blend intermediate between S_A and S_E that consists of all stimului that are common to acquisition and extinction. Following experimental extinction, the resultant response tendency is the algebraic sum of S-R_o (positive) and S-R_c (negative), with the obtained value depending on the prevailing stimulus condition. When the resultant value of $S_{A\cap E}$-R_o is greater than the resultant value of $S_{A\cap E}$-R_c, spontaneous recovery occurs.

---

transfer is practically complete; i.e., the gradient of generalization is relatively flat. If the altered element (or elements) is made discriminative so that the remaining elements become nondifferential or irrelevant, then any change in this element, including spatio-temporal arrangement with other elements, is proportionately very great (here the proportion of common physiological elements for the stimuli in question is presumably implicated), and the gradient of generalization for the discriminative element becomes relatively steep, as of the type specified by Hull (1943). In other words, typical generalization gradients are the result of discrimination training which places the brunt of response specification (stimulus control) on a particular stimulus. (A recent elaboration here is that a highly salient stimulus, one that represented a large proportion of "relevant" stimulation without discrimination training, could also have a sharp gradient.)

Because a number of stimulus elements typically share stimulus control (or are relevant) some change in the total stimulus situation can often produce decrement in performance (generalization decrement). One main source of inhibition, including both the phenomena of forgetting and experimental extinction, is generalization decrement.

quisition and extinction (i.e., the cues after rest represent the intersection of these two sets of cues). Thus spontaneous recovery is typically partial rather than complete. According to the theory, only when acquisition trials are widely spaced (no aftereffects unique to acquisition) and extinction trials highly massed is spontaneous recovery going to be complete. Such conditions were in effect in a study by Denny (1959), and spontaneous recovery was complete.

An implication of this analysis which seems to be generally valid is that there should be greater spontaneous recovery when extinction is massed than when it is spaced. Only when extinction trials are massed are the aftereffects of frustration a distinctive and unique component of S_E.

Another implication is that there should be greater spontaneous recovery when reinforcement during acquisition is continuous rather than partial. After training under partial reinforcement, the aftereffects of nonreinforcement are common to both extinction and acquisition. Thus a long rest period that eliminates these aftereffects produces generalization decrement for both S_A-R_o and S_E-R_c. Proportionately, this decrement should be less for S_A than for S_E where every trial is preceded by nonreinforcement, so that some spontaneous recovery should occur. There are at least three studies which show less spontaneous recovery with partial than with continuous reinforcement (Fischer & Cole, 1968; Thompson, 1966a, 1966b).

An interpretation of disinhibition

This analysis is reminiscent of the one Hull (1943) used to explain external inhibition in terms of generalization decrement. It is an attempt to account for the instances in which disinhibition occurs, as well as the instances in which disinhibition fails to occur (Boice, 1968; Leibrecht, 1969; Skinner, 1936). In essence, these effects are explained by the differential amounts of generalization decrement suffered by R_o and R_c when the extra stimulus is applied during extinction. Results of several recent studies are consistent with this interpretation: Kimmel and Greene (1964) have shown that amount of disinhibition is a direct function of the strength of R_o; Pennypacker (1964) has found that the same stimulus which acts as an external inhibitor during acquisition serves as a disinhibitor following partial extinction; and Singh and Wickens (1968) have data which clearly suggest an intimate connection between external inhibition and disinhibition.

In the study by Singh and Wickens, the extra stimulus (buzzer) was introduced into a stable FI-3-min. schedule either in the first or last half of the 3-min. period. When introduced into the first half where the rat was inhibiting, the effect was disinhibition; when introduced into the last half, the effect was inhibition. The important aspects of these data are that the opposite effects were essentially equivalent in magnitude and occurred for the same extra stimulus for the same response (lever pressing). Such findings make sense if both external inhibition and disinhibition are assumed to be due to generalization decrement; and with respect to the response elicited by the extra stimulus (S_{E+}), they rule out compatibility and incompatibility with R_o as the sole explanations of disinhibition and external inhibition, respectively.

A detailed analysis of the phenomenon of disinhibition is presented in Figure 3. Whether or not disinhibition occurs depends on the resultant response tendency for the algebraic sum of S-R_o (positive) and S-R_c (negative) for the stimulus conditions that prevail. In Figure 3, the formulae that accompany each graph represent the algebraic summation of R_o and R_c, yielding the resultant values of R_o for S_E and S_{E+}. When the conditions that prevail are such that the resultant value of R_o is both greater than zero during S_{E+} and greater during S_{E+} than during S_E, disinhibition occurs. When the resultant value of R_o is less during S_{E+} than during S_E or is less than zero during S_{E+}, disinhibition fails to occur. In the figure, dashed-line verticals have been erected at the appropriate stimulus positions and the intersection of these verticals with the generalization gradients yields the numerical values of response tendency used in these formulae.

According to this analysis, disinhibition fails to occur when the extra stimulus makes the resultant stimulus complex more like S_E than S_A. For example, when an extra stimulus makes *S* more emotional, the resultant stimulus complex is probably more like S_E than S_A (*S* is relatively emotional during S_E because of frustration). This would seem to have been the case with the type of extra stimulus used in the experiments by Skinner (1936) and Boice (1968). Ordinarily, however, it is more likely that the extra stimulus will produce a stimulus complex that is more similar to S_A than S_E (Figure 3). One way to view this is to assume that R_c is most strongly conditioned to the cues that are unique to extinction (less competition from R_o). Thus the introduction of an extra stimulus represents a greater proportionate change in the set of cues that are relevant for R_c than in the larger set of cues that are relevant for R_o.

A final word: The extinction of escape-avoidance behavior

There is considerable evidence that the concepts of interference and backchaining apply as well to escape-avoidance behavior (Denny, 1971; Denny, Koons, & Mason, 1959). And this extension of elicitation theory to experimental situations that involve aversive stimuli serves to distinguish the present theory of extinction from that of Amsel (1958) and Spence (1960). In escape-avoidance, it is assumed that R_c (relaxation or relief) is elicited by the removal of the aversive, or conditioned aversive, stimulus. When pitted against fear, this R_c produces a variety of extinction-like effects (e.g., poor performance in single compartment avoidance situations, temporary effects of punishment, and extinction itself). In other words, the main source of R_c in the extinction of escape-avoidance behavior, as in positive approach learning, is the removal of the original US, yielding a general theory of extinction.

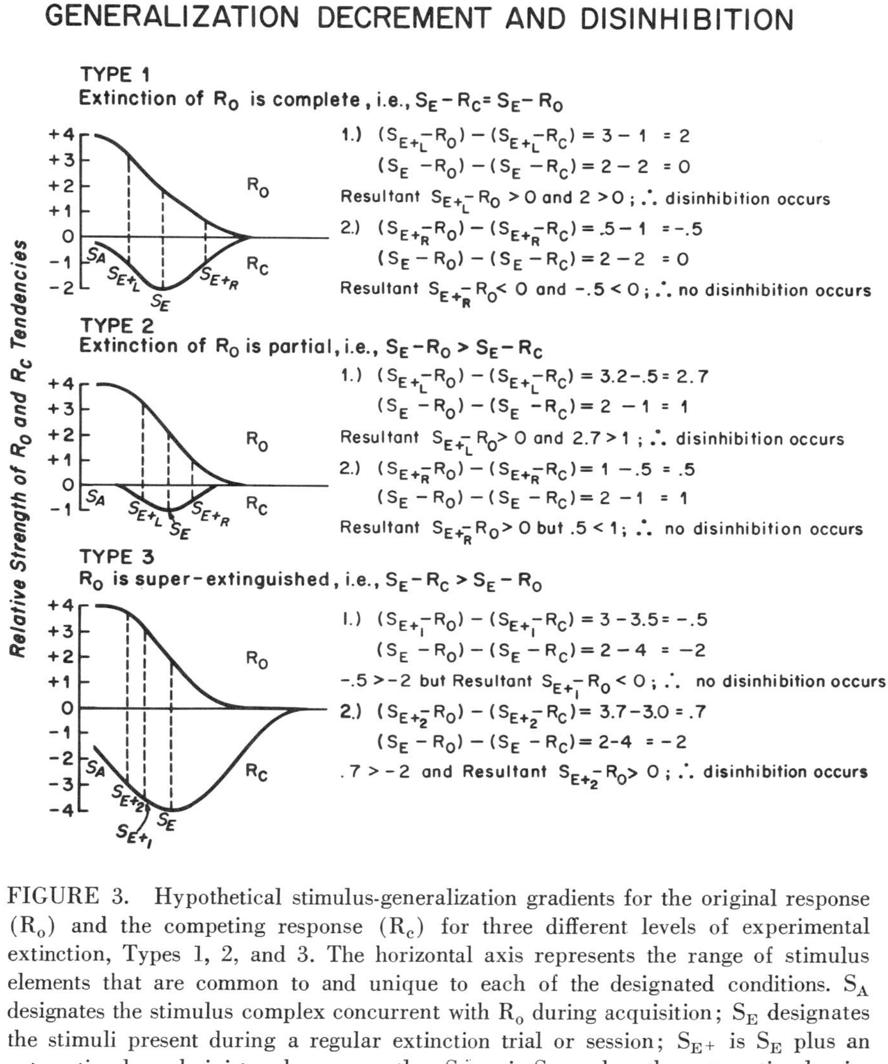

FIGURE 3. Hypothetical stimulus-generalization gradients for the original response (R_o) and the competing response (R_c) for three different levels of experimental extinction, Types 1, 2, and 3. The horizontal axis represents the range of stimulus elements that are common to and unique to each of the designated conditions. S_A designates the stimulus complex concurrent with R_o during acquisition; S_E designates the stimuli present during a regular extinction trial or session; S_{E+} is S_E plus an extra stimulus administered concurrently; S_{E+_L} is S_{E+} when the extra stimulus increases the similarity between S_A and S_E (the S_{E+} is to the left of S_E, i.e., on the side of the R_c gradient toward S_A); S_{E+_R} is S_{E+} when the extra stimulus decreases the similarity between S_A and S_E (the S_{E+} is away from S_E on the right side of the R_c gradient); and S_{E+_1} is a stimulus complex which is more similar to S_E than SE_{+_2} is.

REFERENCES

Adelman, H. M. Resistance to extinction as a function of the type of response elicited by frustration stimulation and level of reinforcement. Unpublished doctoral dissertation, Michigan State College, 1954.

Adelman, H. M., & Maatsch, J. L. Resistance to extinction as a function of the type of response elicited by frustration. *Journal of Experimental Psychology*, 1955, *50*, 61–65.

Adelman, H. M., & Maatsch, J. L. Learning and extinction based upon frustration, food reward, and exploratory tendency. *Journal of Experimental Psychology*, 1956, *52*, 311–315.

Ammons, R. B. Acquisition of motor skill: II. Rotary pursuit performance with continuous practice before and after a single rest. *Journal of Experimental Psychology*, 1947, *38*, 393–411.

Amsel, A. The role of frustrative nonreward in noncontinuous reward situations. *Psychological Bulletin*, 1958, *55*, 102–119.

Amsel, A. Frustrative nonreward in partial reinforcement and discrimination learning: Some recent history and a theoretical extension. *Psychological Review*, 1962, *69*, 306–328.

Amsel, A. Partial reinforcement effects on vigor and persistence: Advances in frustration theory derived from a variety of within-subjects experiments. In K. W. Spence & Janet T. Spence (Eds.), *The psychology of learning and motivation.* Vol. I. New York: Academic Press, 1967. Pp. 1–65.

Amsel, A., Ernhart, C. B., & Galbrecht, C. R. Magnitude of frustration effect and strength of antedating goal factors. *Psychological Reprints*, 1961, *8*, 183–186.

Amsel, A., & Prouty, D. L. Frustrative factors in selective learning reward and nonreward as discriminanda. *Journal of Experimental Psychology*, 1959, *57*, 224–230.

Amsel, A., & Roussel, J. Motivational properties of frustration: I. Effect on a running response of the addition of frustration to the motivational complex. *Journal of Experimental Psychology*, 1952, *43*, 363–368.

Amsel, A., & Ward, J. S. Motivational properties of frustration: II. Frustration drive stimulus and frustration reduction in selective learning. *Journal of Experimental Psychology*, 1954, *48*, 37–47.

Bacon, W. E. Resistance to extinction following blocking of the instrumental response during acquisition. *Journal of Experimental Psychology*, 1965, *69*, 515–521.

Barrett, G. V., & Carlson, N. J. Effect of escape versus non-escape responses from the goal box during extinction. *Psychological Reports*, 1966, *19*, 447–454.

Boice, R. Conditioned licking in wild F_1 and domestic Norway rats. *Journal of Comparative and Physiological Psychology*, 1968, *66*, 796–799.

Bolles, R. C. *Theory of motivation.* New York: Harper & Row, 1967.

Campbell, P. E. Sequences of delayed reward and extinction confinement: Effects on pattern running and extinction performance. *Psychonomic Science*, 1969, *17*, 34–35.

Capaldi, E. J. A sequential hypothesis of instrumental learning. In K. W. Spence

& Janet T. Spence (Eds.), *The psychology of learning and motivation.* Vol. 1. New York: Academic Press, 1967. Pp. 67–156.

Capaldi, E. J. An analysis of the role of reward and reward magnitude in instrumental learning. In J. H. Reynierse (Ed.), *Current issues in animal learning.* Lincoln: University of Nebraska Press, 1970. Pp. 357–389.

Capaldi, E. J., & Poynor, H. B. Nonreward confinement duration: The complement of reward magnitude. *Psychonomic Science,* 1965, *3,* 515–516.

Cotton, J. W., Lewis, D. J., & Metzger, R. Running behavior as a function of apparatus and of restriction of goal box activity. *Journal of Comparative and Physiological Psychology,* 1958, *51,* 336–341.

Daly, H. B. Learning of a hurdle-jump response to escape cues paired with reduced reward or frustrative nonreward. *Journal of Experimental Psychology,* 1969, *79,* 146–157. (a)

Daly, H. B. Is instrumental responding necessary for nonreward following reward to be frustrating? *Journal of Experimental Psychology,* 1969, *80,* 186–187. (b)

Denny, M. R. The role of secondary reinforcement in a partial reinforcement learning situation. *Journal of Experimental Psychology,* 1946, *36,* 373–389.

Denny, M. R. Learning through stimulus satiation. *Journal of Experimental Psychology,* 1957, *54,* 62–64.

Denny, M. R. One bar press per day: Acquisition and extinction. *Journal of Experimental Analysis of Behavior,* 1959, *2,* 81–85.

Denny, M. R. A theoretical analysis and its application to training the mentally retarded. In N. R. Ellis (Ed.), *International review of research in mental retardation.* Vol. 2. New York: Academic Press, 1966. Pp. 1–27.

Denny, M. R. A learning model. In W. C. Corning & S. C. Ratner (Eds.), *Chemistry of learning.* New York: Plenum Press, 1967.

Denny, M. R. Relaxation theory and experiments. In F. R. Brush (Ed.), *Aversive conditioning and learning.* New York: Academic Press, 1971.

Denny, M. R., & Adelman, H. M. Elicitation theory: I. An analysis of two typical learning situations. *Psychological Review,* 1955, *62,* 290–296.

Denny, M. R., Koons, P. B., & Mason, J. E. Extinction of avoidance as a function of the escape situation. *Journal of Comparative and Physiological Psychology,* 1959, *52,* 212–214.

Denny, M. R., & Leckart, B. T. Alternation behavior: Learning and extinction one trial per day. *Journal of Comparative and Physiological Psychology,* 1965, *60,* 229–232.

Denny, M. R., & Martindale, R. L. The effects of the initial reinforcement on response tendency. *Journal of Experimental Psychology,* 1956, *52,* 95–100.

Denny, M. R., & Ratner, S. C. *Comparative psychology.* (Rev. ed.) Homewood, Ill.: Dorsey Press, 1970.

Denny, M. R., Wells, R. H., & Maatsch, J. L. Resistance to extinction as a function of the discrimination habit established during fixed-ratio reinforcement. *Journal of Experimental Psychology,* 1957, *53,* 451–456.

Deutsch, J. A., & Wiener, N. I. Analysis of extinction through amnesia. *Journal of Comparative and Physiological Psychology,* 1969, *69,* 179–184.

Estes, W. K. Effects of competing reactions on the conditioning curve for bar pressing. *Journal of Experimental Psychology,* 1950, *40,* 200–205.

Estes, W. K. Statistical theory of spontaneous recovery and regression. *Psychological Review,* 1955, *62,* 145–154.

Fischer, M. J., & Cole, M. Spontaneous recovery as a function of fixed ratio. *Psychonomic Science*, 1968, *10*, 33–34.

Gray, J. A. Sodium amobarbital and effects of frustrative nonreward. *Journal of Comparative and Physiological Psychology*, 1969, *69*, 55–64.

Guthrie, E. R. *The psychology of learning.* (Rev. Ed.) New York: Harper & Row, 1952.

Haggard, D. F. Experimental extinction as a function of the type of response elicited in the goal box. *Psychological Record*, 1959, *9*, 93–98.

Hull, C. L. Goal attraction and directing ideas conceived as habit phenomena. *Psychological Review*, 1931, *38*, 487–506.

Hull, C. L. The concept of the habit-family hierarchy, and maze learning. *Psychological Review*, 1934, *41*, 33–54, 134–152.

Hull, C. L. *Principles of behavior.* New York: Appleton-Century, 1943.

Kimble, G. A., & Horenstein, Betty R. Reminiscence in motor learning as a function of length of interpolated rest. *Journal of Experimental Psychology*, 1948, *38*, 239–244.

Kimmel, H. D., & Greene, W. A. Disinhibition in GSR conditioning as a function of the number of CS-UCS trials and temporal location of the novel stimulus. *Journal of Experimental Psychology*, 1964, *68*, 567–572.

Leibrecht, B. C. Dishabituation of the head-shake response in the rat. Unpublished doctoral dissertation, Michigan State University, 1969.

Longstreth, L. E. Partial reinforcement effect and extinction as a function of frustration and interfering responses. *Journal of Experimental Psychology*, 1964, *67*, 581–586. (a)

Longstreth, L. E. Extinction as a function of goal box behavior. *Psychonomic Science*, 1964, *1*, 379–380. (b)

Maatsch, J. L. An exploratory study of the possible differential inhibitory effects of frustration and work inhibition. Unpublished MA thesis, Michigan State College, 1951.

Maatsch, J. L. Reinforcement and extinction phenomena. *Psychological Review*, 1954, *61*, 111–118.

Maatsch, J. L. An experimental test of the differential effects of work and frustration upon learning. Unpublished doctoral dissertation, Michigan State University, 1955.

Maatsch, J. L., Adelman, H. M., & Denny, M. R. Effort and resistance to extinction of the bar-pressing response. *Journal of Comparative and Physiological Psychology*, 1954, *47*, 47–50.

Martindale, R. L. An experimental study of the effect of the initial reinforcement on subsequent response tendency under differential conditions of food expectancy. MA thesis, Michigan State College, 1950.

Marx, M. H. Resistance to extinction as a function of delay of reinforcement and the opportunity to retrace in the runway. *Psychonomic Science*, 1967, *8*, 287–288. (a)

Marx, M. H. Increased resistance to extinction as a function of the opportunity to retrace in the runway. *Psychonomic Science*, 1967, *9*, 397–398. (b)

Marx, M. H. An experimental test of the interfering-response theory of extinction. *Psychonomic Science*, 1968, *10*, 233–238.

McCain, G. Partial reinforcement effects following a small number of acquisition trials. *Psychonomic Monograph Supplements*, 1966, *1*, 251–270.

Pennypacker, H. S. External inhibition of the conditioned eyelid reflex. *Journal of Experimental Psychology*, 1964, *67*, 33–40.

Premack, D. Toward empirical behavior laws: I. Positive reinforcement. *Psychological Review*, 1959, *66*, 219–233.

Premack, D., Schaeffer, R. W., & Hundt, A. Reinforcement of drinking by running: Effect of fixed ratio and reinforcement time. *Journal of Experimental Analysis of Behavior*, 1964, *7*, 91–96.

Rilling, M., Askew, H. R., Ahlskog, J. E., & Kramer, T. J. Aversive properties of the negative stimulus in a successive discrimination. *Journal of Experimental Analysis of Behavior*, 1969, *12*, 917–932.

Rohrer, J. H. A motivational state resulting from non-reward. *Journal of Comparative and Physiological Psychology*, 1949, *42*, 476–485.

Schlosberg, H., & Pratt, C. H. The secondary reward value of inaccessible food for hungry and satiated rats. *Journal of Comparative and Physiological Psychology*, 1956, *49*, 149–152.

Singh, D., & Wickens, D. D. Disinhibition in instrumental conditioning. *Journal of Comparative and Physiological Psychology*, 1968, *66*, 557–559.

Skinner, B. F. A failure to obtain "disinhibition." *Journal of General Psychology*, 1936, *14*, 127–135.

Skinner, B. F. *The behavior of organisms; an experimental analysis.* New York: Appleton-Century, 1938.

Skinner, B. F. Are theories of learning necessary? *Psychological Review*, 1950, *57*, 193–216.

Spence, K. W. The nature of discrimination learning in animals. *Psychological Review*, 1936, *43*, 427–449.

Spence, K. W. *Behavior theory and learning.* Englewood Cliffs, N.J.: Prentice-Hall, 1960.

Sutey, B. K. Frustration reduction or frustration elicitation as a reinforcing state of affairs. Unpublished MA thesis, Michigan State University, 1967.

Theios, J., & Bower, G. H. A test of the competing response-interference hypothesis of extinction. *Psychonomic Science*, 1964, *1*, 395–396.

Thompson, M. E. Spontaneous recovery and partial reinforcement effects in the runway. *Psychonomic Science*, 1966, *5*, 33–34. (a)

Thompson, M. E. Reminiscence and partial reinforcement in a discrete bar press situation. *Psychonomic Science*, 1966, *6*, 481–482. (b)

Tombaugh, T. N. Resistance to extinction as a function of the interaction between training and extinction delays. *Psychological Reports*, 1966, *19*, 791–798.

Wagner, A. R. Conditioned frustration as a learned drive. *Journal of Experimental Psychology*, 1963, *66*, 142–148.

Weinstock, S. Acquisition and extinction of a partially reinforced running response at a 24-hr. intertrial interval. *Journal of Experimental Psychology*, 1958, *56*, 151–158.

Wike, E. L., Mellgren, R. L., & Wike, S. Runway performance as a function of delayed reinforcement and delay-box confinement. *Psychological Record*, 1968, *18*, 9–18.

Cognitive Inhibition in Classical Conditioning

GREGORY A. KIMBLE

The single hypothesis to be examined in this paper had its origins many years ago. Sechenov (1935), an approximate contemporary of Darwin's, for example, had this to say:

> When the impression [effect of a stimulus] is absolutely unexpected the reflex movement is effected exclusively through the nervous centre connecting sensory and motor nerves. But if the stimulation is expected, a new mechanism interferes with the phenomenon seeking to suppress and inhibit the reflex movement [p. 43].

In making this statement Sechenov was thinking in strictly neuroanatomical terms. In anticipation of Sherrington, he had developed the concepts of synapse and reflex arc. He had also outlined a sophisticated theory of reflex action according to which the reflex is mediated at more than one level of the central nervous system. Although at times he argued that the higher levels of control could enhance or augment the magnitude of a reflex, more characteristically he emphasized the inhibitory influence of higher centers upon lower ones. Thus, preparing for the receipt of a reflex-producing stimulus (a higher level activity) diminishes the effectiveness of that stimulus.

As an example of the type of relationship Sechenov was proposing, we may cite just one example from Konorski (1960). This investigator observed the unconditioned salivary reflex of a dog before and after decortication. The general pattern of salivation appears in Figure 1. Following decortication, eating continued for considerably longer than prior to the operation and there was a strong tendency for salivation to continue following the termination of

The empirical materials reported in this chapter were obtained in experiments supported in part by NIMH grants, No. 8090 to the author and No. 15315 to Dr. L. C. Perlmuter.

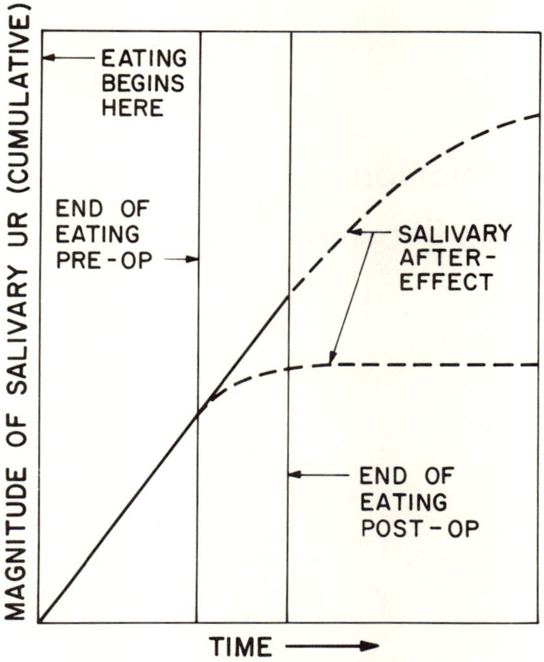

FIGURE 1. Inhibition of eating and unconditioned salivation by the cerebral cortex. The solid line depicts the course of salivation during eating. The dashed line shows salivation after the cessation of eating. The lower function is for the intact animal; the upper function was obtained following decortication. Note that the decorticated animal eats for a longer period of time and shows a pronouncedly greater salivary aftereffect. (Adapted from Konorski, 1960.)

eating. It was as if the cerebral cortex were exercising a suppressive inhibitory effect both upon eating and upon unconditioned salivation.

The conception that reflex activity is mediated at several neural levels has persisted in the Pavlovian literature and has been extended to include conditioned as well as unconditioned reflexes. A contemporary schematic expression of this conception appears in Figure 2. This sketch, from a book by Asratyan (1949), suggests that the conditioned salivary reflex is formed by the establishment of temporary neural connections at cortical and subcortical levels. The original point made by Sechenov, extended to this context, would lead to the expectation that the cortical connections would exercise an inhibitory influence over those at a subcortical level.

The data to be presented in this paper make a strong case for the conclusion that this expectation is valid. The time has come however to translate the Pavlovian concept of "cortical inhibition" into a behavioral one of "cognitive

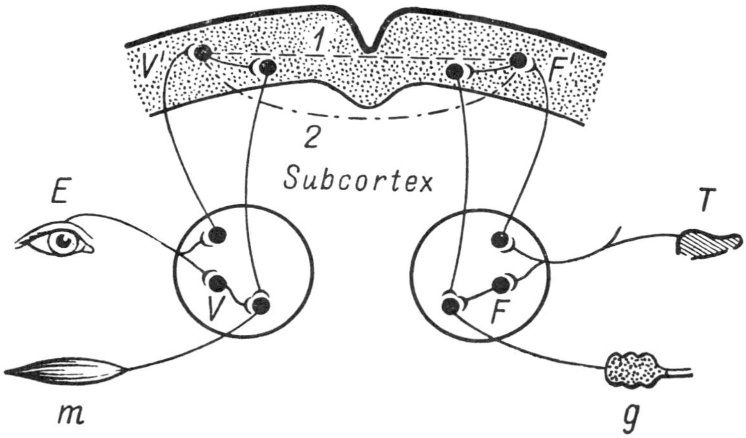

FIGURE 2. Scheme representing the connections formed in the establishment of a classically conditioned reflex according to Asratyan (1949). EVM, the subcortical visual unconditioned reflex arc. EV^1M, the cortical visual unconditioned reflex arc. TFG and TF^1G, subcortical and cortical unconditioned reflex arcs. V^1-1-F^1, cortical conditioned connection. V^1-1-F^1, V^1-2-F^1, subcortical conditioned connection.

inhibition" on the not unreasonable assumption that cognitive activities require the participation of the neocortex in their operation. According to this translation the idea to be presented is that cognitive processes would tend to interfere with classical conditioning. In a sense this point may be taken as an extension and elaboration of Spence's theory of inhibitory set (Spence, 1966). Whereas Spence applied such reasoning chiefly to the process of extinction, however, there also seem to be important implications for the process of acquisition. An adequate development of this idea necessitates the spelling out of some of the complexities of classical conditioning that are basic to it.

THE COMPLEXITIES OF CLASSICAL CONDITIONING

Pavlovian conditioning is commonly accepted as the very simplest form of learning. If this characterization is correct, the actual complexity of the process may come as disquieting news to students of still more elaborate forms of learning who sometimes argue that more complex forms of learning are somehow based upon classical conditioning. For it turns out that classical conditioning is simple only in terms of procedures. The behavioral changes that occur as a result of these procedures, by contrast, are complexly determined and demand the recognition of at least three major sets of variables and of at least two contributing processes. Moreover, these variables and processes interact in intricate ways that remain to be understood, except in general outline.

Three classes of variables

Proceeding from events that can be specifically localized in time to those that are less and less definite, there is some value in recognizing that the independent variables which govern the progress of classical conditioning fall into at least three crude classes: (a) "on-trial" variables, events that take place on a single conditioning trial; for example, US intensity and the CS-US interval. (b) "Within-experiment" variables, events that involve several trials or the entire experimental session, such as patterns of reinforced and nonreinforced trials in an experiment on partial reinforcement, instructions to the subject, and changes in various experimental parameters. (c) "Extra-experimental" variables, events that have happened outside the experimental situation; for example, training that resulted in a certain type of personality (e.g., anxious), the subject's physical condition, and his frame of mind. It may be of importance in this connection to mention that a sound understanding of the great majority of these latter events will probably be lacking for a long time. The most fruitful strategy at the present stage of development in psychology appears to be to attempt to measure the later influences of these variables through the use of personality tests, attitude questionnaires, and other devices for the assessment of individual differences. Even when we have learned more than we know now about the effects of these personal differences upon conditioning, there will still remain the task of linking the differences themselves to experimental, and perhaps genetic, causes. Obviously, this is no small undertaking.

It would be a stroke of scientific luck if it were possible to sort the influences of the three classes of variables identified above in terms of their control of separate basic processes. Unfortunately, this is not possible. In the following section on levels of conditioning, I shall propose that it is essential to distinguish between associations developed at a cognitive level and those responsible for the elicitation of a CR. On-trial variables and the longer-term sets of variables have influences on both types of association.

Levels of conditioning

In the Pavlovian tradition, as mentioned earlier, it is conventional to think of classical conditioning as occurring simultaneously at several levels, these levels being conceived as levels in the central nervous system. Processes that appear to correspond to these levels are, if anything, easier to identify at a more nearly behavioral level. For example, human *S*s frequently complete their sessions in a conditioning experiment without producing a single CR. These same *S*s, however, have no difficulty in describing the experiment in considerable detail (Hartman & Grant, 1962a). Obviously, such *S*s learned something in the experiment, but what they learned was not the same thing as the CR. In common-sense terms, they acquired a certain knowledge or cognitive understanding of the conditions of the experiment. In the words of Tolman, they acquired an "expectancy" or a knowledge of what leads to what in the experimental situation. When a CR is learned, it is a separate acquisition, different from this cognitive form of learning.

A parenthetic methodological note. No doubt the initial reaction of many readers of the paragraph above will be that it is a curious statement to find in a volume of papers written as a tribute to Kenneth W. Spence. For it seems to embrace the concepts of expectancy and stimulus-stimulus learning, both of which are commonly seen as ideas to which Spence was opposed. The prospect of such a reaction appears to demand at least some comment. Several points seem pertinent. The first point is simply that Spence (e.g., 1950) characteristically took the position that the S-R interpretation seemed more fruitful to him than the S-S view, but that the differences between the two theories were differences of emphasis rather than matters of direct conflict. At times, he even went so far as to suggest the possible existence of stimulus-stimulus learning:

> Certainly simple types of perceptual learning would appear possibly to involve intersensory associations. I seriously doubt, however, whether learning is exclusively of this type, or even that the majority of it is. Indeed, what little experimental evidence there is on the point, even in the field of such simple learning as conditioning, would appear to support more strongly the S-R conception than the S-S [1950, pp. 164–165].

This passage captures the essence of Spence's typical stance. The tendency to view him as staunchly and completely devoted to S-R and as adamantly and unalterably opposed to S-S is a distortion of fact. Further evidence that Spence was sensitive to the processes emphasized in cognitive theory is to be found in his use of the r_g-s_g mechanisms and in his acceptance of the concept, K, in connection with incentive motivation.

Second, at least in the field of classical conditioning, it is obviously time to give up whatever remaining preoccupation there may be with the S-S vs. S-R learning controversy. Analysis of the physiological bases of conditioning reveals that they involve mechanisms in which the distinction between S and R is nearly meaningless (Young, 1965). Partly for this reason and partly because it seems to me to be unnecessary, I do not wish to be put in the position of taking sides on this issue. In what follows I shall simply maintain that, as a matter of fact, both cognitive learning and conditioning typically take place in the same situation. My interest will be in the question of how these two forms of learning interact.

The operational facts of the matter seem to demand the distinction made above between cognitive learning and conditioning in the more usual sense. Subjects' verbal descriptions of the circumstances of the experiment provide the operational identification of the first of these forms of learning. The development of the CR affords similar status to the second. The basis for making a distinction between them is that at least the cognitive form of learning can take place in the absence of conditioning in the usual sense. Examples of classical conditioning situations in which fairly elaborate statements of the experimental arrangement can be obtained without the establishment of a CR include the following: backward conditioning, conditioning on a partial schedule of reinforcement, and conditioning with a very long CS-US interval. Whether the reverse of this is true, that is, whether a CR can be formed in the absence of an understanding of the conditions of the experiment, is a question to which I wish to return in a moment. In anticipation of that discussion, however, let me mention here that I am inclined to doubt it.

A related question concerns the applicability of this separation of cognitive learning and conditioning to studies of lower animals who cannot communicate in words. In this context the old observations of Zener (1937) seem important. Zener described the behavior of the dog in the classical conditioning experiment with careful attention to detail. Among other things, he noted that the dog betrayed its understanding of the sequence of experimental events by a number of behavioral signs: looking at the CS when it came on, approaching the food delivery mechanism, and so on. These reactions occurred before the development of a CR and, on a given trial, whether or not a CR occurred. To me, these reactions argue for the conceptual separation of the CR from the other behavioral acquisitions of the subject in the conditioning experiment. To Zener and to many others, by contrast, the same data were taken to mean that the CR is an organismic, holistic reaction in which the elements of cognitive understanding and expectancy are of predominant importance.

At the time Zener offered his interpretation, an argument raged between the "S-R theorists" and the "expectancy (S-S) theorists." The former were the intellectual progeny of Pavlov, Thorndike, and Watson. Their most effective spokesman was Guthrie. Hull and Spence are commonly considered as belonging in this camp; but, as Spence (1950) pointed out, Hull became an S-R theorist only in the context of a set of gratuitous neurophysiological additions to his theory. Spence himself, as we have seen, leaned toward the S-R hypothesis but took no absolutely firm position on this issue. The expectancy theorists were heavily influenced by Gestalt psychology; their chief advocate in the field of learning was Tolman. Underlying this dispute was the unvoiced assumption that one systematic position must be right and the other wrong, at least for large classes of experimental situations. The main conciliatory theoretical gesture came from a small group of two-process theorists. These theorists (e.g., Schlosberg, 1937) held out a possible compromise according to which S-R theory was correct for some forms of learning and expectancy theory was correct for others. The usual position was that classical conditioning involves the development of expectancies and instrumental learning stimulus-response connections.

Even fairly recently (Kimble, 1967) the two-process resolution seemed an attractive theoretical possibility, at least to me. Now, however, the time seems to have come to give up that happy compromise. As the evidence accumulates, it begins to appear that even two-factor theory is an unrealistic oversimplification. Classical and instrumental conditioning are both much more complicated than expectancy theory, S-R theory, or two-process theory treated them as being. A strong argument can be made that cognitions and stimulus-response connections are both formed in any learning situation and that the results of learning experiments depend upon contributions of both types.

Relationships among levels. Presently available evidence suggests that the relationships among these levels of conditioning may be summarized in three points: (a) the most general effect of cognitions upon conditioning is inhibitory. This is the main point of this paper and will be developed in detail in what follows. (b) In spite of this general inhibitory influence, there is other more limited evidence to indicate that cognitive understanding is an essential preliminary to the establishment of a CR. It is possible, for example, to take the results of Chatterjee and Eriksen (1960), who studied GSR and semantic conditioning in human subjects, to mean that the *S* gave a CR only to words that he recognized as possibly dangerous and followed by shock. Previously (Kimble, 1962), I cited certain Russian work on interoceptive conditioning as evidence for *classical* conditioning without awareness and, therefore, without the necessity for cognitive understanding. Unsuccessful attempts at repeating this work, together with a set of serious reservations about the meaning of awareness in this context, have now considerably diminished my enthusiasm for this position. (c) If there are two phases of classical conditioning, as several theorists (Jones, 1962; Liu, 1964) have proposed, it seems very reasonable to suppose (although this is not the supposition of the theorists just mentioned) that the first of these is a cognitive phase and that the second phase is conditioning in the usual sense. One type of evidence for such an interpretation will appear in several sets of results to be presented in this paper. It is that the inhibitory influences attributed to cognition appear very early in the conditioning experiment. Acquisition curves obtained under conditions assumed to differ in the extent to which such processes operate tend to be separate after the very first few trials. This fact seems to require the postulation of some rapidly acquired disposition against responding that must be treated as different from the CR.

OVERVIEW OF THE ARGUMENT

Briefly summing up the points covered so far: there is accumulating reason to believe that the process of classical conditioning is quite complicated. On this basis I have suggested that such conditioning requires the identification of three sets of variables (on-trial, within-experiment, and extra-experimental) and two contributing processes (cognitive learning and CR formation). The general argument I wish to make is that cognitive learning inhibits CR formation. On the other hand it seems improbable that the different sets of variables are equally strict in the cognitive demands they place upon the *S* or equally generous in the opportunities they provide for cognitive understanding. These demands and opportunities are quite limited in a simple conditioning situation, where about all that happens is that the US follows the CS after a brief period of time. The use of a ready signal, conditioning with a partial schedule of reinforcement, or the use of a discrimination procedure (all within-experiment manipulations) offer many more opportunities for the operation of cognitive influences. Consequently, the empirical material presented in this paper will concentrate on such variables. We shall begin with such a discussion and then turn to an interpretation of results obtained in experiments involving on-trial and extra-experimental variables.

WITHIN-EXPERIMENT VARIABLES

In discussing the results of the first study of eyelid conditioning employing the probability-learning masking task, Spence, Homzie, and Rutledge (1964) attributed the greater resistance to extinction of *S*s conditioned under such distracting conditions to their tendency *not* to recognize the change from conditioning to extinction and, therefore, *not* to adopt an inhibitory set. This interpretation clearly anticipates that being offered here. The study itself also stands as a prototype of those to be considered in this section. The experimental circumstances were manipulated in such a way as to produce over a series of trials, but probably not within a single trial, a difference in the *S*s' understanding of the experimental arrangement.

The inhibitory influence of ready signals

The inhibitory effect of ready signals upon eyelid conditioning is possibly the best documented of the inhibitory influences of within-experiment variables. A series of studies, of which Turner's (1966) is one of the most comprehensive, has shown that the use of such a signal reduces the level of conditioning by something like 20 percent, using a probability measure as the index of conditioning. Turner conditioned different groups of *S*s with a ready signal (a 1-sec. burst of white noise) preceding each trial by 1.0 to 7.5 sec., or without such a signal. Certain of the results of this experiment appear in Figure 3. Two points are of particular interest: (a) There is a marked reduction in performance for the group conditioned with a ready signal. (b) The difference in performance is already present on the first block of 15 conditioning trials. Subsequent fine-grain analysis of these early trials revealed that the difference was

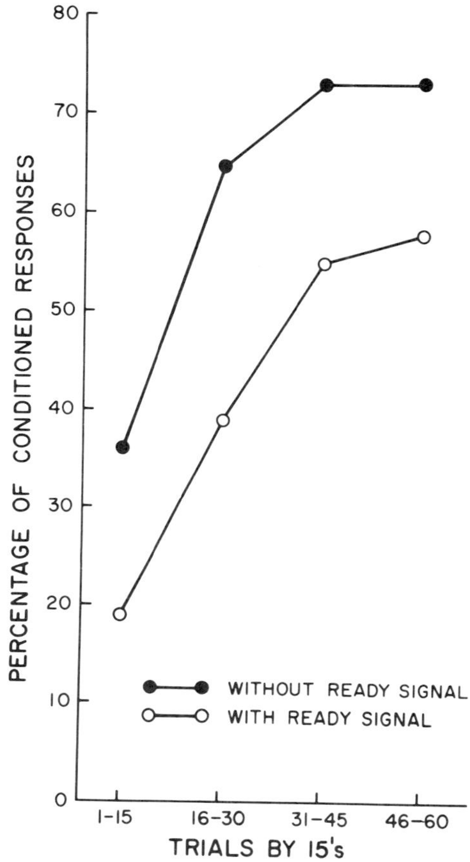

FIGURE 3. The acquisition of the classically conditioned eyelid response in groups conditioned with and without a ready signal. (Redrawn from data published by Turner, 1966.)

actually present after just 3 trials. Obviously the ready signal has an almost immediate effect. From its first appearance this effect seems to be approximately constant, as revealed by the roughly parallel courses of the two functions throughout conditioning.

The dependability of the inhibitory effect of a ready signal is one of the strongest pieces of evidence for the validity of Sechenov's general proposition that preparedness interferes with reflex behavior. The further interpretation that this influence depends upon *cognitive* preparedness requires additional evidence. One suggestion of such support is to be found in an unpublished eyelid conditioning experiment by Perlmuter, Krems, and Kimble. In this experiment *S*s were conditioned with three different types of ready signal, the word "ready," a white noise, and an airpuff. There were also two control groups, one an ordinary conditioning control, the other a conditioning group with interpolated airpuffs. Acquisition functions for these five groups appear in Figure 4. It should be noted that a degree of inhibition occurred in all groups but that the greatest amount occurred in the group conditioned with the verbal ready signal. This result surprised us, even though we had predicted it in planning the experiment. What it seems to tell us is that the verbal ready signal is reacted to in a way that is particularly inhibitory. To the extent that cognitive processes are verbal processes, this supplies support for the hypothesis that ready signals have their effects through a mechanism specifically involving cognition.

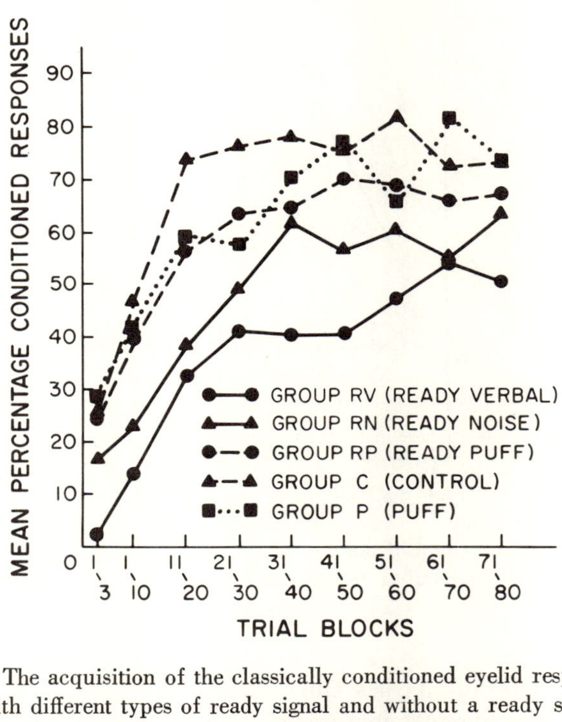

FIGURE 4. The acquisition of the classically conditioned eyelid response in groups conditioned with different types of ready signal and without a ready signal under two different conditions. Note, in addition to the ordering of the groups, the immediacy with which the effects appear. (Perlmuter, Krems, & Kimble, unpublished.)

Partial reinforcement

A second within-experiment manipulation with a marked inhibitory influence in *classical* conditioning is the use of a partial schedule of reinforcement. A typical experiment was done by Fowler (1964) for his doctoral dissertation. Fowler conditioned *S*s' eyelid responses under either continuous or a 50 percent quasi-random schedule of reinforcement and with two different interstimulus intervals, .4 and 1.1 sec. The results of the study appear in Figure 5. Obviously the partial schedule inhibited conditioning but more so in the 1.1-sec. condition than in the .4-sec. condition. This may mean that the mediating inhibitory cognitive activity takes time and had a better chance to demonstrate its influence with the longer interval.

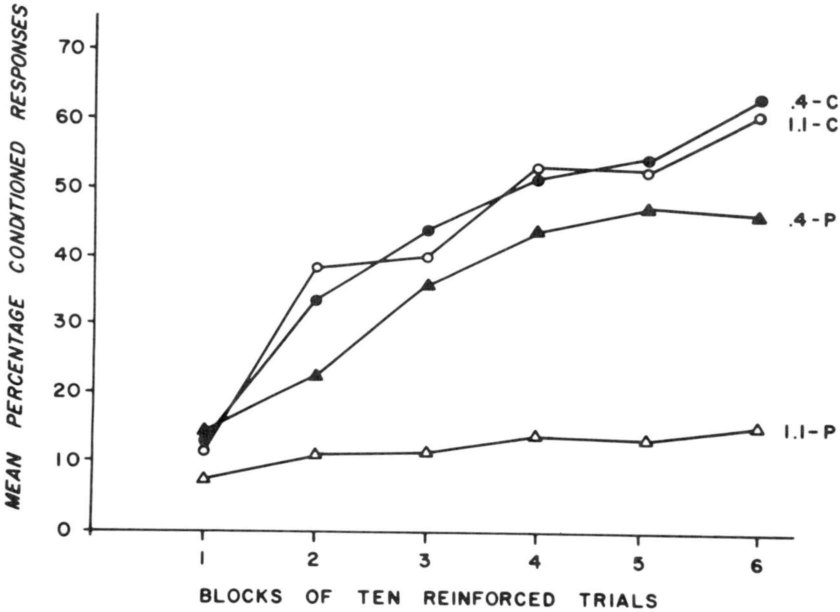

FIGURE 5. Acquisition of the classically conditioned eyelid response in groups conditioned with interstimulus intervals of .4 and 1.1 sec. and with 50 or 100 percent reinforcement. (Fowler, 1964.)

These results differ from Turner's in that the effect of the schedule did not appear until after 10 trials. This is not surprising, however, because it takes more trials for the *S* to learn anything about the sequence of reinforced and nonreinforced trials. Taking this into account, the results in Figure 5 again show that the influence under discussion appears early in conditioning and obviously before the conditioning process represented in the percentage of conditioned responses is anything like complete.

A particularly important point about the inhibitory effect of partial schedules is that regular sequences (e.g., double-alteration sequences) of reinforced and nonreinforced trials are particularly disastrous to the progress of classical conditioning (Hartman & Grant, 1962a). Since it is possible to "track" such schedules by counting, this in a different way calls attention to the important inhibitory role of cognitive processes in classical conditioning.

Differential conditioning

Differential conditioning provides a somewhat different context in which to examine the inhibitory influence of procedures that call cognitive mechanisms into play. In *Conditioning and Learning* (Kimble, 1961) I treated classical discrimination learning in terms of the noncognitive theory advanced by Spence (1936) and offered this summary of underlying assumptions:

> (1) that every reinforcement leads to an increment in the (excitatory) tendency to repeat the reinforced response, (2) that every non-reinforcement leads to an increment in the (inhibitory) tendency not to respond, (3) that both of these tendencies generalize to other stimuli, (4) that the magnitude of the inhibitory tendency is less than that of the excitatory tendency (otherwise learning could not occur in any partial-reinforcement situation, S+ and S— being the same stimulus, where reinforced and non-reinforced trials occur in a ratio of 1:1 or less), (5) that the excitatory and inhibitory tendencies interact algebraically, and (6) that discriminatory reactions are based on the resolution of the competing tendencies in favor of the reaction to the stimulus which has the stronger tendency conditioned (or generalized) to it [p. 364].

At the time of that writing, the most complete test of this "conditioning-extinction" theory in a classical situation was the eyelid conditioning study of Gynther (1957). In this study the positive and negative stimuli were small lights separated by about two inches. One light was consistently reinforced, the other nonreinforced. Gynther obtained results that supported the following predictions from the theory: (a) performance under the reinforced stimulus was lower in discriminative conditioning than under ordinary conditioning with continuous reinforcement. (b) There was a substantial level of generalized responding to the nonreinforced stimulus. (c) Increasing the ratio of reinforced to nonreinforced trials from 1:1 to 3:1 raised the level of responding both to S+ and S—. (d) The introduction of discrimination trials following preliminary conditioning to S+ alone lowered the level of responding to S+, theoretically because of the effect of inhibition generalized from S—. (e) Increasing the physical difference between S+ and S— increased the differential in performance to the two stimuli. When S+ and S— were identical (partial reinforcement) there was, of course, no differential conditioning and overall performance was lowest of any condition in the experiment.

Such confirmation of the theory giving rise to the experiment was so impressive that perhaps we may be forgiven for failing to pay sufficient attention to (or probably even to notice) a problem of interpretation. Much of what happened in the experiment happened a little too rapidly, the effects of several manipulations being detectable within a very few trials. Similar results in extinction, of course, are what led Spence (1964) to the conclusion that the rapid loss of response strength was the result of cognitive factors which he then sought to exclude with the introduction of the masking task. Although the importance of such factors could have been inferred from incidental results in Gynther's dissertation, it took me a decade and a dozen more experiments to reach this conclusion and finally to give cognitive and attitudinal variables the importance they deserve even in ordinary conditioning (Kimble, 1967, Ch. 46).

The extension of this way of thinking to differential conditioning was strongly suggested by the work of Hartman and Grant (1962b) which showed that the optional CS-US interval for such conditioning was longer than for ordinary conditioning. This, from two different perspectives, suggests either of two interpretations: (a) it might be that differential conditioning calls a mediating cognitive process into play, that it takes time for the *S* to identify the stimulus as positive or negative, and that this accounts for the longer optimal interval; (b) it might be that the inhibition of responses to S− is a time-consuming process and that this inhibition, generalized to S+, slows responses to the point where a longer interval is optimal. The argument advanced here implies that these two interpretations may not be incompatible, that cognitive processes are inhibitory with respect to classical CRs and that one is in effect the equivalent of the other.

Although it would be incorrect to describe it as the test of this idea, my most recent experiment in conditioning (Kimble, Leonard, & Perlmuter, 1968) is quite illuminating with respect to this point. This was a differential conditioning experiment for certain groups in the sense that different conditioned stimuli signaled reinforcement after interstimulus intervals of 0.5 or 1.2 sec. Other groups were conditioned at just one interval or the other. The results of the experiment corresponded to certain expectations derived from the classical theory: (a) performance was lower under the discrimination procedure than under the conditioning procedure, (b) there was substantial generalization of responses conditioned at the short interval to the stimulus associated with the long interval. It is important to note, however, that the first of these results could not, as conditioning-extinction theory requires, result from nonreinforcement, since both stimuli were reinforced. This fact, together with the details of the data, led us to conclude that the inhibition generated in differential conditioning results not from nonreinforcement, but from the cognitive process of making a discrimination.

ON-TRIAL VARIABLES

Unfortunately for the particular argument being made here, the values of on-trial variables in the typical conditioning experiments are usually carefully selected to produce good learning. This means that inhibitory influences tend to be minimized. There are, however, two or three lines of evidence that suggest the operation of the same principles as were discussed in the section on within-experiment variables.

One of these involves the history, in the conditioning experiment, of the so-called orienting reflex, commonly taken as an index of paying attention to the CS. As conditioning proceeds there is a tendency for this reflex to disappear, suggesting diminished attentiveness and decreased cognitive involvement.

More substantial evidence is provided by the phenomenon of "conditioned diminution" of the unconditioned reflex, reported by Kimble and Ost (1961). The essential nature of this effect, illustrated in Figure 6, is that the magnitude of the unconditioned reflex is smaller on trials with the CS than on trials without it. Once more the important point may be that the CS provides the individual with a signal that enables him to prepare for the US and that this very preparedness exercises an inhibitory influence upon the reflex reaction.

The most recent study of conditioned diminution of the UR (Hupka, Kwaterski, & Moore, 1970) compares the effect in the human eyeblink and in the conditioned nictitating membrane reaction in the rabbit. These data show that the phenomenon occurs in the first of these reactions and not in the second, a result that may come from the presumably greater cognitive involvement of human subjects in experiments of any type.

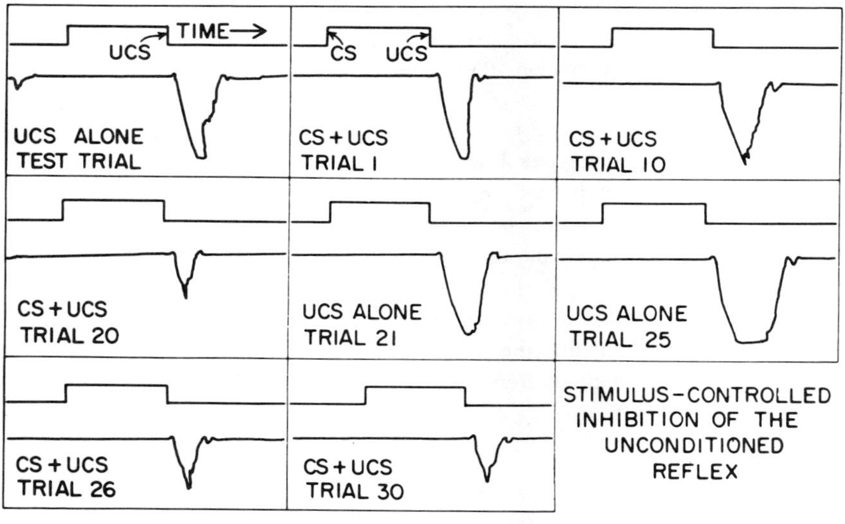

FIGURE 6. Conditioned diminution of the unconditioned eyelid reflex. The subject who produced this record gave no CRs, but did show marked differences in the amplitude of the unconditioned reflex on trials with (CS + UCS) and without (UCS alone) the unconditioned stimulus. Note the rapidity with which this effect occurs by comparing amplitudes on Trials 20 and 21 and Trials 25 and 26. (For further discussion of this effect, see Kimble & Ost, 1961.)

Although he cites the evidence in support of quite a different interpretation, Bruner's comments upon the inhibition of the sucking activities of infants seem to support the general argument being offered here:

> At birth, and for some days after, the infant sucks with eyes tight shut. If the infant looks, tracks, or listens, sucking is disrupted. . . . With the three- to five-week-old baby, the eyes may be open while sucking, but there is a high likelihood that when fixation or tracking occurs, sucking stops [Bruner, 1968, p. 18].

Again, it looks very much as though orienting behavior, which I would take as a simple form of cognitive activity, has an interfering effect—this time, again, upon an unconditioned reflex.

Possibly the most important influence of this cognitive, inhibitory mechanism as it relates to on-trial variables may be that it contributes to the determination of the form of the interstimulus-interval function. It is well known, of course, that the level of conditioning decreases for many responses if this interval is more than about .5 sec. It is not obvious why this should be so. Certainly time intervals of this magnitude do not tax the associative powers of the organism. On the other hand, such intervals do allow the organism to assume a condition of readiness for the receipt of the US and a byproduct of this condition could be an inhibition of the CR.

Obviously, the influences described in this section must be taken as merely suggestive of the operation of a cognitively controlled inhibitory mechanism. A general strategy for direct experimental examination of the effect, however, is equally obvious: experiments arranged to establish conditioned reflexes under conditions of lowered cognitive involvement (perhaps using something like Spence's masking task) should lessen the degree of conditioned diminution of the UR, and they should produce better conditioning at long CS-US intervals. To the best of my knowledge the indicated experiments have not been done.

Extra-experimental variables

The situation with respect to the role of the extra-experimental variables is even less satisfactory than in the case of on-trial variables so far as the hypothesis advanced here is concerned. At present the chief possibility for studying such effects appears to be through the investigation of individual differences in conditioning. In this area, work has been dominated by the investigation of the influence of anxiety upon conditioning. Results of numerous studies have shown, without much doubt, that *S*s with high anxiety as measured by some test such as the Taylor scale of manifest anxiety condition better than those with low levels of anxiety.

The important question left unanswered in these studies is the appropriateness of the designation "anxiety." For some time I have suspected that what the tests employed in these studies actually measure is tendency toward impulsive reactivity to events in the environment as opposed to a more thoughtful or cognitive style. Admittedly, this suspicion is without much empirical basis. What is badly needed is a study employing some measure developed deliberately as a test of this dimension of personal variation, and a comparison of the effectiveness of this measure in the prediction of conditionability with measures obtained with tests of manifest anxiety. If, in addition, scores on the anxiety scale were available for the same *S*s, it should be possible to obtain an indication of the extent to which the two tests measure the same traits as well as which measure has greater predictive power.

Chronological age is another extra-experimental variable that has a demonstrated effect upon classical conditioning. Children are better conditioners than young adults, who in turn are better conditioners than aged *S*s. The interpretation being offered here suggests a partial solution to the puzzle of why young children are better conditioning subjects than young adults. They characteristically function without a fully developed level of cognitive control. Whether the inferior conditioning of aged subjects (Kimble & Pennypacker, 1963) fits the same pattern raises an interesting question, but there is some evidence that the answer to this question may be in the affirmative. For one thing, the old *S*s in the study of Kimble and Pennypacker did show a greater tendency toward diminution of the UR than the younger *S*s, an influence that now seems the result of cognitive involvement. For another thing, in retrospect it seems definite that many of our older *S*s went considerably out of their way to make the simple conditioning situation an intellectual challenge. They showed much greater concern than did college students about the adequacy of their performance; they wanted to know how they were doing and whether their performance met acceptable standards of normality.

SUMMARY AND A BASIC QUESTION

In this paper, I have attempted to show that cognitive activity tends to inhibit and interfere with the acquisition and performance of classically conditioned reflexes. This process is complicated in two main ways: (a) the inhibiting cognitive process seems necessary to the establishment of the very conditioned reactions it inhibits, and (b) the mode of operation of this inhibiting process is through several sets of variables: on-trial, within-experiment, and extra-experimental. The evidence for cognitive inhibition is most substantial for the within-experiment variables, possibly because they are most susceptible to verbal (cognitive) encoding. More limited data, however, also point to the usefulness of the basic idea in the more complete context.

Assuming that the evidence advanced here for cognitive inhibition of the CR is sufficient to require that the hypothesis be taken seriously, a basic question seems worth raising: why should this relationship between cognition and conditioned reflexes exist? The answer to this question raises several issues to which the remainder of this contribution is devoted.

At one level of analysis, it seems inevitable that the cognitive inhibition of conditioned reflexes is a matter of the suppression of the CR by competing reactions. In some cases this seems very clear. Pennypacker (1967), for example, studied the external inhibition of the classically conditioned eyeblink. In this experiment *S*s were conditioned at a 1.0-sec. CS-US interval, using a light as a CS and an airpuff as a US. On critical trials a brief tone was sounded halfway through the interval. On these trials the *S*s gave very few CRs. A general explanation in terms of the argument offered here would be that the novel stimulus gained the attention of the *S* and that this paying attention (a cognitive process) interfered with the evocation of the CR. In his analysis, however, Pennypacker was able to show that the external inhibition (the tone) usually elicited its own reaction (also a blink), and that this appeared to be responsible for the inhibition of the CR. One suspects that the basic mechanism at work when cognition inhibits the CR may always be something like this.

Whatever virtues there are in this type of explanation, I find myself more attracted to a different way of looking at the problem, one that seems to give it broader significance. The critical feature of this different viewpoint is that it considers the conditioned reflex not as a peculiar and isolated type of reaction but as a part of a group of responses that might be called automatic behavior. This collection includes unconditioned reflexes and heavily overlearned motor behavior as well as the CR. These reactions all take place under circumstances where the individual reports no intention or active personal intervention. Reportedly, they occur without thought and without awareness and are commonly referred to as involuntary.

Obviously, this feature of automatic behavior has a certain biological adaptive value in that it allows the organism to engage in more important attention-demanding activities while the automatized reactions proceed "on their own." At the same time, it would seem of equal biological significance for nature to have arranged things so that these automatic activities would be interrupted under circumstances requiring greater intellectual involvement. Circumstances requiring thought, attention, and decision making are precisely those in which thoughtless, automatic, involuntary reactions seem most maladaptive. Within this framework the relationship outlined in this paper seems to take on great significance in that it identifies a set of processes that enable the individual to operate effectively in a complex world.

REFERENCES

Asratyan, E. A. *I. P. Pavlov, his life and work.* Moscow: Foreign Languages Publishing House, 1949.

Bruner, J. S. Processes of cognitive growth: infancy. In *Eighth annual report 1967–1968 of the Harvard University Center for Cognitive Studies*, 1968.

Chatterjee, B. B., & Eriksen, C. W. Conditioning and generalization of GSR as a function of awareness. *Journal of Abnormal and Social Psychology*, 1960, *60*, 396–403.

Fowler, W. R. The interstimulus interval and schedule of reinforcement in eyelid conditioning. Unpublished doctoral dissertation, Duke University, 1964.

Gynther, M. D. Differential eyelid conditioning as a function of stimulus similarity and strength of response to the CS. *Journal of Experimental Psychology*, 1957, *53*, 408–416.

Hartman, T. F., & Grant, D. A. Effect of pattern of reinforcement and verbal information on acquisition, extinction and spontaneous recovery of the eyelid CR. *Journal of Experimental Psychology*, 1962, *63*, 217–226. (a)

Hartman, T. F., & Grant, D. A. Differential eyelid conditioning as a function of the CS-UCS interval. *Journal of Experimental Psychology*, 1962, *64*, 131–136. (b)

Hupka, R. B., Kwaterski, S. E., & Moore, J. W. Conditioned diminution of the UCR: differences between the human eyeblink and the rabbit nictitating membrane response. *Journal of Experimental Psychology*, 1970, *83*, 45–51.

Jones, J. Contiguity and reinforcement in aversive conditioning. *Psychological Review*, 1962, *69*, 176–186.

Kimble, G. A. *Hilgard and Marquis' conditioning and learning*. New York: Appleton-Century-Crofts, 1961.

Kimble, G. A. Classical conditioning and the problem of awareness. In C. W. Eriksen (Ed.), *Behavior and awareness*. Durham, N.C.: Duke University Press, 1962.

Kimble, G. A. *Foundations of conditioning and learning*. New York: Appleton-Century-Crofts, 1967.

Kimble, G. A., Leonard, T. B. III, & Perlmuter, L. C. Effects of interstimulus interval and discrimination learning in eyelid conditioning using between- and within-*S*s designs. *Journal of Experimental Psychology*, 1968, *77*, 652–660.

Kimble, G. A., & Ost, J. W. P. A conditioned inhibitory process in eyelid conditioning. *Journal of Experimental Psychology*, 1961, *61*, 150–156.

Kimble, G. A., & Pennypacker, H. S. Eyelid conditioning in young and aged subjects. *Journal of Genetic Psychology*, 1963, *103*, 283–289.

Konorski, J. The cortical "representation" of unconditioned reflexes. In H. H. Jasper & G. D. Smirnov (Eds.), *The Moscow colloquium on electroencephalography of higher nervous activity*. Supplement No. 13, *The International Journal of Electroencephalography and Clinical Neurophysiology*. Montreal: The EEG Journal, 1960. Pp. 81–90.

Liu, I. M. A theory of classical conditioning. *Psychological Review*, 1964, *71*, 408–411.

Pennypacker, H. S. External inhibition of the conditioned eyelid reflex. *Journal of Experimental Psychology*, 1964, *67*, 33–40.

Schlosberg, H. The relationship between success and the laws of conditioning. *Psychological Review*, 1937, *44*, 379–394.

Sechenov, I. *Selected works*. Moscow: State Publishing House, 1935.

Spence, K. W. The nature of discrimination learning in animals. *Psychological Review*, 1936, *43*, 427–449.

Spence, K. W. Cognitive versus stimulus-response theories of learning. *Psychological Review*, 1950, *57*, 159–172.

Spence, K. W. Cognitive and drive factors in the extinction of the conditioned eye blink in human subjects. *Psychological Review*, 1966, *73*, 445–458.

Spence, K. W., Homzie, M. J., & Rutledge, E. F. Extinction of the human eyelid CR as a function of the discriminability of the change from acquisition to extinction. *Journal of Experimental Psychology*, 1964, *67*, 545–552.

Turner, B. B. Effects of a ready signal upon eyelid conditioning. *Journal of Experimental Psychology*, 1966, *72*, 11–14.

Young, F. A. Classical conditioning of autonomic functions. In W. F. Prokasy (Ed.), *Classical conditioning*. New York: Appleton-Century-Crofts, 1965. Pp. 358–371.

Zener, K. The significance of the behavior accompanying conditioned salivary secretion for theories of the conditioned response. *American Journal of Psychology*, 1937, *50*, 384–403.

The Orienting Reflex and Thinking as Determiners of Conditioning and Generalization to Words

IRVING MALTZMAN

This essay will describe some of the research conducted in my laboratory over approximately the past 10 years. The work began as an investigation of the conditions giving rise to semantic conditioning and generalization, but of necessity, and in unforeseen ways, touched upon many other problems. The investigation of semantic conditioning and generalization was undertaken after almost a decade of research on topics such as complex higher mental processes, mental set, problem solving, and originality (e.g., Maltzman, 1955, 1960). A research program on semantic conditioning and generalization was initiated, its purpose to return to the study of "first principles." The Hullian learning theory approach that we employed in the study of the higher mental processes rested upon the assumed basic principles of semantic conditioning and generalization. Looking back upon this assumption of the primacy of principles of conditioning after almost a decade of research on semantic conditioning and generalization, we must now conclude that adult thinking is not a consequence of semantic conditioning and generalization as ordinarily envisaged, but to a

The studies reported here were made possible in part by funds provided by Public Health Service Research Grant MH 04684 from the National Institute of Mental Health and from the Carnegie Corporation of New York. For the analyses of the results of experiments reported here, computing assistance was obtained from the Health Science Computing Facility, UCLA, sponsored by National Institute of Health Grant FR–3.

I am greatly indebted to the many students who made this research possible: Sharon Brewster, D. Feeney, J. Gould, Ola Johnson, W. Kantor, B. Langdon, Carol Mochizuki, D. C. Raskin, J. Scull, M. Smith, C. Vincent, W. Watts, S. Weissbluth, C. Wolff, and Helen Yee. I am also indebted to Mrs. Lynn Ng for her creative computer programing which greatly facilitated the analyses of experimental results. I am especially indebted to Dr. Mary P. Mandell for her ability to disagree and for her fundamental theoretical and experimental insights. Much of what is said here represents her contributions.

far greater degree these "simple" processes are themselves a consequence of complex processes including thinking and attention.

It became apparent during the course of the present program of research that the "basic" principles of animal conditioning upon which the usual type of S-R learning theory formulation of semantic conditioning and generalization was based are inadequate for the task at hand. The principles of conditioning developed in animal studies cannot be applied in any straightforward fashion to conditioning, simple or semantic, in normal humans possessing speech, or more accurately, the ability to think—which we shall not attempt to define here. Possession of speech or the ability to think radically changes the nature of the principles of conditioning. Further, our research convinced us that the usual principles of conditioning, associative strength, drive, inhibition, etc., derived as they were primarily from animal conditioning and human eyelid-conditioning experiments, cannot be applied to many of the details of human conditioning involving physiological measures of the orienting reflex. There is an insufficient number of concepts available for an adequate interpretation of human behavior in various kinds of conditioning situations. This insufficiency is even more apparent when the more complex kinds of behaviors found in complex problem-solving situations are considered. It also became increasingly evident that the apparent clear-cut distinctions between concepts, such as between learning and drive, associative and nonassociative variables, and so forth, cannot be consistently maintained in the face of a variety of complexities of human behavior. The generality of these concepts and distinctions among them tend to be limited to the kinds of situations from which they were originally derived. Finally, it became our conviction that a molar behavior theory eschewing all reference to current advances in related disciplines, particularly physiological psychology, physiology, and neurophysiology, cannot possibly attain its goal of a self-contained set of behavioral laws that will adequately predict and explain behavior, and which may then be coordinated with principles of physiology. While a strictly molar behaviorism was clearly defensible during the 1930s and 1940s because of the paucity of reliable relevant physiological information, the situation has changed significantly since the inception of neobehaviorism.

The remainder of this essay will be concerned primarily with the presentation of some of our experimental results which led to this set of current beliefs.

SEMANTIC CONDITIONING

Just when our program of research on the problem of semantic conditioning and generalization was getting underway we became acquainted with the article by Luria and Vinogradova (1959). The authors were concerned with semantic conditioning and generalization of the orienting (OR) and defensive (DR) reflexes.* Their results and interpretation had a marked influence on our thinking and research at that time and since, and made it apparent that it literally is not possible to investigate conditioning and generalization of autonomic responses, at the very least, without considering the role of the OR. At that time the conditions giving rise to the OR, stimulus change and the significance of stimuli, seemed relatively straightforward. The theoretical role of the OR as a form of attention and reinforcement was intriguing, because it permitted a consistent interpretation of many phenomena which seemed highly resistant to reasonable interpretations in terms of the concepts available, particularly problems associated with human reinforcement and motivation. Learning, where there was no external reinforcement administered, which is often the case outside of the laboratory, and motivation, where there was no obvious external source such as deprivation or noxious stimulation, seemed susceptible to reinterpretation in terms of the OR (Maltzman & Raskin, 1965). Since then we have realized that the conditions that may give rise to the OR and the role of attention may be far more complex than initially stated in our own research and in the early Soviet literature that appeared in translation. Of far greater importance for human behavior than externally induced ORs are ORs that are self-generated, that are a consequence of thinking (Galperin, 1969; Hernandez-Peon, 1966; Maltzman & Mandell, 1968; Sokolov, 1969).

In any case, in addition to profoundly affecting our thinking, the Luria and Vinogradova article introduced us to an experimental procedure which we have used and enlarged upon in a number of studies, some of which we shall briefly describe here.

In one experiment reported by Luria and Vinogradova (1959), children were instructed to press a button with their right hand whenever they heard a particular word, e.g., CAT. The physiological measure of the OR obtained from the left hand, digital vasoconstriction, occurred to this critical word along with the motor response. But normal children also showed peripheral vasoconstriction to semantically related words even though they did not press the button. These subjects presumably oriented to the semantically related words as indicated by the greater vasoconstriction to them than to unrelated words, as a consequence of the original training. Thus Luria and Vinogradova demonstrated that the significance of a stimulus may be enhanced by instructions to perform a motor response, in addition to the more usual classical conditioning procedure of pairing a relatively "neutral" stimulus with a noxious UCS. They also demonstrated that semantic generalization of a measure of the OR can be studied without the necessity for employing noxious stimulation.

* We will not describe these concepts at length since there are readily available primary sources for this purpose (Sokolov, 1963, 1969; Voronin, Leontiev, Luria, Sokolov, & Vinogradova, 1965). We are using the term OR to refer to a pattern of physiological changes, particularly the GSR, which has, among a variety of other conditions, stimulus change as an antecedent condition.

The OR induced by overt and implicit activity

We repeated and extended the Luria and Vinogradova study by adding experimental groups engaged in implicit activity and a control group not instructed to engage in differential activity, as well as a group that performed an overt response. The *S*s were college students.

One group was instructed to press a foot pedal whenever they heard the word LIGHT, the condition analogous to the group used by Luria and Vinogradova. A second group was told to free associate implicitly whenever they heard the word LIGHT; a third group was told to count implicitly the number of times LIGHT occurred; and a final control group was told only to sit quietly and listen. Figure 1 shows the mean GSRs obtained by the various groups during the habituation session.

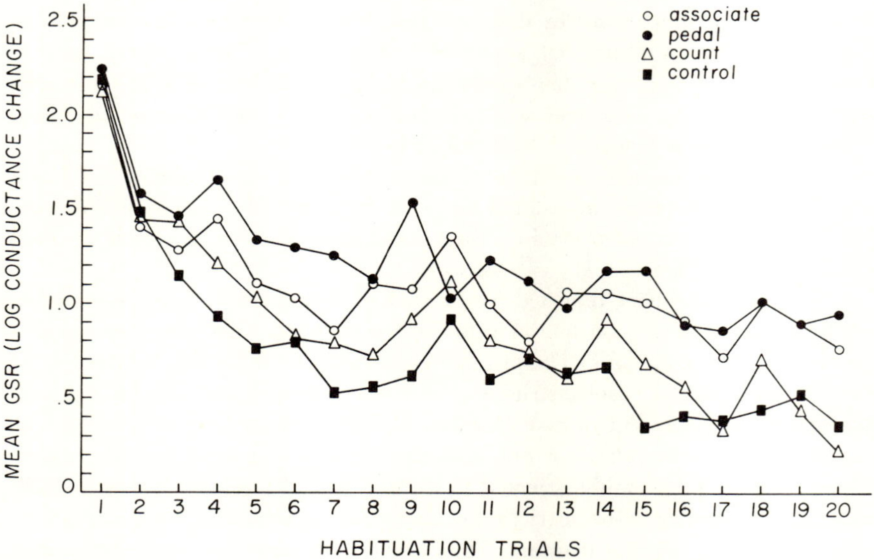

FIGURE 1. Mean GSRs obtained by control and experimental groups during habituation.

The difference in amount of habituation between the control and experimental groups indicates that habituation of the OR is not a simple function of stimulus repetition, at least in humans. The greater responsivity of the experimental groups prior to the occurrence of the critical word suggests that the task instructions had induced a "set" or anticipation of the task to come. Because of the task these students were orienting more intensely to all the words in anticipation of the critical word. We have subsequently found that a variety of factors affect habituation of the GSR-OR. Instructions given the *S*s and their self-instructions and interpretations of what the situation is about may reliably influence habituation (Mandell, 1968). It is important to note that the habituation curves for the experimental and control groups start at the same level and diverge during the course of habituation. We have repeatedly found this to be the case in normal *S*s. The initial OR to a stimulus change is highly resistant to experimental variables such as task instructions and does not show a sex difference. These factors manifest themselves differentially as the habituation progresses. For example, a sex difference will frequently appear in habituation curves, implying that in part different processes are determining the initial OR and the habituation of the OR to subsequent stimulus presentations.

Figure 2 shows the performance of the experimental and control groups

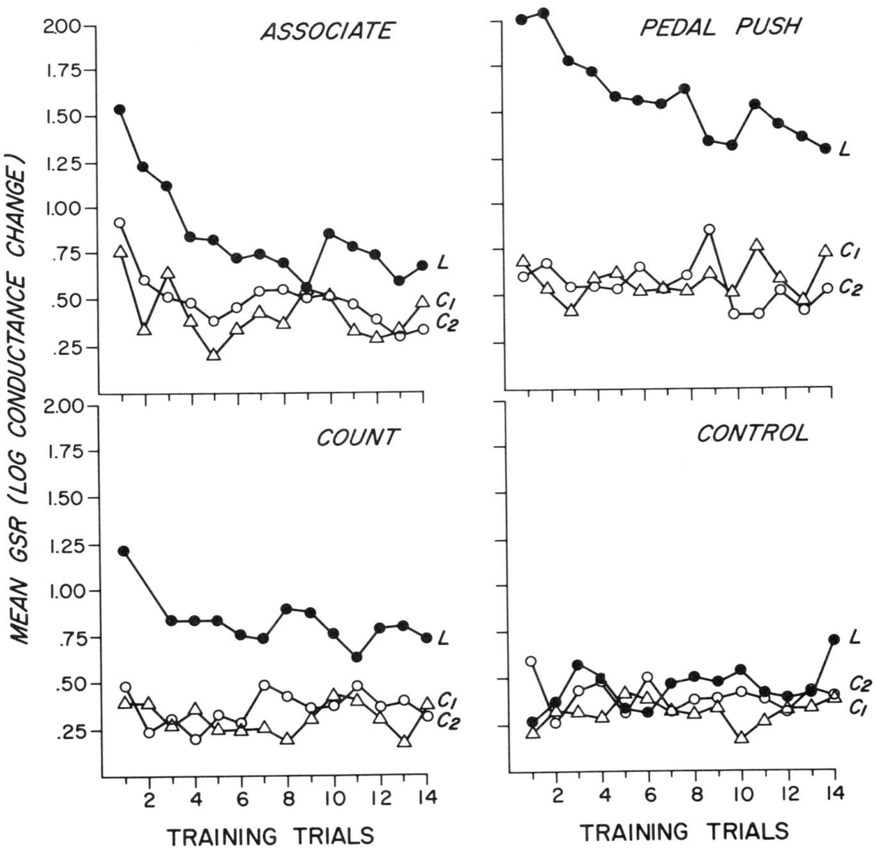

FIGURE 2. Mean GSRs obtained by control and experimental groups during training to the critical word LIGHT (L) and the immediately preceding (C_1) and following (C_2) control words.

during the training or "conditioning" phase of the experiment. These training data show that differential implicit activity as well as overt responding led to differential orienting to the critical word. Such selective attention was not manifested by the control group. An implication of these results, that implicit thinking, counting, and free associating induces GSRs, is relevant to the interpretation of a number of experiments in the literature. The so-called spontaneous GSRs have been employed as an indication of individual differences in personality, particularly individual differences in anxiety, emotionality, or autonomic lability (Mundy-Castle & McKiever, 1953). In a sense these "spontaneous" GSRs may be measures of anxiety, concern, or nervousness, but more directly they may be a consequence of a particular style of thinking, or lack of such a style. That the GSR was differentially evoked to a reliably greater degree in the implicit activity groups as compared to the control group indicates that an autonomic measure such as the GSR cannot be equated in any simple manner with a theoretical concept such as anxiety or emotionality.

This problem illustrates the importance of one of the basic methodological tenets of neobehaviorism: a science such as psychology, given its state of theoretical development, must employ abstract concepts that are definable in terms of their observable antecedent as well as consequent conditions. A concept is not equivalent to its consequent conditions or its method of measurement. The same consequent conditions may be used to define very different concepts, and when different initial conditions are present the same concept cannot be employed without demonstrating the lawful bases for doing so. The fact that anxiety is definable by electric shock and the GSR does not permit one to assume that anxiety is present under all conditions under which a GSR is observed.

Another result from the above experiment with theoretical implications of some import was the finding that several subgroups, including those engaged in implicit activity, subsequently manifested differential semantic generalization when related test words were presented. Some form of learning occurred in the absence of externally administered reinforcement. Since the response measure of semantic generalization was itself a measure of the OR, the implication was that the OR as manifested in the central nervous system, attention itself, must be reinforcing or intimately related to the reinforcement process.

What the phenomenon of semantic generalization of the GSR represents, we would now assume, is a shift in attention. Our hypothesis is that a dominant focus (John, 1967) was established for the critical word; a cortical set developed. Occurrence of an associated word in the generalization test induced a shift in attention to it relative to the filler words.

Historically, two general kinds of theories designed to account for the sequence of "ideas" appearing in consciousness, for the direction of thought, developed during the eighteenth and nineteenth centuries: the formulations of the British associationists, and Wundt's dynamic structural psychology. Neither one was primarily a theory of learning; neither one was especially concerned with how associations are initially acquired. The British associationists employed the notion of association to account for the phenomenon of why one idea would occur and not another. What is now called semantic generalization would be interpreted as a consequence of mediated associations. An alternative interpretation in the Wundtian tradition is that, given the necessary associations, one idea occurs rather than another because attention shifts from one idea to another. The direction of thought occurs in a given manner not solely because the occurrence of one idea evokes an associated idea, but because attention, like a searchlight probing in the darkness, lights upon one idea and then another. The principles determining the direction of the searchlight, in addition to associations, are the principles of the orienting reflex, dominant foci, attention, or cortical sets, all closely related concepts.

"Conditioning" the OR with motor activity

One of the peculiarities of the results of the training or "conditioning" phase of the experiment under consideration is that the experimental groups, while they all showed clear differential responding, greater GSRs to the critical than to the filler words as compared to the control group, also showed a continuous decline in the magnitude of the responses to all words, critical as well as noncritical. We think we now know the reason for the continuous decline during training as the result of the experimental and theoretical analyses conducted by Mandell (1968).

But the fact that there was continuous habituation of the responses to critical and noncritical words during training and that there was no differentiable CS and UCS with their corresponding CR and UCR, among other reasons, led us to modify the procedure in the direction of the more traditional classical conditioning paradigm. An innocuous 70 db, 1000 cps tone rated neutral on an evaluative semantic differential scale was introduced 5.5 sec. after the CS word. College student *S*s were instructed to make a foot-pedal response whenever they heard the tone. Now the GSR-OR evoked by the tone-pedal response complex could be differentiated from the response induced by the CS word, since the responses were scored during the 2.5 sec. immediately following a stimulus. Figure 3 shows the mean GSRs induced by the CS word and the immediately preceding and following control filler words, C_1 and C_2, for verbalizers (V) and nonverbalizers (NV) during conditioning employing the above procedure. Verbalization of the critical stimulus contingencies, "awareness," was assessed by means of a postexperimental interview.

It is clear that reliable differential semantic conditioning was obtained by the verbalization group in the absence of a noxious UCS. The response "conditioned," we believe, is a manifestation of the OR. It is again apparent that an autonomic response such as the GSR, commonly considered to be an index of anxiety, can readily occur in the absence of noxious stimulation.

It might be argued that the UCS, the tone-motor response complex, is still a source of anxiety in the present situation, although of a complex sort, because

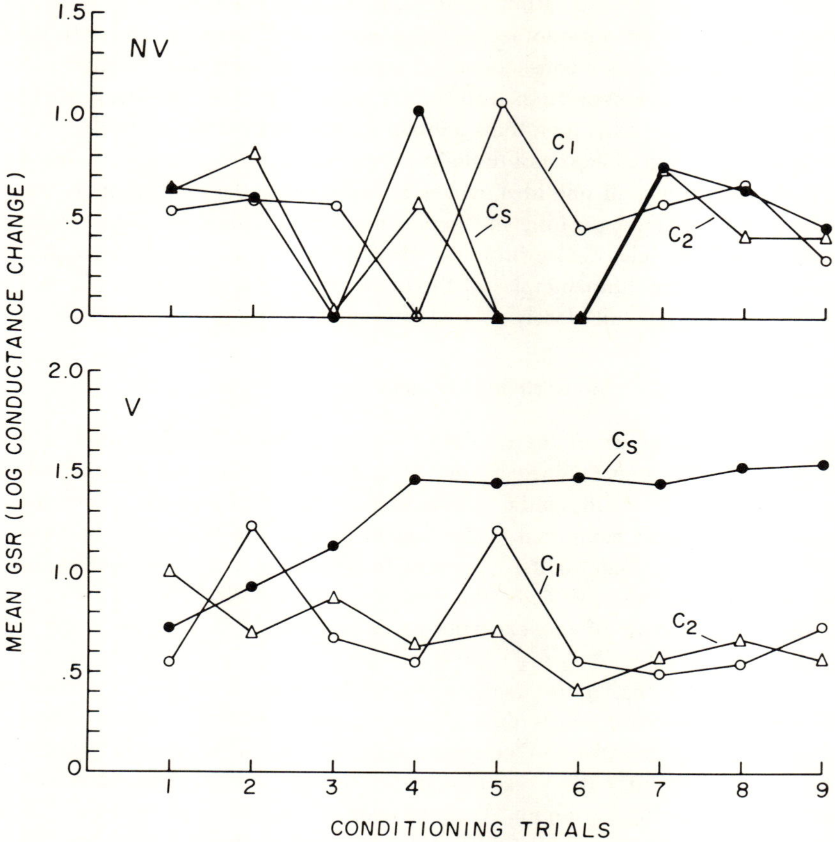

FIGURE 3. Mean GSRs obtained by verbalizers (V) and by nonverbalizers (NV) to the CS and the immediately preceding (C_1) and following (C_2) control words, with a motor response to a tone as the "UCS."

the *S*s were instructed to press the pedal as quickly as possible. The instructions induced anxiety to succeed. Or, an alternative interpretation may be offered: that the CR, the GSR to the CS, is really a manifestation of a preparatory motor response induced by the task. Evidence contrary to the above alternative interpretations stems from conditioning results that we have obtained in the absence of either a motor response or noxious stimulation.

"Conditioning" the OR with implicit activity

In order to more closely approximate semantic conditioning and thinking as it occurs outside the laboratory we eliminated the necessity for an overt response in our tone-motor response experimental paradigm. We used instead a variation of the procedure employed in our first experiment. We again presented a CS word followed by an innocuous tone. However, instead of an overt motor response to the tone, a group of *S*s was instructed to implicitly free associate pleasant thoughts whenever they heard the tone. Figure 4 shows the responses occurring to the CS word obtained by subjects who verbalized (V) the CS-Tone contingency and those who did not (NV). Responses to filler words are omitted for the sake of clarity. A control group that simply heard the tone did not show differential responsivity.

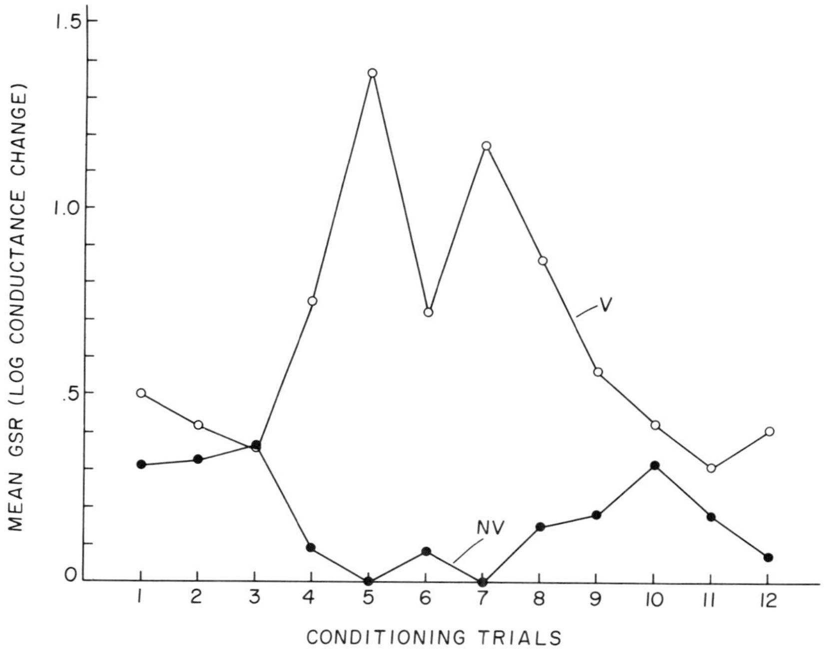

FIGURE 4. Mean GSRs obtained by verbalizers (V) and nonverbalizers (NV) to the CS with instructions to think pleasant thoughts to the tone.

In this, as in all other conditioning-type experiments that we have conducted, only those *S*s who verbalized the relevant stimulus contingencies as a group showed conditioning. Nonverbalizers as a group did not. The point to be considered is that reliable differential semantic conditioning may be obtained in the absence of an overt response or a noxious UCS. Instructions to free associate implicitly to an innocuous tone, hence orient to it, can provide the conditions which may induce anticipatory conditioned responses which we interpret as simply another form of the OR.

An interpretation of classical conditioning of the GSR

The above results suggest that classical conditioning, with college students at least, is a matter of inducing *S*s by one means or another to orient to a given stimulus, the UCS. A noxious stimulus accomplishes this task readily, but a noxious stimulus is not a necessary condition for inducing human *S*s to orient. If there is a consistent relationship present among the stimuli and one of them induces orienting, and if the *S*s discover this relationship and orient to the stimulus signalling the significant stimulus, it too becomes significant; a "conditioned" OR occurs. The "conditioned response" occurs to the CS when the *S* discovers the significance of the CS, that it consistently signals the occurrence of another significant event. He orients to the CS as a consequence of this discovery, as manifested by a GSR (Mandell, 1968).

When a measure such as the GSR is employed, all the relevant responses involved are probably reflections of the OR: the UCR to the UCS as well as the anticipatory and preparatory responses that develop over trials. The orientation that gives rise to the CR immediately following the CS is not a consequence of dishabituation of a previously habituated OR, but a consequence of problem solving.

During habituation prior to the start of conditioning trials *S*s attend to the stimuli because of their novelty, and because they are uncertain as to what will happen. Uncertainty, novelty, and stimulus change are the type of factors responsible for the elicitation of the OR to "neutral" stimuli during preconditioning habituation. In conditioning, however, *S*s come to attend, orient, to the CS because it has acquired significance. They discover (Mandell, 1968) that the CS is a signal for a noxious UCS or some other kind of stimulus that has significance.

In our semantic conditioning experiments with filler words, a *differential* GSR index of the OR then appears to the CS. Whether the physiology of these two ORs, one evoked by a stimulus change, an external stimulus, the other a consequence of problem solving, generated within the brain, are precisely the same cannot be determined at present. We would assume that they are not, even though the final common path, the peripheral expression as a GSR, appears to be the same except possibly for their latency. Whether they should therefore be called the same or different ORs is in part a semantic problem. But to describe the reappearance of the GSR-OR during conditioning as nothing more than the dishabituation of a previously habituated OR entirely misses the point of what is taking place in human conditioning. To establish arbitrary latency criteria to distinguish a CR from an OR simply compounds the error.

The reason that second interval or preparatory responses persist in a partial reinforcement situation is not, as has been claimed (McDonald & Johnson,

1965), that they are true CRs as distinguished from an OR, but that the UCS in a partial reinforcement situation is less predictable than in continuous reinforcement, and the *S* may be thinking differently after the CS as compared to before the UCS. Shifts in the frequency and magnitude of first and second interval responses during the course of conditioning and as a function of different experimental conditions occur for similar reasons. The kind and amount of orienting, active as well as passive, changes during an experimental session and as a function of the various experimental variables, because the kinds of integrative cortical activity change.

The fundamental relationship between the appearance of conditioning and verbalization in the individual *S*, as well as the fact that in our initial experiment the response to the critical word declined whereas in a conditioning paradigm it increases, has been clarified in a study conducted by Mandell (1968).

Among a variety of other conditions, Mandell included one group that was completely instructed with respect to the critical stimulus contingencies. They were told to perform a pedal response to the tone, and they were further informed of the critical word that would always precede the tone. Another group was treated in a manner that corresponded to the conventional conditioning procedure. Subjects here were told to respond to the tone, but were not informed either that a specific word would always precede the tone or of the contingency between the critical stimuli. They were required to discover the contingency. Following the completion of the experiment the *S*s were intensively interviewed.

Mandell found that the response to the critical CS in the instructed group was at a maximum on the first trial and showed a progressive decrement, habituation, thereafter. The maximum amplitude ultimately attained by the Discovery group curve was essentially the same as the Instructed group on that particular trial. Subjects who were instructed concerning the CS-Tone contingency and *S*s who discovered and instructed themselves about the correct contingency showed almost identical GSR curves following the discovery by the later group. Subjects who failed to verbalize the critical contingency showed no reliable evidence of differential semantic conditioning. The GSR curves obtained by the Instructed and Discovery groups provide striking evidence of the importance of instructions, experimenter or self-induced, on the GSR measure of the OR.

Mandell's analyses of the interviews with her *S*s in relation to their individual conditioning curves demonstrated that the smooth negatively accelerated group conditioning curve is essentially an artifact of averaging the curves obtained from individuals who discovered the critical Word-Tone contingency on different trials. The discovery, when it occurred, was usually accompanied by a GSR of asymptotic magnitude. Discovery of the relevant contingency is similar to an "aha" phenomenon, insight, which is accompanied by an OR manifested as a large GSR.

Mandell's analyses indicated that the *S*s were engaged in problem-solving activity, and when the problem was solved there invariably was a large and abrupt increase in the magnitude of the GSR to the critical word. Individual conditioning curves tended to be all-or-none. Hilgard's (1948) notion of a provisional try appears to be appropriate to conditioning as well as complex learning. Subjects have a variety of hypotheses or anticipated outcomes which they test. It appears that when the *S* discovers the correct stimulus contingency or thinks that he has, a GSR-OR follows the CS. Conditioning of the OR as manifested by the GSR does not follow the principle of the continuous acquisition of habit strength. The conditioning of a response such as the GSR is primarily a consequence of thinking and changes in attention. This description of the problem-solving activity that produces the GSR-OR manifested as conditioning corresponds in some respects to Woodworth's (1947) characterization of conditioning as a two-phase trial-and-check process.

Everyone who manifests conditioning in their GSR can also verbalize the relevant CS-UCS contingency because having actively engaged in verbal problem solving and having successfully solved the problem, they can subsequently describe the solution. Awareness does not cause conditioning. Problem solving and the discovery of the correct solution causes "conditioning" and the "awareness" of the correct contingencies. Subjects who do not verbalize the CS-UCS contingency and who do not show conditioning of the GSR also typically engage in problem solving or other forms of implicit activity during the experiment, but they do not hit upon the verbal solution of the problem.

In other studies we have found that not every *S* who engages in problem-solving activity and who verbalizes the relevant stimulus contingencies shows conditioning of their GSR. Two possibilities may account for the lack of differential responsivity in these *S*s. They may be unresponsive in the GSR mode, and if some other measure of the OR were employed conditioning might be manifest in it. In some instances this appears to be the case, since *S*s show little if any GSR to the stimuli presented. A second possibility is that the style of thinking or the manner in which they engage in problem solving precludes the development of a differential OR. Research employing multiple measures of the peripheral and central manifestations of OR accompanied by procedures for obtaining detailed protocols might resolve the problem of why it is that some *S*s who verbalize the relevant contingencies do not manifest evidence of conditioning in their GSR index of the OR.

Results of the analyses of conditioning in individual *S*s when the more usual noxious UCS is employed yielded results comparable to those obtained by Mandell.

Subjects in an experiment with a 110 db. white noise as the UCS were classified as High Orienters or Low Orienters in terms of the magnitude of their GSR to the first word in the habituation series of words that preceded conditioning. Of the 80 *S*s all but two failed to verbalize the CS-UCS contingency, and they also failed to show evidence of differential conditioning. It is worth noting that in addition to showing larger responses, high OR *S*s also showed greater differentiation in their responses to the critical and noncritical words than the low OR *S*s. If high and low orienters differed only in peripheral responsivity, there would be no reason for the kind of superior differential conditioning manifested by the high OR subgroup.

Results obtained from the low OR *S*s indicated that the capacity to verbalize the relevant stimulus contingency does not guarantee the occurrence of differential conditioning in a given response mode. Verbalization in this sort of conditioning situation is a necessary but not a sufficient condition for differential conditioning.

It was also evident in the conditioning of individual *S*s that the UCS did not uniformly reinstate the previously habituated GSR-OR to words. Following the introduction of the UCS the immediately following control word showed an augmented response. Several trials later, and only for verbalizers, there may occur an augmented response to the CS. None of these characteristics of conditioning seen in the records of individual *S*s are in accord with the dishabituation conception of the OR in relation to conditioning. Certainly, if the OR during conditioning is the result of dishabituation produced by the UCS, then the GSR should reappear to all words equally, CS and filler, and all *S*s, unaware as well as aware. But it does not.

Grings (1969) has summarized a variety of GSR conditioning experiments which show that the UCR, the response to the UCS, decreases during conditioning under standard procedures. Greater UCR magnitudes are obtained when the CS-UCS interval is varied, when unpaired random UCSs are presented, and on trials where the CS is omitted. All of these variations suggest that the UCR is simply a strong OR. Experimental variations producing increases or decreases in the magnitude of the GSR-UCR are changes that increase or decrease the predictability of the UCS, a condition that would affect the OR (Sokolov, 1960, 1963, 1969). As conditioning progresses the UCR-OR decreases, because any repeated and predictable stimulus will show habituation of the OR that it induces. Varying the CS-UCS interval within *S*s decreases the predictability of the UCS, and presenting the UCS in an unpaired random fashion still further increases the stimulus uncertainty, leading to larger UCR-ORs and slower habituation.

The progressive decline in GSR-UCRs, whether induced by a noxious UCS or the tone-motor stimulus complex, corresponds to habituation with innocuous nonsignificant stimuli. Because a stimulus qualifies as a UCS is no reason for the changes it induces in the OR to differ radically from the effects of other kinds of stimuli. Whatever else an exteroceptive UCS must do, it must also evoke ORs. Subjects must pay attention to it if conditioning is to occur, and variations or lack of variations in the UCS and the stimulus setting in which it occurs will affect the OR that it induces.

The above brief summary of research and speculations suggests that classical conditioning of the GSR is primarily the study of conditions that induce changes in attention, those induced by the *S*'s problem-solving activity as well as the ones induced by changes in physical stimuli, the CS and UCS.

SEMANTIC GENERALIZATION

We have recently presented a review of learning theory accounts of semantic generalization, and found them wanting (Maltzman, 1968). Research results that we have obtained since that review have strengthened our belief that current theories are incapable of adequately accounting for many phenomena of semantic generalization.

The most popular current theory, Osgood's (Osgood, Suci, & Tannenbaum, 1957) representational mediation theory, as well as its alternatives (e.g., Bousfield, 1961) assume that a CS word evokes an implicit mediator—in Osgood's theory, a meaning response. Stimulation produced by this meaning response is associated with the CR during conditioning. Other words will evoke that CR as a function of the similarity in their connotative meaning responses. A quantitative method is available for assessing the similarity in connotative meaning, the semantic differential, and the index of semantic distance that can be derived from it.

Generalization measured by the semantic differential

In all of our semantic conditioning and generalization studies we obtain ratings of relevant words on semantic differential scales in addition to the physiological measures. From the very beginning, it was apparent that the ratings obtained on the semantic differential were more complexly determined than assumed by the relevant theory. In our initial experiment we simply presented the rating scales following the experiment and asked the *S*s to rate words that were listed, including filler words, the CS, and the generalization test words. Many *S*s asked how to rate the words: according to the way they felt about the words in the experiment or how they felt about the words in general. We quickly changed the instructions to specify ratings of the words with respect to how they made the *S*s feel during the experiment. But the theory does not qualify the connotative meaning of the words as being a function entirely of the experimental setting. If the theory did this, then it would greatly complicate matters, and conditioning of meaning could no longer serve as the simple building block for more complex formulations of thinking and problem solving.

Since the theory that semantic generalization of autonomic responses as a function of connotative similarity is not qualified in any manner, it follows that if semantic conditioning occurs following pairings with a noxious UCS, then all connotatively similar words will show increased negative evaluations on the semantic differential whether or not these generalization test words occurred within the experimental context, or were heard over the earphones in the experiment.

Context effects have been studied in several experiments in our laboratory. In an experiment by Lodwig (1969) the CS word CARPET was paired with white noise interspersed among filler words, and RUG was the generalization word interspersed among other filler words. Before and after the experiment these related and unrelated filler words and FLOOR were presented for rating on an evaluative semantic differential scale. The CS word and the generalization word CARPET which appeared in the experiment showed reliable evidence of semantic conditioning and generalization, respectively, in terms of their semantic differential ratings. FLOOR, not present in the experiment, did not show evidence of generalization. We invariably have obtained semantic conditioning and generalization on the semantic differential when a highly noxious UCS was employed. The failure to obtain it for words not present in the experiment strikingly reflects the context effect. In Lodwig's experiment a relatively large number of conditioning trials were employed in a relatively complex design, so that differentiation between the words presented in the experiment and those that were not part of the experiment presumably could readily occur.

A different result was obtained in another semantic conditioning and generalization experiment conducted in our laboratory. Subjects received conditioning trials with one CS word and then switched to a second CS word for 10 additional reinforced trials. For some groups the two CS words were semantically related; for some they were not. Semantic generalization test words interspersed among filler words were presented following the second block of conditioning trials. As in the previous experiment *S*s were asked to rate the CS and generalization test words on an evaluative scale of the semantic differential along with semantically related words that were not presented in the experiment proper. In the present study the new generalization test words not presented during the experiment proper showed reliable semantic generalization. Ratings of these test words showed a reliable increase in negative evaluation along with the CS and generalization test words employed in the experiment. Such findings would appear to support a theory which assumes that generalization is a consequence of connotative similarity between words.

However, in addition to the semantic differential ratings of the words on an evaluative scale, the *S*s in this and other of our experiments are also asked to rate the extent to which they had expected the word to be followed by the UCS. Every *S* who showed evidence of semantic generalization on the semantic differential, i.e., assigned a negative rating to a generalization word whether it occurred in the experiment or not, stated that he expected the noise to follow the word. If questioned further, these *S*s stated that they expected the noise to follow the generalization word because it was similar to the CS word which was followed by the noise; therefore, the noise might also occur after the generalization word. Subjects who did not expect the noise to follow the generalization word did not rate the word negatively. Semantic generalization in terms of semantic differential ratings therefore appears to be a consequence of problem solving, and a critical ingredient is the fact that the *S*s anticipated the noise to follow the generalization test word, or thought that they had anticipated the noise following the new generalization test word.

Generalization of the GSR, likewise, occurs only in *S*s who state that they anticipated the UCS following the generalization word. However, not every *S* who is aware as defined in this manner shows generalization of the GSR. When the innocuous tone and pedal response is used as the UCS in the manner described in previous experiments, the evaluative scales of the semantic differential do not provide evidence of semantic conditioning or generalization. But *S*s reporting a high probability of anticipating the tone after the CS or generalization word are the only ones who may show semantic conditioning or generalization of the GSR.

Generalization of the GSR-OR

Semantic generalization of the GSR index of the OR has been obtained in several of our experiments where the conditions do not provide for the possibility of generalization of a conditioned response from a CS word to a related word as a consequence of mediation by a representational mediation process, connotative meaning, or some form of implicit verbal response.

In one study semantic generalization was obtained in the absence of any opportunity for conditioning to occur between the hypothetical mediating response and the CR to be transferred (Maltzman, Langdon, & Feeney, 1970).

All *S*s were instructed to perform a pedal response when they heard a particular word, LIGHT. Following an habituation series of unrelated words the control group received 14 presentations of LIGHT interspersed among unrelated words. A generalization test word, LAMP, interspersed among neutral words, was then presented. The experimental group received the habituation series followed directly by the generalization test. They never received the critical word LIGHT to which they could make a motor response. The two groups did not differ significantly, both showing differential semantic generalization.

In the above experimental group the connotative meaning of LIGHT was not changed because it was not paired either with a noxious or any other kind of stimulus or with a stimulus or instructed response which would augment the response to the critical word. The fact that the control group, comparable to the experimental group in our initial experiment and in the study of Luria and Vinogradova, showed no more differential semantic generalization than the present experimental group suggests that conditioning trials do not condition. Conditioning trials provide the opportunity for *S*s to discover the significance of the CS. The CS always precedes the UCS which is already significant, noxious, etc., or it is significant as a consequence of special instructions. The CS is discovered to be a signal for the impending UCS and it therefore evokes an OR. The *S* attends to it. When a word in some manner related to the CS occurs, the *S* orients to the new word because it too is significant: it may also be followed by the UCS, and serve as a cue. The present experiment indicates that the CS word can acquire significance via instructions, and this is sufficient to provide the basis for generalization. We believe that Ukhtomski's conception of a dominant focus (John, 1967) is of basic importance to the occurrence of generalization in the above experiment, as well as a variety of other behavioral phenomena. Behaviorally, the notion of a dominant focus of cortical excitability is analogous to a concept of set. The *S*s in the previous experiment were set for LIGHT by the task instructions. Occurrence of LAMP induced an OR because it is an associate of the word for which they were set.

Another study in our laboratory has demonstrated that semantic generalization may occur in the absence of any possibility of mediation by connotative meaning or implicit associative responses (Maltzman, 1968). Following conditioning with the CS word PLANT, one group of *S*s received five unreinforced trials with an associate, STEM; a second received unreinforced generalization test trials with TREE; and a third received five presentations of an unrelated word, MUSIC, interspersed, as in all cases, among other unrelated words.

As indicated in Figure 5 all three groups showed a reliable increase in the magnitude of the GSR to the critical word as compared to the unrelated control words. These results are based upon all *S*s, aware as well as unaware, and those who reported that they anticipated that the noise would follow the repeated test word as well as those that did not. Excluding the unaware *S*s would heighten the apparent generalization effect. It was found that a greater percentage of "aware" *S*s were in the TREE and STEM groups than in the MUSIC

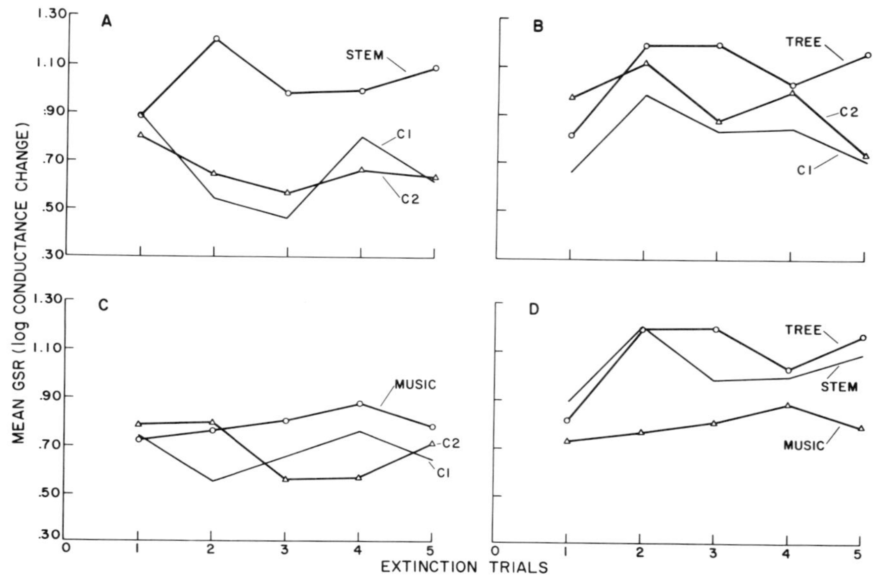

FIGURE 5. Semantic generalization of the GSR based upon similarity with the CS due to repeated presentations (Maltzman, 1968).

group, indicating that the associative connection between the training and test words played a role in determining the number of *S*s who became aware. Subjects who showed generalization in the MUSIC group, both on the semantic differential and in terms of the GSR, were *S*s who reported that they anticipated the noise following the word MUSIC. The reason that they came to anticipate that the UCS would occur after MUSIC is that MUSIC was repeatedly presented, and the only other word that was repeated was followed by noise; therefore they thought that it too would be followed by noise. In a sense, then, an abstract similarity between MUSIC and PLANT was established by the generalization test situation itself. As the generalization test progressed the similarity was established and the probability of *S*s discovering and orienting to the test word increased. However, with a relatively large number of test trials the GSR would presumably decline. The OR would habituate when it was learned that the UCS would not follow the test word.

In all of our generalization studies the generalization test avoids the novelty or stimulus change parameter of the OR by interspersing the new generalization test word among other unrelated new filler words. This control is essential, because the introduction of the test word as the only new word will evoke an OR on the basis of stimulus change per se quite aside from its semantic or other connections with the CS word (Maltzman & Langdon, 1969). An obvious experimental implication is that if filler words were introduced periodically and then repeated, the above experimental effect of generalization based upon abstract similarity would not occur.

DISCUSSION

We have attempted in the previous sections to present some of the experimental results which have led us to conclude that the GSR-OR is not in any simple fashion conditioned or associated to the CS when normal adults are employed in classical conditioning situations. Conditioning of the GSR, at least in the type of situation that we have employed, is a product of problem-solving activity. This autonomic response measure, which has in the past been taken as a measure of emotionality or anxiety, must always, like any other dependent variable, be considered in terms of the initial conditions under which it arises. With noxious stimulation the problem is difficult to analyze because a strong emotional component as well as an orienting one may be manifest in the GSR. An advantage of our conditioning-like situations is that use of an innocuous UCS reduces the complexity of the physiological processes generating the response measure and provides relatively unambiguous conditions for the manifestation of an OR.

Nevertheless, the traditional interpretation of the GSR as a measure of emotion is not entirely incorrect. This is so, paradoxically, because the traditional distinctions between thinking or cognitive activity, and emotion, drive, or conative activity, can no longer be maintained in any simple fashion. There are physiological processes of emotion, attention, and thinking in all of the activities under consideration. At the human level integrative cortical activity must be intimately related to the production of emotion, attention, and arousal, as well as thinking. The possibility of corticofugal activation, the possibility of facilitation of the brain stem reticular formation by cerebral cortical activity, has been demonstrated in infrahuman organisms (French, 1958). The possibility is even greater in humans due to their increased cephalization. It is therefore reasonable to assume production of the GSR-OR by integrative cortical activity (problem solving). It is even more reasonable to suppose that the anxiety neurotic generates his own anxiety in part by his thoughts about impending disaster or ruminations over supposed past disasters. In like manner the normal individual's anticipation or thinking of negative evaluation induces emotionality. Many of the physiological indices of the OR and attention are the same as the emotional response constituting the emergency reaction (Cannon, 1963; Feigenberg, 1969) reflecting increased activity of the sympathetic nervous system. There are obvious elements of continuity between the OR and the classical emotional responses of the emergency reaction. There are also obvious elements of continuity between thinking and attention. The functional school of psychology emphasized that thinking arises when habitual responses fail. The occurrence of a problem or a sudden change in the environment leads to thinking (Dewey, 1933). But these are also conditions under which an OR would arise.

All of these processes, thinking, attention, and emotion, are present in classical conditioning of the GSR, and, for that matter, probably all human exteroceptive classical conditioning. A GSR presumably is occurring, that is, orienting is taking place, whether or not it is measured, as are the underlying neurophysiological processes. The type of situation we have employed and the results that we have obtained suggests that classical conditioning in normal adults, or at least college students, is a problem-solving situation, and the GSR as an indication of the OR reflects the relationship between attention and problem solving. Once beyond the initial stimulus changes in an experiment, the GSR-OR increasingly reflects actively-produced ORs rather than stimulus-bound novelty-induced ORs. The role of self-generated ORs is of far greater importance as a determiner of complex human behavior than stimulus-induced shifts in attention. The distinction between different ORs, between externally induced and internal attention, between passive and active attention that is induced outside the brain and within is an important one, but one that has received insufficient attention (Hernandez-Peon, 1966; James, 1950; Maltzman & Mandell, 1968). Orienting reflexes may occur to incongruities in environmental stimuli, but also to the discrepancy between an anticipation and an outcome and the congruity between an anticipation and an outcome, and undoubtedly as a consequence of still more complex problem-solving activities.

The conception of an OR has fundamental and far-reaching importance not only because it provides a measure of a response to stimulus change and forces a reconsideration of the interpretation of a variety of experimental phenomena (Maltzman & Langdon, 1969; Maltzman & Raskin, 1965). It has such significance because it and other physiological measures such as contingent negative variation (Walter, Cooper, Aldridge, McCallum, & Winter, 1964) provide an objective measure of the occurrence of some forms of higher mental processes. Because of this characteristic it permits an integration of some of the desirable features of cognitive and S-R psychologies. A laudatory feature of cognitive theorizing, by and large, has been its disinclination to fit the complexities of human behavior into oversimplified and misleading theoretical prescriptions, thereby ignoring critically important variables. Its disadvantage has been its inclination towards theorizing that is loosely related to observable phenomena, that is too often highly ambiguous. S-R theories, while having the appearance of far greater precision of meaning, have tended to ignore phenomena of importance unless they occurred within circumscribed experimental paradigms. The conception of an OR with its specifiable physiological measures, although containing many unsolved problems, nevertheless has the virtue of permitting the experimental analysis of some of the complexities of human behavior of whose existence cognitive psychologists have long assured us, with something of the objectivity long espoused by S-R psychologists.

Classical conditioning with normal college students cannot, we believe, reveal the basic principles of habit acquisition, drive, inhibition, etc., which correspond to principles found in animals, and which will form the basis from which more complex principles may be derived for the explanation of complex behavior. Soviet psychologists and physiologists including Pavlov recognized this long ago (Cole & Maltzman, 1969). Pavlov's distinction between principles of the first and second signal systems emphasized that different principles that take precedence will be present in animals possessing speech as compared to those that do not. Razran (1955) has long asserted that conditioning may proceed at different "levels" within as well as between species, and has considered the conditions under which conditioning with and without perception may occur. Spence (1966) has also subjected cognitive factors in eyelid conditioning to experimental analysis.

While human classical conditioning of the GSR cannot reveal basic principles universal to the animal kingdom, it does reveal "principles" of attention and thinking that have some generality, that are not peculiar to classical conditioning. Germana (1968) has recently reviewed the literature on verbal learning studies that have employed concomitant physiological measures. Characteristically, it has been found in these studies that, for example, the GSR increases up to the point at which the last error is made. Once the verbal material is learned the GSR decreases. But this is exactly what happens in classical conditioning of the GSR under certain conditions. Once the *S* has learned what is happening, the situation is predictable and the generalized OR reflected as a CR habituates. The speed and extent of habituation will be a function of such factors as the intensity and predictability of the UCS.

An obvious problem has remained unanswered in this discussion: what is the relation between the GSR-OR, attention, and classical conditioning when such non-OR measures are employed as the salivary response, eyeblink, or some other instrumental response? Classical conditioning of the GSR may reflect primarily the effects of attention and problem solving, but how then does one account for performance changes when instrumental responses are employed? We lack a simple answer and the space for a complex one. A very preliminary and tentative approach to this question has been suggested elsewhere (Maltzman, Langdon, & Feeney, 1970). A provocative program of research and theory related to this problem may be found in the works of Beritov (1965, 1969).

While the previous discussion has emphasized theoretical differences with neobehaviorism, these need to be placed in perspective. The present theorizing and research stems from a different experimental situation than the one characteristically employed by neobehaviorists. It is based upon the use of highly intelligent and verbal subjects, college students, and has employed a physiological measure peculiarly responsive to manifestations of the OR. An urgent problem of theoretical and practical significance is the examination of concomitant changes in measures of the OR and more conventional performance measures. While the principles of "conditioning" of the OR appear to be different from those evolved from instrumental conditioning and the conditioning of "voluntary" responses such as the eyeblink, relating the two remains the problem.

In an analogous manner, Spence (1937) was one of the first investigators to note the importance of preparatory or observing responses, receptor exposure adjustment acts, behavior corresponding to Pavlov's original notion of the orienting-investigatory reflex. Behavioral measures of observing responses were initially used by Russian investigators to validate the physiological measures of the OR, and neurophysiologists still employ such a procedure. The relationships between these two indices of attention, physiological and behavioral, remain to be investigated under a variety of experimental conditions.

We have repeatedly noted the importance of the relationship between the ability to verbalize the relevant experimental contingencies and conditioning and generalization of the GSR-OR. It does not follow that we believe that all conditioning involves "awareness." A great advantage of the conditioning *procedure* is that it may be employed with a great variety of subject populations, including college students, mental retardates, psychotics, infants, and infrahuman organisms. We would not expect the same principles of attention, learning, and problem solving to manifest themselves with these diverse subject populations or with different response measures. It must remain for future research and theoretical analyses to determine the nature of the generalizations that can safely be made within and across different populations of subjects and measures.

REFERENCES

(Beritov) Beritashvili, I. S. Concerning psychoneural activity of animals. In M. Cole & I. Maltzman (Eds.), *A handbook of contemporary Soviet psychology.* New York: Basic Books, 1969. Pp. 627–670.

(Beritov) Beritoff, J. S. *Neural mechanisms of higher vertebrate behavior.* Boston: Little, Brown, 1965.

Bousfield, W. A. The problem of meaning in verbal learning. In C. N. Cofer (Ed.), *Verbal learning and verbal behavior.* New York: McGraw-Hill, 1961. Pp. 81–91.

Cannon, W. B. *Bodily changes in pain, hunger, fear and rage.* (2nd ed.) New York: Harper & Row, 1963.

Cole, M., & Maltzman, I. (Eds.). *A handbook of contemporary Soviet psychology.* New York: Basic Books, 1969.

Dewey, J. *How we think.* (New ed.) New York: Heath, 1933.

Feigenberg, I. M. Probabilistic prognosis and its significance in normal and pathological subjects. In M. Cole & I. Maltzman (Eds.), *A handbook of contemporary Soviet psychology.* New York: Basic Books, 1969. Pp. 354–369.

French, J. D. Corticifugal connections with the reticular formation. In H. H. Jasper, L. D. Proctor, R. S. Knighton, W. C. Noshay, & R. T. Costello (Eds.), *Reticular formation of the brain.* Boston: Little, Brown, 1958. Pp. 491–505.

Galperin, P. Y. Stages in the development of mental acts. In M. Cole & I. Maltzman (Eds.), *A handbook of contemporary Soviet psychology.* New York: Basic Books, 1969. Pp. 249–273.

Germana, J. Psychophysiological correlates of conditioned response formation. *Psychological Bulletin,* 1968, *70,* 105–114.

Grings, W. W. Anticipatory and preparatory electrodermal behavior in paired stimulation situations. *Psychophysiology,* 1969, *5,* 597–611.

Hernandez-Peon, R. Physiological mechanisms in attention. In R. W. Russell (Ed.), *Frontiers in physiological psychology.* New York: Academic Press, 1966. Pp. 121–147.

Hilgard, E. R. *Theories of learning.* New York: Appleton-Century-Crofts, 1948.

James, W. *The principles of psychology.* Vol. I. New York: Dover, 1950.

John, E. R. *Mechanisms of memory.* New York: Academic Press, 1967.

Lodwig, A. K. Experimental manipulations of the OR during semantic conditioning. Unpublished doctoral dissertation, University of California, Los Angeles, 1969.

Luria, A. R., & Vinogradova, O. S. An objective investigation of the dynamics of semantic systems. *British Journal of Psychology,* 1959, *50,* 89–105.

Maltzman, I. Thinking: From a behavioristic point of view. *Psychological Review,* 1955, *62,* 275–286.

Maltzman, I. On the training of originality. *Psychological Review,* 1960, *67,* 229–242.

Maltzman, I. Theoretical conceptions of semantic conditioning and generalization.

In T. R. Dixon & D. L. Horton (Eds.), *Verbal behavior and general behavior theory.* Englewood Cliffs, N.J.: Prentice-Hall, 1968. Pp. 291–339.

Maltzman, I., & Langdon, B. Semantic generalization of the GSR as a function of semantic distance or the orienting reflex. *Journal of Experimental Psychology,* 1969, *80,* 289–294.

Maltzman, I., Langdon, B., & Feeney, D. Semantic generalization without prior conditioning. *Journal of Experimental Psychology,* 1970, *83,* 73–75.

Maltzman, I., & Mandell, M. P. The orienting reflex as a predictor of learning and performance. *Journal of Experimental Research in Personality,* 1968, *3,* 99–106.

Maltzman, I., & Raskin, D. C. Effects of individual differences in the orienting reflex on conditioning and complex processes. *Journal of Experimental Research in Personality,* 1965, *1,* 1–16.

Mandell, M. P. Instructions, attitudinal factors and anxiety in a "semantic conditioning" situation involving physiological and performance measures. Unpublished doctoral dissertation, University of California, Los Angeles, 1968.

McDonald, D. G., & Johnson, J. C. A re-analysis of GSR conditioning. *Psychophysiology,* 1965, *1,* 291–295.

Mundy-Castle, A. C., & McKiever, B. L. The psychophysiological significance of the galvanic skin response. *Journal of Experimental Psychology,* 1953, *46,* 15–24.

Osgood, C. E., Suci, G. J., & Tannenbaum, P. H. *The measurement of meaning.* Urbana: University of Illinois Press, 1957.

Razran, G. Conditioning and perception. *Psychological Review,* 1955, *62,* 83–95.

Sokolov, E. N. Neuronal models and the orienting reflex. In M. A. B. Brazier (Ed.), *The central nervous system and behavior* (3rd conference). New York: Josiah Macy, Jr. Foundation, 1960. Pp. 187–276.

Sokolov, E. N. *Perception and the conditioned reflex.* New York: Macmillan, 1963.

Sokolov, E. N. The modeling properties of the nervous system. In M. Cole & I. Maltzman (Eds.), *A handbook of contemporary Soviet psychology.* New York: Basic Books, 1969. Pp. 671–704.

Spence, K. W. The differential response in animals to stimuli varying within a single dimension. *Psychological Review,* 1937, *44,* 430–444.

Spence, K. W. Cognitive and drive factors in the extinction of the conditioned eyeblink in human subjects. *Psychological Review,* 1966, *73,* 445–458.

Voronin, L. G., Leontiev, A. N., Luria, A. R., Sokolov, E. N., & Vinogradova, O. S. (Eds.) *Orienting reflex and exploratory behavior.* Washington, D.C.: American Institute of Biological Sciences, 1965.

Walter, W. G., Cooper, R., Aldridge, V. J., McCallum, W. C., & Winter, A. L. Contingent negative variation: an electric sign of sensori-motor association and expectancy in the human brain. *Nature,* 1964, *203,* 380–384.

Woodworth, R. S. Reinforcement of perception. *American Journal of Psychology,* 1947, *60,* 119–124.

Reinforcement in Classical Conditioning

CHARLES C. PERKINS, JR.

This essay will present the rationale for describing all learned behavior change as resulting from a secondary reinforcement-like process. This theoretical position has grown out of the law of effect, the sort of general functional principle of reinforcement advocated by Spence in his Silliman lectures (Spence, 1956). It may also be considered an extension of ideas Spence (1947) proposed in his analysis of delayed reward learning but did not develop further.

The law of effect will be used as our point of departure, but the discussion of its applicability to classical conditioning procedures will lead to the introduction of a somewhat different formulation. This formulation is stated in terms of transmission of differential attractiveness (i.e., reinforcement value) from consequences to their antecedents. Finally, we will reexamine the law of effect to evaluate its applicability to all learned behavior change.

Although alternate positions may be tenable, I take it for granted that there is no serious argument about the descriptive accuracy of the law of effect as a way of summarizing the major results of instrumental learning procedures. Application of the law of effect to classical conditioning, however, is not such a simple matter. Therefore, our emphasis will be on the utility of the law of effect and similar principles for explanation of the results of classical conditioning procedures.

DIFFERENTIAL VERSUS ABSOLUTE REINFORCEMENT

The two upper rows (A and B) of Table 1 represent the alternative sequences which follow conditioned stimulus (CS) presentation in a reinforced classical conditioning procedure, depending on whether or not the subject makes a conditioned response (CR). "Reinforced" as used in this context refers to a procedure in which the CS is followed by an unconditioned stimulus (US), and thus its meaning is quite different from when the term "reinforcement" is used in formulating the principle of reinforcement, i.e., the law of effect.

TABLE 1. RELEVANT COMPONENT STIMULI DURING THE CS AND AFTERWARDS (e.g., during US on acquisition trials).

			Time: During CS	Time: During US or $\overline{US}$
	US	CR		
A	yes	yes	CR anticipation of US	aftereffect of CR US
B	yes	no	$\overline{CR}$ anticipation of US	aftereffect of $\overline{CR}$ US
C	no	yes	CR anticipation of $\overline{US}$	aftereffect of CR $\overline{US}$
D	no	no	$\overline{CR}$ anticipation of $\overline{US}$	aftereffect of $\overline{CR}$ $\overline{US}$
			Column 1	*Column 2*

The top row (A) represents a "reinforced" trial on which the subject makes a CR. Row B represents a reinforced trial on which the subject does not make a CR. Both are after a conditioning series when the US will be anticipated. Rows C and D represent comparable nonreinforced trials when the US is not anticipated (e.g., following a number of extinction trials). It will be noted that every row differs from all others both during CS (Column 1) and afterwards (Column 2). A bar (—) over a symbol should be read "absence of"; absence of the US is represented by $\overline{US}$.

The upper sequence, Row A, represents the events which occur after many acquisition trials when the subject makes a CR on presentation of the CS. At least after many paired CS-US presentations anticipation of the US is assumed to accompany the CS. The CR is followed by US presentation accompanied by those stimuli which are aftereffects of the CR. In the case of salivary conditioning, the salivary response (CR) occurs to the buzzer (CS), at which time the dog also "anticipates" food presentation. The food (US) presentation is accompanied by the stimuli which are aftereffects of the conditioned salivary response. In this case, the aftereffects or a portion of them can be described as saliva-in-the-mouth.

Row B of Table 1 represents the stimulus situations which occur when the subject does not make a CR. Presence versus absence of the CR (CR vs. $\overline{CR}$) distinguishes between the parts of the two sequences which precede US presentation. The two sequences differ during US presentation in that one (Row A) includes the stimulus aftereffects of a conditioned response, and the other the stimulus aftereffects of absence of the conditioned response, $\overline{CR}$.

If one assumes that the law of effect "explains" classical conditioning, he is likely to conclude that CR is followed by a more reinforcing state of affairs than is absence of the conditioned response, $\overline{CR}$. That is, since a CR is acquired, US plus the aftereffects of a CR seems to be more attractive than does US plus the aftereffects of no conditioned response, $\overline{CR}$. At least in the case of salivary conditioning this seems quite reasonable intuitively, as saliva-in-the-mouth should make food more palatable. That is, food "tastes better" and/or goes down more easily when the mouth waters.

It should be noted that this interpretation, like a formulation I have suggested earlier (Perkins, 1955), emphasizes relative or differential reinforcement. That is, the critical difference in attractiveness is assumed to be between the conditions following CR and those following $\overline{CR}$; the critical difference is not the difference between adding the US and not adding it to the stimulus situation. Interpretations emphasizing an increase in the strength of a reinforcing state of affairs (e.g., drive reduction), accompanying US presentation will be designated absolute theories of reinforcement.

It is instructive to note how a choice of a differential or an absolute view of reinforcement inclines one toward acceptance of certain other definitions and principles. An absolute theory of reinforcement implies that CR and $\overline{CR}$ are differentially affected by the same reinforcer which strengthens the CR but not the $\overline{CR}$. An absolute theory requires some sort of division(s) between those responses which are strengthened by reinforcement versus those which are not. It implies that $\overline{CR}$, a class of "incompatible responses" and/or "resting responses," is not strengthened by the same reinforcing state of affairs that strengthens the CR. As Hull's (1943) treatment of extinction illustrates so clearly, this may produce serious logical difficulties.

A differential reinforcement theory implies a counter-conditioning interpretation of extinction. In fact, it implies that there is no difference between the processes going on during acquisition and extinction. The response class strengthened during acquisition consists of these responses which are designated the conditioned response (CR); the response class strengthened during extinction is "incompatible responses," or "other behavior" ($\overline{CR}$). The process going on when the subject selects between Rows A and B of Table 1 could be described equally well as positive reinforcement of the CR or as negative reinforcement of $\overline{CR}$. Similarly, the conditions shown in Rows C and D of Table 1, which summarize the alternate sequences of stimulus situations available during extinction, can be described as involving either positive reinforcement of $\overline{CR}$ or negative reinforcement (weakening) of CR.

A differential reinforcement version of the law of effect implies a simple distinction between reinforcement in classical and in instrumental conditioning. In the case of classical conditioning procedures the basis for the differential reinforcement is a difference in "internal" or inferred stimuli, the aftereffects of the CR versus the aftereffects of $\overline{\text{CR}}$. In instrumental procedures the differential reinforcement is provided by a difference in the external stimuli or environmental conditions (i.e., presence versus absence of the reward or punishment).

A differential reinforcement interpretation of classical conditioning follows naturally from the hypothesis that external and inferred (internal) stimuli have essentially the same functional properties. That is, either an external or an inferred stimulus may serve as a cue for differential responding. Similarly, both shock (external) and hunger (inferred from deprivation) have aversive properties. This hypothesis seems to be generally assumed though it is seldom stated explicitly.

Another implication of a differential reinforcement interpretation of classical conditioning is that the attractiveness (i.e., relative reinforcing effect) of a component stimulus such as the aftereffect of a CR depends on the context in which it occurs. This is clear when we compare the more reinforcing stimulus with the less reinforcing stimulus during acquisition and during extinction of a classical conditioned response. Consider the case of salivary conditioning. Here saliva-in-the-mouth is more attractive than absence-of-saliva-in-the-mouth when food is presented. It is also the case, however, that absence-of-saliva-in-the-mouth is more attractive than saliva-in-the-mouth when no food is presented. For a law of effect theorist acquisition of a CR implies that the aftereffect of a CR is more attractive (and valuable) than the aftereffect of $\overline{\text{CR}}$ during US presentation, but extinction of a CR indicates that the aftereffect of a CR is less attractive than the aftereffect of $\overline{\text{CR}}$ in the absence of the US.

Such interaction of stimulus components can also be observed with other stimuli. Food is attractive (i.e., a strong reinforcer), relative to no food, for a food-deprived rat. Nevertheless food may have little or no attractiveness for a satiated rat. A differential reinforcement interpretation of classical conditioning does not require a special assumption that the attractiveness of a stimulus depends on context. The assumption that attractiveness of a component stimulus may depend on context is also required by other observations. One such observation is that the attractiveness of food depends upon the intensity of hunger stimuli.

VALUE AND ATTRACTIVENESS

The distinction between primary and secondary reinforcement has proven quite useful even though the distinction has not always been clearly drawn. I will make a related distinction which seems particularly useful. The differences between the present distinction and other primary-secondary reinforcement distinctions is great enough to warrant use of different terms. The present distinction therefore is stated in terms of value and attractiveness, which are more convenient words than the more cumbersome expressions "characteristic attractiveness" and "effective attractiveness" which I have used elsewhere (Perkins, 1968).

Since responses always occur in context and acquirable responses seem to have stimulus properties or necessarily produce differential stimuli, we may refer to the differential value of two responses in the same context as well as to the differential value of other parts of stimulus situations. The differential value of two responses in some particular context is measured directly by assuring that both responses occur frequently in the context and have no differential outcome. If, under these conditions, one response becomes dominant to the extent that the other one will occur on no more than a very small portion of trials, then by definition the dominant response has greater value. Examples are the response of not biting the tongue which has greater value than biting the tongue, and of not tensing a sore muscle which has greater value than tensing this muscle. If one has a sore muscle, he will avoid using it if he can attain the same goals without using it. However, the sore muscle may be used if its use is necessary for the individual to attain a goal.

Consider conditions in which two response classes of approximately equal value, such as turning left or right in a maze, are each followed by different stimuli such as food versus no food, or shock versus no shock. If, in addition, the two response contingent stimuli (e.g., food and no food) are followed by the same set of conditions, and if each response-stimulus pair has occurred many times, then if one stimulus is regularly selected it has the greater value by definition. That is, under these conditions, the response which becomes dominant is the one which has been followed by the more valuable stimulus. If the response leading to food occurs regularly, this implies that food is more valuable than no food.

The very definition of the differential value of stimulus situations such as food versus no food, as described above, implies the operation of the law of effect or some similar principle. Response selection could not be used as a measure of the relative value of stimuli if the value of stimuli had no effect on whether or not the antecedent response were selected on subsequent occasions.

At the same time, since value refers to "intrinsic" (nonextinguishable) properties of stimulus situations, the stimuli being compared in value must be followed by stimuli which are equal in attractiveness. That subsequent stimuli are equally attractive can be assured by having the same stimulus follow both the situations which are being compared in value.

By definition, whatever response an organism makes is the most attractive response available. This statement is tautological by itself, but when taken in conjunction with other parts of the present systematic position it has testable implications. It should be noted that the attractiveness of a response, unlike its value, is affected by the consequences or effects which have followed it in the past. For example, a hungry rat that has had appropriate training will run through an alley in which he receives a mild shock if this "running through" response is followed by a substantial food reward (e.g., Knapp, Kause, & Perkins, 1959). By definition, if this response occurs it is the most attractive response available even though it may also have negative value.

In the above example the term "response" was used to designate a behavioral sequence of measurable duration and its feedback or response-produced stimuli. Such a "molar" term is quite different from a more molecular use of the term "response," which designates behavior of infinitesimal duration and does not include response-produced feedback. The molecular response can produce stimuli, but with this use of the term a response is not said to be a stimulus or to have stimulus properties. On the other hand, a molar response is a stimulus (i.e., has stimulus properties).

Molar and molecular uses of the term "response" each have certain advantages. The molar term is more directly operationalized, but the more molecular use seems to have greater possibilities for theoretical development. There is good reason to retain both concepts, but the two should be clearly distinguished.

The relative attractiveness of two stimuli, or more precisely, two stimulus situations, may be compared by having each follow a different response. The set of conditions already described may also be used to illustrate this operational specification of the relative attractiveness of two stimuli when the conditions are described in more molecular terms. The response of entering the shock-food arm is followed first by shock then by food. If this arm is regularly selected (i.e., entered) after many turns in each direction, then by definition shock in that arm is more attractive than no shock in the other arm. In general terms (a) if the attractiveness of two stimulus situations X_A and X_B is stabilized by having each consistently followed by a different set of events, and (b) if one of these stimuli, X_A, follows response R_A, and another, X_B, follows R_B, an incompatible response of the same value as R_A, and (c) if R_A comes to be selected regularly, then by definition X_A is more attractive than X_B. The relative attractiveness of two stimuli is affected both by their (intrinsic) value and by the relative attractiveness of the stimuli which have followed them in the past.

TRANSMISSION OF ATTRACTIVENESS

The basic hypothesis around which the present view is built is that differential attractiveness of stimulus situations tends to be transmitted to antecedent stimuli. Let us consider examples of how this principle describes events in acquisition and extinction of (a) instrumental learning, (b) classical conditioning, and (c) secondary reinforcement. In instrumental reward learning, the reward is more attractive than its absence and the greater attractiveness of the reward is transmitted to the reinforced response-in-context (i.e., the response preceding the reward). When this response gains enough differential attractiveness it occurs regularly. Extinction of an instrumental response such as bar pressing occurs when the conditions following bar press do not differ from those following incompatible responses. Thus, zero difference in the attractiveness of the consequences of the two response classes is transmitted to the responses themselves so that their differential attractiveness approaches their differential value. Bar presses above the operant level apparently have some negative value. Otherwise the operant level would be higher and extinction would not be obtained.

We have already noted that if US-plus-aftereffect-of-CR is a more attractive (and valuable) state of affairs than US-plus-aftereffect-of-$\overline{\text{CR}}$, their differential attractiveness will be transmitted to CR and $\overline{\text{CR}}$ so that the former becomes more attractive. Thus, the former response will show a greater tendency to occur.

Secondary positive reinforcing properties will be acquired by a stimulus such as a buzzer (in some particular context) if the buzzer is regularly followed by presentation of food to a hungry rat who gets no food in the context-without-buzzer. The greater attractiveness (and value) of the food compared to no food is transmitted to buzzer compared to its absence. If a stimulus, tone, is followed by a negative reinforcer, shock, the lesser attractiveness of shock compared to no shock is transmitted to the tone (compared to no tone) which becomes less attractive (i.e., acquires secondary negative reinforcing properties, conditioned aversiveness, or fear-evoking properties).

In addition to summarizing all these types of behavior change, the principle of transmission of differential attractiveness directly implies an empirical generalization which is of some importance. This is that whenever some pair of stimuli X_{A2} and X_{B2} transmit differential attractiveness to antecedent responses, R_A and R_B respectively, so that R_A is acquired at the expense of R_B, then they will also transmit differential attractiveness to antecedent stimuli X_{A1} and X_{B1} so that X_{A1} will gain in attractiveness relative to X_{B1}. For example, if presentation of a flavored liquid such as a saccharine solution strengthens bar pressing, it will also transmit positive reinforcing properties to a tone which precedes it.

If we are to get much mileage from the principle of transmission of attractiveness, it will have to be a bit more specific. For our present limited purposes we need only assume that when time intervals are short, on the order of a minute or less, very nearly 100 percent of the differential attractiveness of a pair of stimulus situations, X_{A2} and X_{B2}, such as food and an empty goal box, will be transmitted to the antecedent pair of stimulus situations, X_{A1} and X_{B1}. This is assumed regardless of whether the members of the antecedent pair of X_1s differ with respect to responses (which are said to be differentially reinforced as when X_{A1} is turning right at a choice point and X_{B1} is turning left) or with respect to stimuli (which are said to acquire differential secondary reinforcing properties). In other words the assumption of an approximation of 100 percent transmission implies that at asymptote there may not be any gradient of effects of delay of reward or punishment as such when there are distinctive stimuli during the delay. In addition should there be a gradient under these conditions it is assumed that it would be very nearly horizontal. This is not to imply that delay of reward or punishment may not have indirect effects by altering the value of stimulus situations. In fact, as has been pointed out previously (Perkins, 1968), it is difficult to introduce delay of reward or punishment without confounding delay as such with other variables.

OBSERVING RESPONSES

As has been pointed out elsewhere (Perkins, 1955, 1968; Prokasy, 1956) the acquisition of observing responses, R_o, in the absence of differential external reward is implied by a differential reinforcement theory but not by a contiguity interpretation of classical conditioning. Our use of the term R_o is taken from Wyckoff (1952) who defines it as any response which provides reception of positive and negative discriminative stimuli. It should be emphasized that such R_os need not be receptor-orienting responses.

It may be helpful to indicate why R_o should be acquired according to reinforcement theory. An explanation in the language of the present paper is quite explicit and thus serves to clarify the issues. The assumption that classically conditioned responses are preparatory responses (PRs) implies that when a CR occurs the stimulus situation at the time of the US is more valuable than if there had been no CR. The acquisition of R_o permits occurrence of PRs which make the stimulus situation during the US more valuable. Absence of PR for US on nonreinforced presentations of the negative stimulus increases the value of conditions following CS presentation on nonreinforced trials. R_o is differentially reinforced because only when R_o occurs can those PRs which maximize the value of the following stimulus situation be made on both reinforced (US) and nonreinforced ($\overline{US}$) trials.

No comparable gain in value when R_o occurs can be predicted from contiguity theory; such a view does not imply that unambiguous anticipations have greater value than ambiguous ones. According to a contiguity interpretation of classical conditioning the value (and attractiveness) of conditions following a CR is no greater than the value of the conditions which follow its absence. For example, food-plus-saliva-in-the-mouth is no more valuable than food-without-saliva-in-the-mouth.

Described in terms of value and attractiveness the contiguity hypothesis implies that CR-plus-anticipation-of-US is more valuable than anticipation-of-US-without-CR. The rationale for the above assertion follows: If the CR comes to occur as a result of presentations of the CS followed by the US, the CR must be more attractive than $\overline{CR}$ in this context. If in addition the stimulus situation which follows CR is no more attractive than the situation which follows $\overline{CR}$ the greater attractiveness of CR than $\overline{CR}$ must be due to a difference in the value of the situations during the CS.

With reference to Table 1 the value of Row A must be greater than the value of Row B if classical conditioning occurs. According to reinforcement theory the difference in value is in Column 2; according to a contiguity interpretation it is in Column 1.

E-maze experiments

Since Prokasy's (1956) procedure is the prototype for a series of experiments it will be described in some detail. He ran rats in a single choice E-shaped maze which had interchangeable black and white delay and goal box sections for each arm. Runs to either arm were always followed by confinement in a delay box for 30 sec. and by food reward on exactly half the trials. In one arm, the consistent side, the food reward was always associated with black (white) delay and goal boxes and nonreward with white (black). On the inconsistent side the delay and goal boxes were black on half the trials and white on the other half, but brightness cues were uncorrelated with reward. Thus, the consequences of choosing the consistent side differed from the consequences of choosing the inconsistent side in just one way: food was predictable from brightness cues only on the consistent side. The alternatives are summarized in the portion of Figure 1 to the left of the first vertical space. At the choice point, CP, *S* can either make R_o, a turn to the consistent side, or the nonobserving response, R_n, a turn to the inconsistent side. In either case food follows just half the time. A free-forced technique was used to assure that at the end of blocks of eight trials *S* had entered each arm equally often. Prokasy's *S*s acquired a significant preference for R_o; they came to run predominantly to the consistent side.

In analyzing these conditions it will be convenient to use the conditioned salivary response as an example of preparatory (conditioned) responses which are acquired when food is the US. It should be remembered, though, that there are many other components of the preparatory response (PR) for food. These include secretion of the pancreas and gall bladder (Bykov, 1957). Salivation is the most frequently measured response of those which become conditioned when food is the US, but is only one of many such responses.

After differential conditioning to black and white has occurred on the consistent side, there presumably is more salivation before entering a goal box containing food than before entering an empty goal box on this side. Following R_n the same salivary response precedes entrance to baited and empty goal boxes. According to a reinforcement interpretation, the amount of salivation following R_o becomes appropriate in the sense that it maximizes the value of the conditions in the goal box. Following R_n the salivary response is the same on rewarded and nonrewarded trials, and thus cannot maximize the value of the stimulus situation when *S* is in the goal box on both rewarded and non-

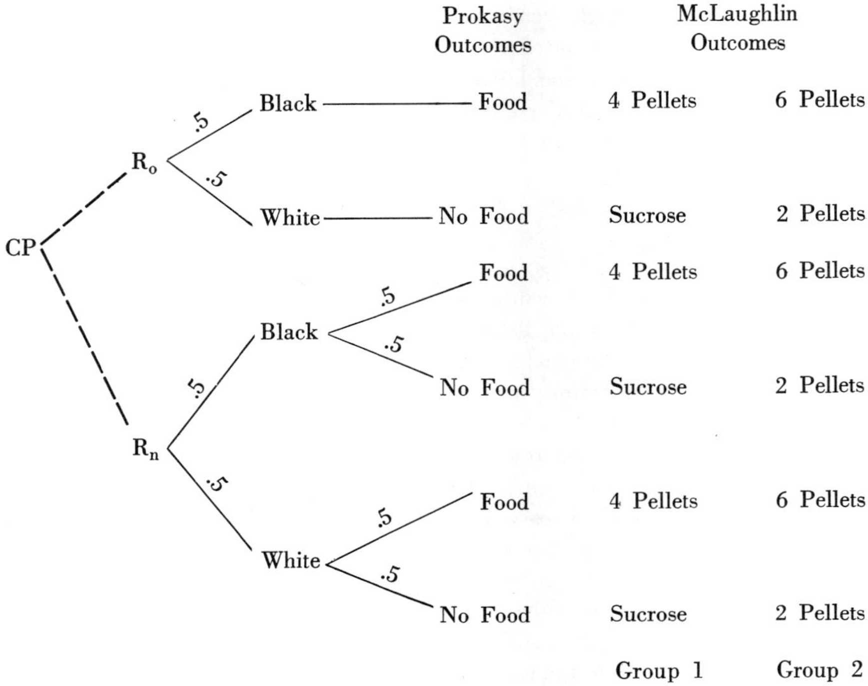

FIGURE 1. Outcomes for different responses in Prokasy's (1956) experiment and for Groups 1 and 2 of McLaughlin's (1968) experiment. Schema represents conditions for a single subject; brightness was counterbalanced across subjects.

rewarded trials. The rat has either less than the optimal amount of saliva-in-the-mouth on rewarded R_n trials, more than the optimal amount on nonrewarded R_n trials, or both. Optimum salivation on both rewarded and nonrewarded trials is possible only following R_o.

Variations of Prokasy's basic procedure have been used to demonstrate that R_o is more rapidly acquired under high drive than under low (Wehling & Prokasy, 1962); with water as well as with food reward (Levis & Perkins, 1965); equally well with any delays between 3 and 81 sec., but not at all with 0-sec. delay (Lutz & Perkins, 1960); and much more rapidly with 25 Noyes pellets than with 5, and not at all with a 1-pellet reward (Mitchell, Perkins, & Perkins, 1965.

It should be noted that in these experiments no instance of an R_n preference was acquired, and that the conditions under which no R_o preference was found (zero delay and very small reward) are conditions under which we would expect preparatory responses (PRs) to produce no measurable increase in the value of conditions at the time of US presentation.

In his dissertation research, McLaughlin (1968) tested certain implications of the PR interpretation of acquisition of R_o. He first ran a preliminary experiment which demonstrated that rats similar in strain, age, sex, and deprivation condition to those subsequently used in his R_o experiment had no clear preference for four 45-mg. Noyes pellets vs. 1.5 cc. of 10 percent sucrose solution, and that such rats came to select a six-pellet reward over the sucrose and the sucrose reward over two pellets. Thus, for the R_o experiment he had available an intermediate-sized food reward approximately equal in value to a specified amount of a sucrose solution and two other magnitudes of food reward, one of greater value and the other of less value than the sucrose.

The general procedure for McLaughlin's main experiment was about the same as Prokasy's except that the set of outcomes was different.

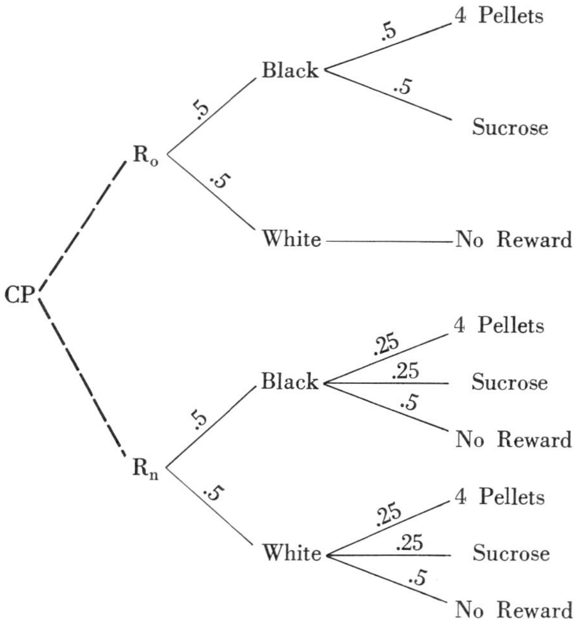

FIGURE 2. Outcomes for different responses for subjects in McLaughlin's (1968) Group 3.

For Group 1 the outcomes were four pellets or sucrose. These outcomes are shown in the first column to the right of Prokasy's paradigm in Figure 1. That is, if the column labeled Group 1 is substituted for the last column in the diagram representing Prokasy's experiment, the resultant diagram describes the outcomes for *S*s in McLaughlin's Group 1. The outcomes for McLaughlin's Group 2 were two or six pellets. The last column in Figure 1 represents these conditions. The alternatives followed R_o and R_n for Group 3 are summarized in Figure 2. The results in terms of percent of R_o responses on the first half of each day's trials are presented in Figure 3. It is clear that Group 1 acquired R_o most rapidly. According to *t* tests, this group made R_o significantly more often than either of the other groups at the end of training. As can be seen in Figure 3, there was also some tendency for Group 2 to acquire R_o. This tendency was of borderline significance; final performance did not differ from chance at the 5 percent level, but the increase in proportion of R_o responses was significant at this level.

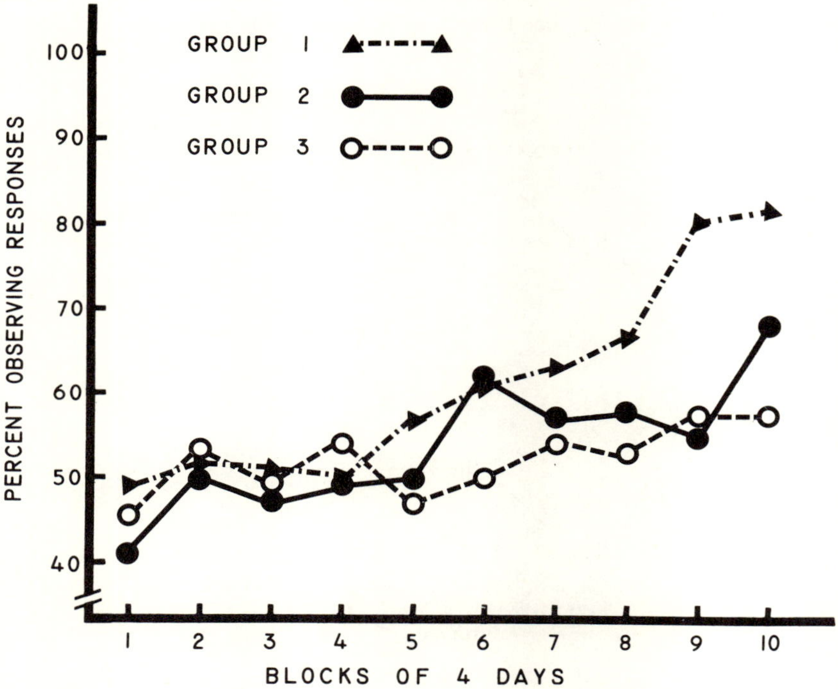

FIGURE 3. Results of McLaughlin's main experiment. Percent of the first half of the day's runs which were to the consistent side (i.e., were R_o), are plotted for successive blocks of 4 days. (Adapted from McLaughlin, 1968.)

The sucrose solution used was relatively weak in concentration and well below the preferred level for rats (Young & Greene, 1953). It was assumed tentatively that salivation, which is presumably a part of the PR for dry food pellets, would dilute the solution further and thus make the sucrose less valuable. In other words, it was assumed that there is at least some incompatibility between PRs for the dry food pellets and for this sucrose solution. The results for Group 1 clearly support this interpretation, since this group acquired R_0 significantly above chance. The lesser tendency for Group 2 to acquire R_0 is to be expected since in this case the PRs for the two alternatives are presumably similar and differ only in magnitude. At the same time some R_0 preference is to be expected as CR amplitude is a function of US (food) magnitude (Gantt, 1938).

Since the results for Group 1 support the hypothesis that preparatory responses for food and for sucrose are partially incompatible and opposite, the PR approach implies that Group 3 will not acquire strong R_0 tendencies. That is, under these conditions information about whether or not there will be reward has no value unless there is also information about the nature of the reward. Only with the more specific information can *S* make PRs which will enhance the value of the reward. As can be seen in Figure 3, the results for Group 3 confirm this expectation. Only a slight nonsignificant tendency to make R_0 above chance level was obtained for this group.

Other R_0 experiments with positive rewards

There have been a number of pigeon experiments on R_0 acquisition. A number of these, such as Wyckoff's initial experiment (1952), a series of experiments by Bower, McLean, and Meacham (1966), and Hendry's (1969) experiment in which R_0 was followed by a multiple FR 10-FR 90 schedule and R_n by mixed FR 10-FR 90, support the generalization that R_0 may be acquired in the absence of differential reward, and, in fact, that it is acquired under a wide variety of conditions.

In an experiment employing dogs, Shapiro, Mugg, and Ewald (1971) reported results directly contrary to those expected from the hypothesized effects of preparatory responses. Their *S*s were run in a two-lever box with a discrete-trial procedure. The dogs received choice trials on which both levers were presented simultaneously, which provided a measure of preference. Forced trials on which only one lever was presented assured adequate experience with each lever. For all three groups pressing either lever was followed immediately on 50 percent of the trials by 4 sec. of white noise and also on 50 percent of the trials by food, delivered 4 sec. after the response. The correlation between noise and food differed following responses on the two levers. Each group of eight dogs had a pair of correlations from *r*s of 1.0, 0.5, or 0.0. In each group there was a marked preference for the *lower* correlation, for the lever with the less informative condition. The absence of a preference would not be surprising. A 4-sec. signal might not provide enough time for a PR, or PR effects might hold over until the next trial, which was always presented within 2 min. Nevertheless the significant preference obtained is exactly the opposite of what one would expect if PRs have any effect. Further work is clearly needed to determine what factors are operating here. I know of no other results directly contrary to PR theory, and from any principle of which I am aware, there seems no good basis for predicting the preference obtained by Shapiro et al.

R_0 providing a warning signal

A number of studies have been reported in which rats were given a choice between an unavoidable shock preceded by a signal and one which was not (Knapp, Kause, & Perkins, 1959; Lockhard, 1963; Lockhard, 1965; Perkins, Levis, & Seymann, 1963; Perkins, Seymann, Levis, & Spencer, 1966). The results of these experiments are quite consistent in indicating that rats typically come to choose signalled shock over unsignalled shock. This effect may not be obtained when the level of shock is low or when shock produces freezing. However, to my knowledge no study has obtained reliable results in the opposite direction, that is, a preference for unsignalled shock over signalled shock.

Seligman, Maier, and Solomon (1971) have interpreted these results in terms of the lesser amount of fear under the signalled shock condition. Although they apparently feel that their interpretation is different from the PR explanation, I see no necessary difference except in the terms used. A decrease in fear in the absence of the signal is, in the language of the present paper, a decrease in shock preparatory responses in the absence of the signal. Seligman, Maier, and Solomon are perhaps more specific in assuming that the difference in value is between absence of fear (i.e., no shock preparation and absence of shock) compared to unjustified fear (i.e., shock preparation in the absence of shock).

The present interpretation does not specify whether the advantage of the warning signal is in facilitating preparation for shock, preparation for no shock, or both. That is, it is here assumed that without differential stimulation, appropriate conditioned preparatory responses may occur either before shock or before nonshock but not before both. Actually, by analogy with the decrease in salivation which occurs with an intermittent reinforcement schedule as opposed to CRF in salivary conditioning, I would expect the preparatory responses to be more appropriate following R_0 on both reinforced and nonreinforced trials.

Wagner, Thomas, and Norton (1967) reported acquisition of an R_0 which provided stimuli which preceded stimulation of the motor cortex. The cortical stimulation tended to throw their dogs off balance so that a warning stimulus had the obvious advantage of permitting postural adjustment.

Cantor and LoLordo (1970) obtained evidence that rats prefer signalled brain stimulation (ESB) to unsignalled ESB. This result was obtained regardless of whether signal onset preceded ESB by .5 or 15.5 sec., with both rewarding and aversive ESB as measured by independent preference tests. Their conditions, especially with a .5-sec. interstimulus interval, would seem to require a "central" preparatory response.

DELAY OF REWARD AND PUNISHMENT

It will be recognized that the effect PRs apparently have on the attractiveness of the situation which follows them has implications for the effect of delaying reward or punishment. This effect is most easily described with reference to the 100 percent transmission hypothesis (Perkins, 1968). This hypothesis states that if there are distinctive delay cues organisms will show, other things being equal, no asymptotic preference between immediate and delayed reward, or between immediate and delayed punishment. There are, however, a number of factors which are not equal in the typical study of delay of reward effects. In fact, as has been pointed out elsewhere (Perkins, 1965), it appears impossible to equate all these factors in experimental investigations of delay of food or water reward.

With delay of punishment the problem is somewhat simpler. In this case the only factor which is likely to have an effect on asymptotic choice behavior if highly distinctive cues are present during the delay is PRs. Assuming both 100 percent transmission and the hypothesized effects of PRs, immediate punishment should be preferred to delayed punishment when there are no cues to indicate just when the delayed punishment is to be presented. The reason for this is that there are cues indicating just when immediate punishment will be provided, and thus in this case *S* may time his PRs more appropriately than he can for delayed punishment. These cues are *S*'s own behavior, the response. Using rats as *S*s, Knapp, Kause, and Perkins (1959) first reported the preference for immediate over delayed shock. Similar results have been obtained by Badia, McBane, Suter, and Lewis (1966), Cook and Barnes (1964), and D'Amato and Gumenik (1960) with human *S*s. Also, Maltzman and Wolff (1970) obtained a preference for immediate aversive loud noise over the same stimulus after a delay of 15–25 sec.

In an unpublished study Badia (1959) gave rats a choice between two responses each of which was followed by the same delayed reward. Either response was also followed by shock 25 percent of the time. Shocks following one response were both delayed and preceded by a warning signal. Shocks following the other response were immediate and were followed by a signal. If the shocks were scrambled no preference was obtained, but with unscrambled shock there was a preference for delayed predictable shock over immediate unpredictable shock. Furedy and Biederman (1969) similarly reported a preference for signalled shock over unsignalled shock when the shock was unscrambled but not when it was scrambled. These studies suggest that scrambling shock may make PRs ineffective, or at least less effective than they are before unscrambled shock.

Badia's (1959) experiment and those in which immediate shock is selected over delayed shock indicate that either immediate or delayed shock may be preferred and that the preferred condition is the condition in which *S* has a better opportunity to make preparatory responses. At the very least, PRs may have a greater effect than a delay gradient when distinctive delay cues are present.

RUNNING SPEED EFFECTS

It has been observed that if food is thrown into a hungry rat's cage, the food may not be eaten immediately. Bolles (1965) has reported careful measures showing median eating latencies of over 15 sec. for these conditions. Such long latencies are quite a contrast to the immediate eating of a well-trained rat when he gets a food reward in a runway, maze, or other apparatus. The delay in eating unexpected food may be explained by assuming that such a delay allows time for PRs which make food consumption more valuable (i.e., make the food more palatable) than if PRs had not occurred. From the present frame of reference the running speed selected at asymptote in a runway experiment is that speed which maximizes the value of the response and its outcome. Thus, under typical conditions faster running tends to be more attractive in that it provides more immediate reduction of aversive hunger stimuli. At the same time faster running tends to be less attractive, at least beyond a certain point, because of increased "effort." Asymptotic running speed is assumed to be the equilibrium point at which those factors which tend to make faster running more attractive are balanced by others which tend to make slower running more attractive. As Seymann (1969) noted, one would expect PRs to decrease running speed under certain conditions.

In particular, if appropriate PRs have not occurred already, running speed should tend to be slower to give the rat an opportunity to make more appropriate PRs by the time the goal box is reached. Little or no such effect would be obtained when the reward conditions are the same on every trial because then appropriate PRs could begin in the start box or even earlier. If reward conditions differ from trial to trial, fully appropriate PRs cannot be made on all trials unless different cues are correlated with different reward conditions. When two different reward magnitudes are used in a within-subjects design and there are more small- than large-reward trials, there should be a tendency for *S* to run slower on large-reward trials if cues indicating the magnitude of the reward on a given trial first became available when the start box door is opened. That is, on a less frequent large-reward condition the rat might be expected to run slower so that PRs could be adjusted to make them appropriate for a large reward.

In Seymann's first experiment, rats received daily training consisting of nine small-reward (5-pellet) trials in one runway and one large-reward (20-pellet) trial in a runway differing in brightness. The large reward never came on the first two runs for the day, but its ordinal position varied irregularly among the other trials. The total runway including the goal box was only 4 feet long and a screen assured that the rats received no differential brightness cues before the start box door was opened.

Seymann's rats ran significantly faster on small-reward trials than on large. He also ran two control groups. In the first, small reward was presented on all trials but on one trial each day the runway differed in brightness. For this group, runway brightness had no significant effect. The second control group differed from the experimental group only in that there were black or white inserts in the start box which were the same brightness as the runway on that trial. All *S*s were in the start box for approximately 10 seconds. The prestart cue group ran faster on small-reward trials than on large ones, but the difference was significantly less than for the experimental group. These results were interpreted as indicating that the experimental *S*s slowed down to make appropriate PRs and the prestart cue group slowed down to a lesser extent because 10 sec. were not long enough for full adjustment of PRs to occur, though it did permit a partial adjustment. However, since for this group the adjustment had presumably occurred in part in the start box, the gain in appropriateness of PRs from extra time in the runway, while still appreciable, was less than for the experimental group.

Seymann ran a second experiment in which the proportion of large-reward trials was 10, 30, 50, 70, or 90 percent for different groups; the procedure was otherwise the same as for the experimental group in his first experiment. He found that the 50 percent group ran at almost exactly the same speed on large- and small-reward trials. The other groups ran faster on the more frequent type of trials, and the greater the difference in frequency, the greater was the difference in speed. These data are represented by the open circles in Figure 4. Since between-subjects results typically indicated that rats run faster for large than for small rewards it appeared that the adjustment in PRs gains more for *S* on large-reward trials than on small-reward trials. In particular, for the 50 percent group the preparation before differential cues are provided would presumably be intermediate between that most appropriate for 5 pellets and that most appropriate for 20. With respect to salivation this would imply excess salivation for 5 pellets but too little salivation for 20 pellets. On a 5-pellet trial no further adjustment could be made; excess salivation cannot be taken back. However, on 20-pellet trials increased salivation should increase the value of the reward.

This interpretation has further implications which were tested by Perkins (1970) in a replication of Seymann's second experiment with the single important difference that prestart cues were available for 30 sec. before the start box door was opened. As is shown by the solid curve in Figure 4, this change in procedure raised the value of speed on large-reward trials minus speed on small-reward trials for those groups with at least as many small- as large-reward trials. The 50 percent group ran faster for the large reward than for small,

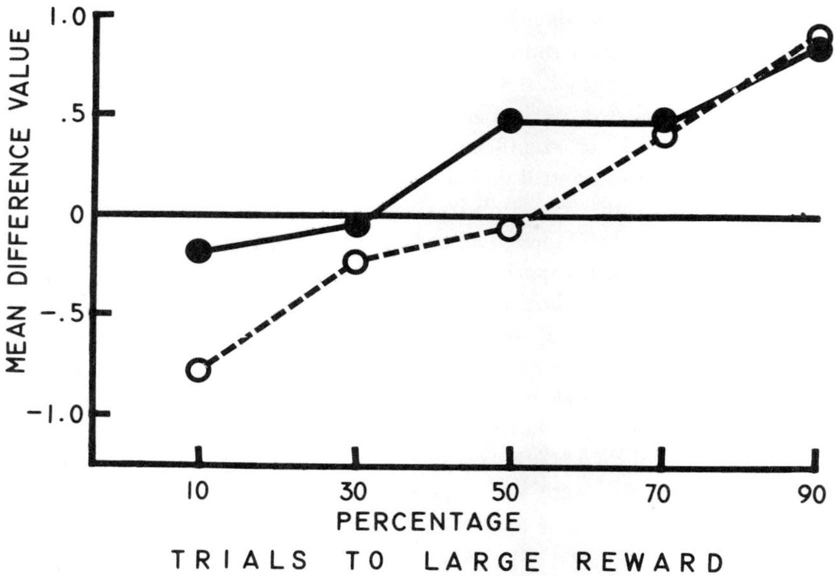

FIGURE 4. Differences in running speed (M ft/sec on large-reward trials minus M ft/sec on small-reward trials at the end of training for Seymann's procedure with no prestart cues (dashed line) and with 30-sec. prestart cues. (Figure after Perkins, 1970.)

indicating that reward magnitude as such has an effect which had been counteracted by PR effects in Seymann's 50 percent group. When 70 or 90 percent of the trials were for a large reward, the prestart cues had no effect on the difference between speed on large- and on small-reward trials. These results are exactly what is to be expected from PR theory. When most trials (70 or 90 percent) are large-reward trials, then appropriate PRs should occur before the start box door is opened whether or not there have been differential prestart cues. However, when at least half the trials are for small rewards, appropriate PRs for large rewards will occur before the start door is opened only if there are differential prestart cues.

Dammann and Perkins (1969) reported a parametric experiment to determine the effect of duration of prestart cues on the difference between speed on large- and small-reward trials. Their groups had prestart cues of 0, 3, 9, 27, or 81 sec. before the start box door was opened. All groups received nine small-reward trials and one large-reward trial each day in a procedure that closely paralleled Seymann's first experiment. Their 0-sec. group ran considerably faster for small than for large reward and there was a progressive decrease in the difference between speed for large and small rewards as duration of start box cues increased. The finding that even with start box cues of 81 sec. duration, the rats still ran as fast (actually nonsignificantly faster) for small as for large reward is puzzling. One possibility, of course, is that even 81 sec. is not long enough for food preparatory responses to be fully adjusted. Such an assumption is consistent with the effect of food-associated cues on amount of food eaten (Valle, 1968).

To summarize, the experimental evidence provides considerable support for the PR hypothesis. The prediction of acquisition of R_0 in the absence of differential reward has received a great deal of empirical support and the relative strength of the effect under different conditions is quite consistent with the hypothesis. Furthermore, implications of the PR hypothesis for delay of punishment effects and for certain running speed effects have been clearly supported by experimental results.

EVIDENCE FOR DIFFERENTIAL VALUE AT THE TIME OF THE CS

The evidence from R_0 experiments indicating that conditions are more valuable at the time of US presentation if the CR has occurred does not preclude the possibility that conditions are also more valuable at the time of CS presentation if the CR is in progress. In fact, it seems likely a priori that there are instances in which some (conditioned) response enhances the value of conditions when a US is anticipated, but detracts from the value of an otherwise identical stimulus situation when the US is not anticipated. That is, with reference to Column 1 of Table 1, there are presumably instances in which Row A is more valuable than Row B at the same time that Row D is more valuable than Row C. It is difficult to determine whether or not this is the case in most instances. Although the value of the total sequence represented by Row A is greater than that represented by Row B, by definition whenever a conditioned response is acquired, the locus of the differential value cannot be specified without additional information. Evidence from R_0 experiments suggesting differential value at the time of the US (Column 2) supports a reinforcement interpretation. However, it does not indicate whether or not there is also differential value at the time of the CS (Column 1), as implied by a contiguity interpretation.

Auto-shaped key pecking in pigeons (Brown & Jenkins, 1968; Williams & Williams, 1969) and auto-shaped key pressing in monkeys (Sidman & Fletcher, 1968) seem to provide instances of greater value of CR-plus-anticipation-of-US relative to anticipation-of-US-without-CR. An effective procedure for producing auto-shaping in pigeons is to present a CS, transillumination of the key, for 6 sec. and follow this by presentation of the food magazine. After a number of such trials most pigeons will start pecking the key when the CS is present. Presumably they will maintain this behavior indefinitely so long as magazine presentation follows the CS. This, of course, is a classical stimulus contingent procedure in which the US is presented regardless of the pigeon's behavior.

In the above case, there is no reason to believe that this particular response makes the grain more palatable. If preliminary pecking facilitated eating in some way, pecking something other than the CS key should serve just as well. Williams and Williams (1969) demonstrated that pigeons continue to peck the CS key in preference to another key and that they will peck the CS key even if their response terminates the CS and prevents presentation of the food magazine. That is, even when the CR serves as an avoidance response for the US of food, this response continues to occur. These findings seem to demand the conclusion that pecking a key which signals a food reward is more valuable than not pecking the key under these conditions, and that this difference in value is of some magnitude.

The occurrence of auto-shaped key pecking and its maintenance in spite of negatively correlated reinforcement indicate that key pecking in the pigeon may be maintained as well by respondent conditioning (i.e., stimulus contingent food presentation) as by an operant procedure (i.e., response contingent food presentation). Key pecking, a much-studied operant, seems to be a good respondent as well. In much "operant" work (e.g., discriminated operants and chaining with pigeons), the two "processes" are hopelessly confounded.

Breland and Breland (1961) have reported acquisition of other behavior changes that seem to be based on greater value of CR than of $\overline{\text{CR}}$ during stimuli which regularly precede food delivery. These include the scratching response in chickens and the rooting response in pigs. It is worth noting that these responses, like key pecking, are not mediated by the autonomic nervous system (ANS). Sheffield (1965) has obtained evidence indicating that the dog's acquisition of a conditioned salivary response which is mediated by the ANS probably depends on the greater value of CR than of $\overline{\text{CR}}$ when food is anticipated. At the same time Miller and Carmona (1967) obtained evidence that the law of effect (i.e., the differential value of subsequent stimuli), can determine whether or not a salivary response occurs.

It is hardly surprising that regardless of whether the response involves smooth or striped muscles, conditions might have greater value at the time of either CS or US presentation on trials on which *S* makes a CR than on trials on which *S* does not. The findings can be most simply described in terms of our distinction between value and attractiveness and the single principle that differential attractiveness is transmitted to antecedent stimulus situations.

The presence of a response may affect the value of a prevailing stimulus situation and/or the value of the stimulus situation which follows. According to the present view, classical conditioning will occur whenever (a) the value of the situation during either the CS or the US is increased by the CR when the US follows the CS and (b) the value of the situation during the CS or afterwards is greater if there is no CR when the CS is not followed by the

US. This latter requirement is included because a response is said to be classically conditioned only if its acquisition depends upon CS-US sequences.

Viewed in this way, the issue of contiguity versus reinforcement interpretations of classical conditioning (i.e., differential value during CS versus differential value during US), is neither an all-or-none question nor a general question. Rather, it is a number of specific questions about the relative value of different pairs of stimulus situations.

The above molar analysis of classical conditioning implies that some instances of classical conditioning are not explained by the law of effect. The auto-shaped key peck does not seem to be followed by a more attractive condition that is incompatible behavior.

It is hardly surprising that the value of a response (e.g., auto-shaped key pecking) depends on other aspects of the situation (e.g., anticipation of food). A built-in species specific characteristic (e.g., asymptotic preference) is all that is required for key pecking to be more valuable than incompatible responses during anticipation of food and less valuable when no food is anticipated. The disadvantage of such an assumption is that it clearly implies that value must be determined empirically, and that the value of a stimulus situation cannot be predicted from the value of its components. This disadvantage reflects on our wish for a predictable world, however, not on the theory's adequacy in describing behavior.

Let us take a different approach and use "response" to designate behavior during an infinitesimal period of time. If a response refers to an event of infinitesimal duration, then the initiation of a CR is a response which is followed by a more attractive situation than is initiation of an incompatible response, $\overline{CR}$. Thus, if one employs a temporally molecular response concept or what Logan (1966) has called a dynamic micromolar theory, it is possible to explain all behavior change in law of effect terms or in terms of transmission of attractiveness to responses which are of infinitesimal duration. Such responses are so short that they have only trivial value and thus within the error of measurement their attractiveness is determined by their effects. It seems to me that this sort of ongoing concept of a response, which implies that response selection is occurring all the time, is reasonable intuitively and at the same time is more useful for analyzing many problems.

In any case we have an interesting example of the interdependence of different aspects of a theory. The law of effect or the principle of transmission of attractiveness seems quite workable as an explanation of all learned behavior change when responses are assumed to be of infinitesimal duration (i.e., when response selection is considered continuous), but not when the response concept employed designates responses which last for some measurable period of time.

It appears that there is no incompatibility between molecular reinforcement theory and molar two-process theory. Each may be correct if it incorporates the appropriate response concept. An emphasis on the distinction between value and attractiveness and the explanation of behavior change in terms of transmission of attractiveness is quite compatible with both approaches. In addition, an interpretation in terms of transmission of attractiveness seems to summarize many findings more simply.

REFERENCES

Badia, P. Intermittent immediate punishment vs. intermittent delayed punishment preceded by a warning signal as a determiner of choice. Unpublished M.A. Thesis, Kent State University, 1959.

Badia, P., McBane, B., Suter, S., & Lewis, P. Preferences behavior in an immediate versus variably delayed shock situation with and without a warning signal. *Journal of Experimental Psychology*, 1966, *72*, 847–852.

Bolles, R. C. Consummatory behavior in rats maintained a-periodically. *Journal of Comparative and Physiological Psychology*, 1965, *60*, 239–243.

Bower, G., McLean, J., & Meacham, J. Value of knowing when reinforcement is due. *Journal of Comparative and Physiological Psychology*, 1966, *62*, 184–192.

Breland, K., & Breland, M. The misbehavior of organisms. *American Psychologist*, 1961, *16*, 681–684.

Brown, P. L., & Jenkins, H. M. Auto-shaping of the pigeon's key-peck. *Journal of the Experimental Analysis of Behavior*, 1968, *11*, 1–8.

Bykov, K. M. *The cerebral cortex and the internal organs*. Translated and edited by W. H. Gantt. New York: Chemical Publishing Company, 1957.

Cantor, M. B., & LoLordo, V. M. Rats prefer signaled reinforcing brain stimulation to unsignaled ESB. *Journal of Comparative and Physiological Psychology*, 1970, *71*, 183–191.

Cook, J. O., & Barnes, L. W., Jr. Choice of delay of inevitable shock. *Journal of Abnormal and Social Psychology*, 1964, *68*, 669–672.

D'Amato, M. R., & Gumenik, W. E. Some effects of immediate versus randomly delayed shock on an instrumental response and cognitive processes. *Journal of Abnormal and Social Psychology*, 1960, *60*, 64–67.

Dammann, C. A., & Perkins, C. C., Jr. Duration of antecedent discriminative stimuli and within-subject reward magnitude differences as determiners of running speed. *Journal of Experimental Psychology*, 1969, *82*, 554–556.

Furedy, J. J., & Biederman, G. B. The preference-for-signalled-shock phenomenon: reinforcing effects of signalling the shock as a function of scrambling the grid. Paper presented at the meeting of the Psychonomic Society, St. Louis, November, 1969.

Gantt, W. H. The nervous secretion of saliva: the relation of the conditioned reflex to the intensity of the unconditioned stimulus. *American Journal of Physiology*, 1938, *123*, 74.

Hendry, D. P. Reinforcing value of information: fixed-ratio schedules. In D. P. Hendry (Ed.), *Conditioned reinforcement*. Homewood, Illinois: Dorsey Press, 1969. Pp. 300–341.

Hull, C. L. *Principles of behavior*. New York: Appleton-Century, 1943.

Knapp, R. K., Kause, R. H., & Perkins, C. C., Jr. Immediate versus delayed shock in T-maze performance. *Journal of Experimental Psychology*, 1959, *58*, 357–362.

Levis, D. J., & Perkins, C. C., Jr. Acquisition of observing response (R_0) with water reward. *Psychological Reports*, 1965, *16*, 114.

Lockhard, J. A. Choice of a warning signal in an unavoidable shock situation. *Journal of Comparative and Physiological Psychology*, 1963, *56*, 526–530.

Lockhard, J. A. Choice of a warning signal or none in several unavoidable-shock situations. *Psychonomic Science*, 1965, *3*, 5–6.

Logan, F. A. Continuously negatively correlated amount of reinforcement. *Journal of Comparative and Physiological Psychology*, 1966, *66*, 31–34.

Lutz, R. E., & Perkins, C. C., Jr. A time variable in the acquisition of observing responses. *Journal of Comparative and Physiological Psychology*, 1960, *53*, 180–182.

Maltzman, I., & Wolff, C. Preference for immediate versus delayed noxious stimulation and the concomitant GSR. *Journal of Experimental Psychology*, 1970, *83*, 76–79.

McLaughlin, D. L. Some necessary conditions for the acquisition of observing responses. Unpublished doctoral dissertation, Emory University, 1968.

Miller, N. E., & Carmona, A. Modification of a visceral response, salivation in thirsty dogs, by instrumental training with water reward. *Journal of Comparative and Physiological Psychology*, 1967, *63*, 1–6.

Mitchell, K. M., Perkins, N. P., & Perkins, C. C., Jr. Conditions affecting acquisition of observing responses in the absence of differential reward. *Journal of Comparative and Physiological Psychology*, 1965, *60*, 435–437.

Perkins, C. C., Jr. The stimulus conditions which follow learned responses. *Psychological Review*, 1955, *62*, 341–348.

Perkins, C. C., Jr. A conceptual scheme for studies of stimulus generalization. In D. I. Mostofsky (Ed.), *Stimulus generalization.* Stanford: Stanford University Press, 1965. Pp. 38–54.

Perkins, C. C., Jr. An analysis of the concept of reinforcement. *Psychological Review*, 1968, *75*, 155–172.

Perkins, C. C., Jr. Proportion of large-reward trials and within-subject reward magnitude effects. *Journal of Comparative and Physiological Psychology*, 1970, *70*, 170–172.

Perkins, C. C., Jr., Levis, D. J., & Seymann, R. G. Preference for signal-shock vs. shock-signal. *Psychological Reports*, 1963, *13*, 735–738.

Perkins, C. C., Jr., Seymann, R. G., Levis, D. J., & Spencer, H. R., Jr. Factors affecting preference for signal-shock over shock-signal. *Journal of Experimental Psychology*, 1966, *72*, 190–196.

Prokasy, W. F., Jr. The acquisition of observing responses in the absence of differential external reinforcement. *Journal of Comparative and Physiological Psychology*, 1956, *49*, 131–134.

Seligman, M. E. P., Maier, S. F., & Solomon, R. L. Unpredictable and uncontrollable aversive events. In F. R. Brush (Ed.), *Aversive conditioning and learning*. New York: Academic Press, 1971.

Seymann, R. G. Effect of differences in reward magnitude with correlated cues on running speed. *Journal of Experimental Psychology*, 1969, *81*, 504–509.

Shapiro, M. M., Mugg, G. J., & Ewald, W. Instrumental preferences and conditioned preparatory responses in dogs. *Journal of Comparative and Physiological Psychology*, 1971, *74*, 227–232.

Sheffield, F. D. Relation between classical conditioning and instrumental learning. In W. F. Prokasy (Ed.), *Classical conditioning: A symposium.* New York: Appleton-Century-Crofts, 1965. Pp. 302–322.

Sidman, M., & Fletcher, F. G. A demonstration of auto-shaping with monkeys. *Journal of the Experimental Analysis of Behavior*, 1968, *11*, 307–309.

Spence, K. W. The role of secondary reinforcement in delayed reward learning. *Psychological Review*, 1947, *54*, 1–14.

Spence, K. W. *Behavior theory and conditioning.* New Haven: Yale University Press, 1956.

Valle, Fred P. Effect of exposure to feeding-related stimuli on food consumption in rats. *Journal of Comparative and Physiological Psychology*, 1968, *66*, 773–776.

Wagner, A. R., Thomas, E., & Norton, T. Conditioning with electrical stimulation of motor cortex: Evidence of a possible source of motivation. *Journal of Comparative and Physiological Psychology*, 1967, *64*, 191–199.

Wehling, H. E., & Prokasy, W. F. Role of food deprivation in the acquisition of observing responses. *Psychological Reports*, 1962, *10*, 399–407.

Williams, D. R., & Williams, H. Auto-maintenance in the pigeon: sustained pecking despite contingent non-reinforcement. *Journal of the Experimental Analysis of Behavior*, 1969, *12*, 511–520.

Wyckoff, L. B. The role of observing responses in discrimination learning. *Psychological Review*, 1952, *59*, 431–442.

Young, P. T., & Greene, J. T. Quantity of food ingested as a measure of relative acceptability. *Journal of Comparative and Physiological Psychology*, 1953, *46*, 288–294.

Discrete Trials and Their Relation to Free-Behavior Situations

JOHN R. PLATT

It is the custom of experimental psychologists to evolve classification schemes for their experimental paradigms and then to catalogue results and to abstract theoretical systems in terms of these paradigms. A good example of this procedure is provided by considering the distinction between classical and instrumental conditioning. These two sets of operations, clearly differing in respect to the experimenter's control of relationships between particular behaviors and their stimulus consequences, are used to define two different behavioral processes.

Such distinctions are of course in some degree necessary, for without them consistent functional laws would be extremely elusive and chaos would probably result. On the other hand, an extreme application of this procedure would mean that every behavioral experiment would have to be considered a different paradigm in that certain operational divergences could undoubtedly be identified. This extreme would of course totally eliminate the abstract generality which is so essential to scientific knowledge.

Thus, the problem at any stage of development of an area of scientific knowledge becomes one of distinguishing that number of distinct paradigms which maximizes generality without producing a chaos of empirical inconsistencies. At a given time the distinction between classical and instrumental conditioning may need to be respected as an essential or process distinction so as to allow the development of a consistent body of empirical laws for each

Preparation of this chapter and unpublished research reported herein was supported by United States Public Health Service Grant No. MH–15380, John R. Platt, principal investigator.

Stephen Bitgood, Jennifer Davis, and Peter Senkowski were responsible for the unpublished data reported in this chapter. Their assistance is gratefully acknowledged.

paradigm. At some point, however, the problem of integrating these two sets of laws must be faced. The search for generality and order will not be completed so long as two such sets of laws at the same level of discourse are posed as independent. The commonalities of these two paradigms should be made as specific as possible. To the extent that this is not possible, essential differences should be clearly shown. This basic integrative goal of scientific investigation has been well stated by Sidman (1960) : "We must be able to classify our variables in such a manner that we can recognize similarities in their *principles of operation*, in spite of the fact that their physical specifications may be quite different."

Kenneth Spence was particularly attuned to this need for abstraction of common principles of operation and paradigm integration. He contributed greatly to such ends by his repeated efforts to analyze discrimination learning paradigms into simple instrumental components, and to examine relationships between classical and instrumental conditioning by developing a theory which postulated the operation of classically conditioned anticipatory goal responses in instrumental paradigms.

Another paradigm distinction, that between instrumental and operant conditioning, or at least between discrete-trials and free-behavior procedures, has been a rather enigmatic and largely ignored issue in behavior theory. Since these two paradigms have emerged from the work of groups differing with respect to procedure, apparatus, design philosophy, and theoretical persuasion, each group has usually been content simply to ignore the results of the other's paradigm. This attitude clearly will not produce the kind of generality previously described as desirable. However, those not particularly interested in the issues of either of the groups often make indiscriminate use of both paradigms without regard for the possible implications of their differences. This attitude is of course likely to produce what was previously described as a chaos of empirical inconsistencies.

The present essay is an attempt to consider some of the more obvious functional relationships between free-operant and discrete-trials paradigms. Following a brief statement of several previous suggestions for relating these two paradigms, an existing notation will be suggested as adequate to the conceptualization and simulation of discrete-trials behavior in typical free-operant settings. This notation will then be used to suggest the relevance of both free-operant and discrete-trials data to the specification of some important similarities and dissimilarities between typical implementations of the two paradigms. In addition, some new problems raised by these considerations will be indicated so as to illustrate the greater understanding of both free-operant and discrete-trials situations which would emerge from their conceptual integration.

PREVIOUS INTEGRATIVE ATTEMPTS

It would be a serious error to suppose that no one has given attention to the need for conceptual continuity between discrete-trials and free-operant paradigms. Recently there have been a surge of discrete-trials studies using typically free-operant situations such as lever pressing or key pecking in operant chambers. These studies come both from the discrete-trials camp (e.g., Gonzalez, Bainbridge, & Bitterman, 1966; Platt, Senkowski, & Mann, 1969; Porter & Hug, 1965) and from operant investigators (e.g., Jenkins, 1970). In these studies "discrete trials" seems to mean nothing more than that in interpolated periods, marked by distinctive stimuli, responses are not allowed or at least not reinforced. The apparent implication is of course that discrete-trials procedures are simply operant discriminations or discriminated timeout (TO) procedures. It will be suggested here that considerably more than this is involved in transition from customary discrete-trials situations to an operant paradigm.

Although the studies just mentioned have not had as their principal goal the illumination of systematic relationships between discrete-trials and free-operant paradigms, they do suggest one approach to that problem. Specifically, by investigating procedural variations on free-operant paradigms and comparing the results obtained with those from typical discrete-trials situations, one might eventually arrive at statements of limited generality as to parallels and discrepancies beween the results of the two. There is certainly nothing wrong with such a procedure, but this author feels that more efficient progress toward developing more general laws might be made by attempting to abstract such relationships from existing knowledge about the two situations, along with a little educated guessing as to points of congruence between them. Such an approach would closely resemble what Spence (1957) has called the empirical-construct type of theorizing, in which guessed-at relationships are posed as empirical abstractions to be rejected or modified on the basis of the outcome of further experimentation suggested by them.

This latter type of approach to the problem of integrating free-operant and discrete-trials results is exemplified by several existing treatments. Keller and Schoenfeld (1950) wrote an entire introductory textbook from an operant viewpoint at a time when very few data were available from free-operant situations. They thus drew extensively on discrete-trials runway data and provided a theoretical analysis of both situations in terms of common principles. The runway was treated as a homogeneous chain of operants with terminal reinforcement—the proper free-operant analogue being something like a fixed ratio (FR) schedule of reinforcement in which every *n*th response is reinforced with food. Their treatment thus used the theoretical process of behavioral chaining to suggest an equivalence between at least one free-operant and one discrete-trials situation.

A somewhat similar analysis has been offered by Spence in a discussion of response decrements under nonreinforcement:

> While considerable experimentation has been conducted with partial or mixed schedules of reinforcement and nonreinforcement it has, unfortunately, mostly been carried on with the free-responding type of Skinner-box situation. It is my own belief that this latter phenomenon, important as it is, has little or nothing to do with extinction but rather is related to the problem of the length of the chain that can be established in instrumental sequences. Essentially what these studies have demonstrated is that one can establish very long instrumental chains. Translated into the runway situation these types of studies are not nearly so dramatic as they appear in the context of the lever box, for what they have shown is that one can train a rat to take a great many steps, i.e., run a long way, to get a piece of food [1956, pp. 122–123].

This particular view of the relationship between discrete-trials and free-behavior situations has been further expanded by Logan and Wagner. After advocating the frequently-held view that discrete trials may be simulated in a free-behavior situation simply by introducing an operant discrimination, these authors say:

> Consider another alley analog of the bar-pressing situation: a bar press is like taking a step (or possibly running a foot) in an alley. On this assumption, a variable-ratio schedule is not a partial reinforcement condition but instead varies the length of the response chain rather than the number of discrete responses. The alley analogue of a VR schedule would be to vary the length of the alley from trial to trial—but the rat would eventually be rewarded every time he was put in the alley. Should it make a difference whether the rat is rewarded on half the trials he is put in a 1-foot alley or whether he is rewarded every trial but with alley length varied so that it averages 2 feet? The average number of feet run per reward is the same, but the rat might learn quite different things [1965, pp. 56–57].

Logan and Wagner seem to be suggesting the comparability of discrete-trials runways and operant FR schedules while proposing an implementation of discrete-trials in operant situations which centers instead on the establishment of a discriminated TO or intertrial interval (ITI). It is only too apparent that the operant reinforcement schedule in effect, the existence of a discriminated TO and any relationships between the two may be independent of each other. Which characteristics are being considered essential for distinguishing discrete-trials from free-operant situations? In a purely definitional sense, the existence of ITIs may of course be taken to be this characteristic, but such a definition is not guaranteed to have any functional significance. The question is, What discrepant characteristics of the two types of situations must be considered in order to account for similarities and dissimilarities between the behaviors they produce in terms of a common set of principles? To this end, a given feature, such as an ITI, may or may not be significant.

Unfortunately, this question of functionally significant discrepancies between free behavior and discrete trials cannot be approached in a completely general manner, but only in relation to particular behavioral criteria or reference phenomena. That is to say, the functional significance of manipulating some factor which is identified as differing between two types of situations can only be evaluated with respect to the effect of that manipulation on one or more behavioral processes chosen by the experimenter because of some relevance he attaches to them. What is an important discrepancy between two situations for one behavioral process may not be critical for some other process. Furthermore, the processes chosen for such a reference may be of varying degrees of abstraction. Some degree of abstraction is already implied when the processes chosen can be identified in two different situations. Any degree of abstraction beyond this minimum is desirable to the extent that it increases the generality of a resulting integration of the two situations, but undesirable to the extent that it may omit other critical factors with a resulting appearance of empirical chaos.

In this essay, we will use various behavioral criteria to assign functional significance to similiarities and dissimilarities between free-operant and discrete-trials paradigms. Most important among these criteria will be the ability of certain stimulus relationships to maintain and pattern behaviors, and the consequences of various operations of reinforcement omission in each of the two paradigms.

A COMMON NOTATIONAL SYSTEM

The preceding section showed that most attempts to specify operant analogues to discrete-trials paradigms have centered on FR schedules with TOs or ITIs after reinforcements. This scheme seems eminently plausible in that the runway typically involves some relatively fixed amount of homogeneous responding (steps), terminating in reinforcement, and followed by a distinctly cued period in which reinforcement is not available. In a later section of this essay, the significance of such TO periods will be examined in greater detail. For the moment, the characterization of the trial itself will be of primary concern.

Knarr and Collier (1962) have suggested that locomotion may be a different sort of response than such typical operants as lever pressing. They proposed the existence of two distinct classes of responses. The first class contains repetitive serial reflexes of a fixed, genetically determined topography such as licking, chewing, running, etc., in which the chaining stimuli are those produced by the preceding response. These sequences are not chained by external stimuli, although they can be brought under the control of specific discriminative stimuli, e.g., presentation of food or opening of a start-box door. The second class contains responses of novel flexible evolutionary topography, such as right and left turns in a maze or sequential discrimination behavior, which are chained by external stimuli.

Knarr and Collier suggested that arbitrary operants such as lever pressing were members of the second class for which the chain could shift from external to internal stimulus control with extensive training under such conditions as FR schedules of reinforcement. The importance of this distinction between response classes was said to be in their controllable parameters. "The first [class] acts as a unit, i.e., occurs in bursts of constant rate, the appropriate parameters being burst rate, burst duration, and burst latency; while for the second the individual response acts as a unit, the appropriate parameters being the probability and/or latency of occurrence [p. 586]." Although it would be difficult to determine empirically the correctness of Knarr and Collier's suggestions, acceptance of them implies one would only be able to identify common parameters for the comparison of operant FR and runway data after the FR performance had been well established.

Even if units of locomotor behavior are established much like those of operants under FR schedules, a potentially important operational difference still remains between the reinforcement contingencies in the two situations. While the FR contingency is based on a fixed number of identifiable responses, this is not quite the case with a runway where reinforcement is contingent on a fixed distance (FD) being traversed (Williams, 1966). If it were assumed that all *S*s made equal-sized steps and no retracing occurred, this fixed distance would be identical to a fixed number of response units. However, since these locomotor units are not readily measurable, it might be better to maintain a distinction between FD and FR for the time being. Such a distinction would also allow a context for possible response unit differences, such as those proposed by Knarr and Collier, without biasing against eventual equation of FR and FD contingencies.

Somewhat more difficult than the formulation of an operant analogue for a single discrete trial is the specification of contingencies across trials. It is this problem to which Logan and Wagner (1965) were referring when they asked whether a difference would result between rewarding a rat on half the trials in a 1-ft. alley or on every trial in an alley varying in length with an average of 2 feet. Consider a slightly different but related question. Is the difference between rats running to continuous reinforcement and those running with single alternation of reinforced and nonreinforced trials the same as that between the former and those running to continuous reinforcement in an alley twice as long? The answer to this question is clearly "no." Several studies (Capaldi, 1958; Tyler, Wortz, & Bitterman, 1953) show that single alternation subjects come to run very slowly on nonreinforced trials, while there is no evidence (Hull, 1934) that doubling the length of a runway eventuates in reduced running speeds over its first half. Much the same sort of results can be shown for discrete-trials lever-pressing situations. The suppression of first-response latencies on nonreinforced trials under single alternation of reinforcement has been demonstrated by Gonzalez, Bainbridge, and Bitterman (1966).

Some unpublished results from the author's laboratory show such a depression of response speeds for all responses on nonreinforced trials in a discrete-trials, single-alternation condition. Six male hooded rats, maintained on 12 gm. of food per day, were trained to make five lever presses which produced a blackout and lever retraction. At the beginning of every second blackout, three 45-mg. food pellets were delivered. Twenty such trials were administered each day at a rate of one every 60 sec. Any trial not completed within 30 sec. was terminated without reinforcement. Figure 1 shows mean response speeds for successive responses in the ratio on reinforced and nonreinforced trials over Days 17 to 20. Slower response speeds on nonreinforced trials are quite apparent throughout the ratio, in a manner quite comparable to results obtained with single alternation of reinforcement in a runway. Also, as in the runway, rats in discrete-trials lever-pressing situations show no tendency to be slower on the first half of a trial than rats required to make only half as many responses (Platt & Senkowski, 1970b, Exp. I; Weiss, 1961).

Many other examples of differences between trial length and schedule of

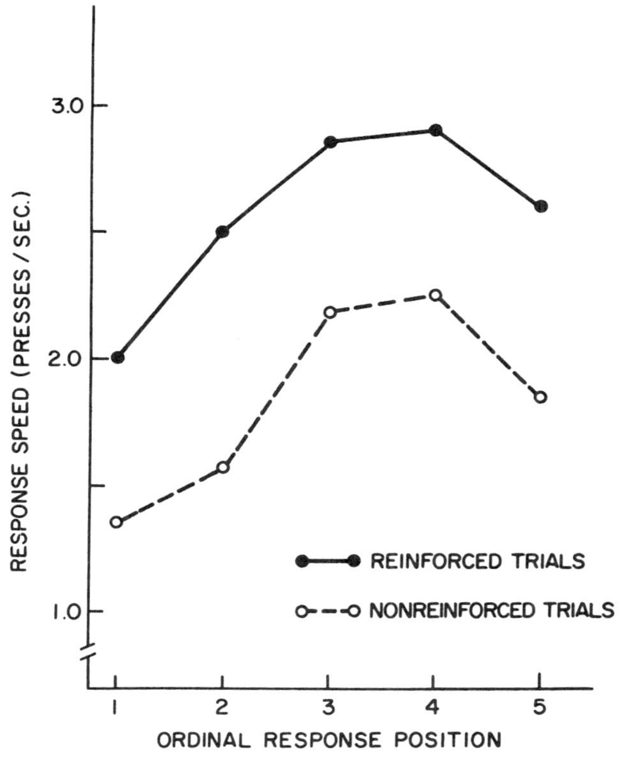

FIGURE 1. Mean speeds for successive lever press in a ratio requirement on reinforced and nonreinforced trials over Days 17 to 20 of training under single alternation of reinforcement.

reinforcement across trials could be presented. However, the single phenomenon just cited should suffice to indicate that variations in discrete-trials reward schedules cannot be thought of simply as variations in the distance requirement of a FD or variable distance (VD) schedule. Analogously, considerable confusion is likely to result if one attempts to compare variations in discrete-trials reinforcement schedules with variations in FR or VR requirements in operant situations. For example, the fact that free-operant resistance to extinction is an increasing function of FR (Mowrer & Jones, 1945; Skinner, 1938) or VR (Hearst, 1961) size in acquisition might have little to do with the increase in resistance to extinction of a runway response when some of the acquisition trials are nonreinforced (Lewis, 1960).

Returning to the original problem of specifying a notation which will allow conceptualization and simulation of discrete trials in typically free-operant settings, we find that ratio schedules promise to be a reasonable representation of the intratrial structure of a discrete-trial runway, but some way is needed to express and simulate the additional reinforcement contingencies being imposed upon the ratio components of such a schedule. As a matter of fact, just such a problem of "schedules of schedules" has occasionally interested operant investigators, and Kelleher (1966) has provided a particularly clear notational system for such situations, labelling them "second-order schedules." Following Kelleher: "A 'second-order schedule' treats a pattern of behavior engendered by a schedule contingency as a unitary response that is itself reinforced according to some schedule of reinforcement [p. 476]." Thus, the runway single alternation experiments discussed previously may be viewed as fixed ratios of fixed distance schedules or FR (FD). Similarly, the discrete-trials lever-pressing analogue of Figure 1 may be denoted FR 2 (FR 5). Still following Kelleher, the fact that these schedules both involved a stimulus change at the end of each first-order component could be designated by referring to them as FR 2 (FD x:S) and FR 2 (FR 5:S). However, since this stimulus change was a TO in the latter case, it could more accurately be denoted FR 2 (FR 5:TO), and a control analogous to a continuously reinforced group with twice the runway length could be denoted as CRF (FR 10:TO).

The major advantage of this notational system is that it emphasizes a number of factors, identifiable in both free-operant and discrete-trials situations, which may be quite important to their integration. These factors include: (a) the nature of the first- and second-order schedule components, (b) the presence or absence of a stimulus change at the end of the first-order component, (c) whether or not this change is the same on reinforced and nonreinforced occasions, (d) whether this stimulus change involves a TO, and (e) whether successive second-order components are distinctively cued.

Before turning to a consideration of the roles of some of these factors in the two paradigms, it is reasonable to ask whether the notion of second-order schedules really does provide a common representation for the two paradigms.

The single-alternation example above certainly suggests that it does, but further evidence would be welcome. One set of phenomena which should be maximally sensitive to similarities and dissimilarities of the type which second-order schedules represent is the effects of various acquisition manipulations on resistance to extinction (R_n). A principal question concerns the relationships between increases in R_n under partial reinforcement in the two paradigms. Are these the same phenomenon in both cases, and can the notation of second-order schedules be used to indicate their points of functional congruence and discrepancy?

Logan and Wagner (1965, p. 57) have already been cited as differentiating an operant VR from a runway partial reinforcement condition by suggesting that the former varies the length of a continuously reinforced behavior sequence while the latter varies the reinforcement frequency of a constant length sequence. This distinction is well represented in the current notation by the distinction between CRF(VR) and VR(FR) or VR(FD). But does this distinction have any functional significance? Logan and Wagner suggested that free-operant and discrete-trials extinction procedures tap rather different variables. In the former case, "EXT" in the present notation, one is seeking to find how long a sequence the *S* will execute without reinforcement. In a runway situation this might be thought of as asking how far the *S* would run down an endless runway. Logan and Wagner suggested that this free-operant extinction technique would probably be most sensitive to those manipulations which vary length of behavior sequence or first-order schedule component, as in the case of simple VR schedules. On the other hand, discrete-trials extinction, denotable as EXT (FR:TO) or EXT(FD:TO), was said to answer the question of how many response sequences of a particular length a *S* would execute without reinforcement. This latter extinction technique might thus be expected to be most sensitive to manipulations of the reinforcement frequency of behavioral sequences or second-order schedule components.

Logan and Wagner's suggestions concerning partial reinforcement fit well within the present formulation and, if correct, would represent a significant integration of free-operant and discrete-trials intermittent reinforcement effects. Unfortunately this author knows of no published research bearing directly on this hypothesis. Orthogonal investigations of the effects of first- and second-order schedule components with both free-operant and discrete-trials extinction procedures are needed. Such investigations have been initiated in the author's laboratory and some early results can be presented here.

The first step was to demonstrate the usual discrete-trials partial reinforcement extinction effect (PREE) in a typical operant situation, while controlling possible first-order, VR-like increments in R_n for the partial reinforcement condition. Fifteen adult male White Carneaux pigeons were reduced to 80 percent of their free-feeding weights and auto-shaped (Brown & Jenkins, 1968) to peck a white key. The birds were then randomly and equally assigned to three treatment groups for 18 sessions of acquisition training. In one group,

CRF(FR 30:S, TO), each session consisted of 30 trials and on each trial 30 key pecks extinguished the key light and produced a 4-sec. presentation of an illuminated food hopper, followed by a 10-sec. blackout of the chamber. This condition was intended to be analogous to continuous reinforcement in a runway of constant length. Runway partial reinforcement was simulated in a second group, VR 2(FR 30:S, TO), which was identical to the first except that on a random half of the trials the food hopper was illuminated, but not raised so as to make the food accessible. A third group, CRF(VR 60:S, TO), was required to make the same number of responses to obtain the same number of reinforcements as Group VR 2(FR 30:S, TO), but all trials terminated with food presentation. This group thus received 15 trials per session with varying numbers of responses being required per trial. Following this training all *S*s received four sessions of 30 trials each under EXT(FR 30:S, TO). That is to say, after 30 key pecks the key light was extinguished and the food hopper was illuminated for 4 sec., but never raised. A 10-sec. blackout concluded the trial. During extinction, if the response requirement was not completed within 120 sec., the hopper light and blackout were presented noncontingently.

The mean number of trials to successive criteria of consecutive trials without any responses are shown in Figure 2 for each of the three groups. In these terms, Group VR 2(FR 30:S, TO) was considerably more resistant to extinction than each of the other two groups, which in turn did not differ reliably from each other. The mean total numbers of key pecks over the four sessions of extinction yielded the same conclusion. These values were 3602, 2831, and 2774 for Groups VR 2(FR 30:S, TO), CRF(FR 30:S, TO), and CRF(VR 60:S, TO) respectively.

These results clearly demonstrate a discrete-trials PREE which cannot be accounted for on the basis of simple VR-like effects. This provides perhaps the clearest data to date that probability of reinforcement per discrete trial is not equivalent to probability of reinforcement per free response. More specifically, the findings support Logan and Wagner's suggestion that usual discrete-trials extinction paradigms are sensitive to the former, but not to the latter. Whether or not the reverse is true for the usual free-operant extinction paradigm cannot be decided until the completion of studies using such extinction techniques.

In any case, the available data certainly suggest the functional significance of conceiving the relationships between free-operant and discrete-trials paradigms in terms of second-order schedules. At this point attention should be turned to the use of second-order schedules in isolating necessary conditions for various phenomena. For instance, is the TO or ITI necessary for the discrete-trials PREE obtained in the study just presented? If not, then free-operant studies of the role of intermittency of the pairing of primary (S^R) and conditioned reinforcers (S^r) in determining the effectiveness of that S^r (Fox & King, 1961; Zimmerman, 1957) may be much more intimately related to discrete-trials PREE than to phenomena observed in typical operant-extinction studies.

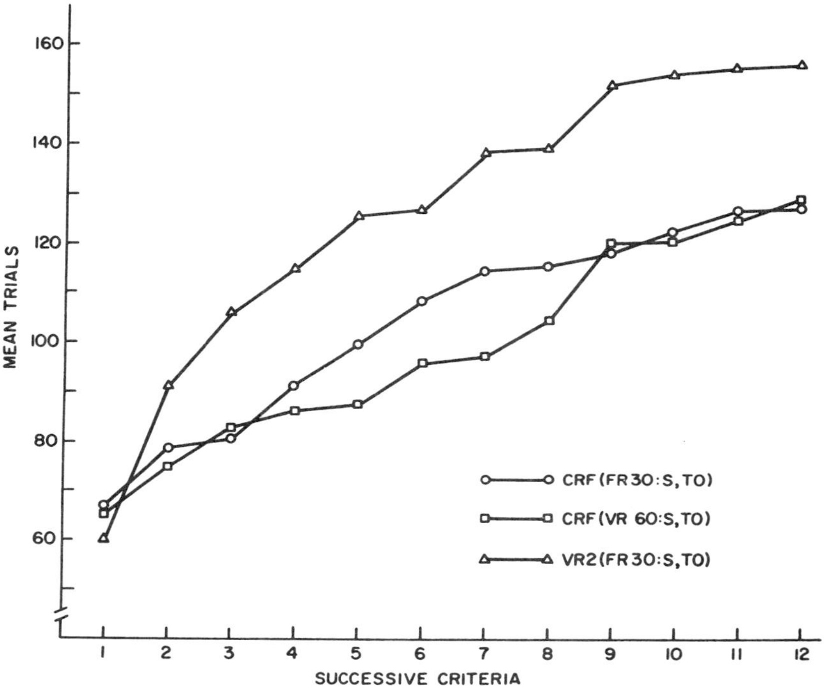

FIGURE 2. Mean numbers of trials to reach successive criteria of consecutive numbers of trials without responding in discrete-trials operant extinction for three second-order schedules of acquisition reinforcement.

STIMULI ASSOCIATED WITH REINFORCEMENT

In considering the roles of some of the factors which the second-order schedule concept suggests are relevant to integrating discrete-trials and free-operant results, little explicit consideration will be given to types of first- and second-order schedule components. With the exception of Logan (1960), almost no systematic variation of type of first-order schedule has been done in discrete-trials situations. Conversely, there is very little operant research on second-order components. It can thus be seen that few data exist that permit comparison of free-operant and discrete-trials results in respect to reinforcement schedules. On the other hand, considerable data do exist from both paradigms concerning the role of certain other factors related to the termination of the first-order component.

The first such factor is the role of stimuli distinctively paired with S^R. In the present notation these are the stimuli denoted by an "S" following the first-order component; e.g., FR 2(FR 10:S) means that every tenth response produces a brief, distinctive stimulus event, such as a hopper light, and every other occurrence of this stimulus is paired with S^R. Typically, discrete trials have always involved such a stimulus. In the case of a runway this function is served by the situational cues of the goal box. In addition, even if no explicit stimulus is provided by *E*, the *S*'s own behavior may produce one (Platt & Senkowski, 1970b, Exp. V, VI). In the present section two effects of such stimuli will be indicated.

In the first place, stimuli distinctively associated with S^R meet the operational requirements for becoming conditioned reinforcers (S^r). That is, such stimuli would be expected to have some of the same behavior-maintaining and patterning properties as S^R, as long as the effects of the S^r-S^R pairing are not allowed to extinguish. The operant literature concerning such effects has been extensively reviewed by Kelleher and Gollub (1962) and that for discrete trials by Wike (1966).

The clearest demonstration of the maintaining and patterning effects of such S^rs in second-order schedules is provided by Kelleher (1966) who studied the key pecking of pigeons under FR 30(FI 2:S) and FR 15(FI 4:S). Thus a 0.7-sec. stimulus light was presented for the first response after either 2 or 4 min. had passed since its last presentation. Every fifteenth or thirtieth light presentation, respectively, was then followed by access to grain. Under either schedule the positively accelerated responding characteristic of an FI schedule developed in each first-order component. When the S^r was not so presented, lower, relatively constant rates of responding prevailed in each component. The only difficulty with interpreting these data as evidence for the maintaining and patterning effects of S^r is that when this stimulus change was presented at the completion of each FI except the one terminating with S^R, some maintenance of the FI pattern was still evident. Kelleher suggested that this latter result was produced by certain histories of his birds.

It has often been suggested that the apparent maintaining and patterning effects of stimuli associated with S^R may be due to their role as conditioned evoking stimuli for responding (Bugelski, 1956) or as discriminative stimuli for increased activity (Wyckoff, Sidowski, & Chambliss, 1958). There are many variations on this sort of hypothesis and the reader should refer to one of the reviews mentioned above for a complete survey of the relevant data. Another study by Kelleher (1961), however, serves to indicate the unlikelihood that all S^r effects can be accounted for by such alternatives.

Kelleher gave pigeons extensive training under a condition in which the first key peck after 5 min. had passed since the last S^R produced a 4-sec. operation of a grain hopper (FI 5). In subsequent extinction sessions, the sound of the now empty grain hopper was presented on various operant-reinforcement schedules. When the sound was presented only if the bird had not responded for 5 or 10 sec., response rates were low. When the sound was presented on various FR schedules, response rates were high. And under FI presentation a positively accelerated rate of responding was produced over the interval between S^r presentations. In addition, when the schedule of presentation was changed during extinction, the new pattern of responding emerged only gradually. All of these results taken together are very difficult to interpret solely in terms of stimulus control of subsequent behavior by the sound of the grain hopper.

Another aspect of stimuli associated with S^R is that they come to occasion behavior concerned with obtaining and utilizing the S^R. On the one hand, such stimuli stand in a relationship so as to be classically conditioned to behaviors elicited by the S^R. Such a mechanism was the basis of Spence's (1956) r_g-s_g theory of incentive motivation, and Hull (1943) had earlier used this function of stimuli associated with S^R to provide a theoretical account of their S^r properties. In either case it was the facilitative aspects of such classically conditioned behaviors that was emphasized, as indicated by the fact that r_g is usually defined to contain only those components of the behaviors elicited by S^R which do not compete with the instrumental or operant response on whose occurrence S^R is contingent.

On the other hand, stimuli associated with S^R are also in a position to become S^Ds controlling overt instrumental behaviors (R_T), reinforced by obtaining S^R. Examples of such behaviors include approaching, seizing, chewing, etc. The anticipatory occurrence of such behaviors might have a considerable effect on both the learning and final form of the instrumental response under study, depending on their degree of compatibility with that response. To the extent that both the instrumental responses used and the opportunities for anticipatory R_Ts may be somewhat different in typical free-operant and discrete-trials situations, a consideration of their role may be critical to an integration of these situations.

Denny, Wells, and Maatsch (1957) have investigated the role of R_T in the development and extinction of free-operant FR responding. In a 2-ft. alley with a lever at one end and a food cup at the other, rats were conditioned to press the lever on a CRF and then a FR 5 schedule for food, with approaches to the food cup (R_T) being recorded. The results indicated a clear decrease in the number of food-cup approaches per S^R as training proceeded on the FR. This decrease was most pronounced early in the ratio requirement.

Platt and Spence (1967) have suggested that the role of anticipatory approach may be quite different in operant chambers and runways since in the former case it is incompatible with the operant response, while it is indistinguishable from the locomotor runway response. Other evidence suggests, however, that additional R_Ts serve much the same interfering function in runways that food-cup approach does in operant chambers. This evidence arises indirectly from the shape of response speed gradients over free-operant and discrete-trials FRs and those over a discrete trial in the runway. In all three cases the gradients have tended to be of an inverted U-shape. The terminal decrement in such gradients has been assigned to the competing role of R_Ts in free-operant FRs (Davison, 1969), discrete-trials FRs (Platt & Senkowski, 1970b), and runways (Hull, 1934). In the latter case it was speculated that the responsible R_T was the stopping and posturing necessary to consume the S^R. Platt and Senkowski's account of the development and maintenance of discrete-trials FR gradients in terms of a quantification of stimulus control of R_T by response-produced stimulation may thus be equally applicable to free-operant FRs and discrete-trials runways.

In addition to this integrative role of R_T, its study may also lead to a better understanding of the relations between free-operant and discrete-trials extinction. Following acquisition training in the Denny, Wells, and Maatsch study, extinction was administered with the sound of the food delivery mechanism continuing to be presented for every fifth lever press, EXT(FR 5:S), for rats that had received various amounts of CRF(FR 5:S) training; for those who had received only the CRF(FR 1:S) training, the sound was delivered for every lever press, EXT(FR 1:S). The results indicated R_n to be an increasing function of amount of CRF(FR 5:S) training, although number of food-cup approaches in extinction was a constant for all groups. If number of food-cup approaches is taken as an indicator of number of behavior sequences in extinction, then its insensitivity to FR training is in agreement with the Logan and Wagner hypothesis since second-order schedule components were identical (CRF) for all groups. The effect of FR training on total number of lever presses in extinction would thus be reasonably assigned to degree of learning of a longer response sequence (Mowrer & Jones, 1945). Put somewhat differently, these data suggest that maintaining the contingency of stimuli distinctly associated with S^R is sufficient to convert free-operant extinction performance to that typical of discrete trials.

AVERSIVE PROPERTIES OF STIMULI PREVIOUSLY ASSOCIATED WITH REINFORCEMENT

The S^r and R_T functions of stimuli associated with S^R are not the only ones which have been assigned to them. In order to assess either of these functions it is necessary to present the stimuli previously associated with S^R in its absence. But such presentation has been postulated to produce an aversive or frustrating (R_F) state of affairs which organisms will actively avoid (Amsel, 1958; Amsel & Ward, 1965; Terrace, 1963a, 1963b). The postulation of both behavior maintaining (S^r) and avoidance producing (R_F) properties of nonreinforced presentations of previously reinforced stimuli gives rise to a paradox which has often been noted, most recently by Amsel (1968) and Lott (1967). This paradox will be returned to later, but for the moment attention will be directed to documenting this postulated aversive effect.

The assumed aversive properties of nonreinforcing stimuli previously associated with S^R was probably most clearly demonstrated in discrete trials by Wagner (1963) who showed that rats would learn a new response of hurdle jumping to escape a light previously presented in the goal box of a runway on the nonreinforced trials of a partial reinforcement schedule. The controls provided in Wagner's study were not adequate to demonstrate that prior pairing of the goal box stimuli with S^R was a necessary condition for the acquired aversiveness of the light, but recent experiments by Daly (1969) do provide such a demonstration. Daly was able to show acquisition of a new hurdle-jumping response to escape the goal box of a runway in which 60 food reinforced trials had previously been followed by 18 nonreinforced trials. Such learning did not occur in rats receiving the same number of runway trials without S^R.

Leitenberg (1965) has reviewed the operant literature purporting to show avoidance of and escape from stimuli associated with periods of nonreinforcement. Leitenberg was unable to find any free-operant studies showing escape from or avoidance of stimuli associated with such TOs and correctly indicated that those studies showing escape or avoidance of TO itself might be equally well interpreted as the result of such responding producing an increase in the density or immediacy of positive S^R. Thus it appears that there has not been an unambiguous free-operant demonstration of the aversiveness of a discrete stimulus as a result of previous association with S^R.

A recent study from the author's laboratory (Platt & Senkowski, 1970a) provides a clear demonstration of avoidance of a stimulus as a result of its prior association with S^R in a discrete-trials lever-pressing situation. These results strengthen the case for the postulated aversion in discrete trials, and partially compensate for the apparent lack of relevant evidence in typically free-operant situations. In this study, two groups of food-deprived rats were trained to make eight lever presses in the presence of a 4-KHz. tone, after which the lever was retracted. Ten sec. later the lever was reinserted and the tone changed to 10 KHz. Eight additional presses retracted the lever and extinguished the tone and house lights for approximately 40 sec., after which the entire cycle was repeated. Ten such cycles or trials were run per day and the second eight responses of a trial always terminated with presentation of three 45-mg. food pellets. The probability of food presentation at the end of the first eight responses was set at 0, 50, or 100 percent. One group of rats (AD) received an ascending and then a descending series on this percentage variable (0, 50, 100, 50, 0), while the other group (DA) received the conditions in the order 100, 50, 0, 50, 100. Each value was run until the mean latencies of the first response in both ratios and the mean response rates within the ratios showed no monotonic trend for 20 sessions. Within the present formulation this paradigm may be viewed as analogous to a double alley (Amsel & Roussel, 1952) with continuous reinforcement in the second alley and reinforcement frequency manipulated in the first alley.

Figure 3 shows the mean time between lever presentation and the first press for the first ratio of a trial over the last 20 sessions at each reinforcement frequency. The actual percentage received in each successive phase for each of the two groups is indicated along the abscissa. The only statistically reliable differences between these means, either between or within subjects, are the longer response times associated with 0 percent S^R when S^R had previously been received at the end of the first eight responses. These two means are indicated by solid shading and are to be contrasted with the initial occurrence of 0 percent reinforcement in Group AD which is indicated by diagonal lines. Response rate within the first eight responses of a trial displayed a similar pattern of results.

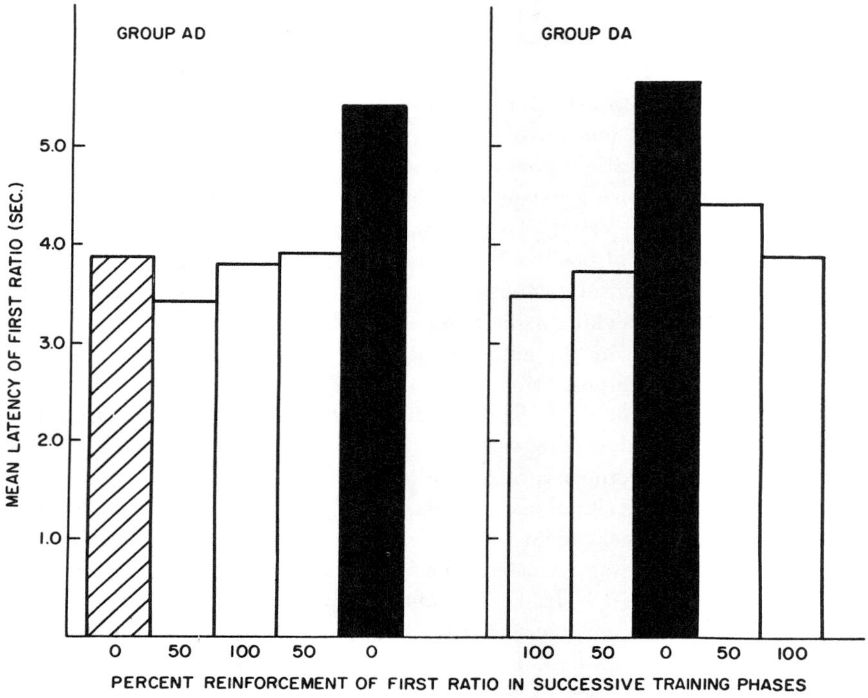

FIGURE 3. Mean latency of first response in a discrete-trials, lever-pressing analogue to the double-alley runway as a function of successive reinforcement frequencies for the first behavioral sequence of a trial. Group AD received an ascending followed by a descending order of reinforcement frequencies, while the reverse was true from Group DA. The second behavioral sequence of a trial was always reinforced.

That the slower responding in the solid-shaded means of Figure 3 represents an avoidance of stimuli previously associated with S^R is strongly argued by the fact that such slowing actully delayed S^R for the second eight responses and only occurred following a reinforcement history for the first eight responses. It would thus appear that there is indeed clear evidence for both the maintaining-patterning effects of stimuli associated with S^R and for their aversive effects. This paradox must eventually be resolved by additions to or modifications of the operational definitions of S^r and R_F on the basis of experimental isolation of the variables determining which sort of effect will be observed. For present purposes, it should be quite clear that any generalizations between free-operant and discrete-trials paradigms will need to consider carefully the history and current role of stimuli which have been associated with S^R.

STIMULI PRESENTED ON THE SAME CONTINGENCY AS REINFORCEMENT

It may be asked whether stimuli terminating the first-order components of a second-order reinforcement schedule perform any behaviorally significant function not dependent on their association with S^R. It will be remembered that some reinforcing effect of a stimulus (red key) terminating the first-order components of a second-order schedule has been found, even if a different stimulus (white key) terminated the reinforced component (Kelleher, 1966). Kelleher suggested that this effect might have resulted from his birds' prior experience with red keys in other experiments. Another possibility is that sufficient stimulus generalization occurred from the flash of a white key light to that of a red key light for the latter to function as a S^r, although this seems unlikely in view of the pigeon's sensitive color discrimination. In any case, these results suggest the possibility of a reinforcing role for first-order schedule terminators in addition to that which might be expected on the basis of any association with S^R.

Similarly suggestive findings were reported by Ferster and Skinner (1957) who found that pigeons' performances on FR schedules were sustained when food reinforcements were replaced half of the time by periods of blackout. This procedure was similar to the VR 2(FR 30:S, TO) condition reported earlier in this essay, but differed from it in that the hopper light was presented only at the end of reinforced ratios and the blackout only at the end of nonreinforced ones. Thus, the hopper light (S^r) was not presented at the end of nonreinforced ratios and the blackout could not have been serving as an S^r since it never preceded or accompanied S^R. It could be that the ratio performance in Ferster and Skinner's study was maintained because of some unique property of blackout, because of maintenance of the FR behavioral sequence by partial reinforcement, or because the response-produced stimuli associated with the end of the FR had become S^rs. What is needed is a demonstration of this effect with stimuli other than blackouts and with controls to show that the exteroceptive stimulus was indeed responsible for maintenance of the FR performance. These problems are dealt with in a recent set of studies by Neuringer and Chung (1967).

After pigeons were trained to peck on a 1-min. variable-interval schedule of reinforcement (VI 1), a procedure was introduced in which a peck was required to initiate a 5-sec. interval such that the first peck after this interval would produce either food or some brief stimulus change such as a blackout, a buzzer, or a darkened key light. Determination of whether the S^R or a simple stimulus change would occur on a particular occasion was made by the same VI programmer used in initial training so that essentially the same temporal pattern of S^R was maintained. This general procedure can be represented in the present notation as VI 1(tand FR 1 FI 5″). The tandem (tand) designation simply refers to the requirement of a response to initiate the FI, and the use of a FI rather than a FR was presumably prompted by the greater distinctiveness of the pattern of responding generated by a FI.

Using this general procedure Neuringer and Chung were able to show a doubling of the constant VI 1 rate of responding with a positive acceleration within each FI component over a range of blackout durations (0.25 to 7.0 sec.). They also demonstrated similar effects with a buzzer or darkened key replacing the blackout periods. Further, these response patterns and rates were not maintained in the absence of blackout or other distinctive stimulation at the end of the nonreinforced FIs, and the responding maintained with such stimuli was indistinguishable from that obtained when all of the tand FR 1 FI 5″ components were reinforced. It is thus clear that distinctive stimuli terminating a first-order schedule component can under some conditions display strong behavior-maintaining and patterning properties not dependent on their prior association with S^R.

The question then arises as to what the necessary conditions are for such reinforcing effects. Neuringer and Chung suggested that a stimulus will serve as a reinforcer when it is made contingent on a behavior sequence identical to one which receives S^R. To obtain evidence for this proposition, they compared two conditions in which the schedules of blackout presentation were the same, but in only one case was the same behavior sequence required to produce S^R and blackout. One schedule was a VI 1(FR 11) while in the other schedule blackouts were programmed in the same way, but S^R was presented for the first response after the VI had set up. Thus, in the control condition, 11 responses were required for blackout, but only one for S^R. When an FR 11 led either to blackout or S^R, the usual high rate of responding with positive acceleration was found, but in the control condition neither effect was apparent.

Although more work is needed, it would appear that distinctive stimuli contingent on behavior sequences identical to reinforced ones will themselves acquire maintaining and patterning properties. This is particularly relevant to the current problem since, as Neuringer and Chung have indicated, many studies of S^r have confounded the association of neutral stimuli with S^R and the contingency of neutral stimulus presentations on reinforced behavioral sequences. This has of course always been true of discrete-trials runways where the first-order component is always the same FD schedule.

In respect to these phenomena, one interesting possibility deserves mention. To the extent that apparent S^r properties of a stimulus might be due to its presentation on the same contingency as S^R, rather than its contiguity with

S^R, the S^r-R_F paradox could be resolved by a respecification of the operations which may have been mistakenly identified as S^r. Of course some demonstrations of S^r do not meet the boundary conditions for Neuringer and Chung's phenomenon. Examples would include Kelleher's (1961) demonstration of S^r effects on schedules introduced for the first time in experimental extinction and other such "new-learning" experiments. However, it then becomes necessary to ask whether a reinforcer established by the Neuringer and Chung technique might not then be able to serve for a time as a reinforcer for new behavioral sequences.

TIMEOUT AND INTERTRIAL INTERVAL

One final topic requires special consideration with respect to terminators of first-order schedule components in free-operant and discrete-trials paradigms. This is the issue of ITIs and their relationship to free-operant TOs. It is often assumed that these two operations are identical, but actually the notion of a TO is much broader, as is indicated by Leitenberg's definition:

> There is no single set of operations which adequately defines time-out (TO) from positive reinforcement. The essential feature is a period of time in which positive reinforcement is no longer available. Within this boundary can fit such diverse experimental operations as extinction, S^{Δ} in discrimination training, and intervals between reinforcement in various schedules of reinforcement [1965, p. 428].

Within the framework of this essay, an ITI in such discrete-trials situations as the runway always and only occurs at the end of a first-order schedule component. As such, the ITI immediately follows either S^R or S^r and is contingent on a particular behavioral sequence. Thus, ITI would only reasonably be simulated by or related to data from free-operant TOs fulfilling these same boundary conditions. Data based on randomly presented TOs or simply operant-extinction procedures are operationally quite dissimilar to ITIs, so that their possible interrelations would require demonstration.

With these restrictions in mind one can inquire as to what special effects such an ITI or TO might have in addition to those which have already been discussed for first-order component terminators in general. One such effect would of course be a reduction in nonassociative sequential effects from trial to trial. Examples of such effects would include the degree to which the events of one trial or schedule component determine the stimulus complex of the next (Capaldi, 1967; Ferster & Skinner, 1957; Jenkins, 1970); the accumulation of short-term, satiation, and fatigue effects; and pauses in responding produced by consumption of S^R (Platt & Spence, 1967). Of far greater systematic importance for the integration of discrete-trials and free-operant results, however, is the possibility that ITIs may have unique aversive or reinforcement properties. This concern has been expressed by Azrin and Holz:

> Historically, time-out from positive reinforcement has been considered in a static sense; that is, simply as a period of time that separates the opportunities to respond. Such is the case, for example, in restricted trial procedures, such as runways, alleys, choice procedures, etc. in which the time-out is designated as an intertrial interval. Although the restricted trial methods have necessarily utilized time-out periods, the possible dynamic properties of this time-out had not been realized. Only recently has it been discovered that a time-out stimulus may possess reinforcing or aversive properties and may, therefore, control the frequency of responses by arranging that stimulus as a consequence of the responses [1966, p. 390].

Turning first to possible positive reinforcing properties of TO, such as discussed in the last section, it will be remembered that these effects seemed to result from any stimulus change presented on the same contingency as S^R. These effects would thus not seem to require any special consideration of ITI in addition to that given any first-order schedule terminator.

Possible unique aversive effects of ITI cannot be so readily dismissed. As mentioned previously, Leitenberg (1965) reviewed a large amount of literature on the effects of TO from positive reinforcement and found some evidence for such effects. Most of this evidence is based on TOs which do not meet the previously specified boundary conditions for ITI, but some relevant data are available.

Kaufman and Baron (1968) have recently provided one of the clearest demonstrations to date of TO avoidance, and have also investigated the effects of preceding a TO with S^R. This latter manipulation is of particular importance because ITIs are characteristically preceded by S^R. After rats learned a simple operant discrimination in which lever presses were continuously reinforced in the presence of a white noise (S^D), but never in the presence of a 500-Hz. tone (S^Δ), a procedure was instituted in which every third lever press was nonreinforced. When this nonreinforced response was followed by a period of S^Δ, the time between the second and third response was an increasing function of the duration of the S^Δ period. When the nonreinforced response was not followed by an S^Δ period, its IRT was the same as the other IRTs in the three-response sequence. These data clearly showed avoidance of the TO, since lengthening the third IRT actually resulted in a loss or delay of positive reinforcement, as in the author's previously described discrete-trial lever-pressing study. The most important result for present consideration, however, is that when Kaufman and Baron reinforced all three responses in the sequence, an S^Δ period following the third response did not produce any lengthening of the third IRT.

The results just reviewed suggest that an ITI will have no aversive properties when preceded by S^R. Several other aspects of these results produced some consternation, however. For one thing, the aversiveness of the TOs in Kaufman and Baron's study seems to be at odds with the reinforcing functions found for such presentations in the Neuringer and Chung study reviewed in the last section. One can only speculate as to which of the many differences between the two studies was responsible for this discrepancy. A good possibility is that Kaufman and Baron's rats had a long history of nonreinforced responding in S^{Δ}, while Neuringer and Chung's pigeons seldom, if ever, responded in blackouts. Terrace (1963a, 1963b) has argued that such responding is necessary to the development of aversive properties by a TO, and this view is not inconsistent with Amsel's (1958, 1965) position. If this analysis is correct, the Neuringer and Chung study is more relevant to ITIs since responding is typically prevented during ITIs in discrete-trials situations. In any case this point strongly suggests that operant attempts to simulate discrete trials should prevent rather than merely nonreinforce responding in ITIs, unless all trials are to terminate in S^{R}.

CONCLUSIONS AND SUMMARY

Following a discussion of the need for systematic integration of discrete-trials and free-operant paradigms, previous attempts to provide such integration were briefly reviewed. These attempts typically emphasized the role of intertrial intervals, as well as possible analogies between such discrete-trials situations as the runway and operant ratio schedules.

It was suggested that second-order reinforcement schedules or "schedules of schedules" provide a reasonable conceptualization and notation for comparing and contrasting specific procedures from the two paradigms. Within this framework a discrete trial was cast as analogous to an operant first-order schedule component. The usefulness of this formulation was illustrated by the problem of comparing intermittent reinforcement effects from free-operant situations with those of discrete trials. Data were presented to support the argument that operant studies have typically dealt with intermittency in first-order schedule components, while discrete-trials studies have dealt with variations in second-order components.

After the paucity of data concerning first-order schedule variations in discrete-trials and second-order variations in free-operant situations was mentioned, the role of stimuli terminating first-order schedule components or trials was examined. Data were reviewed to show that such stimuli may function as conditioned reinforcers and as discriminative stimuli for consummatory behaviors as a result of their association with primary reinforcement. It was also shown that such stimuli may have aversive properties when primary reinforcement is withheld. Also, on the basis of recent data, a resolution was proposed for the paradox raised by the similarity of the operations for positive conditioned reinforcement and conditioned aversion. These data suggested that the positive reinforcing effects of such stimuli may be a result of their presentation on the same contingency as primary reinforcement, rather than their contiguity with it.

Finally, the role of intertrial intervals and their relation to operant timeouts were considered. It was suggested that the former were special cases of the latter. On the basis of data presented, it was emphasized that attempts to simulate intertrial intervals with timeouts should prevent responding in the timeout unless primary reinforcement is always presented at its onset. When this restriction was respected, no aversive function seemed to be indicated for intertrial intervals.

REFERENCES

Amsel, A. The role of frustrative nonreward in noncontinuous reward situations. *Psychological Bulletin,* 1958, *55,* 102–119.

Amsel, A. Secondary reinforcement and frustration. *Psychological Bulletin,* 1968, *69,* 278.

Amsel, A., & Roussel, J. Motivational properties of frustration: I. Effect on a running response of the addition of frustration to the motivational complex. *Journal of Experimental Psychology,* 1952, *43,* 363–368.

Amsel, A., & Ward, J. S. Frustration and persistence: Resistance to discrimination following prior experience with the discriminanda. *Psychological Monographs,* 1965, *79* (4, Whole No. 597).

Azrin, N. H., & Holz, W. C. Punishment. In W. K. Honig (Ed.), *Operant behavior: Areas of research and applications.* New York: Appleton-Century-Crofts, 1966. Pp. 380–447.

Brown, P. L., & Jenkins, H. M. Auto-shaping of the pigeon's key-peck. *Journal of the Experimental Analysis of Behavior,* 1968, *11,* 1–8.

Bugelski, B. R. *The Psychology of Learning.* New York: Holt, 1956.

Capaldi, E. J. The effect of different amounts of training on the resistance to extinction of different patterns of partially reinforced responses. *Journal of Comparative and Physiological Psychology,* 1958, *51,* 367–371.

Capaldi, E. J. A sequential hypothesis of instrumental learning. In K. W. Spence & J. T. Spence (Eds.), *The Psychology of Learning and Motivation.* Vol. 1. New York: Academic Press, 1967. Pp. 67–156.

Daly, H. B. Learning of a hurdle-jump response to escape cues paired with reduced reward or frustrative nonreward. *Journal of Experimental Psychology,* 1969, *79,* 146–157.

Davison, M. C. Successive interresponse times in fixed-ratio and second-order fixed-ratio performance. *Journal of the Experimental Analysis of Behavior,* 1969, *12,* 385–389.

Denny, M. R., Wells, R. H., & Maatsch, J. L. Resistance to extinction as a function of the discrimination habit established during fixed-ratio reinforcement. *Journal of Experimental Psychology,* 1957, *6,* 451–456.

Ferster, C. B., & Skinner, B. F. *Schedules of reinforcement.* New York: Appleton-Century-Crofts, 1957.

Fox, R. E., & King, R. A. The effects of reinforcement scheduling on the strength of a secondary reinforcer. *Journal of Comparative and Physiological Psychology,* 1961, *54,* 266–269.

Gonzalez, R. C., Bainbridge, P., & Bitterman, M. E. Discrete-trials lever pressing in the rat as a function of pattern of reinforcement, effortfulness of response, and amount of reward. *Journal of Comparative and Physiological Psychology,* 1966, *61,* 110–122.

Hearst, E. Resistance-to-extinction functions in the single organism. *Journal of the Experimental Analysis of Behavior,* 1961, *4,* 133–144.

Hull, C. L. The rat's speed-of-locomotion gradient in the approach to food. *Journal of Comparative Psychology,* 1934, *17,* 393–422.

Hull, C. L. *Principles of behavior.* New York: Appleton-Century, 1943.

Jenkins, H. M. Sequential organization in schedules of reinforcement. In W. N. Schoenfeld & J. Farmer (Eds.), *Theory of reinforcement schedules.* New York: Appleton-Century-Crofts, 1970. Pp. 63–109.

Kaufman, A., & Baron, A. Suppression of behavior by timeout punishment when suppression results in loss of positive reinforcement. *Journal of the Experimental Analysis of Behavior,* 1968, *11,* 595–607.

Kelleher, R. T. Schedules of conditioned reinforcement during experimental extinction. *Journal of the Experimental Analysis of Behavior,* 1961, *4,* 1–5.

Kelleher, R. T. Conditioned reinforcement in second-order schedules. *Journal of the Experimental Analysis of Behavior,* 1966, *9,* 475–485.

Kelleher, R. T., & Gollub, L. R. A review of positive conditioned reinforcement. *Journal of the Experimental Analysis of Behavior,* 1962, *5,* 543–597.

Keller, F. S., & Schoenfeld, W. N. *Principles of psychology.* New York: Appleton-Century-Crofts, 1950.

Knarr, F. A., & Collier, G. Taste and consummatory activity in amount and gradient of reinforcement functions. *Journal of Experimental Psychology,* 1962, *63,* 579–588.

Leitenberg, H. Is time-out from positive reinforcement an aversive event? A review of the experimental evidence. *Psychological Bulletin,* 1965, *6,* 428–441.

Lewis, D. J. Partial reinforcement: A selective review of the literature since 1950. *Psychological Bulletin,* 1960, *57,* 1–28.

Logan, F. A. *Incentive: How the conditions of reinforcement affect the performance of rats.* New Haven: Yale University Press, 1960.

Logan, F. A., & Wagner, A. R. *Reward and punishment.* Boston: Allyn and Bacon, 1965.

Lott, D. F. Secondary reinforcement and frustration: A conceptual paradox. *Psychological Bulletin,* 1967, *67,* 197–198.

Mowrer, O. H., & Jones, H. M. Habit strength as a function of the pattern of reinforcement. *Journal of Experimental Psychology,* 1945, *35,* 293–311.

Neuringer, A. J., & Chung, S. Quasi-reinforcement: Control of responding by a percentage-reinforcement schedule. *Journal of the Experimental Analysis of Behavior,* 1967, *10,* 45–54.

Platt, J. R., & Senkowski, P. C. Effects of discrete-trials reinforcement frequency and changes in reinforcement frequency on preceding and subsequent fixed-ratio performance. *Journal of Experimental Psychology*, 1970, *85*, 95–104. (a)

Platt, J. R., & Senkowski, P. C. Response-correlated stimulus functioning in homogeneous behavior chains. In J. H. Reynierse (Ed.), *Current Issues in Animal Learning*. Lincoln: University of Nebraska Press, 1970. Pp. 195–231. (b)

Platt, J. R., Senkowski, P. C., & Mann, R. Discrimination, contrast and chaining: Effects of prior training without discriminanda and response-contingent delay of discriminandum presentation. *Journal of Experimental Psychology*, 1969, *82*, 38–45.

Platt, J. R., & Spence, K. W. Intertrial interval and response competition in discrete-trials lever pressing. *American Journal of Psychology*, 1967, *80*, 110–114.

Porter, J. J., & Hug, J. J. Effects of number and percentage of rewarded trials on the acquisition and extinction of lever pressing using a discrete-trial procedure. *Journal of Experimental Psychology*, 1965, *70*, 575–579.

Sidman, M. *Tactics of scientific research: Evaluating experimental data in psychology*. New York: Basic Books, 1960.

Skinner, B. F. *The behavior of organisms*. New York: Appleton-Century, 1938.

Spence, K. W. *Behavior theory and conditioning*. New Haven: Yale University Press, 1956.

Spence, K. W. The empirical basis and theoretical structure of psychology. *Philosophy of Science*, 1957, *24*, 97–108.

Terrace, H. S. Discrimination learning with and without errors. *Journal of the Experimental Analysis of Behavior*, 1963, *6*, 1–27. (a)

Terrace, H. S. Errorless transfer of a discrimination across two continua. *Journal of the Experimental Analysis of Behavior*, 1963, *6*, 223–232. (b)

Tyler, D. W., Wortz, E. C., & Bitterman, M. E. The effect of random and alternating partial reinforcement on resistance to extinction in the rat. *American Journal of Psychology*, 1953, *66*, 37–65.

Wagner, A. R. Conditioned frustration as a learned drive. *Journal of Experimental Psychology*, 1963, *66*, 142–148.

Weiss, R. F. Response speed, amplitude, and resistance to extinction as joint functions of work and length of behavior chain. *Journal of Experimental Psychology*, 1961, *61*, 245–256.

Wike, E. L. *Secondary reinforcement: Selected experiments*. New York: Harper & Row, 1966.

Williams, D. R. Relation between response amplitude and reinforcement. *Journal of Experimental Psychology*, 1966, *71*, 634–641.

Wyckoff, L. B., Sidowski, J., & Chambliss, D. J. An experimental study of the relationship between secondary reinforcing and cue effects of a stimulus. *Journal of Comparative and Physiological Psychology*, 1958, *51*, 103–109.

Zimmerman, D. W. Durable secondary reinforcement: Method and theory. *Psychological Review*, 1957, *64*, 373–383.

Cognitive Factors in Conditioning: The Use of Masking Tasks in Eyelid Conditioning

LEONARD E. ROSS

INTRODUCTION

Beginning in 1963, Kenneth Spence and his students published a series of articles dealing with the acquisition and extinction of the conditioned eyelid response. These experiments were performed under masking-task conditions that were designed to minimize or eliminate cognitive factors which could complicate the discovery of laws and the formulation of theory relating to this simple response. Although concern with the effects of the *S*s' sets, attitudes, and general cognitive involvement in the conditioning situation dates from the earliest human conditioning research, this work by Spence has led to the renewed interest of many investigators in this topic. The importance of a revival of research concerned with the role of cognitive factors in conditioning has become increasingly evident as data accumulate demonstrating the importance of this class of variables in extinction, partial reinforcement, and differential-conditioning situations. The present paper discusses some of the early studies that employed masking-task procedures, reviews the considerations that led to Spence's utilization of masking tasks, summarizes the data from this series of studies, and discusses masking-task data recently obtained in the Wisconsin laboratories. The major interest is in experimental procedures in which the *S* is actively engaged in an extraneous or masking task, rather than those which, through misinformation about the nature of the study

The preparation of this essay and the Wisconsin research reported in it were supported by Public Health Service Research Grant 10235 from the National Institute of Mental Health and NIH Training Grant No. 5 TO1 HDOO 117 from the National Institute of Child Health and Human Development. The author wishes to thank Susan Wilcox, Lois Putnam, and Michael Nelson for their helpful comments.

or instructions, manipulate the *S*'s set so that he behaves in a certain manner with respect to the response itself.

EARLY WORK WITH MASKING TASKS AND CONDITIONING

Even a cursory examination of the conditioning literature of the 1930s reveals the interest of experimenters in what might be broadly labeled as the effects of cognitive factors on conditioning. In fact, interest in such matters appears to have been a major concern of many of those then working with human conditioning. As early as 1919, Hamel discussed the conditioned response in terms of the conscious anticipation of the UCS, and interest in such factors persisted as classical conditioning studies proliferated during the 1930s.

In 1939 Cole presented a very interesting and useful survey of positions dealing with the role and nature of "subjective factors" in conditioning (i.e. those of distraction, expectancy, attitude, and verbalization); and in the following year Hilgard and Marquis's highly regarded and influential book, *Conditioning and Learning*, appeared with its widely quoted chapter entitled "Voluntary Action."

Views regarding the implications of voluntary cognitive factors for the investigation of conditioning phenomena were of major interest with respect to the use of masking tasks in conditioning situations. While some experimenters such as Hamel (1919) considered these procedures to be essential in the establishment of conditioned responses and others (e.g. Mowrer, 1938; Tolman, 1932) stressed the importance of expectancy in theorizing about the nature of the conditioning process, the majority of the investigators of this period considered subjective factors to be an undesirable feature of human conditioning experiments. According to Cole, many investigators believed subjective factors interfered with "pure conditioning," led to the variability or unpredictability of data, or prevented conditioning altogether. Hilgard and Marquis stated, "With human subjects, the results of any conditioning experiment will tend to be complicated by the influences of voluntary factors [1940, p. 270]." In addition, Razran commented that *S*s' sets and attitudes "masked a number of otherwise established conditioning attributes," and suggested that while attitudes could be of interest in their own right, they must be "ruled out when the properties of conditioning *as such* are to be studied [1939c, p. 161]."

Considering the prevalence of such views, it is not surprising that many investigators used a variety of procedures which were intended to reduce or eliminate these presumably undesirable activities of the *S*. Again quoting Hilgard and Marquis, "the discovery and formulation of conditioning principles depend upon the devising of experimental situations in which voluntary influences are impossible or are eliminated [1940, p. 270]."

Hilgard and Marquis described the procedures adopted to achieve this goal. First, *S*s (such as animals and infants) could be selected who did not have the capacity for the appropriate voluntary actions. Second, a response could be selected over which the *S* had a minimum of voluntary control; and third, the experimental situation could be arranged so that the *S* did not engage in subjective or voluntary behavior that interfered with the conditioning process. Several procedures were possible with the last approach. Naive *S*s could be obtained by selecting those who had no previous experience with conditioning situations, or the *S* could be instructed to have a passive attitude and not control any responses he might make. Alternatively, weak or incidental stimuli could be used, or the *S* could be misinformed, distracted, or given some irrelevant task to perform. It is this last stratagem that is of interest for the present paper, since the concern of early experimenters with cognitive factors and their influence on conditioning led to the utilization of a variety of extraneous masking tasks which were intended to occupy the *S* so that he would not engage in such potentially interfering activities.

One of the earliest examples* of the use of a masking task to hide the nature of a conditioning study appears in a GSR experiment by Freeman (1930), in which the *S*s were told that the shock UCS was the result of faulty apparatus. In addition, since it was considered advisable to keep the subjects in complete ignorance of the nature of the problem, a "false assignment" was given which consisted of the presentation of a short series of nonsense syllables after each trial, a task which supposedly represented the continuation of a memory experiment in which the *S*s had previously served. Freeman was not too satisfied with this procedure and suggested that it might be better to trust that the *S* would not question the purpose of the study and thereby "complicate the setting," since one could carefully choose *S*s and "a good observer never questions the experimenter's purpose [p. 537]." Also in 1930, Scott reported the establishment of conditioned finger reflexes while the *S* was in a state of hypnosis. The conditioned response then was evoked in the succeeding waking state although the *S*s supposedly could not recall the conditioning process. While the classification of hypnosis as a masking task is somewhat questionable, the *S*'s awareness of the conditioning contingencies was apparently manipulated by the hypnosis procedure

Thorndike's book, *Fundamentals of Learning* (1932), contains a report by Lorge of a generally unsuccessful attempt to condition the finger-lifting response. As part of the procedure the *S* brought or was given an "interesting"

* Although Schlosberg (1928) permitted *S*s to read or draw pictures during knee-reflex conditioning, these activities do not appear to have been intended to divert the *S* from conditioning. Subjects in the preliminary experiments where this procedure was described were familiar with the conditioned reflex, and Schlosberg stated that no attempt was made to keep the purpose of the experiment a secret. Nevertheless, he reported *S*s' comments to the effect that they gave the highest and most frequent conditioned responses when "their attention was diverted toward their reading material or when they were lost in thought."

book to read during the conditioning session. This aspect of the experiment was not discussed, however.

Finally, Razran used masking tasks extensively during the 1930s in his work with the human salivary response. Razran discusses this procedural feature (1939c), wherein the use of masking tasks (along with the presentation of a series of conditioned stimuli rather than a single one) is given credit for highly successful conditioning which conformed with Pavlov's main behavioral findings and was in contrast with the irregular and rather unsuccessful conditioning obtained before these masking procedures were instituted. In addition to misinforming the *S*s by stating that the purpose of the study was to investigate eye fatigue or the influence of music on digestion, Razran had *S*s participate in tasks of memory or maze solution. With the former type of task (e.g., Razran, 1939b, 1940), the *S* was informed that learning and memory were involved, and nonsense syllables were exposed with stimulus lights as part of the compound stimulus. The maze task (e.g., Razran, 1936, 1939a) required considerable *S* participation in that the *S*'s task was to learn a finger-cue maze, which consisted of a 20x20 matrix of screws. The *S* was to trace a path with a stylus from the extreme upper left to the extreme lower right. Green and red lamps at the top of the board signalled correct and incorrect contacts (although the problem was not necessarily solvable), and also served as conditioned stimuli for the consumption of food.

From the above it can been seen that masking tasks were used in a variety of conditioning situations during the 1930s (although not in eyelid-conditioning studies). Their use was intended to reduce or eliminate subjective factors on the part of the *S* which were believed to complicate the conditioning situation to the point of interfering with or preventing the collection of good data.

Nevertheless, masking tasks do not appear to have been employed again to any extent until the work of Spence in the early 1960s. While the reason is not obvious, there are two factors that may have been to a large extent responsible. First, the influence of set and attitude was believed to be greater the more "voluntary" the response (e.g., Miller & Cole, 1936), and the increasing popularity of eyelid conditioning and its classification as a semivoluntary response may have reduced experimenters' concern about direct voluntary influences.

Second, and probably more important, the eyelid-conditioning studies of the late 1930s and the 1940s which were concerned with the set or attitude of the *S* manipulated these factors by establishing a facilitory or inhibitory set through instructions, or by informing the *S* of the stimulus contingencies. These studies, particularly those of Cole (1939), Grant (1939), Hilgard (1938), Hilgard, Campbell, and Sears (1937, 1938), and Hilgard and Humphreys (1938), were extensively cited and undoubtedly were largely responsible for determining the manner in which experimenters attempted to control these S variables in conditioning studies during the next two decades. The consistent finding of these experiments was that although set and attitudinal factors could have significant effects on the data, they were not the dominant factors in conditioning. Thus Wickens (1939) replied to Razran's (1935) contention regarding the dominance of set in conditioning by pointing out that *S*s could neither prevent themselves from establishing conditioned responses nor stop giving such responses once they started. Of particular importance was the series of differential conditioning studies carried out by Hilgard and his colleagues at Stanford. These studies demonstrated that the ability to describe the experimental contingencies could not ensure discrimination, and that instructions of various sorts could not override the discrimination although they could affect the level of performance.

Although these studies established that conditioning was something more than set, attitude, or expectancy, little in their data suggested to later experimenters that cognitive factors could play an important role with other paradigms, such as those involving partial reinforcement or extinction effects, where instructions might not be effective. More important, perhaps, was the fact that the results of the studies showing that these cognitive variables could be experimentally manipulated suggested that their unwanted intrusion could be controlled through these very procedures (i.e., by the use of naive *S*s and the adoption of "neutral" instructions designed to produce a passive *S*). Whatever the reason these procedures, rather than masking tasks, were adopted by subsequent investigators.

Considerations leading to Spence's use of masking tasks

While Spence accepted these earlier studies at face value, there is little doubt that he continued to be concerned with the problem of the *S*'s cognitive involvement in the experimental situation. Not only were neutral and even misleading instructions used in his laboratory, but attempts were made to gather data from students enrolled in introductory psychology early in the semester, before conditioning was discussed. In fact conditioning experiments were sometimes halted for the few weeks it took students to forget the paradigm, to the point where a relatively small percentage could identify the experiment as classical conditioning in postexperimental questioning. For similar reasons, student nurses were not used as *S*s since they roomed together and appeared to communicate more among themselves about experiments than did other students.

Finally, a "voluntary" *S* criterion was adopted. This was designed to permit consideration of the data without including those *S*s who gave responses that were predominantly of an operant or voluntary form. Actually, the experimental conditions employed in the Iowa laboratories minimized this kind of responding. Thus a low or moderate intensity airpuff was used, and the experimental situation was made as comfortable as possible for the *S*. Although the exclusion of the small numbers of *S*s classified as voluntary rarely affected the general results of the studies, it was a precaution that at least ensured that the experimenter would not be caught unaware if differential numbers of such responders were obtained in various groups through chance or as a function of the experimental conditions. In addition to being a common-sense check on the nature of the data being collected, this criterion was important in view of the theoretical use of parameters found through curve-fitting procedures, since these parameter values could be affected by small numbers of voluntary-form *S*s.

The considerations that led Spence to adopt masking tasks were discussed at some length in his *Psychological Review* paper, "Cognitive and Drive Factors in the Extinction of the Conditioned Eye Blink in Human Subjects" (Spence, 1966a). This paper, as well as his comments in lectures and remarks to students, makes it clear that the major event which led him to use masking tasks was the failure of the delayed (2500-msec. CS-UCS interval) UCS extinction procedure to have its predicted effect when it followed 100 percent reinforcement in acquisition. The original published study involving the delayed-UCS procedure (McAllister, 1953) had demonstrated, as predicted from Spence's emotionality theory of drive, that *S*s who continued to receive the UCS during extinction showed significantly slower extinction than *S*s receiving the usual UCS-omission extinction treatment. These results were obtained following an 80 percent reinforcement schedule in acquisition, however, and a subsequent study using 100 percent reinforcement (Reynolds, 1958) did not find a difference in extinction between omitted and delayed UCS-extinction procedures.

This failure of Reynolds to obtain slower extinction with the delayed as compared to the omitted UCS procedure was very puzzling, and was in large part responsible for Spence's consideration of the effects of nonreinforcement in classical conditioning. As Spence pointed out a number of times, his theorizing had not treated the effects of nonreinforcement in classical aversive conditioning situations to any great extent. In fact, his chapter, "The Roles of Reinforcement and Non-Reinforcement in Simple Learning," which appeared in his 1960 book, *Behavior Theory and Learning*, discussed nonreinforcement in classical aversive conditioning only in terms of the lower asymptote of performance obtained under partial reinforcement as compared to that found with continuous reinforcement. It was however quite clear at that time that partial reinforcement led to very different effects in instrumental-reward as compared to classical aversive conditioning. Spence commented that the laws concerning the growth of inhibition in these situations should be quite different since it was implausible that frustration, a major factor in instrumental-reward situations, could be involved in not receiving a noxious UCS, which of course is the usual nonreinforcement operation in classical aversive conditioning. A similar argument would hold for the delayed-UCS nonreinforcement procedure.

It was obvious from Reynolds' results that other variables were operating in extinction and would have to be considered in any theoretical account of the effects of nonreinforcement. The retention of the UCS under the delayed-UCS extinction procedure presumably had several effects: it (a) maintained the level of emotionality and thus the drive level of the *S*, (b) reduced the possibility that the set of the *S* "to receive the UCS" would drop out in extinction, and (c) prevented a generalization decrement that might have occurred upon the onset of extinction when the UCS was omitted. The fact that the delayed-UCS effect was a function of the acquisition reinforcement schedule employed implicated set factors, particularly those that might be due to the *S*'s awareness of the change in conditions from acquisition to extinction.

In addition to these considerations, the importance of set or cognitive variables was suggested by the writer's MA thesis (Ross, 1959) which was done under Spence's supervision and was planned to provide data relevant to questions Spence raised in classroom discussion. The first purpose of the study was to determine the final level of performance that could be obtained under partial reinforcement, since previous partial reinforcement studies had not been carried far enough to ensure that asymptotic performance had been reached. If Hull's theory was correct in assuming that habit strength was a function of the number of reinforced trials and (work) inhibition a function of response occurrence, partial and continuous reinforcement should eventually reach the same performance asymptote. On the other hand, if inhibition was a function of nonreinforced trials the performance of the partial group should increase to an asymptote and then decrease again as inhibition continued to accumulate. The second purpose of the study was to investigate the growth of inhibition by switching from continuous to partial reinforcement. It was believed that performance would show a continuous decline after the switch, making it possible to determine the function relating the growth of inhibition to the number of nonreinforced trials. For both the partial group and the continuous group switched to partial reinforcement, nonreinforcement was of the delayed-UCS type with the UCS following the CS by 2400 msec.

The acquisition data showed that partial reinforcement led to a stable asymptote significantly below that obtained with 100 percent reinforcement (a total of 220 trials were given). A more surprising finding, however, was that within one or two trials, the *S*s switched from continuous to partial reinforcement showed a precipitous performance drop, to the same level shown by the group receiving partial reinforcement from the beginning of training. Obviously these data did not indicate a slowly accumulating inhibition, and it was suggested that set variables related to some degree of voluntary control might be involved.

The finding of a sudden 100 percent to 50 percent switch decrement was characterized by Spence as "rather startling" in a subsequent study (Spence & Trapold, 1961) which replicated the sudden-drop phenomenon and in addition ran *S*s under a number of conditions where the reinforcement schedule was shifted from partial to continuous reinforcement. Under the latter conditions it was found that groups showed a gradual increase in performance, but to an asymptote below that reached by *S*s conditioned with 100 percent reinforcement from the beginning of training.

Taken together these two reinforcement schedule-shift studies added convincing evidence that set or cognitive factors were significantly involved in conditioning situations where nonreinforcement occurred, especially in cases where a disruption was introduced into the conditioning situation. Clearly, reliance on naive *S*s and neutral instructions would not be sufficient if one wished to investigate and theorize about extinction without the complication of cognitive variables.

MASKING TASKS AND EXTINCTION: PROCEDURES

Although the majority of studies utilizing masking tasks which Spence and his students published were concerned with rate of extinction, the first masking-task study from the Iowa laboratory investigated the acquisition performance of *S*s scoring high and low on the Manifest Anxiety Scale as a function of UCS intensity (Spence & Weyant, 1960). No ready signal was given before each trial in this study, since the experimenters wished to find whether the usual performance differences found with high- and low-anxiety *S*s would occur without the ready-signal feature. Subjects were given 100 paired-acquisition trials, with a light CS and an airpuff UCS, interspersed with 65 trials on which a tone alone was given. The *S*s were instructed to pay close attention to the light and tone and to press a (dummy) telegraph key quickly whenever the tone sounded but not when the light and puff occurred. To quote the authors, "the purpose of this discrimination response procedure was to camouflage the experiment and thus reduce the likelihood that *S* would recognize it as a study of conditioning [p. 147]." This objective was accomplished since only three of 72 *S*s reported that they recognized the study involved the conditioning of the eyelid response to the CS, in contrast to the 10–30 percent recognition usually found.

There was no further discussion of this telegraph-key masking procedure in the Spence and Weyant paper. Obviously, however, it was felt that better results could be obtained with a different masking task since the new procedure described below was used in all subsequent studies.

This new procedure was a variation of the Estes-Straughan light-guessing or probability-learning task. Subjects were instructed that the experiment was concerned with the effects of distraction upon performance in a difficult problem-solving situation; they were further instructed that they were to predict, upon the lighting of a centrally located signal lamp, which of two small lamps located to the left and right would light by pressing correspondingly located buttons on the arms of their chair. They were informed that distracting stimuli in the form of a tone and an airpuff to the eye would be given between their response of pressing a button and the lighting of one of the lamps, and were urged to predict to the best of their ability and to attempt to improve their prediction with practice.

The sequence of events on a masking-task conditioning trial was as follows. The central signal lamp would light followed by the presentation of CS and UCS, which in turn were followed by one of the two small lamps. The duration of the signal lamp and the interval from its onset of the CS varied among experiments, being respectively (in msec.) 2000 and 2000 (Spence, Homzie, & Rutledge, 1964 *; Spence & Rutledge, 1964), 4550 and 2000 (Homzie & Weiss, 1965), and 500 and 1500 (Homzie, 1968; Spence, 1966b). The small lamp lit for 1000 msec. in all studies and came on 500 msec. after the offset of the CS, except in one study (Homzie, 1968) where the small lamp was presented 1000 msec. after CS offset. On trials where the guessing game was given without the CS, or without both the CS and UCS, the small lamp lit at the time it would have lit if the CS had been given. The right and left lamps were presented according to a prearranged schedule, the left seven times and the right three times in each block of 10 trials for half the *S*s, with the reverse frequency for the other half. It should be noted that no ready signal was used when this masking task was employed.

Before discussing masking-task data there are several additional methodological features that should be described. First, not only was a masking task employed to reduce the discriminability of the start of extinction, but the CS duration was lengthened in acquisition so that the switch to a 2500-msec. CS-UCS interval at the start of extinction would not involve a change in the CS duration from 550 to 2550 msec. Thus a 2550-msec. CS was used in both acquisition and extinction, the UCS occurring 500 msec. after CS onset on conditioning trials and 2500 msec. after CS onset in nonreinforced trials. This procedure in itself had an effect upon rate of extinction as shown in Experiment I of the Spence, Homzie, & Rutledge (1964) study, although the slower extinction of the delayed-UCS group was of only marginal significance as compared to that of a UCS-omitted group for *S*s not classified as voluntary-form responders on the basis of the Spence and Ross (1959) criterion. Another approach to this problem was Goldstein's (1962) use of a 550-msec. CS on both reinforced (500-msec. CS-UCS interval) and nonreinforced (2500-msec. CS-UCS interval) trials. This procedure was not used in subsequent studies, however.

Actually, the delayed-UCS procedure was found to create a problem in

* Although the first published report of the use of the probability masking task was in a 1963 *Science* article by Spence, it was a preliminary report of data later published in more detail by Spence, Homzie, and Rutledge (1964), and the latter reference will be used throughout this paper.

that the extinction curve for *S*s extinguished with this technique in the context of the masking task leveled off at approximately 35 percent rather than the 10–15 percent spontaneous blink rate obtained when the UCS was omitted, or when it was delayed without the masking task. Since this higher final level was due to the fact that approximately one-third of the *S*s showed no response decrement during extinction, it was concluded that the delayed-UCS procedure was reinforcing or neutral for some *S*s, and that its use would not give a proper picture of the course of extinction. To avoid this difficulty, Spence (1966) developed a new procedure which was intended to maintain the drive level of the *S* and minimize stimulus change from acquisition to extinction without pairing the CS and UCS during extinction. This involved two types of trials during acquisition: half were CS-UCS conditioning trials with a 2550-msec. CS duration and half were masking-task trials with the CS and UCS omitted. In extinction *S*s received the CS but not the UCS on half of the trials, and the UCS without the CS on the other half. Thus, the UCS continued during extinction but was not paired with the CS. The procedure of giving guess-alone trials in acquisition permitted the intertrial interval between UCS presentations to remain the same from acquisition to extinction, and also gave the *S*s experience with guessing-game trials without the UCS during acquisition, a feature which made the shift to extinction less discriminable. Two other extinction groups were used in this particular study. One received half guess-alone trials and half delayed-UCS trials, while the other also had half guess-alone trials but only the CS on the other trials. In extinction the groups receiving the airpuff showed a higher level of performance than the UCS-omitted group, with the unpaired-UCS procedure leading to a lower final level than the delayed-UCS technique. Thus this new procedure of giving CS and UCS separately with the masking task in extinction led to slower extinction as did the delayed-UCS technique, but avoided the reinforcing effects and consequent higher final extinction level that characterized the delayed-UCS procedure.

An interesting aspect of this new technique was that the use of guess-alone trials permitted a measure of the random or spontaneous blink rate within the context of a guessing-game trial to be obtained simply by scoring these trials as if the CS and UCS had been presented. These data showed a constant response rate of approximately 20 percent during acquisition, and 17.8 percent and 13.7 percent during extinction, respectively, for groups that did and did not have the airpuff continued during that period. Such information was important for Anderson's (1963) procedure for determining extinction rates, which was regularly used by Spence. Homzie (1968) also used this procedure to obtain random response rates from guess-alone trials.

Finally, the point was made in these studies that the usual manner of plotting extinction trials underestimated the initial performance drop since the first extinction trial was the same as an acquisition trial for the *S*. On the first extinction trial, the fact that the UCS will be omitted or delayed can have no conceivable effect on the response that *S* makes during the interval *before* the usual point of occurrence of the UCS. The first trial of extinction should therefore be considered an acquisition trial, with extinction plotted in terms of number of previously nonreinforced trials. The procedure adopted by Spence was to begin extinction on the last trial of what would be scored as acquisition so that the performance on the first trial of the first extinction trial block would reflect the fact that one nonreinforcement had occurred. Thus, if acquisition were to be graphed in 10 blocks of 10 trials, the last trial of the last block, Trial 100, would be nonreinforced and Trial 101 counted in graphing the results as the first extinction trial. This was a rather simple point, but an important one which had been overlooked in the past.

MASKING TASKS AND EXTINCTION: DATA AND THEORY

As mentioned above, the majority of studies utilizing the guessing-game masking task were concerned with extinction phenomena. Although initial interest in the procedure resulted from puzzling findings obtained with the delayed-UCS procedure, the data relevant to this question were reviewed by Spence in his 1966 *Psychological Review* paper and will not be presented in detail here. Suffice it to say that, under conditions which minimized the *S*'s awareness of the acquisition-extinction transition, the presence of the UCS in extinction resulted in the predicted increase in resistance to extinction after 100 percent reinforcement (Goldstein, 1962; Spence, 1966a; Spence, Homzie, & Rutledge, 1964).

The major theoretical development to come from the masking-task studies was the elaboration of the concept of inhibitory set, which was postulated to be a higher-order process adopted by the *S* upon recognition of the change at the onset of extinction. This cognitive set not to blink was hypothesized as being responsible for the rapid decrement found under the usual extinction conditions where the transition was very noticeable; but the effects of set could be eliminated or attenuated by procedural features that prevented or delayed its appearance. It should be stressed that inhibitory set was not the only inhibitory factor presumed to be operating in extinction. Nonreinforcement was still hypothesized to lead to a gradually accumulating inhibition (I_n) which was assumed to be an important factor in animal conditioned-response extinction and, with humans at least, in extinction situations where the use of masking tasks and other procedures ruled out the *S*'s cognitive involvement.

The *S*'s recognition of the switch from acquisition to extinction had been accorded an important role in accounts of extinction behavior for some time. Thus it provided the basis for the discrimination hypothesis, which was offered to account for the partial reinforcement effect (PRE), that is, the greater resistance to extinction found after partial reinforcement as compared to that found after continuous reinforcement. In the case of the inhibitory-set hypothesis the fact that inhibitory set presumably could be manipulated by use of the masking task made it possible to test the usefulness of the concept in accounting for extinction phenomena such as the PRE. The PRE was postulated to reflect the greater discrimination of the shift to extinction on the part of the continuously reinforced *S*s and their quicker and/or more complete adoption of an inhibitory set not to respond. The simple prediction followed that if the masking task eliminated inhibitory set, then the PRE should also be eliminated.

Results consistent with this prediction were found in two studies. Goldstein (1962) found no partial-continuous extinction differences under masking-task conditions when the UCS was omitted in extinction, and Spence and Platt (1967) similarly failed to find a difference between partial and continuous groups in extinction when a masking task was used and the separate CS and UCS extinction procedure developed by Spence was employed. Although Goldstein found the PRE when a masking task was used with the delayed-UCS procedure, Spence and Platt (1967) attributed these contrary results to the reinforcing effects of the delayed-UCS procedure, which were discussed above.

There are other supporting lines of evidence for the inhibitory-set interpretation of the PRE in human classical conditioning. Thus Spence (1966a) cited the Thomas and Wagner (1964) findings that extinction of the eyeblink in rabbits showed the same rate for 50 percent and 100 percent acquisition schedules; the fact that a significant PRE had not been found for classical defense responses in fish and pigeons (Gonzalez, Longo, & Bitterman, 1961; Longo, Milstein, & Bitterman, 1962); and the finding that the conditioned responses of severely retarded humans extinguished at the same rate after partial and continuous reinforcement (Ross, Koski, & Yaeger, 1964). These results with animals and with human retardates were consistent with the inhibitory-set notion since the PRE should not be found in animals and the severely retarded where the higher psychological processes necessary for inhibitory set would be lacking. The same argument is applicable with respect to the fact that the rate of extinction is similar for animals and humans when the latter are run under masking-task conditions.

In addition to the inhibitory-set concept and its implications for extinction and the PRE, use of the masking task led to other theorizing about extinction. Thus Spence used the rate of extinction data from his 1966 masking-task study to examine (a) the question of whether the development of simple inhibition, I_n, was a function of the presence of the UCS, and (b) alternative assumptions regarding the interaction of I_n with drive and habit strength. For the former purpose frequency measures were transformed into superthreshold reaction potential measures ($\overline{E}_L$) as described by Spence (1956) and a curve fitted to these points for the group which received the UCS during extinction. By changing the parameter representing drive level to a lower value, but keeping that for the rate of growth of I_n the same, an excellent fit was found for the group that had the UCS omitted during extinction. This finding implied that the procedures resulted in different drive levels but not different rates of development of inhibition.

With respect to the interaction of inhibition, drive, and habit strength, two alternative formulations were examined. The first, $\bar{E}_L = D(H - I_n)$ implies that the $\bar{E}_L$ values of two groups under different drive levels should be a decreasing function of the number of nonreinforced trials during extinction $(\bar{E}_L{}^1 - \bar{E}_L{}^2) = (D_1 - D_2)\ (H - I_n)$; the alternative relationship, $\bar{E}_L = DH - I_n$ predicts a constant relationship as a function of number of reinforced trials, $\bar{E}_L{}^1 - \bar{E}_L{}^2 = (D_1 - D_2)H$. When $\bar{E}_L{}^1 - \bar{E}_L{}^2$ was plotted it was found to decrease systematically as a function of extinction trials, thus supporting the $\bar{E}_L = D(H - I_n)$ formulation. It should be stressed that this type of theorizing, involving the simple algebraic derivation of the implications of different relationships among theoretical concepts, required the elimination of confounding cognitive factors that could have obscured the relationships. The use of the guessing-game masking task and the new UCS procedure presumably accomplished this, and Spence believed that the extinction procedure used in the 1966 study provided the most satisfactory picture that had been obtained of the extinction of the human conditioned-eyelid response.

One final masking-task extinction study should be mentioned. In contrast to the effects of overlearning in instrumental-reward situations, Spence and Rutledge (1964) found no difference in extinction (delayed-UCS procedure) after 50 as compared to 150 acquisition trials. Since no comparison groups were run without the masking task, existence of a possible relationship between inhibitory set and the rate of extinction after differing numbers of acquisition trials cannot be determined from this study. However since Spence, Rutledge, and Talbott (1963) did find extinctions related to the number of original conditioning trials when the delayed-UCS procedure was used in extinction but the masking task was not employed, it would appear highly probable that there is such a relationship.

An interesting question arises in considering the necessary antecedent condition leading to the *S*'s adoption of inhibitory set. The necessary condition, presumably, is the *S*'s awareness of the sudden change in reinforcement contingencies at the start of extinction. The question has to do with the requirement of a sudden change in reinforcement conditions. It would seem likely that a change from 100 percent to 50 percent reinforcement would be sufficient to elicit inhibitory set, and certainly the sudden-shift data obtained by the writer (Ross, 1959) and Spence and Trapold (1961) fit well with the inhibitory-set position. Inhibitory-set effects would also be expected when nonreinforced trials are introduced into separate-phase differential conditioning where the *S* receives continuous reinforcement to the positive stimulus before the introduction of the negative cue. In fact, Homzie (1968) investigated separate-phase differential conditioning within the context of a masking procedure on the assumption that the use of the masking procedure would eliminate cognitive-set factors in the situation. Excellent agreement was found with Spence's (1936) excitatory-inhibitory theory of discrimination learning, but unfortunately for the purpose of testing the inhibitory-set notion, there were no masking-non-masking comparisons in the study. Other borderline cases with respect to the involvement of inhibitory set are: (a) the acquisition of a response under partial reinforcement and (b) mixed-phase differential conditioning where nonreinforced trials are received from the beginning of the experimental session. In these situations *S*s might or might not adopt an inhibitory set not to respond. The particular events that cause the *S* to self-instruct, with or without consciousness that he is so doing, are not known. Perhaps the *S*'s awareness of blinking when no airpuff occurs leads to the adoption of inhibitory set, and a sudden change in contingencies is necessary for this awareness. On the other hand a similar cognizance might occur in partial- or mixed-phase differential conditioning simply because the *S* responds to the negative cue during the early trials and that cue is not followed by a UCS (or is followed at a long interval), so that the *S* is aware that the blink occurred independently of the airpuff and consequently adopts a set not to respond. The effects of masking tasks in mixed-phase differential conditioning will be discussed in the next section of the paper.

MASKING TASKS: WISCONSIN STUDIES

The author's primary interest in masking tasks and their effects on conditioning stems from attempts to compare the eyelid-conditioning data of subject populations differing widely in age and IQ. Although the procedures and parameters commonly used in the eyelid conditioning of college students can be employed with little change across wide age and IQ ranges (e.g., normal and retarded children), psychologists have hoped that conditioning data might reveal something of a basic nature about the developing organism, his nervous system, and his ability to process incoming stimuli. For these purposes differences that simply reflect varying kinds or amounts of cognitive involvement in the situation are of minor interest and represent a kind of complication that is to be avoided as much as possible. While changes in cognitive behavior with age and differences in the cognitive behavior of normal and retarded children are extremely interesting and important problems in their own right, it is questionable whether eyelid conditioning represents an efficient way to study such phenomena, at least with our present state of knowledge about such processes.

The author's concern with the problem of cognitive factors in developmental and normal-retardate conditioning comparisons began when the work of Spence and his students described above made it apparent that the rate of extinction of the conditioned-eyelid response was profoundly affected by the *S*'s cognitive involvement in the situation. At that time the author had just collected data (Ross, Koski, & Yaeger, 1964) which demonstrated that severely retarded *S*s did not show the PRE and, in addition, that acquisition for these *S*s was almost identical under 50 percent and 100 percent reinforcement conditions. While these data might have been interpreted as demonstrating that retardates do not possess the inhibition mechanisms of college students, an alternative possibility was that some aspect of the experimental situation used with the retardates served a masking-task function. The feature that was suspect was the showing of a motion picture during the conditioning sessions, a procedure that was adopted because it greatly facilitated work with the retardates both in terms of their tolerance of the conditioning headset and their willingness to remain in the experimental room for any length of time. To see if the motion picture had masking-task effects on sophomores, two groups of college students were run, with one group receiving conditions identical to those used with the retardates and the other the same conditions except for the omission of the motion picture. The data showed that while the motion picture slowed extinction for the college students only to a relatively small extent, both movie and nonmovie college groups showed the PRE and a large and significant decrement in acquisition with a 50 percent schedule as well. Thus these data demonstrated large differences in the effects of partial reinforcement on the acquisition and extinction performance of retardates and normals of approximately equal chronological age and suggested that the movie did not have very much of a masking effect on the performance of college students in this particular situation.

While these findings demonstrated that use of the movie procedure did not change college student partial reinforcement and extinction data so that it was similar to that found with retardates, the possibility that the movie served as a masking task for the retardates but not for the students could not be ruled out. In fact, even without the motion picture any differences between such populations might be the result of different degrees of awareness of, or cognitive involvement in, the conditioning situation. This possibility poses an extremely difficult problem. How in the absence of an independent measure of the degree of masking accomplished do we equate two populations with respect to this factor? Although there is no clear-cut solution at present it is obvious that knowledge regarding the limits of masking-task effects and their specific relationships to conditioning phenomena in college students would greatly aid in interpreting conditioning data obtained from normal children and retardates. If the data obtained from these latter populations closely resemble those obtained from student groups run under masking-task conditions, it would be difficult not to conclude that the conditioning paradigms used were insensitive to age and IQ differences, or that the processes being tapped were largely invariant with age and IQ. Clearly more information must be obtained before such population comparisons are understandable in terms of the basic learning processes involved. With this uncertainty it would be unwise to consider retardate-college student differences in their response to partial reinforcement as evidence for a retardate deficiency in either the development of inhibition or the stimulus-processing requirements of the situation.

A similar problem exists with respect to differential-conditioning paradigms. In work with retardates Ohlrich (1968) found only minimal differential conditioning (slightly less than a 20 percent difference to the positive and negative cues) with the best of the three CS-UCS intervals used (1100 msec. better than 500 or 800 msec.), and then only after 300 conditioning trials. In contrast, college sophomores run under identical conditions showed excellent discrimination (approximately 40 percent) after only 100 trials.

The question of how to interpret these differential-conditioning data led to several studies which evaluated the effects of masking tasks on discrimination performance. No masking-task studies involving mixed-phase differential conditioning had been reported prior to the work discussed below, and it could be hypothesized that the better differential conditioning of the college students was largely a function of cognitive involvement (i.e., inhibitory set). The PRE effect had been demonstrated by Spence to be such; that is, it was abolished with the use of masking task. Thus, a similar demonstration might be possible in the case of differential conditioning. Actually, such a result was considered rather unlikely since, as discussed earlier, no sudden contingency change occurs in mixed-phase differential conditioning in contrast to the situation at the onset of extinction. If differential responding was found to be affected to any large degree by a masking task, it would suggest that some variation or combination of attentional, perceptual, or inhibitory-set states is a prerequisite for differential responding to two cues, at least with respect to the speed with which a conditioned-eyelid discrimination is typically established by college students.

When work with masking tasks began, the author decided to use a new task rather than adopt the probability guessing-game procedure. While the guess-alone trials of the Spence (1966b) and Homzie (1968) studies provided data which indicated that the guessing-game stimuli did not acquire response strength in their own right, their use with the CS and UCS embedded within the trial resulted in a compound stimulus, whose effects could possibly have interacted with some of the experimental conditions. It was also desirable to use visual stimuli in some cases and the addition of a visual CS+ and CS− to the masking-task stimuli would have presented the *S* with a rather complex visual input. Even with auditory CSs the visual guessing-game stimuli would have interfered with the showing of a motion picture during conditioning.

In view of these difficulties a time estimation masking task was adopted. The following illustrates the instructions given to the *S* with this procedure.

> This is an experiment involving time estimation. We are interested in how you estimate various time intervals when distracting stimuli are presented. For your time-estimation task all you have to do is sit quietly and look straight ahead at the screen. At various times lights will appear in front of you, along with other distractors. Your task is to judge time intervals after the lights go off. After you think 2 sec. have gone by, press the button on the right arm of the chair. After you think 5 sec. have gone by, press the button on the left arm of the chair.

Subjects in comparison groups who do not receive the masking task are told that the purpose of the experiment is to find out their reactions to certain lights. In studies where heart-rate is recorded with electrodes attached to the *S*'s right arm, the *S* is asked to press the left-hand button once after 2 sec. have elapsed and once again after 5 sec. have elapsed following the presentation of the CS. In all cases the *S* is asked to remove his watch before conditioning starts.

This masking task has an advantage in that it is not specifically tied to extra auditory or visual cues, although the instructions probably cause the *S* to attend to the stimuli more than might be the case with other procedures. It has the second advantage that little or no instrumentation is required. The *S*'s button-press responses cause lamps in the experimenter control room to light so that compliance with the instructions can be checked, but no record of the time estimation is made. Subject reports indicate that the task is successful in convincing most *S*s that time estimation is the purpose of the experiment.

The first study to use this time-estimation masking task compared the mixed-phase differential-conditioning performance of college students under masking-task and no-masking-task conditions (Ross, Wilcox, & Mayer, 1967). A large and significant ($p<.05$) difference in differential responding to the positive and negative cues was found as a function of masking-task conditions with the mean difference over the last 20 trials being 7.5 percent for masking task *S*s and 42.5 percent for *S*s not given the masking task. While these results suggested that the masking task for all practical purposes eliminated differential conditioning, the stimuli employed were "complex"; that is, they were combinations of two colors and two forms with one dimension, either color or form, relevant (one value, CS+, always reinforced; the other, CS−, never reinforced), and the remaining dimension irrelevant (each irrelevant cue occurring 50 percent of the time with CS+ and 50 percent of the time with CS−). Thus it was possible that the dramatic effects of the masking task in reducing discrimination could have been specific to use of such complex stimuli and that little if any attenuation of differential conditioning would be found with a single relevant dimension. To investigate this possibility, a second study (Mayer & Ross, 1969) was conducted which varied the complexity (presence or absence of an irrelevant dimension) and CS-UCS interval (500, 800, 1100 msec.), as well as the masking-no-masking-task factor. Two results are of importance for the present paper. First, poorer differential conditioning was found with the masking task under each combination of experimental conditions. The main effect of the masking task was significant, but its interactions with other variables were not. Secondly, not only did the masking task reduce differential responding, but its use revealed a relationship between stimulus complexity and the interstimulus interval. This interaction, which was again found in a partial replication of the study, reflected optimal differential conditioning for the simple and complex stimuli with the 800- and 1100-msec. CS-UCS intervals respectively.

The studies discussed above all involved visual conditioned stimuli. In order to see if similar effects could be found with the auditory stimuli previously used with children, a study (unpublished) was run by Michael Nelson which involved the masking-no-masking-task factor, CS-UCS intervals of 300, 500, and 800 msec., and fast and slow stimulus-rise times. The CS+ and CS− were 800- and 2100-Hz. tones (counterbalanced) and a movie was shown along with the masking task. The differences in responding to the CS+ and CS− in the last 20 trials for the 300-, 500-, and 800-msec. CS-UCS interval groups were, respectively, 9.6 percent, −4.2 percent, and 10.4 percent for the masked *S*s and 4.6 percent, 12.9 percent, and 24.2 percent for the nonmasked *S*s.

Thus in this experiment as in the previous studies with visual stimuli, the masking task had a significant deleterious effect upon differential conditioning. In this case the reduction in differential responding occurred even though the nonmasked *S*s viewed a movie, which might have had some masking function. The small and reversed difference at the 300-msec. CS-UCS interval reflects the fact that very little differential conditioning was obtained under either condition at this value, but the differences were substantial at the other CS-UCS intervals.

Since the best nonmasking differential performance was found at the 800-msec. CS-UCS interval, 24 additional *S*s were run at that CS-UCS interval with the masking task, half with a slow (50 msec.) and half with a fast (<10 μsec.) time from the onset of the CS until it reached maximum amplitude, i.e., CS rise time. Differential conditioning was carried out over a 3-day period, with 100 trials given each day, in order to see if good masking-task differential-conditioning performance could be obtained with such an extended number of trials. This was not found to be the case, since the response levels to the positive and negative cues appeared to be stable from approximately the middle of Day 2 through the third day. The mean difference score averaged over all trials of Day 3 was 9.45 percent as compared to the 24.2 percent difference found for the corresponding nonmasked *S*s on the last 20 of their 100 conditioning trials. Thus, it does not appear that the masking-task effect is simply one of slowing the rate at which the discrimination is established.

The other time-estimation masking-task studies that have been completed in this series were run by Lois Putnam and were intended to examine the effects of the time-estimation procedure on single-cue acquisition performance. In the first of these unpublished studies, *S*s were given single-cue continuous reinforcement with subgroups receiving combinations of fast and slow stimulus rise times, and CS-UCS intervals of 300, 500, and 800 msec. The performance of the masked and nonmasked *S*s was very similar for all experimental conditions, with the masking effect nonsignificant, $F(1,132) = .39$. A subsequent unpublished study, also by Lois Putnam, which was designed to replicate the 300-msec. condition, compared continuous and partial reinforcement under masking and no-masking conditions. These data showed a somewhat (approximately 15 percent) higher level of performance on the part of the masked *S*s, but the difference only reached the .10 significance level. The performance of both the continuous and partial groups was facilitated to a small and approximately equal degree by the masking-task condition. Further, the groups receiving partial reinforcement showed a large performance decrement, compared to the conditioning level of the continuous reinforcement *S*s, under both masking and no-masking conditions. These data contrast with the acquisition data obtained by Spence and Platt (1967), where very similar 100 percent and 50 percent reinforcement performance was found under guessing-game masking-task conditions, and those of Goldstein (1962), where a nonsignificant (less than 10 percent) terminal difference was found between continuous and partial reinforcement groups run with the guessing-game masking task.

One further aspect of the data should be mentioned: the masking task reduces the number of *S*s classified as voluntary-form responders. The percentage of *S*s so classified has been found to vary considerably with experimental conditions (fewer voluntary-form *S*s are typically found under partial-reinforcement or differential-conditioning paradigms) and *S* population (students are more likely to be voluntary-form responders if they are sophisticated with respect to classical conditioning). While the percentage of *S*s classified as voluntary-form responders varies somewhat with conditioning paradigm and population sampled, the masking-task effect has been very consistent. In the Mayer and Ross (1969) study, 12 of the 48 no-masking-task *S*s were classified as voluntary-form responders by the derivative criterion (Hartman & Ross, 1961), while only 2 of the 48 masking-task *S*s were so classified. In the partial replication of this study, in which all *S*s received the masking task, only one of 32 *S*s was so classified. In the Nelson study 13 of the 72 *S*s run without a masking task were classified as voluntary-form responders, while only 8 masking-task condition *S*s were so classified. In the Putnam single-cue data the numbers for no-masking-task and masking-task *S*s were 14 of 24 and 7 of 24 respectively. Thus it can be seen that the use of the masking task has substantially reduced the number of *S*s classified as voluntary-form responders.

In summary, the time-estimation masking task consistently has large effects in reducing the degree of differential responding and the number of *S*s classified as voluntary-form responders. On the other hand, this masking task apparently has little if any effect on single-cue continuous or partial reinforcement, and if some small facilitation occurs it does so equally under continuous and partial reinforcement conditions.

It is difficult to compare the effects of the time-estimation masking task with those of the guessing-game masking task since the latter has not been used with mixed-phase differential conditioning. However, the single-cue acquisition and extinction data that are available suggest that the effects are not at all the same. Thus the lack of effect of the time-estimation masking task on acquisition under partial reinforcement is in contrast to the Goldstein (1962) and Spence and Platt (1967) results, and extinction data from the Putnam studies shows little difference in the rate of extinction of masked and nonmasked *S*s, in contrast to the large effects found in the Iowa studies.

There are several possible reasons for this discrepancy in single-cue data. The time-estimation masking task may simply not be effective enough as a masking task to produce the same single-cue acquisition and extinction results, or the guessing-game procedure used by Spence and his coworkers may be effective only when the delayed-UCS procedure and (or) a long CS duration are used.

If the time-estimation task is simply less effective as a masking task, it is surprising that it has such large effects in reducing differential conditioning and the number of voluntary responders. Possibly, however, the time-estimation masking task has its effect in differential conditioning because it directs the *S*'s attention to the positive and negative cues in such a way that the discrimination is affected. When differentiation fails to occur with the masking task, the *S* responds to both CS+ and CS−, the response curves to both stimuli rising together. This implicates the failure of some processing or inhibition factor related to the CS−, and Ross and Wilcox (in press) have suggested that the time-estimation masking task may reduce discrimination by preventing the habituation of the orienting response to the CS−. Since such habituation is postulated to be necessary for, or to index, the turnoff mechanism by which responses to a nonreinforced stimulus cease, differentiation would fail to occur when the *S*'s attention to *both* cues is maintained. It remains to be seen if other types of masking tasks which do not direct the *S*'s attention to the stimuli will have a similar effect on differential conditioning.

If, however, it is a reduction of the *S*'s cognitive awareness of stimulus contingencies that is responsible for the masking tasks' effect on differential conditioning, an important question is raised concerning the extent to which the *S*'s awareness, attention, or perceptual response to the relationship between the stimuli is necessary for differential responding. It is interesting in this respect that a study by Dawson and Grings (1968) found that a paper and pencil speed mental test prevented differential GSR-conditioning (i.e., the effects of masking CS-UCS pairings and the use of a pseudoconditioning procedure did not differ). It may well be that differential conditioning requires some sort of awareness or perceptual response on the part of the *S* to the stimulus relationship, whereas a similar requirement does not exist for single-cue conditioning. While such a requirement has been proposed for some time in the case of autonomic discrimination where a mediational state has been postulated as the mechanism leading to differential conditioning, a similar requirement in the case of skeletal muscle responses would be rather surprising given the common view that differential skeletal conditioning is relatively automatic and does not necessarily involve cognitive processes. It is quite possible, of course, that the requirement might be of an attentional or perceptual nature somewhat different from cognitive awareness, which the *S* can report.

CONCLUDING COMMENTS

The demonstration that masking tasks have major effects on eyelid-conditioning data undoubtedly will lead to a greater awareness and investigation of the role of cognitive factors in this conditioning situation. Obviously it is important to understand how such factors affect conditioning, especially for those interested in the comparison of populations whose cognitive involvement in the conditioning situation may differ. Even in research with homogeneous populations where the concern is with other conditioning processes, it must be realized that experimental treatments may differentially elicit set or cognitive involvement so that the differences obtained are largely due to cognitive factors. In some cases the conditioning results may be unaffected by masking-task procedures, while in other cases the phenomena may be found only when masking tasks are used. In the long run, however, it will be necessary to study the processes underlying conditioning data if progress is to be made beyond a crassly empirical approach which observes that certain manipulations were carried out and certain results obtained.

In the past some experimenters have shown reluctance to admit the existence of, or work with, cognitive variables. This is understandable because such factors have sometimes been used in blatantly circular explanations of behavior. Rejection of the mentalism that exists as an easy substitute for experimental work in psychology is undeniably justified if one wishes continued progress toward a scientific understanding of behavior. Nevertheless, it is long past time for those interested in conditioning phenomena to recognize, by the actual investigation of these variables, that human *S*s do adopt sets and that cognitive factors do play a very important role in determining the data obtained with many otherwise simple conditioning paradigms. Too often the *S*'s subjective involvement in the conditioning situation has been ignored in the name of objectivity, with the excuse that only imperfect means were at hand for evaluating such involvement. Admittedly the investigation of cognitive factors in conditioning is an extremely difficult and time-consuming endeavor, much more so than simply varying the values of physical stimuli and the temporal relationships among them. However, experimenters working with classical conditioning paradigms have fallen far behind those in other experimental areas in dealing with the *S*'s set, self-instructions, and general cognitive involvement. The masking-task work initiated by Spence clearly highlights the fact that it would be most unfortunate for this state of affairs to continue.

This is not to say that use of masking tasks represents an easy answer to the methodological problems that arise from the *S*'s involvement in the conditioning situation. All that is presently evident is that their use offers an interesting approach that appears to have potential for a more far-reaching experimental attack than that possible through the use of instructions to the *S* or postexperimental questionnaires. Surely experimenters will utilize masking tasks not only for methodological reasons, but in the hope that much may be learned about the basic nature of conditioning as we come to understand the effects of masking tasks on conditioning.

For some it was surprising that Kenneth Spence became involved in the investigation of cognitive factors in conditioning and that he so labeled the variables. The meaning of the word "cognitive" has changed greatly since earlier times when it represented theoretical positions that stressed perceptual field conditions, as compared to those that emphasized associative processes between stimuli and responses. With the decline of general systematic learning theory where the disputes engendered were often more verbal than empirically testable, the term "cognitive" has come to refer to areas of investigation and classes of variables whose influence on the performance of relatively mature human subjects Spence never denied. As such, much of the affect connected with its use has been lost, and the antagonistic responses which the term aroused during the learning controversies of the 1940s and 1950s no longer occur. Certainly Spence's research did not represent a change in the nature of the evidence which he accepted for use in theorizing or a change in the scientific rigor of his approach to understanding psychological phenomena.

It is characteristic of the contributions of Kenneth Spence that his masking-task work has promise both with respect to the methodology of obtaining needed data and to substantive inquiry about the nature of the conditioning process. His experiments utilizing masking tasks showed the same tight reasoning and consistent progression toward the development of theory that was present in his other research, and as so often was the case, the contribution of his studies will be far greater than their own empirical findings as they continue to stimulate other research workers to investigate these phenomena.

REFERENCES

Anderson, N. H. Comparison of different populations: Resistance to extinction and transfer. *Psychological Review*, 1963, *70*, 162–179.

Cole, L. E. A comparison of the factors of practice and knowledge of experimental procedure in conditioning the eyelid response of human subjects. *Journal of General Psychology*, 1939, *20*, 349–373.

Dawson, M. E., & Grings, W. W. Comparison of classical conditioning and relational learning. *Journal of Experimental Psychology*, 1968, *76*, 227–231.

Freeman, G. L. The galvanic phenomenon and conditioned responses. *Journal of General Psychology*, 1930, *3*, 529–539.

Goldstein, H. The effects of set factors and reinforcement schedules on the acquisition and extinction of the conditioned eyelid response. Unpublished doctoral dissertation, University of Iowa, 1962.

Gonzalez, R. C., Longo, N., & Bitterman, M. E. Classical conditioning in the fish: Exploratory studies of partial reinforcement. *Journal of Comparative and Physiological Psychology*, 1961, *54*, 452–456.

Grant, D. A. The influence of attitude on the conditioned eyelid response. *Journal of Experimental Psychology*, 1939, *25*, 333–346.

Hamel, I. A. A study and analysis of the conditioned reflex. *Psychological Monographs*, 1919, *27* (Whole No. 118).

Hartman, T. F., & Ross, L. E. An alternative criterion for the elimination of "voluntary" responses in eyelid conditioning. *Journal of Experimental Psychology*, 1961, *61*, 334–338.

Hilgard, E. R. An algebraic analysis of conditioned discrimination in man. *Psychological Review*, 1938, *45*, 472–496.

Hilgard, E. R., Campbell, R. K., & Sears, W. N. Conditioned discrimination: The development of discrimination with and without verbal report. *American Journal of Psychology*, 1937, *49*, 564–580.

Hilgard, E. R., Campbell, R. K., & Sears, W. N. Conditioned discrimination: The effect of knowledge of stimulus-relationships. *American Journal of Psychology*, 1938, *51*, 498–506.

Hilgard, E. R., & Humphreys, L. G. The effect of supporting and antagonistic voluntary instructions on conditioned discrimination. *Journal of Experimental Psychology*, 1938, *22*, 291–304.

Hilgard, E. R., & Marquis, D. G. *Conditioning and learning*. New York: Appleton-Century, 1940.

Homzie, M. J. Separate-phase differential eyelid conditioning within the context of a masking procedure. *Journal of Experimental Psychology*, 1968, *76*, 630–635.

Homzie, M. J., & Weiss, G. UCS intensity and the associative strength of the eyelid CR with a masked conditioning procedure. *Journal of Experimental Psychology*, 1965, *69*, 101–103.

Longo, N., Milstein, S., & Bitterman, M. E. Classical conditioning in the pigeon: Exploratory studies of partial reinforcement. *Journal of Comparative and Physiological Psychology*, 1962, *55*, 983–986.

Mayer, M. J., & Ross, L. E. Effects of stimulus complexity, interstimulus interval, and masking task conditions in differential eyelid conditioning. *Journal of Experimental Psychology*, 1969, *81*, 469–474.

McAllister, W. R. The effect on eyelid conditioning of shifting the CS-UCS interval. *Journal of Experimental Psychology*, 1953, *45*, 423–428.

Miller, J., & Cole, L. E. The influence of a "voluntary" reaction upon the development and the extinction of the conditioned eyelid reaction. *Journal of Genetic Psychology*, 1936, *48*, 405–440.

Mowrer, O. H. Preparatory set (expectancy)—a determinant in motivation and learning. *Psychological Review*, 1938, *45*, 62–91.

Ohlrich, E. S. The effect of CS-UCS interval on the single cue and differential eyelid conditioning of retarded children. Unpublished doctoral dissertation, University of Wisconsin, 1968.

Razran, G. H. S. Conditioned responses: An experimental study and a theoretical analysis. *Archives of Psychology*, 1935, *28* (No. 191).

Razran, G. H. S. Attitudinal control of human conditioning. *Journal of Psychology*, 1936, *2*, 327–337.

Razran, G. H. S. Studies in configural conditioning. II. The effect of subjects' attitudes and of task-sets upon configural conditioning. *Journal of Experimental Psychology*, 1939, *24*, 95–105. (a)

Razran, G. H. S. Studies in configural conditioning. VI. Comparative extinction and forgetting of pattern and of single-stimulus conditioning. *Journal of Experimental Psychology*, 1939, *24*, 432–438. (b)

Razran, G. H. S. A simple technique for controlling subjective attitudes in salivary conditioning of adult human subjects. *Science*, 1939, *89*, 160–161. (c)

Razran, G. H. S. Studies in configural conditioning. V. Generalization and transposition. *Journal of Genetic Psychology*, 1940, *56*, 3–11.

Reynolds, W. F. Acquisition and extinction of the conditioned eyelid response following partial and continuous reinforcement. *Journal of Experimental Psychology*, 1958, *55*, 335–341.

Ross, L. E. The decremental effects of partial reinforcement during acquisition of the conditioned eyelid response. *Journal of Experimental Psychology*, 1959, *57*, 74–82.

Ross, L. E., Koski, C. H., & Yaeger, J. Classical eyelid conditioning of the severely retarded: Partial reinforcement effects. *Psychonomic Science*, 1964, *1*, 253–254.

Ross, L. E., & Wilcox, S. M. Conditioned stimulus parameters and the interstimulus interval: The processing of CS information in differential conditioning. In W. F. Prokasy & A. H. Black (Eds.), *Classical conditioning* II. New York: Appleton-Century-Crofts, in press.

Ross, L. E., Wilcox, S. M., & Mayer, M. J. A simple eyelid conditioning masking task and its effects on differential conditioning. *Psychonomic Science*, 1967, *9*, 333–334.

Schlosberg, H. A study of the conditioned patellar reflex. *Journal of Experimental Psychology*, 1928, *11*, 468–494.

Scott, H. D. Hypnosis and the conditioned reflex. *Journal of General Psychology*, 1930, *4*, 113–130.

Spence, K. W. The nature of discrimination learning in animals. *Psychological Review*, 1936, *43*, 427–449.

Spence, K. W. *Behavior theory and conditioning*. New Haven: Yale University Press, 1956.

Spence, K. W. *Behavior theory and learning*. Englewood Cliffs, N.J.: Prentice-Hall, 1960.

Spence, K. W. Cognitive factors in the extinction of the conditioned eyelid response in humans. *Science*, 1963, *140*, 1224–1225.

Spence, K. W. Cognitive and drive factors in the extinction of the conditioned eye blink in human subjects. *Psychological Review*, 1966, *73*, 445–458. (a)

Spence, K. W. Extinction of the human eyelid CR as a function of presence or absence of the UCS during extinction. *Journal of Experimental Psychology*, 1966, *71*, 642–648. (b)

Spence, K. W., Homzie, M. J., & Rutledge, E. F. Extinction of the human eyelid CR as a function of the discriminability of the change from acquisition to extinction. *Journal of Experimental Psychology*, 1964, *67*, 545–552.

Spence, K. W., & Platt, J. R. Effects of partial reinforcement on acquisition and extinction of the conditioned eyeblink in a masking situation. *Journal of Experimental Psychology*, 1967, *74*, 259–263.

Spence, K. W., & Ross, L. E. A methodological study of the form and latency of eyelid response in conditioning. *Journal of Experimental Psychology*, 1959, *58*, 376–381.

Spence, K. W., & Rutledge, E. F. The effect of overlearning on rate of extinction of the eyelid CR. *Psychonomic Science*, 1964, *1*, 315–316.

Spence, K. W., Rutledge, E. F., & Talbot, J. H. Effect of number of acquisition trials and the presence or absence of the UCS on extinction of the eyelid CR. *Journal of Experimental Psychology*, 1963, *66*, 286–291.

Spence, K. W., & Trapold, M. A. Performance in eyelid conditioning as a function of reinforcement schedules and changes in them. *Proceedings of the National Academy of Science*, 1961, *47*, 1860–1868.

Spence, K. W., & Weyant, R. G. Conditioning performance of high- and low-anxious *S*s in the absence of a warning signal. *Journal of Experimental Psychology*, 1960, *60*, 146–149.

Thomas, E., & Wagner, A. R. Partial reinforcement of the classically conditioned eyelid response in the rabbit. *Journal of Comparative and Physiological Psychology*, 1964, *58*, 157–158.

Thorndike, E. L. *The fundamentals of learning*. New York: Teachers College, 1932.

Tolman, E. C. *Purposive behavior in animals and men*. New York: Appleton-Century, 1932.

Wickens, D. D. A reply to Dr. Razran's "Conditioning and attitudes," *Journal of Experimental Psychology*, 1939, *24*, 233–236.

Elementary Associations

ALLAN R. WAGNER

INTRODUCTION

"Elementistic." "Associationistic." Among the adjectives that characterize Spence's systematic preferences, these two point to the most obvious of historical ties. The scientific strategy he proposed was first of all to investigate the strengthening and weakening of elementary associations in relative isolation, and then to attempt to explain instances of more complex learning in terms of the simultaneous operation of multiple associative tendencies.

If Spence's theorizing stands apart from that of others who have shared this advocacy, it is primarily attributable to the sophistication with which he consistently interpreted it. Even in the most restricted learning situations that have been devised, there are innumerable nonlearning variables that influence performance and no simple covariation among the several indexes of learning. Spence recognized that inferences concerning the elementary associations that might be involved could thus be made only within the context of a set of abstract concepts and their postulated interrelationships, developed explicitly so as to deduce the functional relationships observed. Furthermore, the theoretical statements so developed were proposed as potentially useful in the integration of more complex learning phenomena only when taken in conjunction with appropriate composition rules, which specify the assumed manner in which the elementary tendencies interact, and which themselves stand evaluation in each such application of the theory.

Preparation of this chapter and the research reported were supported in part by National Science Foundation Grant GB–14384. The author is especially grateful to Maria Saavedra, whose research has contributed substantially to the formation and evaluation of the theory contained herein, and to Robert Rescorla, with whose collaboration the mathematical treatment was developed.

Granted these characteristics, perhaps the most notable and influential specific achievements of Spence's theorizing involved his ingenious specification of composition rules that would allow for the interpretation of various relatively complex learning phenomena. His classic papers on discrimination learning (e.g., 1936, 1937, 1938) represent an elegant demonstration of the manner in which numerous features of selective learning performance might be accounted for in terms of the summation and competition of gradually strengthening and weakening elementary tendencies. After an extensive period of research and theorizing, instrumental learning was similarly treated as a complex result of the simultaneous change in multiple associative tendencies. It is, in fact, interesting to note that Spence's most recent detailed account (1956; 1960, Ch. 6) of "simple" instrumental-reward learning, which acknowledges the influence of anticipatory reward and anticipatory frustration, in addition to the associative strengths of compatible and incompatible molar behaviors occasioned by a variety of separate cues, incorporates a degree of theoretical complexity far surpassing that of his original analysis of discrimination learning.

By comparison, Spence introduced few novel sentences concerning the assumed strengthening and weakening of the elementary associations that were appealed to in such theorizing. His earliest assumptions (e.g., Spence, 1936) can be viewed (e.g., Hull, 1950; Spence, 1960, Ch. 22) as falling within the general framework of Pavlovian theory: he adopted the position that each pairing of an appropriate antecedent and consequent event (reinforcement) results in an increment in the "excitatory tendency" of the antecedent event, the size of the increment being a bell-shaped function of the magnitude of the existing excitatory tendency. He further assumed that each presentation of the antecedent event alone (nonreinforcement) results in a decrement in this excitatory tendency, the size of the decrement being an increasing linear function of the magnitude of the existing excitatory tendency. Subsequently he followed Hull (1943) in many details, not only with respect to certain of the quantitative functions postulated, but also with respect to various parameters of the reinforcing event which were tentatively assumed to influence the strength of the association. Thus, for example, Spence came to assume that the size of the increment as a result of reinforcement was a decreasing linear function of the magnitude of the existing tendency (Spence, 1952b) and, at least in the case of *aversive* consequent events, a function of their intensity (Spence, 1956) and delay of termination (Runquist & Spence, 1959).

But most frequently (e.g., 1952b, 1956, 1960) he lamented the fact that insufficient data were available to resolve many of the interesting questions concerning the strengthening and weakening of elementary associations. And, when introducing a postulated elementary tendency such as r_g-s_g into a more complex theoretical analysis, it was generally only assumed that the associative tendency involved increased with successive experiences of the appropriate paired events and decreased with successive experiences of the antecedent event alone.*

Much of my research has grown naturally out of this background. Not only has it been generated in large measure as a result of the lack of adequate information concerning the strengthening and weakening of simple associations, but the examples which Spence provided concerning how such information might usefully be applied toward the integration of more complex phenomena added considerably to the felt significance of the endeavor. At an even more concrete level, Spence's arguments (e.g., 1952b, 1956) that simple Pavlovian conditioning might represent a relatively unique source of data from which to draw inferences concerning the formation of elementary associations played a major role in determining the experimental situations employed.

The present paper will describe a portion of this research and theorizing involving Pavlovian conditioning in which my students and I have been engaged for the past several years. More detailed presentations of various features of the work are available elsewhere (e.g., Rescorla & Wagner, 1971; Wagner, 1969a, 1969b), but the opportunity will be taken here to place it in appropriate relationship to an underlying view of associative learning that seems to have influenced the theorizing of Spence, as well as that of many other investigators. That our work, in fact, suggests the possible advantage of an alternative view, provides the substance of the paper.

IMPLICATIONS OF DIFFERENT ACQUISITION-LIMITING PROCESSES

It is the commonest assumption concerning associative learning that repeated pairings of two events will eventually have diminishing incremental effects upon the learned association involved. Thus in a Pavlovian conditioning situation when a CS is consistently followed by a US over a number of trials, it is typically assumed (e.g., Estes & Burke, 1953; Hull, 1943; Spence, 1952b) that the successive increments in the associative strength of the CS will become progressively smaller as the existing associative strength of the CS increases. In a symmetrical fashion, it has frequently been assumed (e.g., Estes & Burke, 1953; Spence, 1936) that repeated exposures to a CS alone will have diminishing decremental effects upon the associative strength of that cue, as the existing associative strength decreases. How one embraces these assumptions may largely dictate one's theory of associative learning.

* An anomaly is the Habit, or sHr, variable in instrumental-reward learning, which was assumed (e.g., Spence, 1956) to increase with each S-R pairing, but was not assumed to decrease with each S-alone occurrence.

Saturation vs. variable-reinforcement views

Such assumptions, it seems, have generally been viewed in terms of a "saturation" principle, with the implication that the signaled event (the US or its absence) is stably effective, but that the signaling event (the CS) can acquire only limited values of associative strength. As the associative strength of the CS approaches its maximum value it is less possible to increment it, and as it approaches its minimum value it is less possible to decrement it.

The same assumptions, however, may also be appreciated to be consistent with a very different interpretation, which attributes the variation in associative change to variation in the potential effectiveness of a US or its absence, depending upon the associative strength of the cues which precede the signaled event. Thus, for example, repeated CS-US pairings may result in smaller and smaller increments in the associative strength of the CS, not because the CS becomes less and less capable of being incremented, but because the US becomes less and less reinforcing as it is announced by a cue which has increasingly more associative strength.

In order to clarify the distinction which is being made it will be helpful to consider an experimental paradigm from which different results would be expected according to the two treatments. Suppose we were to present *S* with successive pairings of a CS, A, followed by a US, until no further increments were observed in some index of the associative strength of the CS, such as a measured CR. Then suppose that on subsequent trial occasions a novel CS, X, were presented at the same time as A, so that both X and A were paired with the consequent US. If Cue A were saturated with associative strength, but the US remained potentially effective, one would expect as a result of such reinforced AX, compound, trials that although Cue A would not be further incremented, Cue X *would* acquire associative strength, and hence the tendency to elicit a CR when presented alone. Alternatively, if the US had become ineffective when preceded by Cue A, as a concomitant of the high degree of associative strength held by A, one would expect not only that Cue A would not be incremented, but that Cue X would also not acquire the tendency to elicit a CR when experienced in compound with A.

As long as concern is restricted to the change in associative strength resulting from training involving a single CS, the two formulations are indistinguishable. However, when an aggregation of stimuli is paired with a US, it becomes meaningful to question whether each individual CS will be incremented in associative strength according to the discrepancy from its own saturation point, or whether the increments in associative strength acquired by all of the CSs will commonly vary as would be expected if the consequent US were changing in effectiveness.

In fact, there are considerable data which indicate that an added cue, such as X in the situation as described above, would *not* acquire appreciable associative strength. This observation, which has come to be referred to as the "blocking effect," was first convincingly demonstrated by Kamin (1968, 1969) in Conditioned Emotional Response (CER) learning and has been replicated in other Pavlovian conditioning situations (e.g., Wagner, 1969b). Furthermore, it is clear (Kamin, 1968; Rescorla & Wagner, 1971) that the greater the associative strength of Cue A, prior to the introduction of AX, compound, training, the less will be the acquired tendency for X alone to elicit a CR. On the basis of such data Kamin (e.g., 1969, p. 293) has proposed that an "expected" US may not be reinforcing, and that in order for a US to promote learning it must be "surprising."

Unfortunately the theoretical significance of the "blocking effect" is clouded by the availability of yet another interpretation. A familiar acquisition-limiting proposition is that *S* has a limited attentional capacity so that attending to one cue may be assumed to decrease the likelihood that *S* will attend to, and hence learn about other available cues. Thus, it can be maintained that reinforcing A alone, prior to reinforcing X in compound with A, "blocks" conditioning to X by causing *S* to attend to A at the expense of attending to X. In fact, Lashley (1942) proposed just such an experimental design to demonstrate the operation of attentional processes. Thus although the blocking paradigm provides a convenient context in which to contrast the saturation and variable-reinforcement interpretations, we will need to consult other experimental arrangements to see how the latter interpretation also differs from an "attentional" modification of saturation theory.

A variable-reinforcement model of associative learning

The variable-reinforcement view which has been introduced can be suited to a variety of more specific interpretations (e.g., Kamin, 1968; Rescorla, 1969a; Wagner, 1969b). Although still highly tentative and incomplete, the most detailed version of such theory has been presented by Rescorla and Wagner (1971) and that version will generally be followed here. A number of important auxiliary assumptions become involved which are themselves open to question, but as far as possible an attempt will be made to avoid more specialized questions and to stress those features of the theory which are considered most central.

The major proposition is that when an aggregation of cues is paired with reinforcement or nonreinforcement, the change in associative strength occurring to each component cue is a linear function of the aggregate associative strength of all of the cues which stood in a conditioning relationship to (imprecisely, "preceded") the signaled event. Consider the case in which there are three cues, A, B, and C, presented in compound and followed by

US_1. Letting V_i represent the associative strength of the designated component or compound, it is assumed that the changes in associative strength, ΔV_i, of the several components may be specified as,

$$\Delta V_A = \alpha_A \beta_1 (\lambda_1 - V_{ABC}),$$
$$\Delta V_B = \alpha_B \beta_1 (\lambda_1 - V_{ABC}),$$
$$\Delta V_C = \alpha_C \beta_1 (\lambda_1 - V_{ABC}).$$

The several parameters in these equations are assumed to be determined by the properties of the specific CS and US under consideration. Each signaled event (including nonreinforcement) is assumed to be associated with a value of λ, which may be identified as the asymptotic level of associative strength that that event will support: as long as V_{ABC} is less than λ each component cue will be increased in associative strength; as long as V_{ABC} is greater than λ each component cue will be decreased in associative strength; and as V_{ABC} approaches λ the resulting ΔVs will approach zero. The value of λ associated with each US event must be empirically determined, but it is reasonable to assume that the λ associated with nonreinforcement is zero and that the value of λ increases with the intensity of the US (Rescorla & Wagner, 1971). The parameters α and β are simply rate parameters, the former dictated by the specific CS involved and the latter by the specific US. If restricted to the unit interval (Rescorla & Wagner, 1971), α and β jointly determine the proportion of the discrepancy between λ and V_{ABC} which will be realized in ΔV_i on each trial.

If a cue, A, were the only cue preceding reinforcement or nonreinforcement, the aggregate associative strength, represented in the above equations as V_{ABC} would equal the associative strength of A, and the changes in associative strength of A would be a linear function of the associative strength of A. Although in this particular instance the present formulation would thus be essentially identical to propositions advanced by Spence (1936, 1952b), two points should be noted. First, as an empirical supposition, it has been proposed (Rescorla & Wagner, 1971; Wagner, 1969b) that a cue can rarely be considered to occur in effective isolation: if no experimentally manipulatable cues are explicitly compounded with A, "situational" cues can be expected to play a similar role (see e.g., Dweck & Wagner, 1970). Secondly, it is important to recognize that in the general case, *ΔV_A is not assumed to be a function of V_A except as V_A influences the associative value of the aggregation of cues which includes A (i.e., V_{ABC}).*

The latter assumption should be appreciated as the critical point of departure from a saturation model. However, the consequences of this assumption will depend upon what additional assumptions are made concerning the allowable values of the component associative strengths and the manner in which these values combine. In order to be able most simply to account for the important facts that the combination of two separately trained cues can be (a) responded to more than either alone (when both are "excitatory," e.g., Hull, 1940), (b) responded to less than either alone (when both are "inhibitory," e.g., Konorski, 1948), or (c) reacted to with some level of responding intermediate to either alone (when one is "excitatory" and the other "inhibitory," e.g., Pavlov, 1927), it will be assumed that a cue may have either positive or negative associative value, and that the associative values of several components combine algebraically. Thus, Rescorla and Wagner (1971) have assumed that $V_{ABC} = V_A + V_B + V_C$.*

Some predictions

Once these assumptions are made, a large number of predictions become obvious. But it is of particular relevance to note here that regardless of the associative value of a component, that value should be potentially capable of being further incremented by reinforcement. That is, it is necessary only to reinforce said cue in compound with other cues of sufficient total "inhibitory" value to yield an aggregate V_{ABC} less than the λ associated with the reinforcing event. Likewise, regardless of the associative value of a component, it should be potentially capable of being further decremented by nonreinforcement. It should be necessary only to nonreinforce said cue in compound with other cues of sufficient total "excitatory" value to yield an aggregate V_{ABC} greater than the λ associated with nonreinforcement. To this extent the associative value accumulable by any component must be considered to be relatively unbounded.

If a component cue may have potentially unbounded positive or negative associative values, the simple combination assumption dictates the same for conceivable aggregations of components. However, the effect of compound stimulus training should be to bring the aggregate associative strength to a value determined by the λ of the reinforcing event involved, irrespective of the direction of this change. Thus, it may be anticipated that reinforced training will cause the associative value of a component cue to increase if the associative strength of the aggregation of cues is less than the λ associated with that reinforcement. However, the same reinforced training should cause the associative value of a component cue to be *decreased* if the associative strength of the aggregation of cues exceeds λ. It also may be anticipated that nonreinforced training will cause the associative value of a component to decrease if the strength of the aggregation of cues is greater than the λ associated with nonreinforcement. Again, however, the same nonreinforced training should cause the associative value of a component cue to be *increased* if the associative strength of the aggregation of cues is less than λ.

* It is possible that "configurational" cues resulting from the relationships among isolable components may also acquire associative strength as a result of compound stimulus training (e.g., Spence, 1952a). When such is the case the appropriate associative value of the configurational cues would be treated like any other component value, as adding to the total value of the aggregation.

This discussion hints at but the beginnings of a theory of simple associative learning applicable to Pavlovian conditioning. Many other variables must be assumed to influence the associative strength of a cue, still other variables will affect *S*'s behavior through nonassociative influences, and it would necessarily have to be specified how these interact to determine the degree of conditioned responding observed to a CS, with different specific response measures (Spence, 1956). Thus, for example, while it may be useful theoretically to assume that associative values are in principle unbounded, performance measures obviously are not. Many of these issues, however, can be bypassed at the present time by restricting our evaluation to experimental arrangements in which the importance of different plausible assumptions is minimized.

EMPIRICAL EVALUATIONS

Four related predictions (in addition to the blocking effect) have been pointed out which follow from the variable-reinforcement view of the Rescorla and Wagner (1971) model, and which run counter to the saturation view underlying conventional theories of associative learning (e.g., Estes & Burke, 1953; Hull, 1943; Spence, 1936). The first two predictions involve the basic implication that the associative strength of a cue is relatively unbounded: specifically it is predicted: (a) that the acquisition of inhibitory properties by a CS may be augmented by nonreinforcing said cue in compound with other, excitatory, cues, and (b) that the acquisition of excitatory properties by a CS may be augmented by reinforcing said cue in compound with other, inhibitory, cues. The remaining two predictions involve the equally basic implication that reinforcement and nonreinforcement *do not* consistently have respective strengthening and weakening effects upon associations. Under certain circumstances it is anticipated (a) that reinforcement may decrease the associative strength of a CS, and (b) that nonreinforcement may increase the associative strength of a CS.

Active inhibition

In presenting data which are relevant to these predictions, it is appropriate to begin with that prediction for which there has been some theoretical precedent (see e.g., Konorski, 1948 and pp. 207–208 below) and for which certain supporting data have been available for some time.

Rescorla (1969) has recently reviewed the literature concerned with the acquisition of active inhibitory properties by a cue, and has concluded that there is little evidence to indicate that simply nonreinforcing a CS in isolation is a sufficient condition to produce such effects. This is to be expected from the present theory, if it is assumed that the λ associated with nonreinforcement has a nonnegative value. If, for example, we continue to assume (Rescorla & Wagner, 1971) that the λ associated with nonreinforcement is zero, then the terminal associative value of a CS repeatedly nonreinforced in isolation should also approach zero.

If, however, a CS is nonreinforced when in compound with other cues, the associative value of that CS should continue to be modified until the associative strength of the *compound* is equal to zero. Thus, for example, when a nonreinforced compound is formed from a novel CS (that may be assumed initially to have a zero associative value) and an exitatory CS, both cues should concomitantly be decremented so that the former cue will necessarily become inhibitory. Furthermore, the magnitude of the negative associative tendency acquired in this case should be greater, the greater the excitatory tendency of the additional cues (i.e., the more negative is the term, $\lambda - V_{ABC}$).

Under some circumstances, in which reinforcement is regularly given in the absence of a nonreinforced CS, it is possible that "situational" cues will acquire excitatory value. Since these cues also occur in conjunction with the CS, the compound of CS plus situational cues may have sufficient excitatory value that nonreinforcement will lead to the acquisition of inhibitory properties by the CS (Rescorla, 1969; Rescorla & Wagner, 1971). However, the theory clearly indicates that the way to maximize the inhibitory value of a CS should be to nonreinforce the designated cue when it is presented in compound with other cues explicitly trained to have robust excitatory effects.

The latter procedure is, of course, exactly what is involved in the conventional paradigm which has proved especially effective in producing a "conditioned inhibitor": one CS, A, is consistently reinforced (+), and the compound of A, plus a second CS, X, is consistently nonreinforced (−). As a result of such A+, AX− training, Cue X may be demonstrated to acquire inhibitory properties, as seen in its tendency to reduce the level of responding in the presence of other independently trained, excitatory cues (e.g., Brown & Jenkins, 1967; Konorski, 1948; Pavlov, 1927).

Turning to the data from our laboratory, Reiss and Wagner (in press), in a study involving eyelid conditioning in the rabbit, found clear evidence that simply nonreinforcing a CS in isolation without concurrent reinforcement experience, in the fashion of the "latent-inhibition" procedure (e.g., Lubow & Moore, 1959; Siegel, 1969) does not result in a true inhibitory cue. That is, such a cue does not acquire the capacity to reduce the degree of responding to subsequently trained, excitatory CSs. At the same time, we have routinely been able to demonstrate (e.g., Rescorla & Wagner, 1971) that a CS which is consistently nonreinforced in compound with a cue which is otherwise reinforced, in the fashion of the "conditioned-inhibition" procedure, does become an inhibitory CS.

That this difference in the effects of nonreinforcement may be attributed to the differential associative strengths of the constellation of cues in which the CS of interest is embedded, has best been demonstrated in a study conducted by Maria Saavedra and reported by Rescorla and Wagner (1971).

Two groups of 20 rabbits were initially trained in an eyelid-conditioning situation with three separately presented CSs, which will be designated as A, B, and C. Each CS was of 1100-msec. duration, and when reinforced, overlapped and terminated with a 100-msec. 4.5-ma. shock, US, applied to the area of the eye. The A and B cues were designed to have different associative strengths as a result of different numbers of reinforced conditioning trials during this initial phase: A was designed to be a relatively strong cue (240 reinforced trials) and B to be relatively weak (8 reinforced trials). The C cue, which, as will be seen, was necessary for the test phase, was also highly trained (548 trials).

Following such training a novel cue, X, was introduced in compound with Cue A for one group of *S*s and in compound with Cue B for the other group of *S*s. In both instances the compound was nonreinforced. Sixty-four such nonreinforced trials were irregularly alternated with a similar number of trials in which the cue (A or B) that was paired with X continued to be presented alone and reinforced.

The X cue should have become a conditioned inhibitor as a result of either training schedule (e.g., Konorski, 1948; Pavlov, 1927). The question was whether or not X would become more inhibitory when nonreinforced in compound with the stronger A cue than when in compound with the weaker B cue. This result would be expected as $(\lambda - V_{AX})$ should have been initially more negative than $(\lambda - V_{BX})$. The prediction was evaluated by returning the C cue, and determining in both groups the reduction in responding to C when in compound with X. The final test phase involved 16 irregularly ordered reinforced presentations of C and of the CX compound.

For all *S*s in this study C was a 20/sec. flashing light, and X a vibratory stimulus in contact with the *S*'s chest. The A and B cues were dissimilar auditory stimuli (a 3160-hz. tone vs. an 11/sec. train of clicks, emanating from spatially separated sources) with the identification of the two stimuli as A and B being counterbalanced within the two experimental groups.

Figure 1 summarizes the results from the several training phases in each of the two groups separately, indicating the mean percentage of conditioned responses to the several cues during the last block of 68 total acquisition trials commonly involving Cues A, B, and C (Phase I); during the total sequence of differential treatment involving either A+, AX− in Group A, or B+, BX− in Group B (Phase II); and finally during the common test sequence with 16 C+ and 16 CX+ trials (Phase III). As may be seen, conditioned responding at the termination of the initial training phase in each group was appropriate to the experimental intention that A have a greater associative strength than B: prior to the introduction of X all *S*s were re-

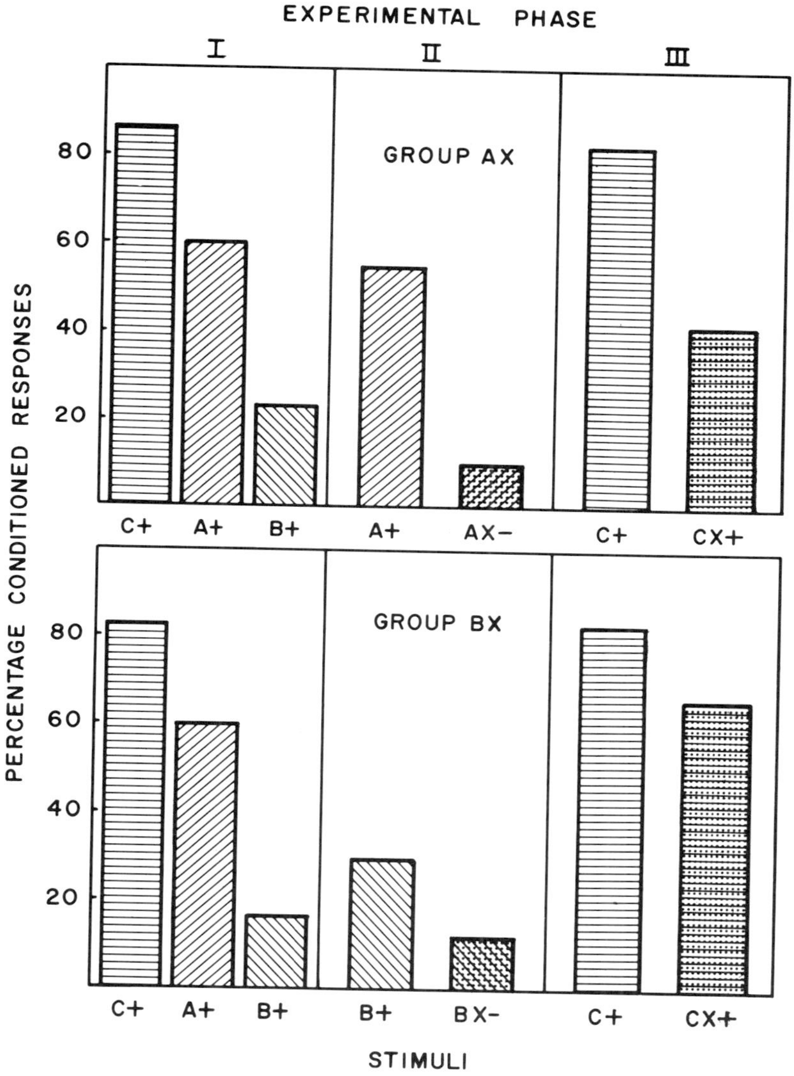

FIGURE 1. Percentage of conditioned eyeblink responses to several CS elements and their combinations, during three phases of training for two experimental groups of rabbits. Phase III testing showed Cue X to be a more potent conditioned inhibitor in Group AX than in Group BX, as a result of being previously nonreinforced in compound with a stronger excitatory cue.

sponding at a higher level to their A than to their B cue. A similar difference between A and B was continued in the performance of the separate groups in the subsequent conditioned inhibition-training phase.

The major data of interest are from the final test phase. During this phase the two groups responded at the same high level to the C cue alone. The presentation of the X cue along with C, however, decreased this responding considerably more in the case of Group AX (which had experienced the nonreinforcement of X in compound with the relatively strong A cue) than in the case of Group BX (which had experienced the nonreinforcement of X in compound with the relatively weak B cue). This predicted difference in the conditioned inhibitory effect of X in the two groups was highly reliable ($F = 8.32$, $df = 1/32$, $p < .01$).

Supernormal conditioning

It would appear, in light of the above data, that there is a firm basis for acknowledging that the acquisition of inhibitory properties by a CS may be augmented by nonreinforcing said cue in compound with other excitatory cues. There is no similar extensive background of data, however, to support the companion prediction that the acquisition of excitatory properties by a CS may be augmented by reinforcing said cue in compound with other inhibitory cues.

There are several studies related to this prediction (e.g., Kamin, 1969; Rescorla & Wagner, 1971; Wagner, 1969b) which show that when an AX compound is reinforced, the degree of associative strength accruing to X alone varies inversely with the associative strength of A. In these previous instances, however, it has either been the case that the associative strength of A has been independently arranged to vary only between some positive value and zero (e.g., Kamin, 1969; Wagner, 1969b), or that comparisons have been lacking (Rescorla & Wagner, 1971) which might demonstrate that *reinforcing AX when A is inhibitory has more of an incremental effect upon the associative strength of X than if X were simply reinforced alone.* This latter possibility, which might be referred to as evidence of "supernormal conditioning" (analogous to the "supernormal" inhibitory learning seen when a CS is nonreinforced in compound with other excitatory cues, as compared to being nonreinforced in isolation) is the strong prediction demanded by the theory.

A recent experiment conducted in collaboration with Maria Saavedra was designed to evaluate this expectation. In procedural details the study was similar to that already described employing eyelid conditioning in the rabbit. In this case, however, the first phase of training for all *S*s was designed so as to develop an inhibitory element. Ten *S*s in each of two groups received 640 conditioning trials. On half of these trials and in irregular order, one CS, B, was presented alone and reinforced; on the remainder of the trials a compound CS, consisting of Cue B plus a second cue, A, was nonreinforced. For half of the *S*s in each group A was a 20/sec. flashing light and B a vibratory stimulus. For the remaining *S*s, this designation was reversed. As a result of such B+, AB– discrimination training, Cue A should have become a conditioned inhibitor.

Immediately following the completion of this training phase, one group of *S*s received 64 trials in which a 3160-hz. tone CS, X, was presented in isolation and reinforced; the second group received 64 trials in which X was presented in compound with A, and the AX compound reinforced. Both groups were then tested (over a total of 64 reinforced trials) for their responsiveness to X alone. According to our theoretical expectation, reinforcing X in compound with the inhibitory A cue should have produced supernormal conditioning to X, exceeding the degree of conditioning resulting from the reinforcement of X in isolation.

This expectation was confirmed. Figure 2 summarizes the conditioned responding observed to the several cues in each of the two groups over the last 16 trials of the initial B+, AB– training (Phase I), the last 16 trials with either AX+ or X+ (Phase II), and finally, the immediately following 16 test trials with X alone (Phase III). The two groups not only performed similarly during Phase I of training, but by the termination of the differential-treatment phase were responding, respectively, at similar levels to the AX compound or to X alone. Quite different degrees of responding were observed, however, in Phase III. While there was little change in the responding to X alone in Group X between the end of Phase II and the adjacent first 16 trials of Phase III, the withdrawal of the A cue in Group AX at this point was accompanied by an abrupt increase in the level of responding, so that there was considerably more test responding to X alone in Group AX than in Group X. The latter difference between the two groups persisted over the total 64 trials of the test phase and was statistically reliable ($t = 2.09$, $df = 18$, $p < .025$).

When reinforcement decreases associations

The further implications of the variable-reinforcement model which are of present concern involve those paradoxical instances in which reinforcement is expected to decrease the associative strength of a CS, and nonreinforcement is expected to increase this strength. The assumption that a component CS will be incremented in strength whenever the quantity $\lambda - V_{ABC}$ is positive, and decremented whenever the quantity $\lambda - V_{ABC}$ is negative, regardless of the value of λ or of the associative strength of the individual component, anticipates such paradoxical instances. This basic feature of the model is in fact critical to many of the relatively complex derivations made by Rescorla and Wagner (1971). To the degree that such derivations are consistent with existing data, there is support for the basic assumption

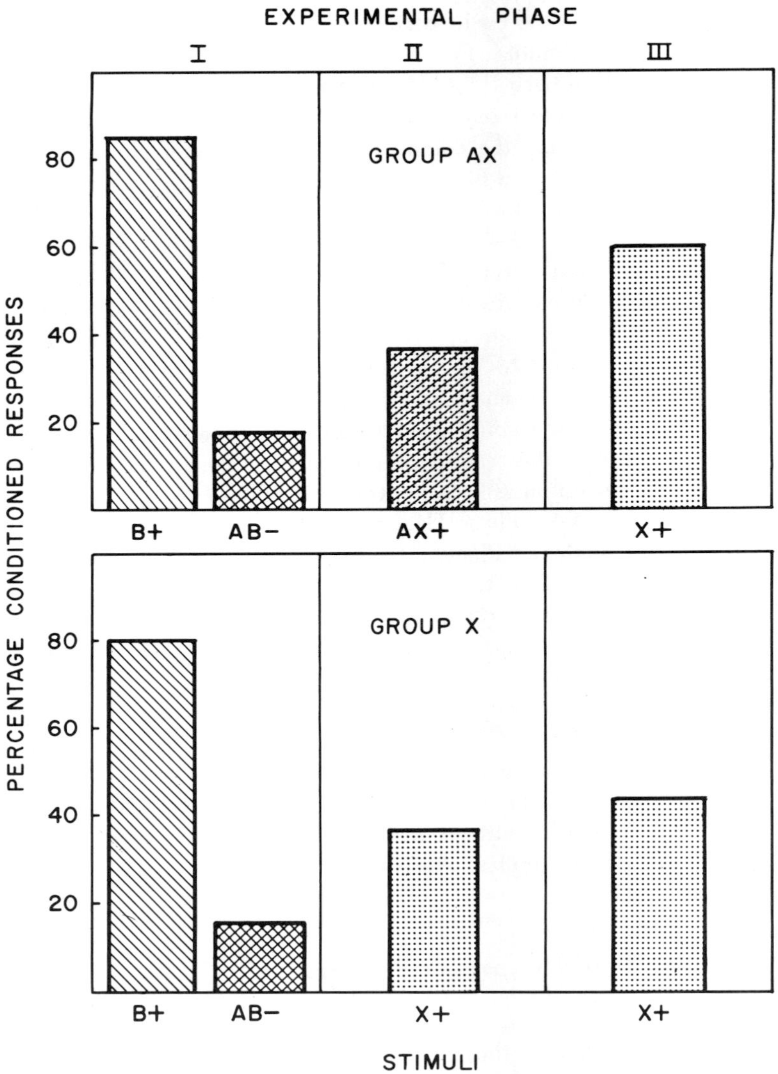

FIGURE 2. Percentage of conditioned eyeblink responses to several CS elements and their combinations during three phases of training for two experimental groups of rabbits. Phase III testing showed Cue X to have acquired a greater excitatory tendency in Group AX than in Group X, as a result of being reinforced in compound with an inhibitory element as compared to being reinforced in isolation.

involved. Yet, it is important to attempt to demonstrate the assumed process in as direct a manner as possible.

The several related studies to which I will subsequently refer were all conducted with rats in CER conditioning. The procedure always involved a standard format in which *S*s were first trained to bar press for food reward on a variable-interval schedule. Conditioning sessions involving the appropriate arrangement of various CSs and a foot-shock US were then administered, during which access to the bar and food was prevented. Finally, the degree of conditioning to the CSs of interest was evaluated in separate test sessions by presenting such cues for the first time while *S*s were bar pressing, and determining the percentage by which bar pressing was reduced in the presence of the CS, as compared to the rate of bar pressing in the immediately preceding interval. During training and testing each CS presentation was of 2 min. duration, and when reinforced, overlapped and terminated with a .5-second US.

That reinforcement may have a decremental effect upon the associative strength of a cue was evaluated in an experiment conducted with the assistance of Carol Dweck and Gayle Morse. Basically the strategy was to reinforce *separately* each of two cues, A and B, over a sufficient number of trials so that the resulting associative value of each could be expected to be relatively asymptotic. At this point, V_A and V_B should *each* have approximated the λ associated with the US involved. Then Cues A and B were additionally reinforced over a further block of trials, with exactly the same US, but now with the two cues presented in compound. If, prior to the latter training, V_A and V_B each approximated λ, V_{AB}, according to the simple summation rule, should have been greater than λ, and $\lambda - V_{AB}$ should have been negative. In this instance V_A and V_B and hence V_{AB} should have been *decremented* on each reinforced compound trial until V_{AB} became equal to λ.

In order to avoid the influence of repeated test sessions upon the measured associative strength, separate groups of 16 *S*s were employed. Group A+B+ received 40 A+ and 40 B+ trials, while Group A+B+/AB+ received these same 80 trials, followed by 40 AB+ compound trials. Each group then received 16 nonreinforced test trials in which the suppressing tendency of the AB compound was evaluated.

To provide appropriate comparison conditions which could be employed to evaluate whether V_{AB} in Group A+B+ was indeed higher than λ, and in Group A+B+/AB+ decreased toward λ, two additional groups of 16 *S*s were run and similarly tested. These groups received AB+ compound training throughout: Group AB+ for 80 trials, and Group AB+/AB+ for an additional 40 trials. It was expected that the terminal associative strength of V_{AB} should have been relatively similar in Group AB+ and Group AB+/AB+, each approaching λ. In comparison the strength of V_{AB} was expected to be higher in Group A+B+ but reduced toward the level of the compound groups by the additional 40 compound trials administered to Group A+B+/AB+.

Incidentally, it should be apparent that the comparison provided by Group A+B+ and Group AB+ represents a variation upon the common "overshadowing" experiment. It has frequently been observed (e.g., Miles & Jenkins, 1965; Razran, 1965) that an isolable CS is less effective after having been reinforced in a compound containing other excitatory elements than when trained alone. This finding, which is consistent with the present formulation, has typically been seen as indicative of an attentional deficit in the compound condition, or, even more simply, as indicative of differential generalization decrements: a group which has specifically been trained to respond to an element alone should perform at a higher level to that element alone during testing than a group which has been trained with only a generalized version of the test element (as it might be viewed when embedded in a compound of additional cues). What the present theory predicts, however, is that an element-trained group (A+B+) will also perform at a higher level to a *compound* of separately trained elements than will a group (AB+) specifically trained with respect to that compound.

For all *S*s in this experiment Cue A was a 3/second flashing light and Cue B was a 2500-hz. tone. The intensity of the US (.5 ma.) was specifically selected as one which would generally support only modest levels of conditioned suppression in the situation employed, and which would therefore favor the detection of any elevated V_{AB} that might be present in Group A+B+.

Figure 3 presents the mean percentage conditioned suppression, over successive blocks of four test trials for each of the four experimental groups. Since all tests were nonreinforced, the conditioned suppression is seen to extinguish. But, as predicted, Group A+B+ showed substantially more suppression to the AB compound than did Group A+B+/AB+, which was treated identically except for the subsequent experience of 40 additional reinforced compound trials. The latter group did not differ notably from either of the two compound-trained groups. Statistical comparisons among the four groups revealed a significantly greater degree of suppression in Group A+B+ than in any of the remaining three groups over the first eight test trials ($p < .001$ in each case), while the minor differences among Groups AB+, AB+/AB+, and A+B+/AB+ did not approach statistical reliability.

When nonreinforcement increases associations

Under conditions suggested by the model, it appears that the pairing of a CS and US may have a decremental effect upon the learned association between the two events. Data which have already been presented should make obvious one set of circumstances under which it would also seem highly likely that the companion phenomenon (nonreinforcement acting to *raise* the associative value of a CS) could occur. That is, suppose that as a result of B+, AB− discrimination training, Cue A had acquired effectiveness as a

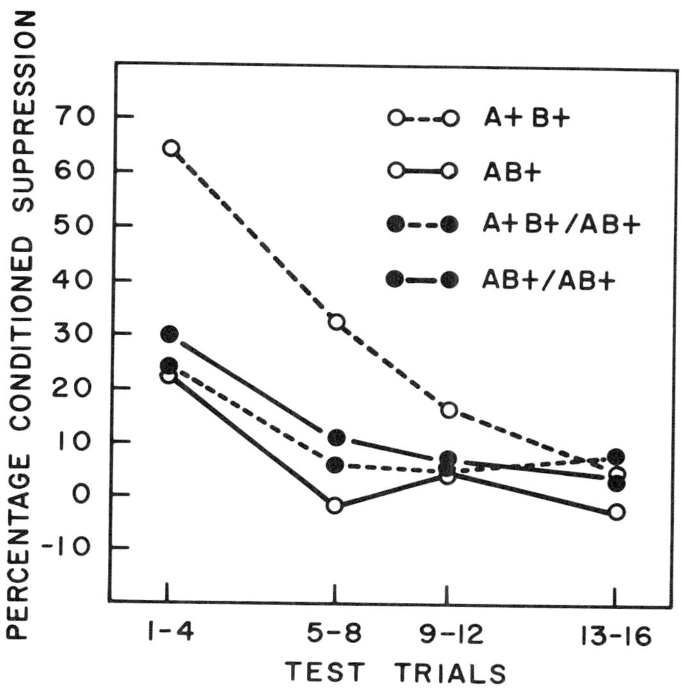

FIGURE 3. Percentage of conditioned suppression of bar pressing to an AB, compound, CS over blocks of nonreinforced test trials, in each of four groups of rats. The groups are distinguished by whether they had been conditioned separately to the elements of the compound (A+B+) or conditioned to the compound (AB+). See text.

conditioned inhibitor, presumably indicative of a negative V_A. Further nonreinforcement of Cue A *in isolation* should be expected to increase V_A toward zero, with a resulting decrease in the tendency of A to act as a conditioned inhibitor.

A recent CER experiment in our laboratory confirmed this expectation. Briefly, the design first involved the training of *two* conditioned inhibitors according to a C+, AC−, BC− discrimination procedure, in which C was a flashing light and A and B different auditory cues. Then Cue A was nonreinforced alone over a series of trials, prior to testing for the suppressing effects of C, AC, and BC upon bar pressing. Cue A was observed to act less as a "conditioned inhibitor" than did Cue B. That is, in testing Cue C produced nearly complete suppression; the addition of Cue A did little to interfere with this effect, while the addition of Cue B substantially removed it.

That an inhibitory trained cue can thus apparently be "neutralized" as a result of nonreinforcement could be viewed as a special case, and as not necessarily reflecting upon the adequacy of the model, in terms of the more general conditions under which nonreinforcement is assumed to have an incremental effect. An experiment by Rescorla (1971) is therefore somewhat more provocative. In this experiment a novel CS, X, was introduced in compound with a previously trained conditioned inhibitor, A, and the AX compound was nonreinforced. Since V_{AX} should initially have been negative, $\lambda - V_{AX}$ during nonreinforcement should have had a positive value, and the associative strength of the inhibitory element, A, should have been incremented toward zero, as in the preceding experiment. But, in this case V_X should also have been incremented on such trials, so that nonreinforcement should have been seen not simply to neutralize an inhibitory cue but to enhance the excitatory value of a novel cue.

Following the usual bar-press training, four groups of 16 *S*s received two phases of CER conditioning, prior to testing. In Phase I, two groups were trained so that a 2/second flashing light CS, A, should have become a conditioned inhibitor: 36 reinforced trials with a 1800 hz. tone CS, B, were irregularly alternated with 36 nonreinforced trials with Cues A and B in compound. In the remaining two groups Phase I training was calculated a conditioned inhibitor: 36 reinforced trials with a 1800-hz. tone CS, B, was presented alone, being reinforced on 36 occasions and nonreinforced on 36 occasions. In the other case, 36 B and 36 AB trials were presented, but all trials were nonreinforced and the US was never experienced.

During Phase II all *S*s received 24 *nonreinforced* presentations of a novel auditory cue, X, consisting of a 250-hz. tone which was interrupted once per second. For one of the two groups in which A had been developed as a condition inhibitor, X was nonreinforced in compound with A (Group B+AB−/AX−). For the remaining such group, X was nonreinforced alone and A was nonreinforced alone on an additional 24 occasions (Group B+AB−/X−). Each of the two groups for which A was presumably a neutral stimulus at the end of Phase I (i.e., Groups B+B−/AX− and B−AB−/AX−) received the same AX nonreinforced trials as did Group B+AB−/AX−.

The expectation from the model was that Cue X, as a result of the Phase II nonreinforcements, would have a greater excitatory strength in Group B+AB−/AX− than in the remaining three groups. This was evaluated over eight suppression test trials, of which Trials 2, 4, 6, and 8 were *reinforced*.

Figure 4 presents the data from the Rescorla experiment replotted in terms of mean percentage suppression, similar to Figure 3. In this case it may be seen that all groups began with X having little suppressive tendency. But with a portion of the trials reinforced, the CER was rapidly acquired. The notable effect is that observable suppression to X was acquired more quickly in Group B+AB−/AX− than in the remaining three groups. The single reinforcement which occurred (on Trial 2) prior to the end of the

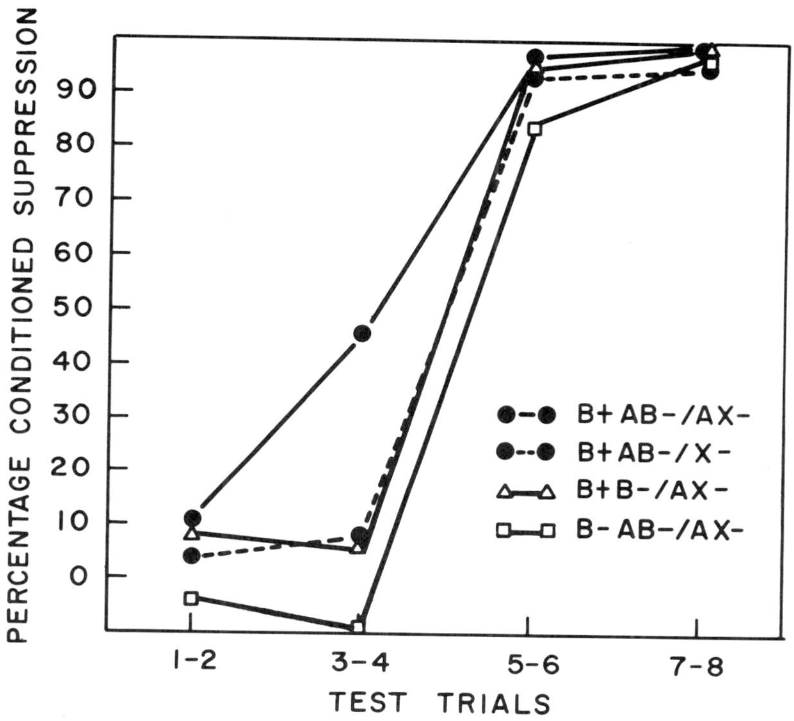

FIGURE 4. Percentage of conditioned suppression of bar pressing to a CS, X, over blocks of partially reinforced test trials, in each of four groups of rats. The groups are distinguished by whether Cue X had previously been nonreinforced alone, in compound with a conditioned inhibitor, or in compound with a neutral cue. See text. (After Rescorla, 1971).

measurement period on Trial 4 was sufficient to promote a sizeable suppression in Group B+AB−/AX− during Trials 3 and 4, but had no similar immediate observable influence on the other groups. Rescorla (1971) reports that this predicted difference was statistically reliable ($H = 11.42$, $p < .01$; beyond this point all groups showed nearly complete suppression.

POSSIBLE MECHANISMS FOR A VARIABLE-REINFORCEMENT PROCESS

The data reviewed in the preceding section join other evidence (e.g., Rescorla & Wagner, 1971; Wagner, 1969a, 1969b) to suggest the measure of deductive advantage enjoyed by the type of theory proposed by Wagner

(1969b) and by Rescorla and Wagner (1971). There appears to be considerable reason tentatively to favor variations in the effectiveness of reinforcement and nonreinforcement, as compared to a saturation process, as the acquisition-limiting factor in associative learning, and accordingly to recast our views concerning the formation of elementary associations.

Yet it is reasonable to ask whether or not the variable-reinforcement proposition might not be rationalized in terms of some more familiar process. There have been a number of conceptual frameworks within which certain variable-reinforcement effects could comfortably be accommodated. And, perhaps they may point to viable ways of accounting for what has simply been postulated as a basic proposition in the Rescorla and Wagner model.

Frustration theory

Spence (1960, Ch. 6) proposed that in appetitional-learning situations the decremental effects of nonreinforcement might be understood in terms of the degree of "frustration" produced. Even in his earliest treatment (1936), Spence assumed that there would be no decremental (inhibitory) effect upon the associative strength of a cue unless the nonreinforcement of that cue was frustrating. In subsequent developments of frustration theory (e.g., 1960, Ch. 6) he made it clear that "frustration" referred to an assumed unitary response-state of the organism, and that the intensity of the frustration reaction produced by nonreinforcement was assumed to increase with increasing anticipation of reinforcement.

It might thus be reasonable to assume that when an aggregation of cues, producing some total anticipation of reinforcement, is followed by nonreinforcement, there would result some total state of frustration, the intensity of which would determine the common degree of inhibition accruing to each of the antedating component cues. Wagner (1963), in fact, followed very analogous reasoning from frustration theory in assuming and demonstrating that active frustrative properties might be acquired by a formerly neutral cue, if that cue were nonreinforced in compound with other cues which elicit anticipation of reinforcement. Such arguments are in line with the treatment of nonreinforcement found in the Rescorla and Wagner (1971) model.

The full implication of this reasoning, however, was never explicitly incorporated into Spence's theorizing. Spence apparently continued to assume, in general accordance with his 1936 treatment, that when an aggregation of cues is nonreinforced, the excitatory strength of each component cue would be decremented, in relationship to the degree to which *its own* nonreinforcement contributed to the total frustrative state. Beyond this, of course, it should also be recognized that the frustration analysis was not meant to apply to aversive learning situations, which have provided the majority of the data cited in the present chapter, and includes no reference to symmetrical variations in the effectiveness of reinforcement.

Center-activity theory

Konorski (1948) was particularly impressed with the difference in the effects of nonreinforcing a CS alone and of nonreinforcing a CS in the context of other excitatory cues, as discussed on p. 194 above. In order to account for this difference, as well as several other facts of Pavlovian training, he presented an analysis of inhibitory learning which shares many features with the model presented here.

According to Konorski, a cue which has a positive associative tendency with respect to a given US is one which leads to an acquired tendency to excite the neural "center" appropriate to that US. As a result of appropriate paired activation of the CS and US centers, excitatory connections are presumably formed between the former and the latter, so that presentation of the CS will come anticipatorily to excite the same center activated by the US.

But, when such an excitatory CS is presented and is *not* followed by the appropriate US, Konorski assumed that the aroused excitation of the US center will rapidly diminish over time. The crucial proposition which Konorski advanced was that the necessary and sufficient condition for decremental associative learning is that a CS be followed in close temporal contiguity by such a fall in excitation of a US center—regardless of the stimulation which initially gave rise to the excitation. When this contiguous experience occurs the CS center is assumed to form inhibitory connections with the US center, which may then function, upon presentation of the CS, antagonistically to any excitatory influences upon that US center.

Given this set of assumptions, it follows that an excitatory cue which is consistently nonreinforced in isolation will eventually be neutralized, but will not acquire a net inhibitory effect. As long as the CS when presented leads to excitation of the US center, nonreinforcement will occasion a fall in this excitation, and an increase in inhibitory connections. But when the inhibitory connections between the CS and US centers are sufficiently developed so that the CS no longer excites the US center, nonreinforcement will no longer be associated with the requisite fall in excitation, and no further inhibitory connections will be formed.

If, however, a neutral CS, which itself has no tendency to excite the US center, is presented in compound with other excitatory cues, so that the net effect is an initial excitation of the US center, then nonreinforcement will involve the fall in excitation necessary to produce new inhibitory connections between each of the cues and the respective US center. In such fashion an elementary CS, nonreinforced in compound with other cues, is assumed to be capable of developing a preponderance of inhibitory connections, and hence becoming an effective conditioned inhibitor.

The similarity of this treatment of inhibitory learning to that described in the Rescorla and Wagner (1971) model should be obvious, even to the extent of anticipating greater conditioned inhibition, the greater the excitatory tendency of the remaining cues in the compound, as seen in the Saavedra experiment (pp. 196–198 above).

It is interesting that Konorski (1948) also suggested that the incremental effects of *reinforcement* depend upon the CS being followed in close temporal contiguity by a *rise* in excitation in the US center. Since CSs and compounds of CSs of different net associative strengths are assumed to lead to different degrees of excitation of the US center prior to reinforcement, it would be reasonable to assume further that a CS-US pairing would have a variable incremental effect upon the associative strength of the cues involved, depending upon the ability of the specific intensity of US employed to raise the level of excitation of the appropriate center beyond that already produced by the CS. Given this assumption it would be difficult to distinguish such a "center-activity" theory from the general formulation which has been offered by Rescorla and Wagner. It would clearly anticipate the blocking effect (pp. 190–191), and, granted appropriate assumptions concerning the combination of excitatory and inhibitory influences, would also be compatible with the finding of supernormal conditioning (pp. 198–199), as well as those instances in which reinforcement and nonreinforcement have apparent paradoxical effects (pp. 199–205).

On the basis of available evidence, however, Konorski (1948, p. 141) explicitly rejected such a treatment of excitatory learning as symmetrical to inhibitory learning. He preferred to assume that reinforcement invariably produces a rise in excitation of the US center of such magnitude that the excitatory value of the cues which precede it is effectively inconsequential. The degree of excitatory learning to each CS was assumed instead to be limited by the saturation point of that cue.

Variable-rehearsal theory

When first introducing the variable-reinforcement notion on p. 191, reference was made to Kamin's seminal proposal (1969, p. 293) that an "expected" US may not be reinforcing, and that in order for a US to promote learning it must be "surprising." Kamin (1969), and more recently Atkinson and Wickens (1969), have elaborated upon this notion to suggest similar mechanisms by which "surprisingness" may influence associative learning.

Ignoring the primitive and transient memory features of the so-called sensory-register, it is common to assume (e.g., Atkinson & Shiffrin, 1968) that information concerning previously experienced events may be retained in memory for future use in either of two stores. A short-term-store (STS) is assumed to hold a limited amount of information temporarily, while the long-term-store (LTS) is assumed to represent a relatively permanent memory of inexhaustible capacity.

Given this distinction, it can be acknowledged that the associative phenomena with which we have been concerned, involving retention over long intertrial intervals, implicate the storage of information in LTS. But it is generally assumed (e.g., Atkinson & Shiffrin, 1968) that the transfer of information to LTS occurs only while that information is resident in STS, and that there are a variety of control processes which influence both the length of time information is held in STS and the content of what is transferred. For example, information in STS may be "rehearsed," and thereby held available longer for transfer to LTS.

Other control processes may also influence the degree to which additional incoming information is excluded from STS, and the amount and kind of information retrieved from LTS to be held in juxtaposition to new information. These factors together may influence the effective distinctiveness and retrievability of the consequent memory image in LTS.

There are many ways in which this complex formulation might address the variable-reinforcement phenomenon. Atkinson and Wickens (1969) have suggested that CS input leads to the formation of a prediction based upon this input and correlated information retrieved from LTS. The comparison of this prediction with the subsequent occurring events (e.g., a US or its absence) then determines whether information about the episode will or will not be transferred to LTS. Specifically, they state that

> the extent to which the outcome fails to agree with the prediction determines the degree and nature of the study the item receives. *Usually large discrepancies between the prediction and outcome dispose the subject to apply control processes that maintain the relevant information in STS and induce the transfer of information to LTS.* . . . The result is to reduce the disparity between the outcome and information now stored in LTS so that if the same stimulus and outcome were to be presented again, the discrepancy would be smaller than the original one [pp. 34–35, italics added].

In the same vein Kamin (1969, p. 293) has suggested that for an increment in an associative connection to occur, it is necessary that the US instigate some "mental work," involving a scanning of its memory store of recent stimulus input. And, that this will occur only when the US is "unpredicted" or "surprising."

Such an approach is also congenial to the Rescorla and Wagner (1971) model. The acquisition-limiting process does not involve any saturation capacity in LTS, but rather the likelihood that reinforcement or nonreinforcement will promote storage, depending upon the degree to which they are predicted by the preceding cues. In contrast, moreover, to Konorski's center-activity treatment, this approach also suggests a rather new set of questions to be asked of Pavlovian conditioning. For example, will there be unique evidence of the short-term availability of the association immediately following a CS-US episode, and will the temporal persistence of this evidence vary systematically with the predictedness of the US? Or, will manipulations which might be thought to otherwise facilitate or interfere with the rehearsal and transfer (consolidation) processes (e.g., McGaugh, 1966; Ost, 1969) interact appropriately with the predictedness of the US, to determine the degree of relatively permanent associative learning?

As stimulating as this account is, however, it does not *in itself* allow for the deduction of the range of data presented on pp. 194–205 or similar data presented by Wagner (1969b) and Rescorla and Wagner (1971). The Rescorla and Wagner model incorporates a number of important detailed assumptions, which in effect specify what "predictions" *S* will make with various aggregations of cues, and how each of the component predictors will be modified so that, as Atkinson and Wickens (1969) say, "If the same stimulus and outcome were to be presented again, the discrepancy would be smaller than the original one [p. 35]." Indeed, both Kamin (1969) and Atkinson and Wickens (1969) appear to favor somewhat different auxiliary assumptions that are less well calculated to account for the data which have been presented here.

Other mechanisms

The several mechanisms which have been cited above by no means represent an exhaustive list of the ways in which a variable-reinforcement process might be rationalized. Space permitting, one might, for example, also profitably consider various tenets of dissonance theory (e.g., Lawrence & Festinger, 1962), attribution theory (e.g., Kelley, 1967), or preparatory-response theory (e.g., Perkins, 1955), among others.

Those which have been cited, however, may be viewed as representative of the range of approaches available, and as offering assurance that investigators working in different data areas and within very different conceptual frameworks have frequently entertained some form of a variable-reinforcement mechanism. What is urged by the treatment of Wagner (1969b) and Rescorla and Wagner (1971) is that we view such mechanisms not as complications to be added to our theories of learning, but as basic and central determiners of the elementary associations involved.

CONCLUDING COMMENTS

It has been useful to call attention to a "saturation" premise that is implicit in conventional treatments of associative learning, and to contrast this viewpoint with an alternative acquisition-limiting notion that we have referred to as a "variable-reinforcement" view. Granting the evidence reviewed on pp. 194–205, it has further seemed appropriate to exemplify the various theoretical mechanisms that could be held responsible for variations in the effectiveness of reinforcement and nonreinforcement, depending upon the degree to which these events are signaled by the preceding cues.

Our theories concerning the formation of elementary associations have perhaps been unfortunately restricted by certain presystematic views. To escape this restriction it is helpful to attempt to make the underlying notions explicit, however inelegant they may then appear, and to attempt to indicate how alternatives may be accommodated within familiar theoretical languages.

A point concerning appropriate emphasis is in order, however, and particularly so in the context of this commemorative volume. Spence was frequently critical of abstract speculations concerning theoretical mechanisms which were misleading or distracted from the critical features of a theory. Thus he pointed out that his own quantitative assumptions concerning the strengthening and weakening of associations were indifferent to such issues as whether S-S or S-R associations were formed (Spence, 1950), how to construe the structure of the associations (Spence, 1952b), or how the reinforcing stimulus provides for the hypothetical changes (Spence, 1956). Likewise it should be recognized that the critical and only essential features of the theory which has been described here are contained in the specific quantitative assumptions which we have made concerning the strengthening and weakening of associations. It is this set of quantitative assumptions which is capable of integrating the findings described herein, as well as many additional facts of Pavlovian conditioning (e.g., Rescorla & Wagner, 1971; Wagner, 1969a, 1969b). Hopefully, it may also point toward a more generally adequate theory concerning the formation of elementary associations.

REFERENCES

Atkinson, R. C., & Shriffrin, R. M. Human memory: A proposed system and its control processes. In K. W. Spence, & J. T. Spence (Eds.), *The psychology of learning and motivation: Advances in research and theory.* Vol. 2. New York: Academic Press, 1968. Pp. 89–196.

Atkinson, R. C., & Wickens, T. D. Human memory and the concept of reinforcement. Technical Report Number 145, Institute for Mathematical Studies in the Social Sciences. Stanford University, Stanford, California, 1969.

Brown, P. L., & Jenkins, H. M. Conditioned inhibition and excitation in operant discrimination learning. *Journal of Experimental Psychology,* 1967, *75,* 255–266.

Dweck, C. S., & Wagner, A. R. Situational cues and correlation between conditioned stimulus and unconditioned stimulus as determinants of the conditioned emotional response. *Psychonomic Science*, 1970, *18*, 145–147.

Estes, W. K., & Burke, C. J. A theory of stimulus variability in learning. *Psychological Review*, 1953, *60*, 276–286.

Hull, C. L. Explorations in the patterning of stimuli conditioned to the G. S. R. *Journal of Experimental Psychology*, 1940, *27*, 95–110.

Hull, C. L. *Principles of behavior*. New York: Appleton-Century, 1943.

Hull, C. L. Simple qualitative discrimination learning. *Psychological Review*, 1950, *57*, 303–313.

Kamin, L. J. Attention-like processes in classical conditioning. In M. R. Jones (Ed.), *Miami Symposium on the prediction of behavior: Aversive stimulation*. Miami: University of Miami Press, 1968. Pp. 9–31.

Kamin, L. J. Predictability, surprise, attention, and conditioning. In R. Church, & B. Campbell (Eds.), *Punishment and aversive behavior*. New York: Appleton-Century-Crofts, 1969. Pp. 279–296.

Kelley, H. H. Attribution theory in social psychology. In D. Levine (Ed.), *Nebraska symposium on motivation*. Lincoln: University of Nebraska Press, 1967. Pp. 192–238.

Konorski, J. *Conditioned reflexes and neuron organization*. Cambridge, England: The University Press, 1948.

Lashley, K. S. An examination of the "continuity theory" as applied to discrimination learning. *Journal of Genetic Psychology*, 1942, *26*, 241–265.

Lawrence, D. H., & Festinger, L. *Deterrents and reinforcement*. Stanford: Stanford University Press, 1962.

Lubow, R. E., & Moore, A. V. Latent inhibition: The effect of non-reinforced preexposure to the conditioned stimulus. *Journal of Comparative and Physiological Psychology*, 1959, *52*, 415–419.

McGaugh, J. L. Time-dependent processes in memory storage. *Science*, 1966, *153*, 1351–1358.

Miles, C. G., & Jenkins, H. M. Overshadowing and blocking in discriminative operant conditioning. Paper presented at the meeting of the Psychonomic Society, Chicago, October, 1965.

Ost, J. W. P. Consolidation disruption and inhibition in classical conditioning. *Psychological Bulletin*, 1969, *72*, 379–383.

Pavlov, I. P. *Conditioned reflexes*. London: Oxford University Press, 1927.

Perkins, C. C., Jr. The stimulus conditions which follow learned responses. *Psychological Review*, 1955, *62*, 341–348.

Razran, G. Empirical codifications and specific theoretical implications of compound-stimulus conditioning: Perception. In W. F. Prokasy (Ed.), *Classical conditioning*. New York: Appleton-Century-Crofts, 1965. Pp. 226–248.

Reiss, S., & Wagner, A. R. CS habituation produces a "Latent Inhibition Effect" but no active "Conditioned Inhibition." *Learning and Motivation*, in press.

Rescorla, R. A. Conditioned inhibition of fear. In N. J. Mackintosh, & W. K. Honig (Eds.), *Fundamental issues in associative learning*. Halifax: Dalhousie University Press, 1969. Pp. 65–89. (a)

Rescorla, R. A. Pavlovian conditioned inhibition. *Psychological Bulletin*, 1969, *72*, 77–94. (b)

Rescorla, R. A. Variation in the effectiveness of reinforcement and nonreinforcement following prior inhibitory training. *Learning and Motivation,* 1971, *2,* 113–123.

Rescorla, R. A., & Wagner, A. R. A theory of Pavlovian conditioning: Variations in the effectiveness of reinforcement and nonreinforcement. In A. Black, & W. F. Prokasy (Eds.), *Classical conditioning II.* New York: Appleton-Century-Crofts, 1971.

Runquist, W. N., & Spence, K. W. Performance in eyelid conditioning as a function of unconditioned stimulus duration. *Journal of Experimental Psychology,* 1959, *57,* 249–252.

Siegel, S. Effect of CS habituation on eyelid conditioning. *Journal of Comparative and Physiological Psychology,* 1969, *68,* 245–248.

Spence, K. W. The nature of discrimination learning in animals. *Psychological Review,* 1936, *43,* 427–449.

Spence, K. W. The differential response in animals to stimuli varying within a single dimension. *Psychological Review,* 1937, *44,* 430–444.

Spence, K. W. Gradual versus sudden solution of discrimination problems by chimpanzees. *Journal of Comparative Psychology,* 1938, *25,* 213–224.

Spence, K. W. Cognitive versus stimulus-response theories of learning. *Psychological Review,* 1950, *57,* 159–172.

Spence, K. W. The nature of the response in discrimination learning. *Psychological Review,* 1952, *59,* 89–93. (a)

Spence, K. W. Mathematical formulations of learning phenomena. *Psychological Review,* 1952, *59,* 152–160. (b)

Spence, K. W. *Behavior theory and conditioning.* New Haven: Yale University Press, 1956.

Spence, K. W. *Behavior theory and learning.* Englewood Cliffs, N.J.: Prentice-Hall, 1960.

Wagner, A. R. Conditioned frustration as a learned drive. *Journal of Experimental Psychology,* 1963, *66,* 142–148.

Wagner, A. R. Stimulus validity and stimulus selection. In W. K. Honig, & N. J. Mackintosh (Eds.), *Fundamental issues in associative learning.* Halifax: Dalhousie University Press, 1969. Pp. 90–122. (a)

Wagner, A. R. Stimulus selection and a "modified continuity theory." In G. H. Bower, & J. T. Spence (Eds.), *The psychology of learning and motivation.* Volume 3. New York: Academic Press, 1969. Pp. 1–40. (b)

DISCRIMINATION LEARNING

Positive Induction, Behavioral Contrast, and Generalization of Inhibition in Discrimination Learning

ABRAM AMSEL

The subject matter of this essay seems especially appropriate to this volume for two reasons. The first is that, of his many interests, perhaps Kenneth Spence's main continuing one was in discrimination learning and differential conditioning, beginning with his great papers in the 1930s. The second reason is that some of the guiding ideas behind the arguments presented here are in the form of a classical conditioning model of mediation in instrumental behavior, a theoretical form which Spence found important throughout his scientific lifetime.

I am going to argue, presenting data from recent experiments, (a) that Spence's conceptions of inhibition and generalization of inhibition in discrimination learning are still solid more than thirty years after he enunciated them, despite recent statements (e.g. Terrace, 1968) stemming from research on behavioral contrast * in operant situations that suggest limitations of this conception; (b) that, indeed, the important phenomena of "behavioral contrast" which have been offered as evidence against generalization of inhibition may not require discrimination learning for their demonstration; and (c) that the Pavlovian counterpart of contrast, "positive induction," may turn out to suffer from the same limitation and to be a phenomenon of instrumental rather than of classical conditioning. I will start with the last of these considerations, as it makes some historical sense to do so.

Preparation of this essay has been supported by Grant GB–3772 from the National Science Foundation. It was written in the spring and summer of 1969.

* The references to behavioral contrast in this essay are to behavioral-contrast effects due to nonreinforcement, or reduced rate of reinforcement, and are not meant to be general enough to include experiments in which contrast-like effects result from direct application of noxious stimulation in one component of a multiple schedule.

PAVLOVIAN INDUCTION

In the course of studying differential conditioning of the salivary conditioned reflex, Pavlov (1927) came across some phenomena which he thought reflected "mutual, or reciprocal, excitation leading to increased inhibition and inhibition leading to increased excitation [p. 188]." Following earlier terminological practice (he referred to Hering and Sherrington), he termed increased inhibitory effects *negative induction* and the increased excitatory effects *positive induction.* The demonstration of positive induction, with which we will be concerned, seems simple and straightforward. On the other hand, there can be some question as to whether negative induction of a direct sort has really been demonstrated (Kimble, 1961, p. 96).

Two features of the positive induction effect are of some special interest in the present context. The first is that in Pavlovian differential conditioning the effect has been demonstrated only when the negative stimulus precedes the positive by a very short interval of time; in the Pavlovian protocols the interval between the negative stimulus and the positive test stimulus is typically 30 sec. (1927, pp. 189–190). The second feature is that positive induction is more likely to occur in the earlier rather than in the later portion of a differential-conditioning experiment; indeed there is some evidence that in long-established discriminations the effect diminishes and even disappears.

For some years we (and many others) have been studying the potentiating effects of nonreinforcement (frustrative nonreward) in a double or tandem runway apparatus. The primary frustration effect (FE) is an increase in vigor of running in the second alley in the series when reward is omitted in the first goal box after the first-alley response (e.g., Amsel & Roussel, 1952). In one important respect, this procedure is similar to that involved in positive induction: a nonreinforcement immediately precedes a reinforced response and increases the strength of that response. It is conceivable that the factor of nonreinforcement preceding reinforcement is at least a part of the inductive effect, and that a similar effect might occur in Pavlov's procedure even though the CS preceding the test CS+ was not a CS−, but was the same CS+ with the usual UCS (reinforcement) omitted on the test trial. That is, it is possible that (a) a Pavlovian procedure in which partial reinforcement in relation to a single CS is substituted for differential conditioning of CS+ and CS− might also produce positive induction, and (b) if this did turn out to be the case, there would be no basis for linking the "induction" to differential conditioning. So much, for the moment, for the first feature of Pavlovian positive induction which interests me.

The second feature involves a coincidence of effects in Pavlov's experiments and ours which is perhaps more remarkable. We have reported several experiments (Amsel, 1962; Amsel & Ward, 1965) in which successive discrimination (differentiation) and the FE are studied side by side within the individual subject. In these experiments, we have been able to show that the FE is present in the early stages of discrimination training, prior to the development of differential responding to S+ and S−; but we have also shown that after the discrimination is clearly established the FE diminishes in strength and even disappears. This is a finding also remarkably like that reported by Pavlov in his demonstrations of positive induction: inductive effects tend to disappear after differentiation has been strongly established (Pavlov, 1927, pp. 193–196).

BEHAVIORAL CONTRAST IN OPERANT CONDITIONING

A very extensive investigation of inductive effects—*induction* is used here in the Pavlovian and not in the Skinnerian sense—has been made in a family of experiments studying *behavioral contrast.* Behavioral contrast is, again, quite analogous to Pavlovian positive induction (Reynolds, 1961), and it refers to an increase in the strength of responding to the more positive component in a multiple schedule (S+) that accompanies a decrease in the rate of responding and/or of reinforcement to the more negative component (S−) during discrimination training. There is this difference between behavioral contrast, as Skinnerians seem to view it, and positive induction as it is studied in the Pavlovian arrangements: in Pavlov's work the inductive effect was seen to be the direct consequence of an immediately preceding inhibitory event. Positive induction referred to an increase in excitatory strength in the presence of the irradiated cortical inhibition left over from the just-terminated CS−. Apart from statements made by Terrace (1966a, p. 321) and by Nevin and Shettleworth (1966), who regard transient, as opposed to sustained, contrast as having something to do with the just-preceding stimulus, behavioral contrast does not seem to be viewed primarily in terms of the just-terminated stimulus, even though the great preponderance of such studies are conducted with single alternation of S− and S+, so that every positive trial-segment is preceded by a negative one. Contrast seems rather to be regarded as relatively independent of the immediately preceding event, to be related to "the fact that the organism has been confronted with a differential reinforcement procedure [Terrace, 1966a, p. 321]," and it has been looked at in three ways: (a) as an increase in responding to S+ *because of a decrease in responding to S−* (Terrace, 1968); (b) as an increase in responding to S+ *because of decreased reinforcement density to S−* (Reynolds, 1961); and (c) as an increase in responding to S+ *because of increased preference for S+ over S−* (Bloomfield, 1967b; Premack, 1969).

Pavlovian positive induction and Skinnerian behavioral contrast are similar in that both refer to an elevating effect on responding to a relatively positive stimulus brought about by some characteristic or feature of a relatively negative stimulus or situation. Pavlov refers specifically to differential conditioning and to the irradiation of excitation and inhibition when he discusses induction. The statements about behavioral contrast are always made in the context of discrimination training, and often in relation to peak shift (Terrace, 1966a, 1968), a phenomenon which does seem, unmistakably, a characteristic of discrimination learning. Interestingly enough, to make the coincidence still more striking, there is evidence from operant-discrimination experiments (Terrace, 1966a) that behavioral-contrast effects, like Pavlovian induction effects and double-runway frustration effects, also diminish after a discrimination has been formed.

THE QUESTION I WANT TO RAISE

As I indicated earlier, it does seem particularly appropriate to take the occasion for this essay as an opportunity to ask the following interlocking questions: Is discrimination training a necessary or only a sufficient condition for demonstrating positive induction and behavioral contrast? And if it turns out to be only a sufficient condition, is it sufficient in all instances of discrimination training or only in certain operant-discrimination procedures and in Pavlovian differentiation experiments which can be thought to be analogous to those procedures? And, finally, is there really any basis from the work on inductive effects to deny the validity of the concept of generalization of inhibition, as Spence employed the term?

I can think of two approaches to get at the real basis for these inductive or contrast effects, particularly with respect to their dependence on differential conditioning (discrimination).

The first approach is to look at what happens to S+ in discrimination learning with successive and discrete-trial presentations of stimuli at intertrial intervals (ITIs) long enough so that the immediate potentiating effects of nonreinforcement possible in Pavlovian and Skinnerian situations can be ruled out. The question here is whether with discrete trials and long ITIs the positive induction-contrast-type of phenomenon will emerge at all.

The second approach is to perform appropriate controlled experiments of the Skinnerian and Pavlovian sort, so that the effects of nonreinforcement on subsequent reinforced responses can be studied with and without differential stimulation related to reinforcement and nonreinforcement. In Skinnerian procedures this second tactic involves experiments that include mixed-schedule controls for the multiple-schedule behavioral contrast conditions. In Pavlovian procedures we would have to conduct experiments duplicating all of the Pavlovian differential-conditioning arrangements, but keeping the two CSs nondifferential with respect to reinforcement and nonreinforcement. In both the Skinnerian and Pavlovian versions of the second case, then, we would mimic the experiments already performed but include conditions in which the stimuli were nondifferential in relation to reinforcement conditions.

It turns out that several of the kinds of experiments described as the first approach have been performed in our laboratory quite unwittingly, embedded in studies designed for quite other reasons. And we have recently quite intentionally set out on the Skinnerian version of the second approach. I am not aware of, nor have we yet performed, any experiments using Pavlovian procedures of the kind described as the second approach.

DISCRETE-TRIAL RUNWAY EXPERIMENTS ON INDUCTION-CONTRAST

Behavioral contrast, according to Terrace, "refers to an increase in the strength of the response to S+ that accompanies a decrease in the strength of the response to S− during discrimination training [Terrace, 1966b, p. 1677]." Of course, such a statement can have meaning only in comparison with measurements of performance to S+ alone, a comparison that can be made either within-*S*s, as Reynolds, Terrace, and others using operant techniques make it, or between groups of *S*s. In the latter case, one group responds to S+ alone, the other to S+ and S− concurrently, a situation in which the response strength to S− decreases. Under the former condition, the first phase should be essentially asymptotic S_1+S_2+ training, and in the second phase there is a shift to S_1+S_2-. Further elevation of response vigor to S_1+ beyond the original asymptotic level is taken as evidence for positive contrast. Under the latter between-*S* condition, if the presence of S−, or of responding to S−, is exerting a behavioral-contrast-type effect on the level of responding to S+, responding to S+ alone should be weaker than responding to S+ in the context of S+S−. The between-*S* experiment, to be properly controlled, should involve an S+ condition which is more properly described as S_1+S_2+; that is, a comparison should be made between *S*s who are always rewarded for responding to both stimuli and *S*s who are always rewarded for responding to S_1+ but never rewarded to S_2-, the comparison being between the S_1+s from both cases.

Fortunately, data are available from several recent experiments which, while they were conducted primarily for other reasons, fulfill all of the above requirements.* All of these experiments were conducted in the same kind of

* While most of the detailed evidence we present for the argument comes from experiments in our own laboratory, there are a number of other experimental studies whose results support the present contention about discrete-trial experiments. Most of these are presented

apparatus under very similar conditions. The apparatus is either a pair of runways, one white and the other black, or split alleys (Kolesnik & Amsel, 1966), each of which can be aligned with a common grey start-box unit. Response time measures are taken over three or five 1-ft. segments (starting, running, and goal) and are converted to speeds (ft/sec). The *S*s are run under hunger conditions defined by 22–23 hr. food deprivation, *with an intertrial interval of 15–20 min. in some studies and of 24 hr. in others.* On half the trials the *S* runs in the white alley, on the other half in the black. In the 15–20 min. ITI condition, four trials are run each day, the sequence of black and white being quasirandom.

In an experiment by Henderson (1966) five groups of *S*s were run under the conditions shown across the top of Figure 1. These groups differed only with respect to the percentage of reinforcement given for response in the S_2 alley, which varied from 100 to zero. Magnitude of reward was 500 mg. of food whenever given. The two extreme groups $S_1$100–$S_2$100 and $S_1$100–$S_2$0 provide the conditions for the contrast comparison described earlier. The intermediate groups provided for comparisons of the basic groups with intermediate percentage-reward conditions. Clearly, in none of the three measures is there evidence of a positive-induction kind of behavioral contrast, but quite the reverse: as the level of responding to S_2 decreases, the level of responding to S_1 also decreases.

Figure 2 provides data from an experiment by MacKinnon (1967). Fortunately, the acquisition phase of this experiment is highly comparable to Henderson's (1966), except that magnitude rather than percentage of reward was varied to S_2 as a between-groups parameter, and the numbers across the top of Figure 2 represent mg. of food reward rather than percentages of rewards. Obviously, then, the extreme groups ($S_1$500–$S_2$500 and $S_1$500–$S_2$0) correspond exactly to Henderson's and comprise the same basic between-groups contrast-effect experiment. The results are similar to Henderson's. There is again no evidence of a behavioral-contrast effect, response to $S_1$500 being weaker when zero reward is given to S_2 than when 500-mg. reward is given to S_2. Again, generalization of inhibition is a plausible explanation for the data, and there is a suggestion that this effect is somewhat greater for very small magnitude of reward than for zero reward, especially early in the response chain.

We have other data of this kind, particularly from experiments on differential percentage-of-reward training with 15–20 min. intertrial intervals (e.g., Galbraith, Rashotte, & Amsel, 1968), and it all tends to support generalization of inhibition rather than the positive-induction or behavioral-

---

in a paper by Black (1968), who reviews the evidence on shifts in magnitude of reward and on contrast effects in differential-conditioning experiments varying magnitude, delay, and percentage of reward. In the studies he cites there is virtually no suggestion of a positive-contrast effect, but clear evidence for negative-contrast effects and generalization of inhibition, which he explains in terms of a simple Spence (1936) model, $\overline{E} = E - I$.

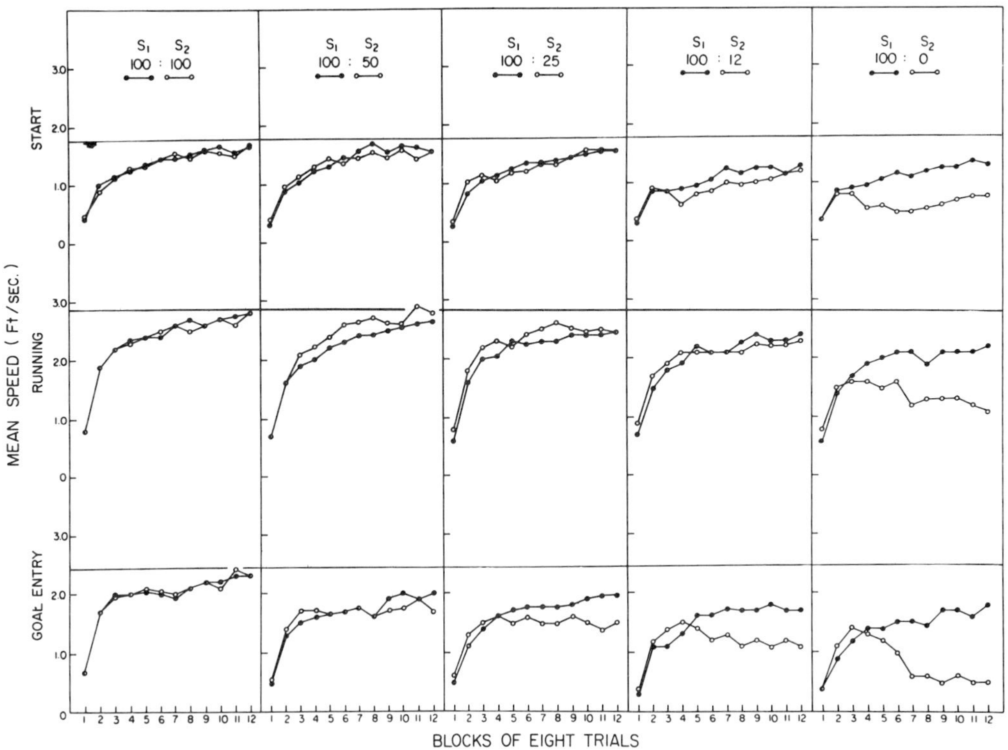

FIGURE 1. Adapted from Henderson (1966), these graphs show within-group (vertical) and between-group (horizontal) comparisons of performance when percent reward to S_2 is manipulated as a between-group parameter while percent reward to S_1 is held constant at 100 percent. The horizontal lines are drawn at the level of terminal performance of the S_1100–S_2100 group to facilitate comparison across groups of performance in the S_1 runway.

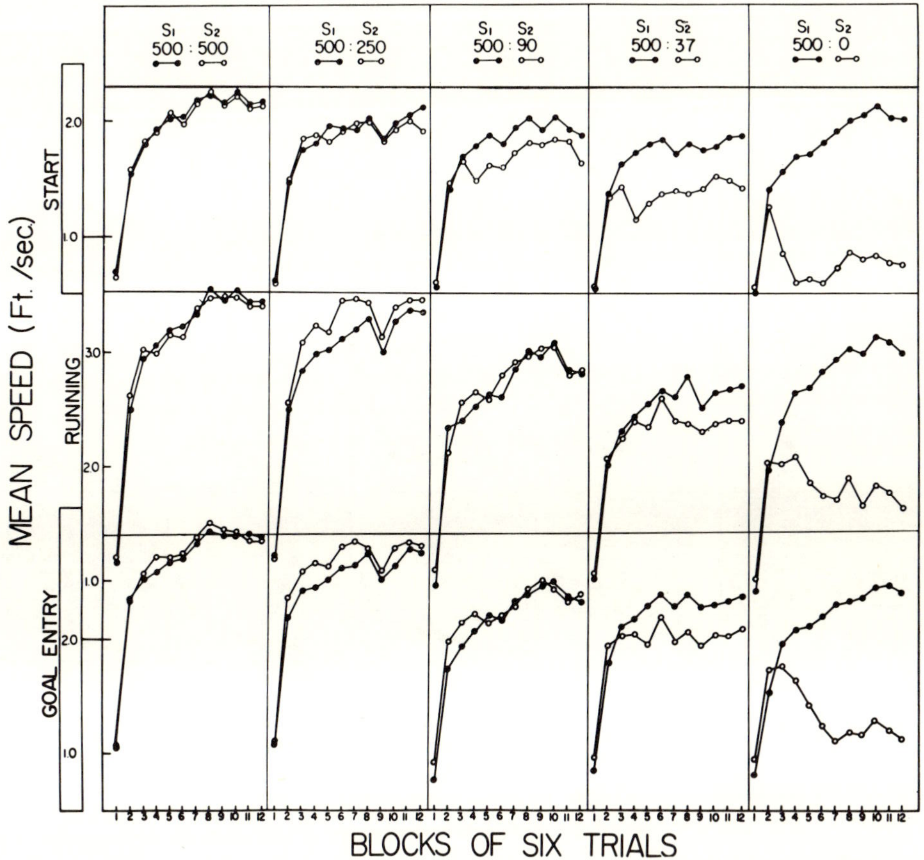

FIGURE 2. Adapted from MacKinnon (1967), these graphs show between-group (horizontal) and within-group comparison of performance when magnitude of reward to S_2 is varied between groups and to S_1 is held constant at 500 mg. Horizontal lines facilitate between-group comparison as in Figure 1.

contrast type of finding. A more recent unpublished experiment of this same sort with M. E. Rashotte and K. J. Galbraith has been conducted on a one-trial-per-day basis and the results of this one seem, if anything, more clear-cut in support of generalization of inhibition. Figure 3 shows for five separate speed measures, from start to goal across a runway, performance to a stimulus signaling 100 percent reward in three groups, the parameter being the present

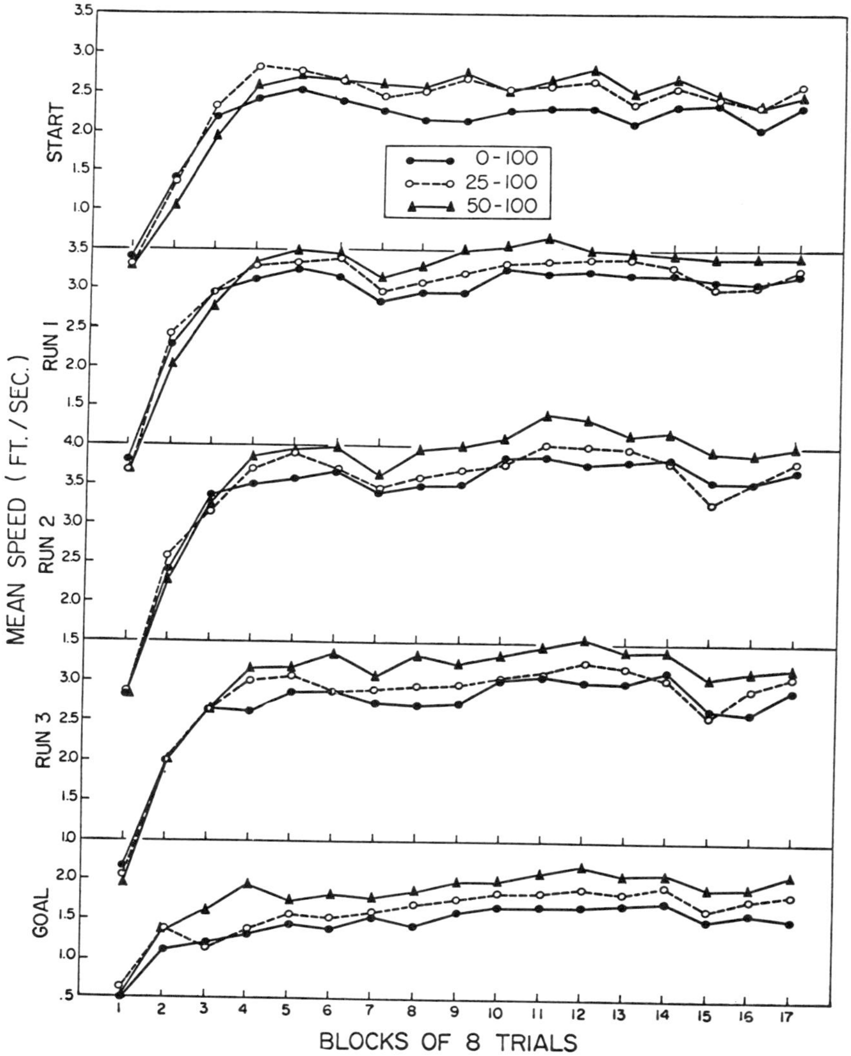

FIGURE 3. Data from an unpublished study with M. E. Rashotte and K. J. Galbraith showing comparisons of performance to a stimulus (S_1) signaling 100 percent reward when percent reward to S_2 is zero, 25, or 50 percent.

reward (zero, 25, or 50) given in each of the three groups to another discriminative stimulus. Clearly, and statistically significantly, speed in the stimulus alley signaling 100 percent reward is directly (not inversely) related to percentage of reward for response to the other stimulus. At one trial a day, as with a 15–20 min. ITI, there is no indication of positive induction-contrast in discrimination learning, but quite the reverse.

Some data taken from a recent doctoral thesis by Galbraith (1969) hammer the point home even further. These have been fashioned into the graphical story told in Figure 4. What is so plain here is that level of responding to S_1+, a stimulus signaling partial reward, depends very strongly on whether, within the same *S*, another stimulus signals continuous reward ($S_{2}{}^{+}_{+}$) or continuous nonreward ($S_{2}{}^{-}_{-}$). Again, the response level to S^{+}_{+} or S^{-} seems to affect the S^{+}_{-} performance by pulling it in its direction, rather than pushing it in the other direction. This goes on for 224 trials without any sign of change.

And finally, lest the runway-type of "contrast" finding be regarded as exclusively a between-*S*-design phenomenon, we can provide some data which are of the within-*S* variety and therefore much closer in form to the usual behavioral-contrast design. In this condition, also taken from Galbraith's work (1969), the sequence of three experimental phases is as follows: (a) S_1+S_2+, (b) S_1+S_2-, (c) S_1+S_2+. This is simply one condition out of many in an experiment performed for reasons having nothing to do with behavioral contrast. Again the intertrial interval was about 20 min. Clearly, a positive-induction-contrast view of this experiment would lead to the expectation that the level of responding to S_1 in Phase 2 would be higher than in Phase 1, given that responding to S_1 in Phase 1 had levelled off over many trials. The expectation would also be that in Phase 3 responding to S_1 would return to the level of Phase 1. The data from these conditions (Figure 5) are clearly not in accord with the first of these expectations, but are in accord with the second.

What is the reason for the difference between the behavioral-contrast effect in the Reynolds-type operant experiment and the opposite effect in runways?* We have never believed it to be a difference between runways

* There are at least a couple of recent experiments (Leonard, Weimer, & Albin, 1968; Senf & Miller, 1967) that have demonstrated effects analogous to Pavlovian positive induction in runways. In both cases the induction was demonstrated in terms of retarding extinction to an S+ by alternating presentations of S+ and S— in the extinction of responding to S+. A specific test for inductive effects during discrimination training by Leonard et al. showed an absence of such effects when the intertrial interval was 3–5 minutes. In both studies, the successful demonstrations of induction in extinction involved an intertrial interval of the order of 10 sec. An even more recent experiment (Ison & Krane, 1969) provides results contrary to positive induction in runway acquisition or extinction training at a 5-to-15 min. ITI, and some evidence of induction in extinction only when the ITI is 30 sec. These studies do suggest that the presence of a *negative stimulus* (nonreinforced), as compared to simply a nonreinforcement, does increase the excitatory strength of an immediately following S+, but the effect has so far been shown only during extinction.

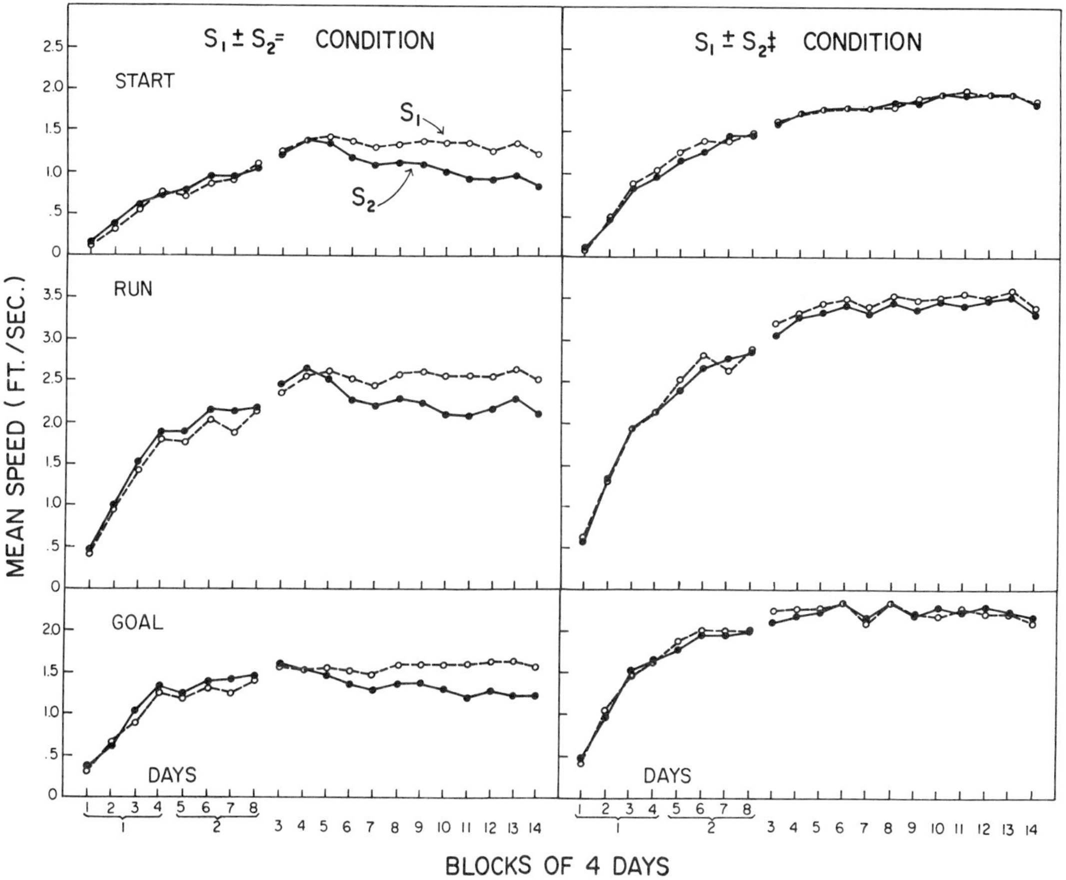

FIGURE 4. Adapted from Galbraith (1969) comparing performance to S_1 (50 percent reward) when $S_2\ddagger$ signals 100 percent reward and when $S_2=$ signals zero reward.

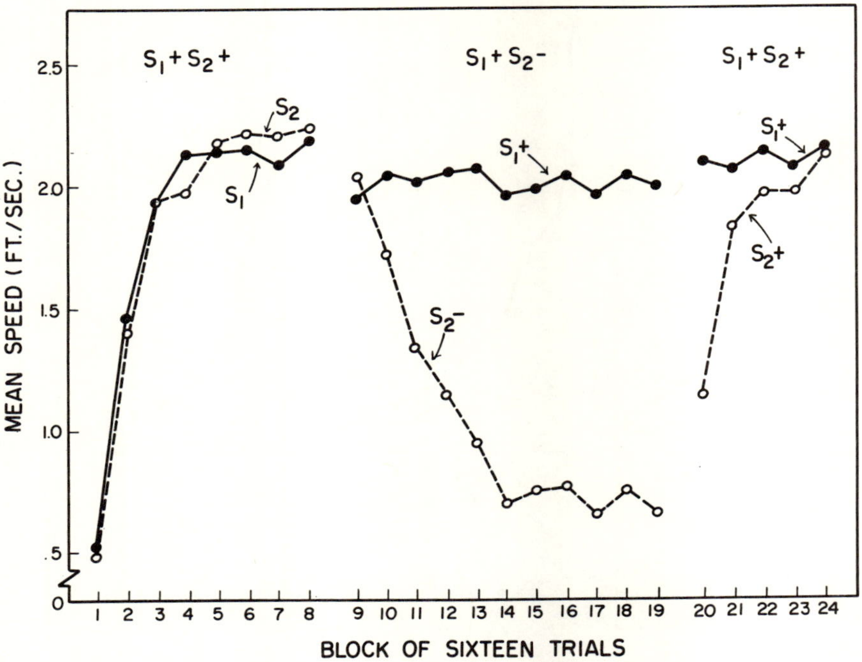

FIGURE 5. Adapted from Galbraith (1969) showing speed of running in an S_1+S_2- discrimination preceded and followed by continuous reward to both stimuli. This is a discrete-trial runway analog of an experiment on behavioral contrast.

and boxes, or between rate and speed measures, but to be a matter of differences within these procedures. As Platt points out in his chapter in the present volume, discrete-trial procedures have usually involved the omission of reinforcement at the end of a well-established, regular behavior sequence (e.g., runway or FR). Operant studies, on the other hand, usually involve a change in the behavioral sequence leading to reward (e.g., increasing an FR or V1 requirement or introducing free-operant extinction). Another major, perhaps related, difference is that data like Reynolds's and Terrace's are collected under conditions which involve a high degree of response "massing" (short intertrial intervals), whereas ours are, relatively, spaced-trial conditions. While the operant procedure is in a sense the ultimate in trial massing, this is not to say that these are the necessary conditions for the behavior contrast effect; any short ITI procedure should be effective if it is simply a matter of allowing the effects of primary nonreinforcement to invigorate immediately succeeding behavior. With trials following each other in rapid succession, the excitatory (emotional, frustrative) effects of nonreward should operate to raise the level of responding to S+. When trials are spaced, these temporally labile effects should dissipate, leaving the more permanent associative effects of generalized conditioned inhibition to yield the relative reduction in speed to the more positive stimulus.

Terrace has suggested a combination of such excitatory and inhibitory effects as the explanation for peak shift: "Subtracting a U-shaped gradient of inhibition from this elevated gradient of excitation would still displace the peak away from S− [1966b, p. 1680]." But generalization of inhibitory effects from S−, by itself, will account for peak shift. The involvement of "excitatory" effects in peak shift is only necessary if one *requires* that the explanations of peak shift and contrast involve only one, and the same, theoretical term, as Terrace has been suggesting. Otherwise, it is possible to account for peak shift in terms of the inhibitory or aversive properties of nonreward, in the manner of Spence's (1936, 1937) model, or of conditioned (anticipatory) frustration (Amsel, 1958, 1967), and to say that contrast is the result of a primary excitatory (frustrative) factor on which the aversive mechanism in peak shift depends. A prediction would then emerge that unlike contrast, which depends on short ITIs, peak shift will be observable in successive discrimination situations irrespective of ITI and of whether free-operant or discrete-trial modes of training are employed. Nevertheless, it would still be the case, as Terrace (1968) has so beautifully shown, that you do not get peak-shift effects unless you also obtain contrast effects, and vice versa.

Terrace sums up what he appears to regard as a contradiction between the data of behavioral contrast and Spence's theory of discrimination by saying: "Behavioral contrast derives its name from the fact that the rates of responding to S+ and S− diverge. According to [Spence's] classical generalization theory, these rates should converge [1966b, p. 1677]." He makes the same point again in connection with a more inclusive treatment of contrast, peak-shift, and errorless discrimination (1966a). The argument of this essay so far has been pointing to the conclusion that behavioral-contrast effects in operant or highly massed-trial conditions and generalized inhibitory effects from discrete-trial conditions can live side by side and be regarded as, respectively, indicants of the primary excitatory and secondary inhibitory effects of frustrative nonreward. Under the discrimination-learning conditions of our runway experiments, which are more like the ones on which Spence's original theorizing were based than on Terrace's conditions, response "rates" do indeed seem to *converge*.

Equally important, perhaps, is the possibility that behavioral contrast, like Pavlovian positive induction, may occur in differential conditioning and discrimination learning but in no way depend on the presence of differential stimuli related to reinforcement and nonreinforcement. These phenomena may depend only on nonreinforcement and its immediate aftereffects. To this possibility we now turn our attention.

IS DISCRIMINATION LEARNING NECESSARY FOR INDUCTION-CONTRAST?

I have been attempting to answer one part of the question put earlier: is discrimination training sufficient for producing positive induction in all instances of discrimination training? The answer is, "No." And now we should pursue the question of whether, even in those circumstances where Pavlovian induction and Skinnerian contrast are clearly and admittedly demonstrable and highly reliable, the phenomena really *require* for their demonstration the presence of differentially reinforced S-R sequences. I am going to suggest that there is certainly no proof one way or the other on this point because the relevant experimental control considerations have up to now not been put into effect.

The Pavlovian experiment demonstrating positive induction really only demonstrates that a conditioned stimulus following shortly on a *nonreinforcement* will evoke a relatively increased magnitude of the conditioned response. The Skinnerian experiment on behavioral contrast really only shows that response level will be higher following a period of reduced reinforcement density. To demonstrate more than this would be to show that the induction-contrast phenomena do not occur in experiments that do not involve differential reinforcement related to discriminative stimuli, but still involve the possibility of immediate invigorating effects of nonreinforcement. This has not yet been done, so far as I know, for the Pavlovian situation, but there is one study in the instrumental-conditioning literature that approximates these conditions. In order to demonstrate an "intermittent reinforcement effect" in discrimination learning, Jenkins (1961) compared resistance to extinction following Discrimination, Intermittent (PRF), and Regular (CRF) conditions. The subjects were pigeons, the response was a single key peck (FR 1), and the discrete trials were separated by intervals of 15 to 60 sec. The differential training in the three groups was preceded by a pretraining phase in which all groups were continuously reinforced for responding to S_1, the stimulus to-be-positive in the discrimination group, and the only stimulus presented in the other two groups. Incidental to the main finding of the experiment, that discrimination training did increase resistance to extinction over CRF training, Jenkins reports a "quickening" of response to S_1+ in the discrimination group: as latency of responding to S_2- increases in the training phase, latency of responding to S_1+ decreases below the latency level at the end of pretraining to S_1+. In the intermittent group there is no quickening, but in fact the reverse: latency increases significantly. While this might seem to be favorable to the view that elevation of responding to S+ in discrimination depends on the presence of an

S− rather than simply nonreinforcement, two factors caution against such a conclusion. First, the experiment was conducted in such a way that "the average time between trials was shorter for Group DISC than for Groups INT or REG [p. 118]." Secondly, the comparisons between latency to S_1+ from the discrimination group and latency in the intermittent group do not isolate specifically the effect of nonreinforcement in terms of an analysis of latencies on trials following reinforcement and trials following nonreinforcement. Of course, it should be emphasized that Jenkins' experiment was not designed to deal primarily with the contrast factor.

We have conducted one version of what would seem to be the properly controlled operant experiment to look at the necessity for discriminative stimuli in positive behavioral contrast. As indicated earlier, such an experiment involves mixed- and multiple-schedule procedures which are completely equated for the number and positions in sequence of reinforcements and nonreinforcements. This experiment (Scull, Davies, & Amsel, 1970) * asks whether behavioral contrast depends on one stimulus signaling reinforcement and another nonreinforcement, or whether the phenomenon is related only to the emotional-frustrative effects of nonreinforcement.

Four groups of rats were trained to bar press in the presence of either of two stimuli (S_1 or S_2) on a fixed-interval (FI) 30-sec. schedule. In a second phase, one group had the discriminative stimuli correlated with reinforced (R) and nonreinforced (N) intervals, and for a second group the FI responding was reinforced on a 50 percent partial schedule (P) to both stimuli. The other two groups were reinforced for responding to both stimuli following every interval, one matched to the experimental groups for number of intervals per day (CL), the other matched for number of reinforcements per day (CS). For analysis, the data from the 30-sec. intervals were split into two 15-sec. segments. Figure 6 shows the data from the first 15-sec. segment. (The data from the second segment offer no additional information for present purposes.) Positive behavioral contrast was observed in the R trials of the discrimination group, and the partially reinforced group showed a comparable increase in response rate over all trials. Further analysis showed that the increased rate in both groups could be accounted for wholly in terms of intervals following nonreinforced intervals.

The fact that positive behavioral contrast can be demonstrated in terms of the greater response rate shown by the discrimination (multiple-schedule) group on positive trials compared with either of the continuous-reward groups confirms the finding from other studies employing multiple fixed-interval-extinction schedules (Hilker, 1968; Reynolds & Catania, 1961). However, the analysis of sequential effects in this experiment showed that the entire contrast effect could be accounted for by increased rate of re-

* The discussion of the experiment presented for purposes of this essay has obvious similarities to the discussion of the experiment presented in greater detail elsewhere.

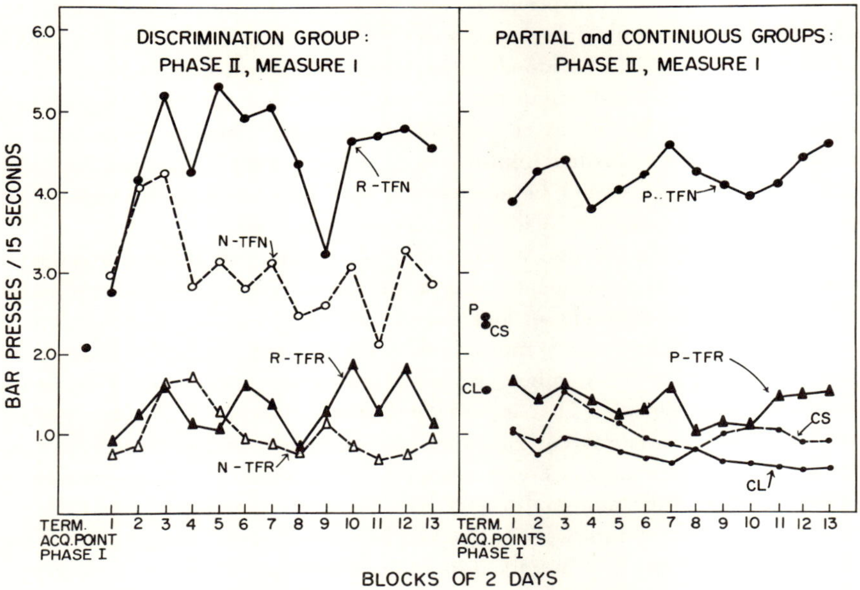

FIGURE 6. Data from Scull, Davies, and Amsel (1970). (See text for details.)

sponding on trials immediately following nonrewarded trials, and that identical effects emerge in a partially rewarded (mixed-schedule) group comparable to the discrimination group. These results suggest (a) that the conditions for the occurrence of behavioral contrast are the same as the conditions under which an FE would be expected to occur, and (b) that in the development of contrast, at least under FI 30-sec. conditions, it does not seem to matter whether or not there are discriminative stimuli.

If contrast is a function of the immediately preceding trial condition and not of *S*'s prior history of reward in relation to differential stimulation, the interpretations of contrast to which we alluded earlier (Bloomfield, 1967b; Premack, 1969; Reynolds, 1961; Terrace, 1966a), which depend on the importance of differential stimulation related to reinforcement and non-reinforcement, are placed in doubt. The appropriateness of the term "contrast" to identify the phenomenon is also called into question. In most of the experiments on which these interpretations are based, the use of single alternation of stimuli, a failure to analyze sequential effects, or both may have masked the short-term nature of the effect.

Terrace (1966a) has reported that response rate was greater on trials following the negative than following the positive stimulus. But he also reported that there was an additional contrast effect in pigeons that was independent of the immediately prior reward condition. In our experiment, there was no evidence of a contrast effect on positive trials following reward. And Platt* indicates that an unreported analysis from a study (Platt, Senkowski, & Mann, 1969) shows that all of the positive contrast in rats can be accounted for by increases to S+ on trials directly following S−. Bloomfield (1967a) has reported a small behavioral-contrast effect in pigeons with 23 hours between components of the schedule. But my colleague Richard Wilton,† who has just completed a study involving conditions very similar to Bloomfield's, has data from eleven pigeons that show no evidence of positive behavioral contrast in nine of the birds. In fact, in some of these nine there is a suggestion of generalization of inhibition. There is only a slight suggestion of positive contrast in the other two subjects.

Possibly these differences in results reflect in part differences between pigeons and rats in their response to discriminative stimuli. Possibly prepotent, species-specific responses such as pecking in the pigeon are affected differently than relatively unnatural responses such as bar pressing in the rat. However, running is a natural response in rats, and there is certainly no evidence of contrast in our runway studies with intertrial intervals of 15 min. or more. Whatever turns out to be the case, here are matters to be considered, and there are implications for the methods of operant research. First, in view of the short-term invigorating effects of frustrative nonreward and punishment (Banks, 1969) that have been demonstrated in double-runway situations, it is apparent that under most operant-research training conditions, any experiments involving intermittent reward or punishment should employ suitably randomized orders of events and sufficiently analytic measuring and reporting of data to permit evaluation of the short-term effects of one trial on the next. This has not been the case in most research on behavioral contrast. Second, as Smith and Hoy (1954) pointed out, a nondiscriminative control group is necessary for the interpretation of operant-discrimination experiments. In our experiment, both discrimination and partial reinforcement groups showed effects that have previously been considered to be characteristic only of discrimination learning.

SUMMARY AND CONCLUDING COMMENTS

We have examined the phenomena of positive induction, behavioral contrast, and the frustration effect and seen that they overlap at several points. My main points, given the similarities between these three conceptions, is

* Personal communication.
† Personal communication.

that there is no very good evidence that the positive induction-contrast phenomena, as studied under both the Pavlovian and Skinnerian experimental arrangements, depend for their demonstration on differential conditioning or discrimination learning. The case has been made that induction-contrast is not demonstrable—and in fact that the reverse effect, generalization of inhibition, is observed—when discrimination training is conducted under well-spaced, discrete-trial conditions in a runway, under either between-*S* or within-*S* conditions. More specific to the Skinnerian work, we have shown that, at least under fixed-interval conditions, behavioral contrast does not appear to depend upon the presence of discriminative stimuli signaling high- and low-reward levels but only on the immediate perseverating effects of nonreward, "immediate" here signifying, perhaps, seconds rather than minutes.

Among the factors leading to the line of inquiry represented by this essay were certain assertions that had been made about the validity of the inhibitory generalization gradient in discrimination learning. I now believe these assertions to be generally incorrect and to be based on a misreading of the generality and meaning of the phenomenon of behavioral contrast. A consideration of these and related matters has led me to imply certain cautions which should perhaps now be made explicit. First of all, arguing from operant procedures to generalized discrimination learning is hazardous, just as arguing from runway procedures to discrimination learning is hazardous, just as arguing from Pavlovian procedures to discrimination learning is hazardous. I believe that it *is* possible to transfer explanatory conceptions, for example, from the box to the runway and back; that there are *not* different basic laws which apply to the two situations. But I believe that in doing so it is important to make the correct translation, particularly if the intention is to evaluate a theory derived from one set of procedures in the light of data derived from other procedures. This point has been made before (e.g., Logan & Wagner, 1965; Spence, 1956), and the essay by Platt in the present volume is an advance toward this translation. There are variables inherent in procedures that may be more discernible to people who are farther from these procedures than to people closer up.

This leads directly to my second caution, which has to do with the necessity for experimental control, even for situations which produce as much response stability as the Skinnerian operant procedures purport to do. Because of this stability, and the attendant possibility of changing behavior from one steady state of responding to another by the variation of an experimental factor, it is tempting to believe that an experiment can be conducted on an individual organism. I have suggested that, at least in the case of the study of induction-contrast, in both Pavlovian and Skinnerian experiments, necessary controls for immediate effects of nonreinforcement make it impossible to experiment on single organisms.

REFERENCES

Amsel, A. The role of frustrative nonreward in noncontinuous reward situations. *Psychological Bulletin*, 1958, *55*, 102–119.

Amsel, A. Frustrative nonreward in partial reinforcement and discrimination learning: Some recent history and a theoretical extension. *Psychological Review*, 1962, *69*, 306–328.

Amsel, A. Partial reinforcement effects on vigor and persistence: Advances in frustration theory derived from a variety of within-subjects experiments. In K. W. Spence, & J. T. Spence (Eds.), *The psychology of learning and motivation: Advances in research and theory*. Vol. 1. New York: Academic Press, 1967. Pp. 1–65.

Amsel, A., & Roussel, J. Motivational properties of frustration: I. Effect on a running response of the addition of frustration to the motivational complex. *Journal of Experimental Psychology*, 1952, *43*, 363–368.

Amsel, A., & Ward, J. S. Frustration and persistence: Resistance to discrimination following prior experience with the discriminanda. *Psychological Monographs*, 1965, *79* (4, Whole No. 597).

Banks, R. K. Invigorating effects of punishment. Unpublished manuscript.

Black, R. W. Shifts in magnitude of reward and contrast effects in instrumental and selective learning. *Psychological Review*, 1968, *75*, 114–126.

Bloomfield, T. M. Some temporal properties of behavioral contrast. *Journal of the Experimental Analysis of Behavior*, 1967, *10*, 159–164. (a)

Bloomfield, T. M. Frustration, preference, and behavioral contrast. *Quarterly Journal of Experimental Psychology*, 1967, *19*, 166–169. (b)

Galbraith, K. J. Mediation in animal discrimination learning. Unpublished doctoral dissertation, University of Toronto, 1969.

Galbraith, K. J., Rashotte, M. E., & Amsel, A. Within-subjects partial reinforcement effects varying percentage reward to the partial stimulus between groups. *Journal of Experimental Psychology*, 1968, *77*, 547–551.

Henderson, K. Within-subjects partial reinforcement effects in acquisition and in later discrimination learning. *Journal of Experimental Psychology*, 1966, *72*, 704–713.

Hilker, D. Behavioral contrast and the frustration effect. Paper presented at the Psychonomic Society Meeting, St. Louis, 1968.

Ison, J. R., & Krane, R. V. Induction in different instrumental conditioning. *Journal of Experimental Psychology*, 1969, *80*, 183–185.

Jenkins, H. H. The effect of discrimination training on extinction. *Journal of Experimental Psychology*, 1961, *61*, 111–121.

Kimble, G. A. *Hilgard and Marquis' Conditioning and learning*. New York: Appleton-Century-Crofts, 1961.

Kolesnik, B., & Amsel, A. A "split-alley" technique for equating brightness in a visual discrimination task. *Psychonomic Science*, 1966, *5*, 187–188.

Leonard, D. W., Weimer, J., & Albin, R. An examination of Pavlovian induction phenomena in differential instrumental conditioning. *Psychonomic Science*, 1968, *12*, 89–90.

Logan, F. A., & Wagner, A. R. *Reward and punishment*. Boston: Allyn and Bacon, 1965.

MacKinnon, J. R. Interactive effects of the two rewards in a differential magnitude of reward discrimination. *Journal of Experimental Psychology*, 1967, *75*, 329–338.

Nevin, J. A., & Shettleworth, S. J. An analysis of contrast effects in multiple schedules. *Journal of the Experimental Analysis of Behavior*, 1969, *9*, 305–315.

Pavlov, I. P. *Conditioned reflexes*. (Translated by G. V. Anrep.) London: Oxford University Press, 1927.

Platt, J. R., Senkowski, P. C., & Mann, R. Discrimination, contrast, and chaining: Effects of prior training without discriminanda and response-contingent delay of discriminandum presentation. *Journal of Experimental Psychology*, 1969, *82*, 38–45.

Premack, D. On some boundary conditions of contrast. In J. T. Tapp (Ed.), *Reinforcement and behavior*. New York: Academic Press, 1969. Pp. 122–145.

Reynolds, G. S. Behavioral contrast. *Journal of the Experimental Analysis of Behavior*, 1961, *4*, 57–71.

Reynolds, G. S., & Catania, A. C. Behavioral contrast with fixed-interval and low-rate reinforcement. *Journal of the Experimental Analysis of Behavior*, 1961, *4*, 387–391.

Scull, J., Davies, K., & Amsel, A. Behavioral contrast and frustration effect in multiple and mixed fixed-interval schedules. *Journal of Comparative and Physiological Psychology*, 1970, *71*, 478–483.

Senf, G. M., & Miller, N. E. Evidence for positive induction in discrimination learning. *Journal of Comparative and Physiological Psychology*, 1967, *64*, 121–127.

Smith, M. H., & Hoy, W. S. Rate of response during operant discrimination. *Journal of Experimental Psychology*, 1954, *48*, 259–274.

Spence, K. W. The nature of discrimination learning in animals. *Psychological Review*, 1936, *43*, 427–449.

Spence, K. W. The differential response in animals to stimuli varying within a single dimension. *Psychological Review*, 1937, *44*, 430–444.

Spence, K. W. *Behavior theory and conditioning*. New Haven: Yale University Press, 1956.

Terrace, H. S. Stimulus control. In W. K. Honig (Ed.), *Operant behavior: Areas of research and application*. New York: Appleton-Century-Crofts, 1966. Pp. 271–344. (a)

Terrace, H. S. Discrimination learning and inhibition. *Science*, 1966, *154*, 1677–1680. (b)

Terrace, H. S. Discrimination learning, the peak shift, and behavioral contrast. *Journal of the Experimental Analysis of Behavior*, 1968, *11*, 727–741.

Continuity Theory and Cue-Dominance

TRACY S. KENDLER

A BRIEF REVIEW OF CONTINUITY THEORY

Discrimination learning is a fertile technique, but it sometimes seems that its major harvest is controversy. Nevertheless, until we find a better way, this method will remain important for evaluating fundamental conceptions about how behavior adapts to changing environmental events. It may be true that after decades of research few controversies have been resolved, but a little patience is in order since some of the issues are as fundamental and venerable as the Kantian-Empiricist controversies. Perhaps it is because the issues are so basic that the scientific community has not yet agreed about how they are to be resolved. Perhaps for the same reason there has been a concentration of ingenious research and clever theorizing in the area. Kenneth W. Spence was a pivotal figure in this effort. In fact, since 1936 much of the theorizing and research in discrimination learning either derives from or reacts to Spence's continuity theory (1936, 1937). His central role is widely acknowledged as witnessed by this quotation: "Modern accounts of discrimination learning have their intellectual beginnings with a paper in 1936 by Spence entitled 'The Nature of Discrimination Learning in Animals' . . . a true classic in the field [Trabasso & Bower, 1968, p. 4]."

Continuity theory can be interpreted literally as the specific formulation offered by Spence in his 1936 article, including the explicitly arbitrary parameter values used to illustrate the argument (e.g., Wolford & Bower, 1969). Or it can be interpreted in the way I think Spence intended, as a set of principles or assumptions subject to amendment, addition, and ulti-

This research was supported by United States Public Health Service Grant HD–01361.

mate specification. This discussion will be based on an interpretation of continuity theory which amalgamates the major tenets of the classical referent for continuity theory (Spence, 1936) with the equally important referent for stimulus-generalization theory (Spence, 1937). According to this interpretation, discrimination learning entails the strengthening or weakening of a set of hypothetical associative bonds between stimulus and response events which will be referred to as excitatory and inhibitory tendencies. These tendencies obey the following principles:

1. *Principle of reinforcement.* If a response is followed by a reward, the excitatory tendency of each of the stimulus components impinging on the organism's sensorium is strengthened by a certain amount.

2. *Principle of inhibition.* If a response is not followed by a reward, the inhibitory tendency of each of the stimulus components impinging on the organism's sensorium is strengthened by a certain amount.

3. *Principle of stimulus generalization.* In the case of continuous dimensions, there is a generalization of acquired excitatory and/or inhibitory tendencies to other similar stimuli in the form of a gradient around each component.

The theory assumes that the *effective* excitatory tendency of any stimulus *component* is equal to the algebraic sum of the positive (excitatory) tendency and negative (inhibitory) tendency. In a similar vein, it assumes that the *total* effective excitatory strength of a stimulus *complex* which is composed of more than one component is the sum of the effective excitatory tendencies of the components. The final assumption relates learning to performance by stating that, in the case of mutually exclusive responses, the response with the greatest total effective excitatory strength will prevail, provided that the difference exceeds some threshold value.

This interpretation does not encompass everything that occurs in discrimination learning. To use Spence's own words, this theory is

> of course, only a skeletal and purely conceptual outline of the processes that lead to the establishment of the discrimination habit. It is not intended to be, and in no sense should be construed as, a descriptive account of the behavior of the animal in the discrimination situation. Moreover, the animal learns many other responses in addition to the final, selective approaching reaction. Prominent and important among these are what have been termed, for want of a better name, "preparatory" responses. These latter consist of the responses which lead to the reception of the appropriate aspects of the total environmental complex on the animal's sensorium, e.g. the orientation and fixation of head and eyes towards the critical stimuli. That is, the animal learns to "look at" one aspect of the situation rather than another because of the fact that this response has always been followed within a short temporal interval by the final goal response. Responses providing other sensory receptions are not similarly reinforced in a systematic fashion and hence tend to disappear [Spence, 1960, p. 294].

Skeletal, hypothetical, or incomplete—it was the closest thing to a formal theory of discrimination learning that psychology had produced up to that time.

CONTINUITY VERSUS NONCONTINUITY THEORY

Continuity theory was initially formulated as an alternative to the noncontinuity theory proposed earlier by Lashley and Krechevsky. Noncontinuity theory conceived of discrimination learning as a problem-solving process entailing successive testing of alternative hypotheses until the correct one was discovered. Learning was assumed to be discontinuous in the sense that practice preceding criterion performance was irrelevant to the actual formation of the association (Lashley, 1929). Associations were assumed to be selective in the sense that they were limited to the abstracted attributes of the relevant stimulus events (Lashley, 1938).

The continuity-noncontinuity controversy produced a series of experiments in the 1940s, recently reviewed by Riley (1968), who comments:

> It is probably fair to say that in 1950 most psychologists in the field of learning, regardless of their particular sympathies, were convinced that the continuity position was essentially correct, . . . [but] even as the continuity position seemed to have been demonstrated beyond doubt, new attacks were being made upon it and new experiments critical of the continuity position were appearing [Pp. 128–129].

The disagreement stems from a number of sources but the most concentrated opposition to continuity theory on the contemporary scene comes from selective attention theorists like Lovejoy (1968), Mackintosh (1965), Trabasso and Bower (1968), and Zeaman and House (1963), for whom the central issue is the role of attention in discrimination learning. None of these theorists maintain the extreme noncontinuity position initially proposed by Lashley. Mackintosh, for instance, concedes that: "There is no possible doubt that some learning about the relevant cue does occur during the presolution period; there is equally no doubt that rats learn something about a second, incidental cue when it is paired with a primary cue [Mackintosh, 1965, p. 129]." Nevertheless his review of the evidence leads him to conclude that while attention to one cue does not prevent an animal from learning anything about a second cue, it does reduce the amount learned.

The modified noncontinuity approach has yielded a number of mathematical models and a quantity of research which is usually interpreted as favoring selective attention theory and casting doubt on the validity of continuity theory. But the modification in the new noncontinuity approach makes the differences between these two stances so subtle that the controversy must take a new form. Resolution of the theoretical differences must now depend on close analysis of competing theoretical formulations as they apply to specific experimental paradigms. Closer analysis makes obvious the fact that selective attention is not represented by one general theory. A number of competing mathematical models share the central thesis that learning entails a selective attention mechanism, but differ in other ways. Moreover, each model tends to be associated with a different experimental paradigm and a different subject population. Lovejoy's models (1968), for instance, are largely associated with overtraining paradigms in which rats are *S*s. The Zeaman and House (1963) model is usually associated with the intra-dimensional-shift paradigm with human retardates as *S*s. Trabasso and Bower (1968) favor the redundant-relevant-cue paradigm, mostly with adult human *S*s. If the issues are to be joined, a common experimental vehicle must be accepted and the range of applicability over species must also be specified.

Spence was quite explicit about limiting continuity theory to nonarticulate organisms but this was never clearly understood. As he put it: "I have long since lost track of how many disproofs there have been of my theory of discrimination learning in nonarticulate organisms that have employed college sophomores as subjects [1956, p. 202]."

It was, in fact, his student, Kuenne (1946) who first showed that while continuity theory could predict the transposition of nonarticulate children, it did not account for the transposition of articulate children. Kendler and Kendler (1962, 1970) spoke to the same point when they proposed the developmental mediational hypothesis of discrimination learning to the effect that while continuity theory applies to infrahuman and very young children's discrimination learning, there is in the course of human development a transition from a single-stage process implicit in the continuity formulation to a representational-mediational process that produces significant changes in learning and transfer.

CUE-DOMINANCE AND THE NONSELECTIVE ASSUMPTION

The present discussion of continuity theory will be confined to rat behavior in a set of variations on the redundant-relevant-cues paradigms illustrated in Table 1. Since differential cue-dominance is a central feature of most selective attention theories, the particular concern will be with the ability of continuity theory to predict cue-dominance in rats. These experimental paradigms were selected because they are excellent vehicles for studying various aspects of this phenomenon.

An example of the basic redundant-relevant-cue paradigm is presented in the first column of Table 1. The *S* is required to learn an initial discrim-

TABLE 1. REDUNDANT-RELEVANT-CUE PARADIGMS

	Basic		Reversal on One Dimension		Optional Shift	
Initial Discrimination	RC+	GT− *	GC+	RT−	GC+ RC−	RT− GT+
Shift Discrimination	none		RC+	GT−	RC+	GT−
Opposed-Cues Test	GC	RT	GC	RT	GC	RT
Interpretation of Choice	Form dominant	Color dominant	Ambiguous	Color dominant	Ed ** Choice	Rv ** Choice

* R, C, G, T refer to red, circle, green, and triangle, respectively.
** Ed and Rv refer to extradimensional and reversal, respectively.

ination between a red circle (RC+) and a green triangle (GT−). Both color and form are relevant to the reinforcement contingencies and both dimensions are perfectly redundant. To learn this discrimination a *S* must bring his choices under the control of either one or both dimensions. If one of these dimensions assumes more control than the other, it is not due to the immediate reinforcement history. To determine the outcome a series of opposed-cues test trials are presented which require a choice between the green circle (GC) and the red triangle (RT). If the subject chooses GC consistently, form is said to be dominant because the correctness of circle outweighed the incorrectness of green. Conversely, if RT is chosen consistently then color is presumed dominant over form.

There is ample evidence of differential cue-dominance. In fact Aristotle observed that given simultaneous stimulation the stronger always tends to extrude the weaker, while Pavlov (1927) showed that one cue in a compound conditioned stimulus can completely overshadow another. On the contemporary scene differential cue-dominance has been demonstrated with a variety of *S*s, e.g., pigeons (Reynolds, 1961), rats (Lawrence, 1949), monkeys (D'Amato & Fazzaro, 1966), and children (Suchmann & Trabasso, 1966). Because continuity theory is sometimes misunderstood, the occurrence of any kind of cue-dominance is assumed to be counterevidence. Actually two kinds of cue-dominance should be distinguished—intrinsic and acquired. Intrinsic cue-dominance, operationally defined in terms of the basic paradigm in Table 1, reflects the relative sensitivity of the organism's receptors to the two sets of cues. For example, if the illustrative discrimination were presented to an organism that sees red and green clearly but can barely differentiate circle from triangle, the colors would be intrinsically dominant over the forms.* It will be shown that the demonstration of intrinsic cue-

* The second paradigm in Table 1, reversal-on-one-dimension, is also a test for intrinsic cue-dominance. This paradigm is used in experiments described in a later section, where it is discussed more fully.

dominance supports rather than contradicts continuity theory.

Acquired cue-dominance is operationally defined in terms of the optional-shift paradigm of Table 1. This more complex paradigm will be taken up in detail later. For now it is sufficient to describe a critical difference between it and the basic paradigm: the initial discrimination establishes one dimension as relevant (e.g., color) and the other as irrelevant (e.g., form) to the reinforcement contingencies. Acquired dominance is manifested if, on the opposed-cues test, the relevant dimension assumes more control than the irrelevant dimension. Whether this kind of dominance occurs in rats and, if so, whether it reflects a central or a peripheral process is still highly controversial. The occurrence of acquired dominance in rats will be explored further after intrinsic cue-dominance is dealt with.

AN INTRINSIC CUE-DOMINANCE MODEL OF CONTINUITY THEORY

Intrinsic cue-dominance can be explained by continuity theory when the effect of stimulus generalization is considered. To do this precisely requires a detailed model, but the general idea can be described fairly simply. When Spence incorporated stimulus generalization into his theory (1937), he dealt with the effect of generalization between the positive and negative cues of a single dimension. However, stimulus generalization also operates among stimulus compounds composed of two dimensions as in the discrimination between RC (+) and GT (−). In this case a certain amount of stimulus generalization occurs between the cues on the color dimension and between the cues on the form dimension. Unless the psychophysical differences between the cues are carefully matched there will be a difference between the amount of generalization that corresponds to the two dimensions. Assume, for example, that there is less generalization between R and G than between C and T. The effect of this difference between the color and form cues is that every reinforced response to RC produces a greater difference in the excitatory tendency between R and G than between C and T. Similarly, every nonreinforced response produces a greater difference in inhibitory tendencies between the color cues than between the form cues. The effect of training is that the differential effective excitatory tendency associated with the color cues will exceed the differential excitatory tendency associated with the form cues. Let this difference between the two differentials be known as the second-order difference. It will be shown that, according to continuity theory, choice behavior on the opposed-cues test depends on the second-order difference. Thus, if the second-order difference favors the color cues the rat will choose RT more often than GC; consequently the color cues will be declared dominant over the form cues.

Kendler, Basden, and Bruckner (1970) cast this theory into a formal model capable of generating verifiable predictions about the transfer behavior of rats trained on differentially dominant dimensions. The intrinsic cue-dominance (ICD) model is intended to apply to the learning and transfer of naive rats in a class of experimental paradigms that entail simultaneous discriminations between pairs of stimuli that differ on two orthogonal visual dimensions as in the case of RT (+) vs. GC (−). Although the ICD model departs in details from Spence's formulations, the essential tenets of continuity theory are maintained.

Hypothetical excitatory tendencies

At the outset of training, a hypothetical excitatory tendency, E, is assumed to evoke the choice response associated with each discriminable cue in the display. These tendencies derive either from innate predispositions or from the previous reinforcement history of the animal and may vary in strength from zero to some maximal value, M_E. The M_E is not given a specific value to allow for the possibility that some modalities may have higher maximum excitatory tendencies than others. For example, it may prove propitious in the future to assume that for rats the maximum excitatory tendency for proprioceptive cues is higher than for visual cues, to account for differences in learning speed characteristic of the two modalities. However, for the sake of simplicity it is assumed that within the visual modality all dimensions have a common maximum. The effect of each reinforced trial is to increase the excitatory tendency of each cue in the reinforced stimulus complex by an amount that is proportional to the difference between E and M_E. That is

$$E_{R_{n+1}} = E_{R_n} + \theta(M_E - E_{R_n}) \text{ and } E_{C_{n+1}} = E_{C_n} + \theta(M_E - E_{C_n}) \quad (1)$$

where n represents a reinforced trial, R and C represent red and circle, and θ is a fractional-rate parameter that reflects individual and, perhaps, species differences in learning facility. The rate parameter for a given organism is assumed to be constant across dimensions.

Each reinforced response to the correct stimulus complex is assumed to have a generalized effect on the excitatory tendency of each cue in the negative stimulus complex, which in this case is a green triangle (GT). In order to avoid unnecessary controversy no particular form is ascribed to the generalization gradient. The only quantitative relationship specified is that the magnitude of generalized excitation increases monotonically with the psychophysical similarity between the cues on a given dimension. This assumption takes the form

$$E_{G_{n+1}} = E_{G_n} + \theta(A_{RG} M_E - E_{G_n}) \text{ and } E_{T_{n+1}} = E_{T_n} + \theta(A_{CT} M_E - E_{T_n}) \quad (2)$$

where θ, the rate parameter is the same as in Equation 1, and A_{RG} and A_{CT} represent two values between 0 and 1 which are related to the psychophysical similarity between the cues specified by the subscripts. Thus A_{RG} represents a value associated with red and green cues. A_{CT} represents a value associated with circle and triangle. Equation 2 ascribes a limiting value to the generalized excitatory tendency of each negative cue (e.g., $A_{RG}M_E$). For illustrative purposes A_{CT} is assumed to be greater than A_{RG}. If on any given reinforced trial the excitatory tendency of the negative cue is less than its generalized limit (i.e., if $E_G < A_{RG}M_E$), there will be an increase in E_G. The amount of increment on any given trial will be proportional to the difference between E_G and its generalized limit $A_{RG}M_E$.

Although it may seem paradoxical, the excitatory tendency of the negative cue can be greater than its generalized limit. This could occur, for example, if an organism is trained initially on R (+) and G (−) and then the reinforcement contingencies are reversed. Suppose that during initial training E_R had come close to M_E. At the outset of the reversed discrimination E_R would be greater than $A_{GR}M_E$. In that case each reinforced choice of G would reduce rather than increase E_R, causing it to approach the generalized limit. In effect this assumption allows for the gradual restoration of the generalization gradient around the reinforced cue whenever there is a shift in reinforcement contingencies.

Hypothetical inhibitory tendencies

The ICD model follows Spence in assuming that there is also a hypothetical inhibitory tendency, I, associated with each discriminable cue in the display. These tendencies to inhibit the choice response also derive from innate predispositions or previous reinforcement history and may vary in strength from zero to some maximal value, M_I. The inhibitory processs parallels the excitatory process in that each nonreinforced response increases the inhibitory tendency of each incorrect cue as follows:

$$I_{G_{m+1}} = I_{G_m} + \phi(M_I - I_{G_m}) \text{ and } I_{T_{m+1}} = I_{T_m} + \phi(M_I - I_{T_m}) \quad (3)$$

where m represents a nonreinforced trial, G and T represent green and triangle, and ϕ is a fractional-rate parameter reflecting individual differences. Note that although the increment to I takes the same form as the increment to E, both the maximum value of I and the rate at which it approaches its maximum may be different than the corresponding values for E.

Each nonreinforced response also results in a generalized effect on the inhibitory tendency of each cue in the positive compound by an amount related to their psychophysical similarity.

$$I_{R_{m+1}} = I_{R_m} + \phi(B_{GR}M_I - I_{R_m}) \text{ and } I_{C_{m+1}} = I_{C_m} + \phi(B_{TC}M_I - I_{C_m}) \quad (4)$$

where ϕ, the rate parameter, is the same as in (3), and B_{GR} and B_{TC} represent two values between 0 and 1 which are related to the psychophysical similarity between the cues specified by the subscripts. It is not assumed that the gradient of inhibition takes the same form as the gradient of excitation. The only assumption is that the magnitude of generalized inhibition increases with psychophysical similarity. For our illustrative case B_{TC} would be greater than B_{GR}.

Coordination of excitatory and inhibitory tendencies

The ICD model makes the conventional assumption that the effective excitatory strength, $\overline{E}$, of a given cue equals the difference between its excitatory and inhibitory tendencies (e.g., $\overline{E}_R = E_R - I_R$). The tendency to choose one cue over another will be determined by the difference, *d*, between their respective effective excitatory tendencies. Thus the difference between $\overline{E}_R$ and $\overline{E}_G$ after n reinforced trials to red and m nonreinforced trials to green takes the following form:

$$d_{RG_{n,m}} = \overline{E}_{R_{n,m}} - \overline{E}_{G_{n,m}} = (E_{R_n} - E_{G_n}) + (I_{G_m} - I_{R_m})$$

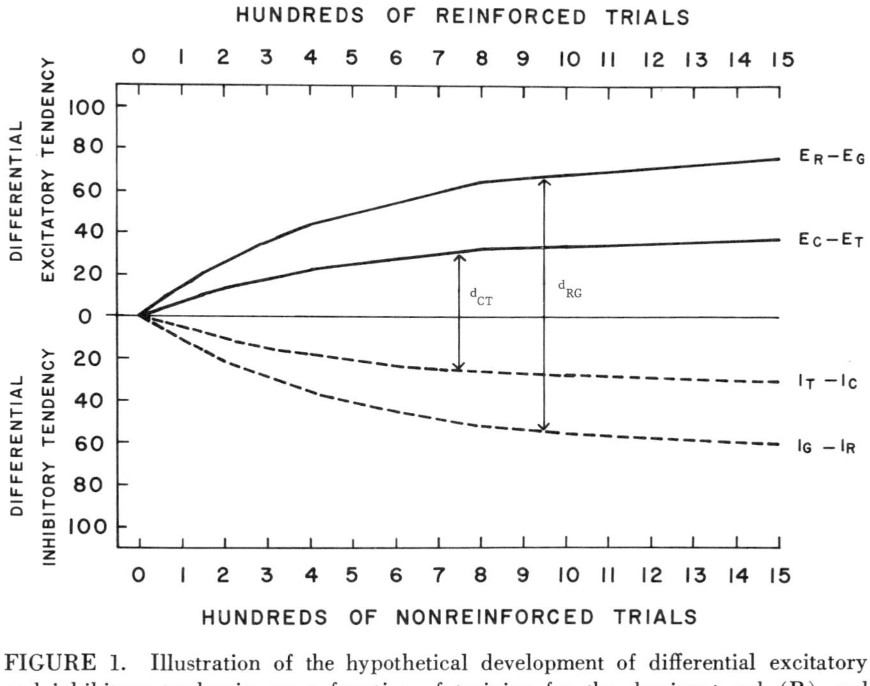

FIGURE 1. Illustration of the hypothetical development of differential excitatory and inhibitory tendencies as a function of training for the dominant red (R) and green (G) cues and for the nondominant circle (C) and triangle (T), when the response to red circle is reinforced and the response to green triangle is not.

If we expand this equation as in (5) it become manifest that d_{RG} is determined by two components. One component is coordinate with cue salience. The other is coordinate with the *E*s and *I*s with which the animal enters the training situation which we shall call initial tendencies.

$$d_{RG_{n,m}} = \underbrace{[1 - (1 - \theta)^n]\, M_E\, (1 - A_{RG}) + [1 - (1 - \phi)^m]\, M_I\, (1 - B_{GR})}_{\text{salience component}} \tag{5}$$

$$+ \underbrace{(1 - \theta)^n (E_{R_{0,0}} - E_{G_{0,0}}) + (1 - \theta)^m (I_{G_{0,0}} - I_{R_{0,0}})}_{\text{initial-tendencies component}}$$

where the subscript 0, 0 refers to the outset of training when n = m = 0.

Equation 5 shows that the magnitude of the salience component decreases with the psychophysical similarity between the positive and negative cues and increases with the number of training trials. Thus, as illustrated in Figure 1, the rate at which *d* increases during the course of training depends on the salience of the cues. If we assume that *d* must attain a given threshold value before choice behavior is affected, then the more salient the cues the more rapid the learning.

According to Equation 5 the effect of the initial-tendencies component is inversely related to the number of training trials. If the animal has no preference, the initial *E* and *I* tendencies for red and green are equal. In this case the entire initial-tendencies component equals zero and choice behavior, or the course of learning, is dependent only on the salience component. If the animal has a preference, the effect could either be to increase or to decrease *d*, depending on whether the preferred cue is correct or incorrect. But in either case as n, m, or both increase, the influence of the initial-tendencies component on *d* decreases. Thus the implications of the model for discrimination learning between cues that differ on one dimension is consonant with two facts (a) learning is more rapid if the rat is trained with, rather than against, his preference, and (b) the speed of learning is positively related to the psychophysical difference between the cues.

The next step is to apply the model to discriminations composed of cues that differ concurrently on two dimensions. This step requires that we make some assumption about how the excitatory tendencies associated with cues on two different dimensions combine.

Stimulus compounding

It is beyond the scope of this essay to provide an analysis of the very complex processes underlying stimulus compounding. The proposed assumption is intended to fit a restricted set of experimental conditions. Given a display composed of two orthogonal dimensions, like color and form, the effective excitatory tendency of each stimulus compound is assumed to equal the sum of its component effective excitatory tendencies (e.g., $\overline{E}_{\mathrm{RC}} = \overline{E}_{\mathrm{R}} + \overline{E}_{\mathrm{C}}$. To approach the necessary complexity, a more comprehensive theory of stimulus compounding will require (a) an interaction term to encompass dimensions that do interact, such as height and width or size and brightness; (b) a system for progressively reducing the increment to be derived from each additional component; (c) a method for incorporating perceptual phenomena such as stimulus contrast; and so on. I shall also delay consideration of the differential effect of learned orientation or scanning strategies on the different components for some future time. At this stage of theoretical development the sensible strategy is to limit theoretical complexity and increase mathematical tractability by selecting experimental situations that minimize the effects of factors such as those described above. Since the present theoretical effort is semiquantitative, the simple additive assumption will be used with the understanding that broader application will require a more complex analysis.

Applying the additivity assumption to the discrimination between RC (+) and GT (−), it follows that $\overline{E}_{\mathrm{RC}} = \overline{E}_{\mathrm{R}} + \overline{E}_{\mathrm{C}}$ and $\overline{E}_{\mathrm{GT}} = \overline{E}_{\mathrm{G}} + \overline{E}_{\mathrm{T}}$. The tendency to choose the correct stimulus complex after n and m trials could then be expressed as

$$\overline{E}_{\mathrm{RC}_{n,m}} - \overline{E}_{\mathrm{GT}_{n,m}} = (E_{\mathrm{R}_n} - E_{\mathrm{G}_n}) + (I_{\mathrm{G}_m} - I_{\mathrm{R}_m}) + (E_{\mathrm{C}_n} - E_{\mathrm{T}_n}) + (I_{\mathrm{T}_m} - I_{\mathrm{C}_m}) = d_{\mathrm{RG}_{n,m}} + d_{\mathrm{CT}_{n,m}} \qquad (6)$$

Equation 6 shows that learning a discrimination between correlated cues on two dimensions would ordinarily be faster than learning a discrimination based on either dimension taken by itself. But the magnitude of the facilitation is dependent on the salience of the cues on the additional dimension. The more salient the additional cues, the greater the facilitation. Adding a pair of cues with low salience to a highly salient pair may produce so little effect on the differential excitatory tendencies as to be undetectable in learning or choice behavior.

Implications for intrinsic cue-dominance

Suppose that after the animal has learned the discrimination between RC (+) and GT (−), a test for cue-dominance is presented. This test entails opposing the cues on the two dimensions by requiring a choice between RT and GC. If the color cues are dominant then RT choices should prevail; if the form cues are dominant then GC choices should prevail. Applying the model to this circumstance entails comparing the composite effective excitatory tendencies of RT and GC as follows:

$$E_{RT_{n,m}} - E_{GC_{n,m}} = (E_{R_n} - E_{G_n}) + (I_{G_m} - I_{R_m}) - (E_{C_n} - E_{T_n}) - (I_{T_m} - I_{C_m}) = d_{RG_{n,m}} - d_{CT_{n,m}} \quad (7)$$

If $d_{RG_{n,m}}$ exceeds $d_{CT_{n,m}}$ by a sufficient magnitude, the rat will consistently choose RT. Thus while Equation 6 shows that choice behavior on the *training* compound depends on the sum of the effective differences associated with each dimension, Equation 7 shows that choice behavior on the *opposed-cues* compound depends on the difference between these effective differences (i.e., the second-order difference). If Equation 7 is expanded, it will show that the second-order difference resolves into the two components previously encountered, namely the salience component and the initial-tendencies component.

$$\begin{aligned} d_{RG_{n,m}} - d_{CT_{n,m}} = {} & [1 - (1-\theta)^n]\, M_E\, (A_{CT} - A_{RG}) + \\ & [1 - (1-\phi)^m]\, M_I\, (B_{TC} - B_{GR}) \Big\} \text{ salience component} \\ & + (1-\phi)^n\, (E_{R_{0,0}} - E_{G_{0,0}} + E_{T_{0,0}} - E_{C_{0,0}}) \\ & + (1-\phi)^m\, (I_{G_{0,0}} - I_{R_{0,0}} + I_{C_{0,0}} - I_{T_{0,0}}) \Big\} \text{ Initial-tendencies component} \end{aligned} \quad (8)$$

Suppose we simplify the implications by assuming that at the outset of learning the excitatory tendencies within each dimension and the inhibitory tendencies within each dimension are equal—that is,

$$E_{R_{0,0}} = E_{G_{0,0}},\ E_{T_{0,0}} = E_{C_{0,0}},\ I_{R_{0,0}} = I_{G_{0,0}},\ \text{and } I_{C_{0,0}} = I_{T_{0,0}}.$$

The initial-tendencies component drops out and the second-order difference depends exclusively on the salience component. Equation 8 shows that if there is more generalization between the form cues than between the color cues, that is, $A_{CT} > A_{RG}$ and $B_{TC} > B_{GR}$, then the second-order difference will be positive. A positive difference, if large enough to reach or exceed the threshold, will effect an RT choice, indicating that the color cues are dominant. Conversely, if the form cues are more salient, the second-order difference in Equation 8 will be negative. If this difference is equal to or greater than the required threshold, the animal should choose GC, indicating that the form cues are dominant.

The magnitude of the second-order difference depends in a systematic way on both the magnitude of the salience difference and on the number of training trials. If the salience difference is large the number of training trials required to effect a differential choice will be proportionately small and vice versa.

In summary, the ICD model, illustrated in Figure 1, predicts that when an animal is trained on a stimulus complex composed of cues from two dimensions, the dimension with less generalization between the cues will have the potential to dominate the dimension with more generalization. Whether the potential dominance is manifested on an opposed-cues test will depend on the interaction of the following three factors: the magnitude of the differential salience of the two dimensions, the initial or predisposing effective excitatory tendencies of the individual components, and the number of training trials that preceded the test.

EXPERIMENTAL VERIFICATION OF THE INTRINSIC CUE-DOMINANCE MODEL

The intrinsic dominance of red-green cues over circle-triangle cues

Experimental tests of the implications of the ICD model would be straightforward if there were a metric for rats comparing either psychophysical differences or degree of generalization between stimuli across different dimensions. Since there is no such metric the first test to be reported was a bootstrap affair (Kendler, Basden, & Bruckner, 1970). The empirical question was whether intrinsic dominance, as defined in the model, could be demonstrated in individual rats of a given strain. Pilot studies suggested that if rats are trained on stimulus compounds that differ simultaneously on color (red vs. green) and form (circle vs. triangle), the color cues would prove to be dominant over the form cues.

It may seem odd to use colored stimuli for a species that is widely believed to be completely insensitive to hue, but nevertheless the choice proved expedient. My colleagues and I began our pilot studies on the color and form stimuli for two practical reasons. First, such stimuli were available from previous research with children, and second, we believed that rats would barely discriminate between the colors on the basis of differences in their luminosity, and that color would therefore be a low-salience dimension. To our surprise color turned out to be much more salient than form according to both the preliminary research and, also, as shall be shown, according to stringent experimental tests. We later found that Granit (1947) had reported that the rat retina is differentially receptive at 600 mu, which he interpreted as evidence of a "red" receptor. Unfortunately, according to illuminometer readings our green stimuli were more intense than our red stimuli, so the results make no substantive contribution to our understanding of rats' color perception per se. However, since the effective stimulus in the case of the circle and triangle is no more certain, the labels "red," "green," "circle," and "triangle" will be used with the understanding that they denote what the human sees, not necessarily what the rat perceives.

The intrinsic dominance of the color cues was measured by a more stringent variation of the usual opposed-cues test as illustrated in the second paradigm of Table 1 (see p. 241). In this variation the cues on a given dimension were established as dominant only if they got fewer reinforcements prior to the opposed-cues test than the cues on the less dominant dimension. To meet this condition each rat was trained to criterion on an initial discrimination between a pair of stimuli that differed simultaneously in color and form, e.g., GC (+) vs. RT (−). After criterion was reached a second discrimination was presented in which the conditions were rearranged so that the reinforcement pattern was held constant for one dimension and reversed for the other, e.g., RC (+) vs. GT (−). In the example the color cues are reversed so this procedure is called a reversal on color. To test for dominance, the opposed-cues test (e.g., GC vs. RT) was presented after one day of overtraining and again after three days of overtraining on the color reversal. The test series consisted of 25 trials in which test and relearning trials were randomly interspersed. If the reversed color dimension exerts more control than the constant form dimension, that is, if the animal chooses RT significantly more often than GC, then the color cues are dominant over the form cues. According to the model such a result is consistent with the hypothesis that there is more generalization between the form cues than between the color cues.

Two male rats of the Fischer strain were randomly assigned to one of four possible stimulus compounds that served as S+: GC, RC, GT, and RT. In order to control for the possibility that the reversal per se produced the preference for the reversed dimension, each rat was run through both a reversal on color and a reversal on form. Half had the reversal on color first and half had the reversal on form first. The first two columns of Table 2 show that every animal on each test made significantly more color- than form-determined choices after a reversal on color. Thus despite a reversal in the reinforcement pattern for the color cues, these cues exerted more influence on choice than the consistently reinforced form cues. The last two columns show that color choices also prevailed when reversal was on the form dimension. Consequently the reversal procedure per se cannot be responsible for the color preference. There is no doubt that the color cues dominated the form cues. In fact the color cues were so dominant that it might appear that the form cues were not discriminable to the rats. That the form cues are discriminable for rats was demonstrated in another experiment, to be described later, where the animals learned a discrimination in which these form cues were relevant and color cues irrelevant (Kendler, Basden, & Bruckner, 1970). But even if rats can discriminate the forms when form is the only relevant dimension, it is possible that when color and form are redundant nothing is

*TABLE 2. PROPORTION * OF COLOR-DOMINANT CHOICES ON TEST TRIALS (Kendler, Basden, & Bruckner, 1970)*

Subjects	After Reversal on Color With Form Constant — Overtraining Trials		After Reversal on Form With Color Constant — Overtraining Trials	
	50	*200*	*50*	*200*
1	.77	.91	.89	.75
2	.85	.92	1.00	.92
3	1.00	.77	.91	.73
4	.91	.90	.92	.92
5	.82	.82	.82	1.00
6	.85	.92	1.00	.45
7	.83	.92	1.00	.92
8	1.00	1.00	1.00	1.00

* All values are significant ($p \leq .05$) except for the value .45 found in Subject 6.

learned about the form cues. Since the model predicts otherwise, some form learning should be demonstrable under these conditions.

To test for form learning when form and color were redundant, four additional rats were trained on the procedure that entailed a reversal on color with form held constant. Instead of opposed-cues tests, these rats were presented with a series of choices between two forms that did *not* differ in color (e.g., RC vs. RT). If they chose the correct form more often than the incorrect form, this would be evidence of form learning. The first two columns of Table 3 show that after the first reversal on color there were more correct than incorrect form choices for the group as a whole, but that only one of the individual choice frequencies (Subject 10) is statistically significant. This result is consistent with the model because, if color and form are redundant,

TABLE 3. PROPORTION OF CORRECT FORM-CHOICES ON TEST TRIALS WITH COLOR CONSTANT (Kendler, Basden, & Bruckner 1970)

Subjects	After First Reversal on Color — Overtraining Trials		After Second Reversal on Color — Overtraining Trials	
	50	*200*	*50*	*200*
9	.50	.46	.64	.85 *
10	.77 *	.54	.75	.38
11	.75	.54	.73	.90 *
12	.64	.62	.46	.77 *

* $p < .05$

criterion should be attained before the difference in excitatory tendencies between the nondominant form cues reaches threshold. Overtraining does not entirely alleviate this condition because even though the *E* of the positive form cue is increased, the *I* of the negative form cue is rarely increased because of the almost complete absence of errors. The ICD model implies that maximal separation depends on an optimal number of reinforcements *and* nonreinforcements. To effect a greater separation between $\bar{E}$s for the form cues, the rats were given a second reversal on color in which the previously correct color was paired with the incorrect form. This increased the number of nonreinforced choices of the incorrect form. Under these conditions, three of the four animals made reliably more correct than incorrect form choices in the last series of test trials. When *S* 10, the maverick of the experiment, was retested the next day he made 80 percent correct form choices. These results indicate that although the color cues plainly dominated the form cues, some learning occurred on the form cues.

The intrinsic dominance of brightness over orientation cues

To test the generality of the model and lay the groundwork for subsequent experimental manipulation of intrinsic dominance, Basden (1969) replicated the reversal-on-one-dimension design with different cues and a different strain of rats. Eight male hooded rats of the Long-Evans strain were trained on stimuli that differed simultaneously on brightness (dim vs. bright center circle) and orientation (horizontally vs. vertically striped annulus surrounding the circle). After attaining criterion on the initial discrimination, half of the rats were reversed on one dimension and half were reversed on the other. The reversal training was followed by the opposed-cues test for intrinsic dominance after criterion and again after 120 overtraining trials.

Table 4 (Columns 1 and 2) shows that the brightness cues were dominant over the orientation cues for each rat. The increase in brightness preference from Column 1 to Column 2 shows that the brightness preference increased with overtraining, a result consistent with the ICD model. The last two columns verify that the brightness preference is not due to the reversal procedure per se.

In this experiment a comparison between the test and retraining performance was used to determine whether the rats had learned anything about the nondominant orientation cues. If performance on the retraining trials, in which the correct brightness and orientation cues are paired, is better than on the test trials, in which the correct brightness is paired with the incorrect orientation cue, then the animal must be responsive to the orientation as well as the brightness cues. The results were that, at criterion, retraining performance was superior to test performance for every rat, testifying to learning on the nondominant orientation dimension. All of these results are quite consistent with the ICD model.

*TABLE 4. PROPORTION * OF BRIGHTNESS-DOMINANT CHOICES ON TEST TRIALS (Basden, 1969)*

After Reversal on Brightness with Orientation Constant			After Reversal on Orientation with Brightness Constant		
Subjects	Criterion	Overtraining	Subjects	Criterion	Overtraining
1	.75	1.00	5	1.00	.92
2	.54	.85	6	.78	.92
3	.75	1.00	7	1.00	1.00
4	.73	.92	8	1.00	1.00

* All values are significant ($p \leq .05$) except for the values .54 and .73 found in Column 1 for Subjects 2 and 4.

Manipulation of intrinsic dominance by varying the difference between cues

The ICD model assumes that intrinsic dominance is a function of the relative magnitude of the difference between the cues on the compared dimensions. If so, it should be possible to manipulate the dominance relationship between two dimensions by varying the physical and, hence the psychophysical, difference between the component cues. Basden (1969) tested this proposition by training 32 hooded rats on an initial discrimination between stimuli that differed concurrently in brightness and orientation. While the orientation cues were identical for all animals, for half of them the brightnesses were relatively less disparate (LD), while for the other half they were more disparate (MD). The animals were trained to criterion on the initial discrimination and then tested for dimensional dominance on the opposed-cues test. Then they were overtrained for 120 trials and tested again.*

The expectation that the brightness cues would be dominant for the MD group and the orientation cues would be dominant for the LD group was confirmed. The mean proportion of brightness-dominant choices for the MD group was .79 at criterion and .88 after overtraining (i.e., brightness was dominant). On the other hand, for the LD group orientation was dominant since the proportion of orientation-dominant choices was .76 at criterion and .86 after overtraining.

* Note that for this test Basden used the more sensitive basic paradigm described in Table 1 and not the more stringent reversal-on-one-dimension paradigm used by Kendler et al., 1970.

Dimensional dominance can be manipulated by varying the difference between the cues on the dimension. The results were also in accord with the ICD model in that preference increased with overtraining and the correct choices on retraining trials exceeded the choices of the dominant cue on the test trials.

ACQUIRED CUE-DOMINANCE

A definition of acquired cue-dominance

The previous sections demonstrated that the facts of intrinsic cue-dominance in rats can be accounted for by a model based on continuity theory. It is time now to deal with the relationship between the model and the facts of acquired cue-dominance in rats. Acquired cue-dominance will be defined in terms of the optimal-shift paradigm illustrated in Table 1. This paradigm differs from the other two only in that during the initial discrimination one dimension is relevant and the other is not. Relevancy is established by presenting, in random alternation, two pairs of stimuli that differ concurrently on two dimensions, and making reward contingent on response to only one dimension. In the example a green choice is always rewarded and a red choice is never rewarded; hence color is relevant. Since obtaining the reward in no way depends on the form cues, they are irrelevant. To determine whether more is learned about the relevant cues, the initial discrimination is followed by a shift discrimination in which only one pair of stimuli is presented and the reinforcement pattern is reversed, e.g., RC (+) vs. GT (−). To learn this discrimination the animal must shift his response. The question is whether the rat is more likely to make a reversal shift within the relevant dimension (e.g., from G to R), than an extradimensional shift to the cue on the previously irrelevant dimension (e.g., from G to C). The shift discrimination is followed by a series of opposed-cues tests which determine whether reversal (Rv) or extradimensional (Ed) choices prevailed. Acquired dominance is demonstrated if Rv choices prevail regardless of which dimension was relevant in the initial discrimination. Acquired dominance, so defined, has been repeatedly demonstrated in human beings (e.g., Kendler & Kendler, 1970). The question now asked is whether acquired dominance, so defined, occurs in rats.

The intrinsic cue-dominance model applied to the optional-shift paradigm

The ICD model predicts that rats will not manifest acquired dominance of the relevant cues if the relevant and irrelevant dimensions are equally salient or, failing such equality, if the dimensions are counterbalanced in the experimental design. A number of affirmative predictions also flow from the model, predictions that depend on the effect of three variables: (a) the number of training trials on the shift discrimination prior to the opposed-cues test, (b) the magnitude of the differential intrinsic cue-salience, and (c) whether the intrinsically dominant dimension was initially relevant or irrelevant.

The predictions derive from the following adaptation of Equation 8 to the opposed-cues test of the optional-shift paradigm:

$$d_{i+i-_{n,m}} - d_{r+r-_{n,m}} = \text{salience component} + \text{initial-learning component} \quad (9)$$

where d represents the difference between the effective excitatory tendencies of the subscripted cues; i and r refer to the cues on the irrelevant and relevant dimensions of the initial discrimination; (+) and (−) represent the positive and negative values on these dimensions during the *shift* discrimination; n and m refer to the number of reinforced and nonreinforced trials on the *shift* discrimination; and the salience and initial-learning components are defined as follows:

$$\text{salience component} = [1 - (1 - \theta)^n] M_E (A_{r+r-} - A_{i+i-}) + [1 - (1 - \phi)^m] M_I (B_{r-r+} - B_{i-i+}$$

$$\text{initial-learning component} = (1 - \theta)^n (E_{i+_{0,0}} - E_{i-_{0,0}} + E_{r-_{0,0}} - E_{r+_{0,0}}) + (1 - \phi)^m (I_{i-_{0,0}} - I_{i+_{0,0}} + I_{r+_{0,0}} - I_{r-_{0,0}})$$

Whether test choices will be primarily Ed, Rv, or neither depends on whether the differential effective excitatory tendency associated with the previously irrelevant cues (d_{i+i-}) is greater than, less than, or equal to the differential effective excitatory tendency associated with the previously relevant cues (d_{r+r-}). If $d_{i+i-} > d_{r+r-}$, and the difference equals or exceeds the threshold, then Ed choices should prevail. Conversely, if $d_{i+i-} < d_{r+r-}$, and the difference equals or exceeds the threshold, then Rv choices should prevail. If the difference between d_{i+i-} and d_{r+r-} is less than the required threshold, then either choice should be equally likely. Whether d_{i+i-} is greater or less than d_{r+r-} depends, in turn, on whether the sum of the initial-learning and salience components is positive or negative in sign. Thus Equation 9 shows that the direction choice behavior should take depends on the sign of the initial-learning component and the sign of the salience component. The contribution of each component can be considered separately.

Consider first the effect of the initial-learning component. At the outset of the shift discrimination, n = m = 0, therefore $(1 - \theta)^n = (1 - \phi)^m = 1$. This term equals whatever value it had attained at the end of the initial discrimination. Since the animal reached criterion on the initial discrimination, the initial-learning component must be greater than zero by some amount.

As training on the shift discrimination proceeds, n and m increase. As n and m increase, $(1 - \theta)^n$ and $(1 - \phi)^m$ decrease and consequently the contribution of the initial-learning term decreases. But until n and m approach infinity, the effect of the initial discrimination is to make Ed choices more probable than Rv choices. Overtraining during the shift discrimination can increase n until it approaches infinity, but there is no way to ensure that m does likewise since the animal will make few, if any, incorrect choices as the overtraining increases. Hence the effect of initial training, if other things are equal, is to incline the animal toward Ed choices, but this effect decreases as training on the shift discrimination increases.

Now consider the salience component. If the two dimensions are equally salient, the salience term collapses to zero. Choice behavior would therefore depend entirely on the initial-learning component. But if the dimensions are differentially salient, Equation 9 shows that the effect depends on both the amount of training on the shift discrimination prior to the test and on the differential salience of the relevant and irrelevant cues. At the outset of the shift discrimination, when n and m equal zero, $[1 - (1 - \theta)^n] = [1 - (1 - \phi)^m] = 0$. Consequently the entire salience component collapses to zero and choice behavior, reasonably enough, is determined exclusively by the initial training. As training on the shift discrimination increases, n and m increase. The effect is to increase the contribution of the salience component. In other words, early in training the initial-tendencies component has a greater weight than the salience component, but as training proceeds the balance swings toward the salience component.

Whether the effect of the salience component is in the direction of Ed or Rv choices depends on whether the dominant cues are irrelevant or relevant. If the relevant cues are nondominant, the sign of the salience component is positive. In this case, tests given early in the shift discrimination should tend to be Ed because of the initial-tendencies component. As training proceeds the effect of the initial-tendencies component decreases, but since the effect of the salience component is in the direction of Ed choices, such choices should continue to prevail, if the differential salience is sufficient.

The prediction becomes more complicated if the relevant cues are dominant, because in this case the salience component and initial-learning component have opposing effects. If the relevant cues are dominant then the sign of the salience component is negative. The effect is, therefore, to increase the tendency to make Rv choices. As before, for tests given at the outset of training on the shift discrimination, when the initial-tendencies component is relatively prepotent, Ed choices should prevail. But as training increases, the prepotency of the salience component increases; therefore the tendency to make Rv choices should increase until, if the salience difference is large enough, Rv choices should prevail. How much training on the shift discrimination is required before Rv choices prevail should depend on the salience difference.

FURTHER EXPERIMENTAL VERIFICATION OF THE INTRINSIC CUE-DOMINANCE MODEL

Color and form cues in the optional-shift paradigm

After it was established that the red-green cues were dominant over the circle-triangle cues, the same cues were used in the optional-shift paradigm with 16 rats of the Fischer strain (Kendler, Basden, & Bruckner, 1970). For 8 rats the color cues were initially relevant; for the other 8 the form cues were initially relevant. The daily training sessions consisted of 60 trials. All animals were trained on the initial discrimination to a criterion of 75 percent correct trials on one day. The next day the shift discrimination was presented. To check on the predictions about the relationship between the amount of training, cue-dominance, and choice behavior on opposed-cues tests, a probe-testing procedure was used throughout the shift discrimination. A test trial was presented after a fixed number of reinforced trials each day (i.e., after reinforced trials 8, 14, 23, 30, 43, and 58). As in the previous research either choice on a test trial was reinforced. Criterion performance on the shift discrimination was 95 percent of the training trials correct. The rats were run for 5 days more after attaining criterion.

As expected the initial discrimination was learned much more easily when the dominant color cues were relevant (mean days = 3.2) than when the nondominant form cues were (mean days = 36.8). No significant difference occurred, however, in mean days to criterion on the shift discrimination between form (14.8) and color (12.2) *S*s.

Table 5 reports the test trial results. To obtain the five training blocks per rat, the total number of reinforced-training trials prior to attainment of criterion were divided into three equal blocks while those in postcriterion training were divided into two equal blocks. The ICD model predicts that the proportion of Rv choices for the form-relevant group should be below .50 in

TABLE 5. MEAN PROPORTION OF REVERSAL CHOICES ON OPPOSED-CUES TESTS ADMINISTERED DURING THE SHIFT DISCRIMINATION (Kendler, Basden, & Bruckner, 1970)

	Training Block of the Shift Discrimination				
Groups	*1*	*2*	*3*	*4*	*5*
Color Relevant	.58	.78	.82	.90	.91
Form Relevant	.30	.14	.04	.03	.03
Combined	.44	.46	.43	.46	.47

every training block. The prediction for the color-relevant group is that the proportion of Rv choices should be relatively low in the first block but should increase as training increases. Both predictions were confirmed. The final prediction is that rats should not manifest acquired dominance. In this experiment positive evidence of acquired dominance depends on the proportion of Rv choices exceeding .50 for both groups combined. Since this proportion (last row of Table 5) was below .50 on every training block, there is no evidence of acquired dominance in these data.

Lovejoy (1968) proposes that acquired dominance in rats is a bounded, second-order effect not likely to mask strong intrinsic-dominance differences. Perhaps the intrinsic-dominance difference in the case of the color and form cues is so robust that it overrides the fragile acquired-dominance mechanism. The next study, in addition to providing another test of the continuity model, also provides an opportunity to test for acquired-dimensional dominance when there is much less intrinsic-dominance difference.

Brightness and size cues in the optional-shift paradigm

This research, conducted before the ICD model was formulated, was designed to compare the performance of rats and children in the optional-shift paradigm. Some of the results were published in a brief report (Kendler, Kendler, & Silfen, 1964), but most of the data reported below are appearing in print for the first time.

The cues in this experiment were squares that differed in size (7.0 vs. 3.8 cm. on a side) and in reflected brightness (black vs. white). One group of 16 rats was tested for intrinsic cue-dominance after having initially been trained with the brightness and size cues concurrently relevant, e.g., large black (+) vs. small white (−). In this experiment, *as well as in the rest of the experiments to be cited*, rats were given 20 trials per day and all training was to a criterion of 18 out of 20 successive correct choices with the last 10 all correct. The day after criterion was attained the rat was presented with a series of 10 opposed-cues tests (e.g., large whole vs. small black) interspersed with 10 relearning trials.

Seven of the 16 rats showed a significant preference for brightness (i.e., 8 or more brightness choices on the 10 test trials); the rest showed no significant preference. The proportion of brightness choices for the group as a whole was .70. Apparently the brightness cues were intrinsically dominant over the form cues but, since the basic paradigm used in this experiment is less demanding than the reversal-on-one-dimension paradigm used by Kendler, Basden, & Bruckner (1970), precise comparison with the color-form cues is not possible.

A second group, composed of 24 rats, was trained on the optional-shift paradigm with the same cues. Half of the animals were trained with the brightness cues and half with the size cues initially relevant. Each stimulus (i.e., black, white, large, and small) served as S+ for 6 rats. The mean number of days to criterion on the initial discrimination for the brightness- and size-relevant groups were 6.2 and 11.9 respectively. These results indicate that the brightness cues were dominant but that the differential dominance is much less than in the case of the color and form cues.

After training on the initial discrimination the rats learned the shift discrimination. The brightness- and size-relevant groups reached criterion in 5.4 and 4.9 mean days respectively; this difference was not statistically significant. After criterion was attained on the shift discrimination, the test series (i.e., 10 opposed-cues trials interspersed with 10 relearning trials), was presented.

The predictions from the ICD model relevant to test performance on this experiment were that: (a) the proportion of Rv choices should be greater for the brightness-relevant group than for the form-relevant group, and (b) the proportion of Rv choices for both groups combined should be less than .50. The obtained proportion of Rv choices was .50 for the brightness-relevant group and .23 for the form-relevant group; for both groups combined the proportion was .36. Thus the results of this experiment were also consistent with the ICD model and, once again, there was no evidence of acquired cue-dominance in rats. But neither of the experiments cited thus far overtrained the animals on the initial discrimination. Since overtraining is important to some of the selective attention models, we will discuss two experiments in the next section that satisfy this condition.

Effect of overtraining during the initial discrimination

Tighe and Tighe (1966) used the optional-shift paradigm with stimuli that varied the orientation of stripes (horizontal vs. vertical) and dimensionality (flat vs. raised surfaces). Three groups, 24 rats per group, varied only in the amount of overtraining on the initial discrimination: 0, 200, and 300 overtraining trials. Half of the animals in each overtraining group were trained with the flat-raised areas relevant and half were trained with the horizontal-vertical cues relevant.

Since the flat-raised group learned in significantly fewer trials than the horizontal-vertical group (means of 70.5 and 138.3, respectively), one may assume that the flat-raised cues were dominant. Consequently more reversal choices would be expected in the flat-raised group than in the horizontal-vertical group. The mean number of reversal choices per group on the test trials were, however, not reported. Instead the results were presented in terms of individual performance categorized as in Table 6. Again the predictions of the ICD model were confirmed. At every level of overtraining more reversal choices occurred in the dominant (flat-raised) group than in

TABLE 6. PROPORTION OF RATS IN EACH CATEGORY OF OPPOSED-CUES TEST CHOICE BEHAVIOR (Tighe & Tighe, 1966)

	Flat-Raised Group			Horizontal-Vertical Group		
Overtraining trials	8 or more Ed choices	Non-selective	8 or more Rv choices	8 or more Ed choices	Non-selective	8 or more Rv choices
0	.00	.67	.33	.83	.17	.00
200	.08	.67	.25	.83	.17	.00
300	.00	1.00	.00	1.00	.00	.00
Combined	.03	.78	.19	.89	.11	.00

the nondominant (horizontal-vertical) group. And at each level of overtraining, when the flat-raised and horizontal-vertical groups were collapsed, fewer animals made eight or more Rv choices than eight or more Ed choices.

Whether overtraining on the initial discrimination affected test behavior depended on which cues were initially relevant. Overtraining had no effect when the horizontal-vertical cues were relevant ($p = .48$, two-tailed). However, when the flat-raised cues were relevant, overtraining resulted in a *decrease* in the number of Rv choices which approached significance ($p = .09$, two-tailed).

How well do these overtraining results fit the ICD model? According to Equation 9 overtraining on the initial discrimination should increase the magnitude of the initial-learning component which, in turn, should decrease Rv choices. But such a decrease would be expected only if the magnitude of this component is not at or near its maximum prior to the overtraining. As Basden (1969) pointed out, whether or not the maximum is approached depends on the stringency of the criterion and on the difficulty of the discrimination. If the discrimination is difficult or the criterion is stringent, overtraining should have little or no effect. But if the discrimination is easy or the criterion is undemanding, overtraining should decrease Rv choices. Since in the Tighe and Tighe experiment the flat-raised discrimination was relatively easy, the horizontal-vertical discrimination was relatively difficult, and the criterion (18/20 correct choices) was stringent, the overtraining results were consistent with the ICD model.

The last study to be cited was performed by Sutherland and Mackintosh (1966) to test the assumption that the main effect of overtraining is to strengthen attention to the relevant dimension rather than to strengthen response attachments. They predicted that if rats are trained in the optional-shift paradigm, those given overtraining on the initial discrimination should subsequently learn more about the reversed cues in the shift discrimination than nonovertrained animals.

The training procedure was essentially as in the Tighe and Tighe (1966) experiment except that a modified Lashley Jumping Stand was used and the cues differed in orientation and reflected brightness. There were two groups, one of which learned the initial discrimination to criterion and the other of which was given 100 overtraining trials. The testing procedure, however, did not entail opposed cues. Instead only one dimension was varied at a time so that if testing was on the brightness cues, orientation was held constant, and vice versa. Twenty test trials were given with the cues of each dimension.

There was no significant difference in initial learning related to any of the variables. The results of the transfer tests were in accord with the ICD model since the rats made significantly more correct choices on tests with the initially irrelevant dimension (18.3) than on tests with the initially relevant dimension (11.2). That is, the irrelevant cues exerted more control than the relevant cues. There was also no evidence of selective attention since there was no difference to speak of between the overtrained (11.1) and nonovertrained (11.3) groups on the trials in which the initially relevant cues were presented.

Taken altogether the results of all of the experiments cited are consonant with the ICD model. No evidence of acquired cue-dominance appeared. Since the null hypothesis cannot be proven this evidence does not establish that there is no mechanism in rats that can produce acquired cue-dominance. On the other hand, it is quite obvious that acquired cue-dominance is much less important to behavioral control in rats than is either intrinsic cue-dominance or preliminary training.

Even though acquired dominance does not seem to be a significant factor in rat behavior, convincing evidence of some measure of inhibition of peripheral sensory reception of irrelevant stimulation may eventually be established. The ICD model would then have to be modified. But if one thinks about what form such a modification would take it becomes clear that it would be necessary to add to rather than change the fundamental conceptions of continuity theory. This addition would entail redefining the "stimuli that impinge on the sensorium" in proximal rather than distal terms and providing some postulates which relate distal to proximal stimulation. If those postulates resemble contemporary selective attention theory, we could argue about whether the result is a modified continuity or a modified noncontinuity theory; but in any case continuity principles will continue to be important in accounting for discrimination learning in rats, and perhaps in other infrahuman species.

SUMMARY AND CONCLUSIONS

The original continuity-noncontinuity controversy concerned the nature of discrimination learning in infrahuman organisms. The controversy hinged on two questions: (a) whether learning is discontinuous in the sense that practice preceding criterion performance is irrelevant and (b) whether associations are selective in the sense that they are limited to the relevant stimulus events. The continuity position, formulated by Spence (1936, 1937) answered "No" to both questions. The noncontinuity position, formulated by Lashley (1929, 1938) answered, "Yes." After a short-lived victory for continuity theory, the controversy has been revived by selective attention theorists who, by and large, advocate a *modified* noncontinuity approach. This approach is exemplified by Mackintosh (1965) who agrees that practice preceding criterion is *not* irrelevant to learning and that the associations formed are *not* limited to the relevant cues. He contends, however, that there is *some* selectivity in the associative process in the sense that the animal learns more about the relevant cues than about the irrelevant cues.

Whether or not there is some selectivity in the associative process is a much more subtle issue than was posed by the original controversy. Settling the new issue requires a more precise analysis of the discrimination learning process and a closer examination of details of the learning data. One consequence is that there is no single selective attention theory; there are, instead, a number of different models associated with different experimental paradigms and subject populations. The models have in common the assumption that *S* learns to attend selectively to the cues that are relevant to the reinforcement contingencies. The present paper proposes to increase the precision of continuity theory by presenting a model, applicable to the redundant-relevant-cue paradigm, designed to explain differential cue-salience (or dominance) in rats.

First a sharp distinction is drawn between intrinsic and acquired cue-salience. Intrinsic cue-salience is related to the sensitivity of the animal's receptors; acquired cue-salience is related to the reinforcement contingencies. The model amalgamates the major tenets of Spence's continuity theory drawn from the classical references on continuity theory (1936) and on stimulus generalization (1937). The specific forms of some of the assumptions are changed, but there are no radical departures from the basic principles of continuity theory. Intrinsic cue-salience is assumed to vary inversely with the degree of stimulus generalization between the cues on a given dimension, that is, the less generalization between the cues the greater their salience. One cue is defined as dominant over another if it is more salient. The model reduces the learning process to two orthogonal components, *viz.*, cue-salience and initial excitatory tendencies. Like Spence's original formulation, this model is an abstraction of a more complex process. It does not as yet incorporate consideration of the chain of responses leading up to the choice response and hence contains no account of orienting or scanning behavior. Nor is there any attempt to provide an account of all perceptual phenomena basic to stimulus compounding. The deliberate decision to exclude such important aspects of discrimination learning was made in order to increase theoretical tractability—on the assumption that experimental situations can be designed which reflect processes incorporated in the theory and minimize those that are not. Experiments are presented which show that, within these limitations, the model provides a good account of the effect of intrinsic cue-salience on the discrimination learning of naive rats.

Acquired cue-dominance, which is central to selective attention theory, has been previously shown to be important in the learning and transfer of mature humans (Kendler & Kendler, 1970). But neither the basic continuity theory nor the proposed model, as it now stands, would predict acquired cue-dominance in naive rats. A series of experiments with rats that used the optional-shift paradigm was reported, the same paradigm that established acquired cue-dominance in humans. The learning and transfer results were consonant with the continuity model. Moreover, no evidence of acquired cue-dominance in rats was obtained.

The modifications in contemporary noncontinuity theory considerably reduce the difference between the two theoretical stances. If the weight of evidence demands it, the proposed continuity model could be adjusted to include a selective attention mechanism which would reduce the differences still further. But the experiments cited show that while intrinsic cue-salience is a significant determiner of learning in rats, there was no manifest effect attributable to acquired dominance. If there is any acquired cue-dominance in rats, it is much less important than intrinsic cue-dominance.

The conclusion is that, for naive rats, learning is largely continuous and, primarily, if not entirely, nonselective.

REFERENCES

Basden, B. H. A nonselective model of differential cue effectiveness in discrimination learning by rats. Unpublished doctoral dissertation, University of California, Santa Barbara, 1969.

D'Amato, M. R., & Fazzaro, J. Attention and cue-producing behavior in the monkey. *Journal of Experimental Analysis of Behavior*, 1966, *9*, 469–478.

Granit, R. *Sensory mechanisms of the retina.* London: Oxford University Press, 1947.

Kendler, H. H., & Kendler, T. S. Vertical and horizontal processes in problem solving. *Psychological Review*, 1962, *69*, 1–16.

Kendler, T. S., Basden, B. H., & Bruckner, J. B. Dimensional dominance and continuity theory. *Journal of Experimental Psychology*, 1970, *83*, 309–318.

Kendler, T. S., & Kendler, H. H. An ontogony of optional shift behavior. *Child Development*, 1970, *41*, 1, 1–27.

Kendler, T. S., Kendler, H. H., & Silfen, C. K. Optional shift behavior of albino rats. *Psychonomic Science*, 1964, *1*, 5–6.

Kuenne, M. R. Experimental investigation of the relationship of language to the transposition behavior of young children. *Journal of Experimental Psychology*, 1946, *36*, 471–490.

Lashley, K. S. *Brain mechanisms and intelligence.* Chicago: University of Chicago Press, 1929.

Lashley, K. S. The mechanism of vision: XV. Preliminary studies of the rat's capacity for detail vision. *Journal of General Psychology,* 1938, *18,* 123–193.

Lawrence, D. H. Acquired distinctiveness of cues: I. Transfer between discriminations on the basis of familiarity with the stimulus. *Journal of Experimental Psychology,* 1949, *39,* 770–784.

Lovejoy, E. *Attention in discrimination learning.* San Francisco: Holden-Day, 1968.

Mackintosh, N. J. Selective attention in animal discrimination learning. *Psychological Bulletin,* 1965, *64,* 124–150.

Pavlov, I. P. *Conditioned reflexes.* (Translated by G. V. Anrep.) London: Oxford University Press, 1927.

Reynolds, G. S. Attention in the pigeon. *Journal of the Experimental Analysis of Behavior,* 1961, *4,* 203–208.

Riley, D. A. *Discrimination learning.* Boston: Allyn and Bacon, 1968.

Spence, K. W. The nature of discrimination learning in animals. *Psychological Review,* 1936, *43,* 427–449.

Spence, K. W. The differential response in animals to stimuli varying within a single dimension. *Psychological Review,* 1937, *44,* 430–444.

Spence, K. W. *Behavior theory and conditioning.* New Haven: Yale University Press, 1956.

Spence, K. W. *Behavior theory and learning: Selected papers.* Englewood Cliffs, N.J.: Prentice-Hall, 1960.

Suchmann, R. G., & Trabasso, T. Color and form preference in young children. *Journal of Experimental Child Psychology,* 1966, *3,* 177–187.

Sutherland, N. S., & Mackintosh, N. J. The learning of an optional extradimensional reversal shift problem by rats. *Psychonomic Science,* 1966, *5,* 343–344.

Tighe, T. J., & Tighe, L. S. Overtraining and optional shift behavior in rats and children. *Journal of Comparative and Physiological Psychology,* 1966, *62,* 49–54.

Trabasso, T., & Bower, G. H. *Attention in learning theory and research.* New York: John Wiley, 1968.

Wolford, G., & Bower, G. H. Continuity theory revisited: Rejected for the wrong reasons? *Psychological Review,* 1969, *76,* 515–518.

Zeaman, D., & House, B. J. The role of attention in retardate discrimination learning. In N. R. Ellis (Ed.), *Handbook of mental deficiency.* New York: McGraw-Hill, 1963. Pp. 159–223.

Essentials of a Theory of Discrimination Learning

FRANK A. LOGAN

INTRODUCTION

In 1936, Kenneth Spence published "The Nature of Discrimination Learning in Animals," a paper destined to become one of the most influential journal articles in the experimental psychology of learning. One reason for this impact was the scientific elegance (parsimony) of the theory: a small number of assumptions led to a large number of implications. Spence assumed that any stimulus was a compound of elements defined by their absolute properties, each of which possessed some individual tendency to evoke a response and which, in combination, resulted in a net tendency to choose that alternative. These tendencies were assumed to increase continuously to all elements of a compound when a response to them was reinforced, and to decrease as a result of nonreinforcement. The resulting excitatory and inhibitory potentials for each element generalized to similar stimulus elements systematically. Except for making some formal assumptions about the functions involved in these processes, and explicitly imposing boundary conditions on the theory, Spence rested his case.

The parsimony of the theory is revealed in the number of phenomena which it subsumed. First is the simple fact that discrimination learning occurs and is easier the more different the stimuli. The theory also implies systematic behavior during the presolution period, that performance might shift suddenly from near chance to near perfect responding, that reversal during the presolution period could retard subsequent discrimination learning, that discriminations would transpose to similar pairs of stimuli (and

Supported by a grant from the National Science Foundation. I am indebted to Philip Wootton for assistance in running subjects.

not to very dissimilar pairs), and that organisms could solve an intermediate stimulus discrimination. The conceptual significance of these implications was not simply their number, but the fact that many theorists of that era had presumed that an absolute, continuous, stimulus-response theory could not possibly handle such phenomena.

For example, some theorists (e.g., Krechevsky, 1932) held that the systematic presolution behavior indicated that organisms attend to selected aspects of the stimulus complex so that behavior is controlled by cognitive "hypotheses." Others (e.g., Lashley, 1929) held that transposition indicated that relative properties of the stimuli were the controlling discriminanda. And still others (e.g., Kohler, 1925) held that sudden solution indicated that learning was an insightful process. With what must have seemed a mighty sword, Spence shattered these preconceptions.

A more fundamental basis for the influence of Spence's 1936 theory was that the assumptions were not ad hoc to discrimination learning. That is to say, Spence assumed that classical and instrumental conditioning were simpler forms of learning from which to derive principles which could be used, probably with additional principles such as the receptor-orienting act, to derive performance under the conditions of discrimination learning. Accordingly, he borrowed his assumptions from Thorndike (1911), Pavlov (1927), and Hull (1943), and hence provided a conceptual integration of these other types of learning situations with discrimination learning.

Finally, compared with other formulations of the time, Spence's theory was formally quite specific and quantitative. It should be noted that he did not really provide analytic solutions or derivations; rather, he made illustrative assumptions about possible parameter values and showed that his theory could at least imply the intended outcomes. In some of these cases, other parametric assumptions would have led to contradictory outcomes. Nevertheless, the implications of the theory were explicit enough so that there could be little question as to whether or not they followed from the premises. Indeed, the special assumptions needed to derive phenomena such as transposition, the overtraining reversal effect, and transfer of discrimination imply constraints upon these findings.

Spence (1937a, 1937b, 1938, 1939, 1940, 1942) published several follow-up articles elaborating additional implications of his approach, but thereafter published relatively little on discrimination learning. This was not because he lost interest in the topic nor because he believed that he had written an adequate theory. Anecdotal evidence on the latter point is provided by the admission that Spence did not actually submit the 1936 article for publication. Rather, he submitted it to Hull for criticism, and it was over a year later, while Spence was still working on improvements, that Hull submitted the original manuscript in Spence's name. Those who knew him were aware that his intention was to write a new theory of discrimination learning.

He turned away from discrimination learning because he believed that the theory of classical and instrumental conditioning was itself inadequate. Since that theory was presumably the source of the principles to be applied to discrimination learning, systematic study of those simpler learning situations should precede further work on this theory. And indeed, important changes did take place within the general Hull-Spence approach during his quarter-century of research in those areas, largely as a result of his own analytic work (e.g., Spence, 1956). Because of his premature death, we have only one preliminary indication (Spence, 1960, Ch. 22) of the direction which his thinking about discrimination learning would take, but we may presume that he would have followed his earlier belief that the principles of classical and instrumental conditioning would apply.

ESSENTIALS OF A THEORY OF DISCRIMINATION LEARNING

Developments in conceptions of learning during the years since Spence's original theory appeared point toward several significant changes. While it is yet impossible to write the resulting theory, some of its essentials can be identified. (It should not be inferred that Spence would himself have agreed with all of these essentials.)

Discrimination as the basic learning process

Spence felt that classical and instrumental conditioning were the simplest learning situations from which basic principles were most readily obtained for application to the more complex situations such as discrimination learning. It now appears that the reverse image is more correct: discrimination is the most basic and fundamental process of learning.

To elaborate on this assertion, we must accept a distinction made elsewhere (Logan & Ferraro, 1969) that classifies stimuli as being initially positive, negative, or neutral with respect to their emotional value. The first (variously called rewarding, reinforcing, beneceptive, pleasant) are ones with positive value in that the organism seeks, chooses, or responds to obtain and maintain them. Emotionally negative stimuli (variously called noxious, aversive, nociceptive, unpleasant) are ones the organism avoids or responds to terminate. This distinction can be traced at least to Thorndike (1911).

In an environment in which emotionally significant events (emS) simply occur or could occur irregularly over time, an organism faces some degree of uncertainty about their occurrence. As an epitome, a variable-interval schedule of reinforcement in an operant-conditioning context confronts an organism with opportunities for reward at unpredictable times. If there is correlated with any schedule of emS another stimulus schedule that conveys information, then optimal adjustment involves responding appropriately on the basis of that information. Most generally, discrimination learning is the stimulus control of behavior resulting from the correlation of discriminative stimuli with emotionally significant events.

Consider classical conditioning in that light. Were there no CS (excluding the case of temporal conditioning), the organism would be completely uncertain about when the US might occur. In the typical procedure, this uncertainty can be eliminated by discriminating the occurrence of the CS from the background environment. If several similar CSs occur, differentially followed by the US, adjustment requires the finer discrimination of which CS has occurred. Classical conditioning may thus be viewed as an instance of discrimination learning, responding to the CS in accord with the information it conveys about the occurrence of the US. Behavioral control in this case is based on purely exteroceptive stimulation.

Control may also be exercised by interoceptive (feedback) stimuli. That is to say, if the occurrence of emS is dependent upon the production of some response, then response-produced stimuli convey information. This is most obviously true in response differentiation where the outcome depends upon the detailed nature of the response, but it is equally true in general. Both operant and instrumental conditioning involve discriminating the relevant feedback stimuli that are associated with reward and punishment.

Finally, it should be noted that information may be conveyed by a combination of interoceptive and exteroceptive stimulation. This combination arises when the effect of a response depends on which of several external stimuli are present. Differential operant and instrumental procedures are familiar illustrations when viewed as conditional discriminations. The basic process is coming under control of informative stimuli.

Accordingly, this view of the centrality of discrimination learning offers promise of reintegrating the many diversities within the Psychology of Learning. Indeed, it suggests that an adequate theory of discrimination learning will, in fact, be a general theory of behavior. Even the presumably complex processes of concept formation and problem solving may be seen as special conditions for the operation of principles of discrimination. While this ideal remains to be realized, it should be the goal.

A dynamic theory of behavior

Consistent with other theoretical approaches of the era, with the possible exception of Tolman (1932), Spence's 1936 theory was a static one: behavior was described in large, discrete steps over time. Specifically, a "trial" was the unit of analysis, behavior on any trial being determined by static excitatory potentials which changed from trial to trial. Increasingly, theoretical descriptions have become more dynamic in the sense of recognizing that behavior occurs more-or-less continuously over time. In effect, a trial in discrimination learning takes place over a period of time during which the organism makes a number of finer-grain responses which culminate in the observed choice behavior. The essence of a dynamic theory in this sense is a description of these ongoing activities from moment to moment.

It is clear that this is a direction in which Spence was moving, with respect to his analyses of both instrumental conditioning and discrimination learning. In the case of the former, his approach assumed that the prevailing stimulus complex at any moment, including feedback stimuli from preceding responses, elicited some strength of the fractional anticipatory goal response which, through the dynamism properties of its response-produced stimuli, contributed incentive motivation to continuation of the ongoing behavior. This incentive construct is discussed somewhat more fully in a later section.

Spence's approach to discrimination learning as a dynamic process during any trial is related to earlier descriptions by Tolman of vicarious trial-and-error behavior as well as to a comparable formulation provided by Bower (1959). Spence assumed that the organism approaches a choice point and, with some probability (p1), orients in one or the other direction. This receptor-orienting act exposes the organism to the interoceptive stimuli in that direction, which in turn may elicit the further approach response with some independent probability (p2). An orienting response, however, is assumed to be subject to rapid fatigue, so that, failing to make an approach response, the organism (with $p = 1 - p2$) reorients toward the other direction, thus exposing himself to the stimuli in that direction. These stimuli have their own probability (p3) of eliciting an approach response or (with $p = 1 - p3$) a further reorientation back toward the original direction. Hence, the organism engages in continuous looking-back-and-forth (VTE) until one or the other discriminandum probabilistically elicits an approach response terminating a trial.

Spence's description was explicitly designed for the case of simultaneous presentation of the discriminanda. But it should be noted that this image of a dynamic description of behavior should equally be applied to all instances of behavior, including differential conditioning in which the discriminanda are presented separately. During any trial, the organism is orienting, reorienting, and otherwise engaging in a continual flow of behavior. One of the most critical features of a satisfactory contemporary theory of learning is its ability to describe the fine-grain of behavior as it occurs continuously over time.

An incentive theory of behavior

The description just given made reference only to the probabilities of orienting, reorienting, and approaching the alternative stimuli. It would of course be possible to construct a learning theory according to which one operated directly upon these probabilities in relation to the outcome of any trial. Doing so would be consistent with the conceptual approach of many contemporary mathematical models of learning.

However, if a theory of discrimination learning is to be a general theory of behavior, it is necessary (and also more consistent with the traditional Hull-Spence approach) to derive probability from an analysis of the competing excitatory potentials and to relate these to their learning and motivational determinants. The most general reason for this is the fact that probabilities are constrained to sum to unity. As a result, any change in one probability necessitates a complementary change in some other probabilities. In contrast, it seems more likely that an outcome such as reinforcement following choice of one alternative strengthens the excitatory potential of that alternative but does not simultaneously weaken (except relatively) the excitatory potential of the other alternative. In similar fashion, probability is limited to a value of unity, whereas it is clear (Logan, 1965) that differences in excitatory potential may well exceed the amount necessary to mediate consistent preference for one or the other alternative. Hence, the goal of integrating the various types of learning situations as instances of discrimination learning would appear most likely to be achieved if the systematic dependent variable were an excitatory potential that could be related to various measures of performance.

Perhaps the most critical component of excitatory potential, at least in the context of discrimination learning, is incentive motivation. According to earlier views, reinforcement served to increase an excitatory process and nonreinforcement to increase an opposing inhibitory process. Increasingly many theorists, including Spence, have come to the view that learning in the sense of habit results entirely from the contiguous occurrence of a response in the presence of a stimulus. The role of reward in such theories is to provide incentive motivation for selecting that stimulus or response in preference to others. In short, organisms come to expect reward as a result of past experiences of reward following particular stimulus-response events.

Accordingly, an adequate theory of discrimination learning must specify the way in which incentive increases and decreases as a result of encountering rewards of various amounts (including nonreward). It must further specify the way in which these changes in incentive generalize to similar stimuli according to their prior value. This assignment is more challenging than might at first appear. As an illustration, consider the following specific problem.

An organism is first trained to respond to one stimulus with a relatively large reward. After performance has stabilized so that incentive has presumably become asymptotic to an appropriate value, the organism is given a series of trials to a similar stimulus with a smaller reward. Indeed, presume that the reward given this second stimulus is precisely the size that will maintain the performance level occurring to it as a result of generalization from the original stimulus. Hence, no further performance changes should occur with respect to this second stimulus. But what effect should this smaller reward have on the incentive to respond to the first stimulus? Intuitively, one might expect a decremental effect to result from a smaller-than-usual reward occurring to a similar stimulus. But there is no way to derive the outcome of this type of study from any extant formulation of incentive.

In any event, one important feature of an adequate theory of discrimination learning is the view that the organism is selecting from among the available exteroceptive and interoceptive stimuli according to the incentive motivation associated with them.

The perceptor-orienting response

The view that behavior is a dynamic process in which the organism is continuously discriminating the information conveyed by events in his environment raises the question of whether the organism responds selectively to more informative aspects of a stimulus complex. The type of VTE behavior described strongly suggests an affirmative answer. And additional data, some mustered around the concept of "attention" and others around the concept of "observing responses," are increasingly insistent.

This question of whether an adequate theory must postulate a stimulus-selection process more central than the receptor-orienting act has plagued the literature of discrimination learning. In one sense, this is surprising, since certainly everyone is personally and intimately familiar with the human's capacity to focus attention on particular aspects of a complex environment. However, the experimental evidence concerning this process (e.g., Mackintosh, 1965), while suggestive and consistent, does not provide unequivocal evidence requiring its postulation. This is especially true with relatively simple stimulus situations with animals, the domain in which Spence worked.

Nevertheless, a larger view of the behavioral domain suggests that not all stimulus-selection processes can be accounted for by overt peripheral responses. Results such as those of Wagner, Logan, Haberlandt, and Price (1968) suggest the need to introduce the concept of a covert perceptor-orienting response. To employ such a concept would not mean that alternative approaches such as the selective analyzer (Sutherland, 1959) or the stimulus-as-coded (Lawrence, 1963) have already received adequate testing. The present approach, however, may be more readily incorporated within a general theory of discrimination learning.

It is assumed that the organism first reacts to his momentary stimulus complex by making a perceptor-orienting response. The model for this response is the visual receptor-orienting response. It is readily apparent that this latter response organizes the visual field into a hierarchy of visual clarity, those objects focused on the fovea being sharpest with clarity diminishing progressively with distance away from that focal point. An analogous but somewhat more central response is here proposed with respect to perception. The perceptor-orienting response organizes the myriad of stimuli bombarding the organism through all sensory modalities into a hierarchy of perceptual clarity.

(The reader for whom this description does not give an intuitive feel might try the following. Press a fingernail from one hand moderately firmly into the palm of the other hand. Holding that pose, first direct attention toward the pressure felt by the finger doing the pressing, then toward the pressure of the fingernail felt by the palm. It is this bringing into relative focus any of several sensory experiences that is the essence of the perceptor-orienting response.)

The perceptor-orienting response provides for a figure-ground relationship within the totality of sensory experiences, much as already familiar with respect to vision. However, it is further assumed that all elements of this stimulus complex participate in any changes in learning processes resulting from reinforcement and nonreinforcement. That is to say, a background element acquires strength as a background element, and behavioral control is dependent upon all elements in the stimulus complex. The extent of control by any element depends on the perceptual clarity of that element.

Let us explore the role of this hypothetical process in terms of two experimental findings (Logan, 1961; Logan, Padilla, & Boice, 1968). The apparatus is shaped like a block number eight, the start box being in the center. As a rat runs around either perimeter path, he makes three right or three left turns and then encounters a Y-shaped choice point exposing two swinging doors, one black and the other white. Passing through one of these doors admits him to the goal box. For discrimination learning, the white and black doors are irregularly in either position at the choice point, and reward in the goal is dependent on the rat going through the correct door regardless of position.

First, one of the perimeter paths is blocked and the rat is run consistently around the other path with, let us say, the black door correct at the choice point. In fact, this is a rather difficult discrimination because the cumulation of three turns in the same direction combined with centrifugal swing makes an opposite position response dominant. Nevertheless, the discrimination is learned. Interest then centers on what will happen if the original path is blocked and the rat is run around the other perimeter path and there encounters the same black-white discrimination problem learned in the original path. The fact is that few rats appear to recognize the problem in this new location, instead reverting to position responding and requiring on the average about half as many trials to relearn the same discrimination in its new location.

According to the present analysis, the rat must have learned to orient both his receptors and perceptors toward the doors in order to learn the original discrimination. But the background contextual cues including feedback from three preceding turns also gained some control over choice behavior. When these latter were changed by reversing paths, performance suffered a substantial stimulus-generalization decrement.

If, however, variation in the background stimulus context is included during original training, the generalization of the discrimination from one location to the other is almost complete. This is true even though location is not varied during original training, but other dimensions of the background such as the presence or absence of lights or noises change from trial to trial. This suggests that variation in the background context enhances the perceptual clarity of the relevant discriminanda so that they gain more complete control over behavior.

Obviously, the concept of a perceptor-orienting response requires considerably more explicit formalization before it can be fully integrated within a general theory of discrimination learning. Most important, the conditions which affect its acquisition need to be specified. But it now appears that some such approach will be required if the total domain is to be adequately encompassed.

Further problems for analysis

Although we cannot review here all of the problems that remain for conceptual and experimental analysis before this type of theory can be formalized, several deserve mention as illustrative. As a prelude, it should be noted that the previously described theoretical approach does not explicitly distinguish between discrimination learning in which the cues are presented simultaneously and differential conditioning in which the cues are presented separately. Indeed, the dynamic analysis of the discrimination situation assumes that the organism effectively converts it into a differential-conditioning situation as a result of successively exposing himself to the discriminanda. He is, in effect, making a go-no-go decision with respect to each stimulus just as is required in the differential-conditioning paradigm.

If that is the case, then what is learned with the two procedures should be very much the same, and accordingly there should be very high transfer from one procedure to the other. The facts, however, are not entirely consistent with this expectation. Generally, animals that have been trained with the differential-conditioning procedure transfer quite effectively to the discrimination procedure, but the reverse is not always true. Perhaps there is an inherent difference in that the differential-conditioning paradigm requires that the response to the negative stimulus be more-or-less completely suppressed, while the discrimination paradigm requires only that a sufficient differential in excitatory potential be built up to produce consistent preference. However, formalizing that interpretation remains to be accomplished.

A related problem concerns the relative ease of learning with the discrimination paradigm as compared with the differential-conditioning paradigm. Presumably, learning should proceed at very much the same rate. Such an expectation may be confirmed when the stimuli are quite different, but when the stimuli are very similar, discrimination learning is faster than differential conditioning. Indeed, the discrimination procedure may be required to produce differential performance when the difference between the stimuli is very small. Perhaps an explanation of this discrepancy could be found in terms of the time separating exposure to the stimuli. Even with highly massed trials, the intertrial interval in differential conditioning must exceed the length of time required for an animal to VTE between the discriminanda in discrimination learning. Of course, if this difference is appealed to, the implication is that comparison of the stimuli may be an important aspect of discrimination learning, an assumption not made by an absolute conception of the stimulus. Very possibly, the final theory will recognize both absolute and relative properties of the stimuli as elements of the total stimulus complex, with the control gained by each dependent upon the difference between the stimuli.

As a final illustrative problem, it would at least be expected that the same general principles would apply to both discrimination learning and differential conditioning. One of the well-established principles of discrimination learning is that organisms are capable of learning to learn during a series of reversals (i.e., to develop a reversal learning set). Such improvement over a series of reversals, however, does not appear to be generally obtainable in the context of differential conditioning (North, 1962). Indeed, performance may progressively deteriorate. While this discrepancy is at least as embarrassing to other interpretations of reversal learning set, its analysis is critical for the type of approach here described.

Summary of essentials

It is apparent that there are a number of difficulties impeding the formalization of an adequate contemporary theory of discrimination learning. At the same time, several important aspects of such a theory can be anticipated. First, a theory of discrimination learning should recognize discrimination as the most basic learning process and aspire to integrate the diverse procedures known to modify behavior. It must be dynamic in treating with behavior as a continuous-over-time interaction of the organism with the environment. It should view the organism as orienting its receptors and perceptors under control of information about emotionally significant events. And these events enable the organism to select appropriate behavior on the basis of the differential incentive motivation engendered.

TRANSFER OF DISCRIMINATION

Successful differential conditioning involving two stimuli that lie close together on a continuum such as tone frequency is more readily achieved if preliminary training is given involving two stimuli further apart on that continuum. Indeed, Pavlov (1927) first noted that a difficult discrimination was sometimes achieved only if preceded by training on an easy discrimination. Subsequently, Lawrence (1952a) showed that even if the difficult discrimination was learnable without pretraining, it was obtained more rapidly by starting with an easy discrimination and moving progressively toward the difficult one. Even counting the trials given on the easier discrimination, difficult discriminations benefit from a shaping procedure.

This finding of transfer of discrimination along a continuum is related to other phenomena such as transposition and is of considerable theoretical significance. Most important, it lends itself readily to an interpretation based on some "attention" process. Specifically, the notion is that the easy discrimination increases the relative salience of the relevant stimulus dimension, focusing attention on that dimension when more difficult problems are introduced. The simple fact of transfer of discrimination does not demand an attentional account; Lawrence (1952b) and Logan (1966) have shown how it could be derived from a habit-inhibition theory such as Spence's (1936), involving assumptions similar to those he used to derive transposition (Spence, 1937). Nevertheless, some observations do not follow directly from such a theory. For example, training on an easy discrimination may facilitate a reversed difficult discrimination, a fact more amenable to attending to the relevant dimension than to the generalization of habit and inhibition built up during the easy discrimination.

Transfer of discrimination is also of considerable practical significance. While far from the laboratory situations, many of the problems encountered in an educational context can be conceptualized as involving relatively difficult discriminations. For example, the child learning to read must discriminate the letters "b" and "d," an accomplishment that is not easy for some young children. More abstract discriminations involving, for example, "right" and "wrong" are sometimes difficult even for adults. Accordingly, basic knowledge about transfer of discrimination could also have important implications for maximally effective training programs.

Unfortunately, however, the available evidence does not go very far toward either of these goals. Logan (1966) showed that the location of the easy discrimination on the continuum relative to the eventual difficult one affected the amount of transfer, but did not provide systematic evidence as to what easy discrimination would maximize transfer. More specifically, how easy should the easy problem be? Lawrence (1952a) showed that a gradual transition from the easy problem toward the difficult one was superior to a sudden shift, but did not provide systematic evidence as to what criteria to employ in such a shaping procedure. Furthermore, a variety of more complex procedures could be designed, such as ones which intermix training on an easy problem with training on a difficult one.

Answers to these more refined questions bear importantly on a theory of discrimination learning. Thus, one could assume that the primary basis for positive transfer of discrimination along a continuum is that an easy discrimination facilitates selective attention to the relevant dimension. Alternatively, the primary basis for this effect could be the generalization of differential response tendencies acquired during the easy discrimination. These hypotheses are not mutually exclusive, but they do lead to somewhat different predictions. The remainder of this paper will explore several such differences and provide some preliminary experimental evidence relevant to them.

Ease of original discrimination

Probably the most obvious question with respect to transfer of discrimination along a continuum concerns the ease of the original discrimination. To be specific, consider an ordered series of 12-tone stimuli differing in pitch by approximately equal logarithmic steps.* The difficult problem requires discrimination between two intermediate tones, 7 and 6, and progressively easier problems can be arranged symmetrically around it (i.e., 8-5, 9-4, 10-3, 11-2, and 12-1). The question is, which of these easier problems will promote the greatest transfer to the difficult one?

Assuming first that the primary basis for the transfer effect is the selective attention to the relevant dimension, it would appear that the easiest problems would be the most beneficial. The greater the difference in the pitch of the tones, the more salient that dimension would be and presumably therefore the greater the selective attention to it. However, if the primary basis for the transfer effect relates to differential response tendencies, then intermediate problems could provide for greater generalization of these to the stimuli involved in the difficult problem.

To obtain evidence on this question, six groups of two rats each were

* The actual tone frequencies employed in the studies to be reported were: 1 = 460; 2 = 525; 3 = 595; 4 = 680; 5 = 760; 6 = 860; 7 = 880; 8 = 1045; 9 = 1273; 10 = 1590; 11 = 1880; 12 = 2190. These were presented in two comparable Lehigh-Valley operant-conditioning chambers run alternately so that the time for a trial in one box contributed to the intertrial interval for the other box. The boxes contained two bars, one associated with each of the tones, and a 45-mg. Noyes pellet was delivered immediately if the rat pressed the correct bar within 5 sec. from tone onset. Pressing either bar terminated the tone and initiated a 24-sec. programmed intertrial interval. Each daily session consisted of 100 trials, 50 to each tone in irregular order.

initially trained on pairs 12-1, 11-2, 10-3, 9-4, 8-5, or 7-6. Their performance was evaluated by a discrimination index (DI), computed as the percent of correct responses minus the percent of incorrect responses, and they were continued on their original problem to a criterion DI of 60 or above for two consecutive days. That the problems reflect progressively more difficult discriminations is shown by the rats averaging 20, 18, 28, 30, 36, and 88 days respectively to reach the stated criterion.

After reaching criterion on the original problem, they were shifted to the next more difficult problem until again attaining a DI of 60, and so on progressively. We can then ask how many days of training were required to reach the criterion DI of 60 on the difficult 7-6 discrimination. Recalling that the group started on the 7-6 problem required 88 days to reach this criterion, evidence of positive transfer is revealed by the other five groups requiring a total of 62, 54, 52, 44, and 40 days respectively to arrive at and master the difficult problem. It is interesting to note that the more difficult the original discrimination, the quicker the 7-6 problem was mastered. It thus appears that, if the procedure involves progressive shaping with the requirement that a relatively stringent criterion be reached at each stage before advancement, it is most efficient to start on a problem of intermediate difficulty.

To some extent, however, this result might reflect the fact that days of training were required simply to establish criterion performance on each problem, and the groups starting on the easier problems had further to go. In an effort to take this condition into account, four new groups of four rats each were trained initially on the 12-1, 10-3, 8-5, and 7-6 discrimination problems. When the rats in the first three groups reached a DI of 60 on their original problem, they were shifted directly to the difficult 7-6 problem. Their performance is displayed in Figure 1.

To demonstrate the relative difficulty of the original problems, learning curves have been constructed by continuing rats that had been shifted to the 7-6 discrimination as if their DI were still 60 on the original problem. But greater interest centers on their performance on the difficult 7-6 problem, which is shown during Blocks 19 and 20, when all rats were on that problem and hence a meaningful average curve could be computed. It will be noted that the group that started on the 8-5 problem outperformed the other groups and is the only one that showed appreciable positive transfer relative to the control group that received all of its training on the 7-6 problem ($U = 4$, $p = .057$).

Perhaps there are procedures intermediate to those employed in these two studies which would be more efficient. But the present evidence suggests that the greatest benefit of positive transfer of discrimination along a continuum occurs from discriminations that are reasonably easy but nevertheless quite similar to the ultimate difficult discrimination. This is the type of result expected by a theory emphasizing generalization of differential response tendencies.

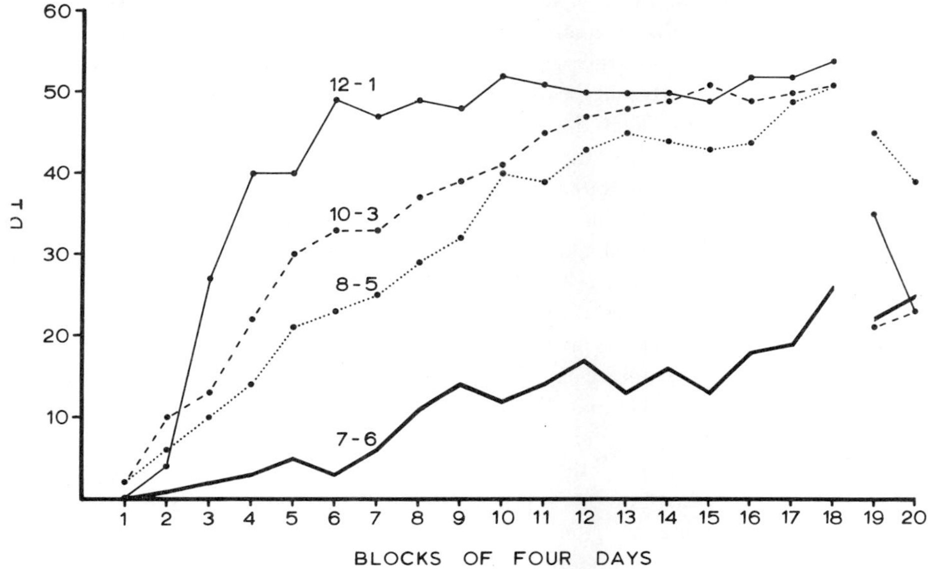

FIGURE 1. The effect of ease of original discrimination on transfer to a difficult discrimination. The heavy curve shows performance when all training was given on the difficult (7–6) problem. The remaining curves show discriminative performance on progressively easier problems, from which each rat was shifted to the difficult problem after reaching a DI of 60. Performance on the difficult problem is shown during blocks 19 and 20 when all rats were on that problem.

Amount of training on original discrimination

A related question concerns the amount of training that should be given on the easy discrimination before transfer is made to the difficult one. Again, different predictions can be made from the two hypotheses. If the primary basis for the positive-transfer effect involves selective attention to the relevant dimension, a greater amount of training on the easy problem should produce greater transfer. Since the same dimension continues to be relevant, attention to it should be strengthened by further training. At least, there should be no detriment resulting from extended training.

However, if the primary basis for the positive-transfer effect is the generalization of differential response tendencies, then there may be an optimal amount of original training before transfer. This is because the range of generalization decreases with extended training, so that the response tendencies would become increasingly specific to the particular stimuli involved in the original discrimination.

To obtain preliminary evidence on this question, three groups of two rats each were all started on the easy 12-1 discrimination and were transferred to the difficult 7-6 problem after 8, 16, or 24 days. Six control rats received all of their training on the 7-6 problem. The results of this study are shown in Figure 2.

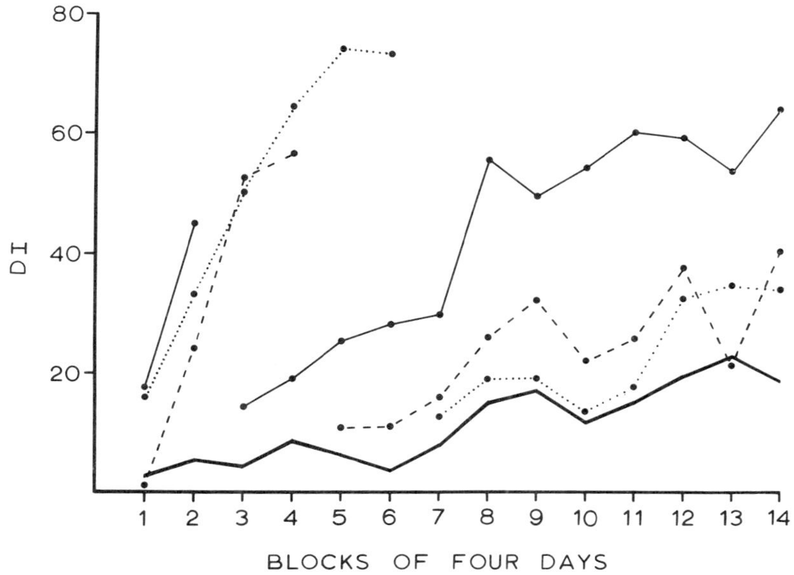

FIGURE 2. The effect of amount of training on the original problem on transfer to a difficult discrimination. The heavy curve shows performance when all training was given on the difficult problem. Three groups started on an easy discrimination, their performance being shown before the break in each line. Their performance on the difficult problem is shown after the break which occurs after different amounts of training for the different groups.

The three experimental groups were reasonably comparable in their performance on the original easy discrimination, although naturally they reached progressively higher levels of performance the greater the amount of training given on it. But interest centers on their performance on the 7-6 problem shown in Figure 2 after the break in each curve. It will be noted that performance is inversely related to the amount of training given on the easy discrimination. Because of the small *N*, the group given 8 days was the only one approaching a significant difference from the control group ($U = 1$, $p = .071$). This result is also more consistent with an analysis based on generalization of differential response tendencies.

Criterion to advance

If, rather than giving a fixed number of days of training on the easy problem, one establishes a criterion to advance in a shaping procedure, an important question concerns the stringency of that criterion. From the point of view of selective attention, a reasonably stringent criterion should be superior since this would ensure that attention had become focused on the relevant dimension during original training. From the point of view of generalization, however, a relatively lenient criterion should be superior since this would prevent learning from becoming focused on any particular absolute stimulus value.

So that this question could be answered, four groups of three rats each were begun on the easy 12-1 problem and shaped toward the difficult 7-6 problem in single steps (i.e., 12-2, 11-2, 11-3, 10-3, etc.). They differed in the criterion employed, being advanced from step to step after attaining a DI of either 30, 40, 50, or 60 on each problem.

By the end of training (Days 73–80) when all *S*s were on the difficult 7-6 problem, their average DI performance scores were 37, 40, 19, and 24 respectively. The two low criterion groups were significantly superior to the two high criterion groups ($t = 9.28$, $p < .05$). It thus appears that, when a progressive shaping procedure is used, a relatively low criterion on the easy problems produces the greatest positive transfer to the difficult discrimination.

In this connection, it is interesting to note the relationship of the present finding to familiar laboratory lore concerning shaping a response: the most common error in that context is to provide excessive reinforcement for an inadequate approximation to the desired response, thus tending to fixate that behavior. The transfer of discrimination procedure may be viewed as a shaping of a discrimination, and the comparability of findings adds further evidence of the relationship between discrimination and differentiation. Both appear most amenable to an analysis based on generalization of differential response tendencies.

Summary of transfer of discrimination

Although the generality of these findings must be considered tentative because of the small number of *S*s employed, especially in relation to the size of the conceptual domain, they do suggest that transfer to a difficult discrimination benefits most from a relatively small amount of pretraining to a relatively low criterion on a problem of intermediate difficulty. Collectively, the results indicate the importance of including a generalization process in any complete understanding of transfer of discrimination along a continuum.

It should not be inferred, however, that the present results completely discount the importance of some selective process such as the perceptor-orienting response earlier introduced. It is quite probable that the pitch of the tones did dominate in the rats' perceptual field. Rather, the findings indicate that over and above any such mechanism, learning is reflected by an association of a response with the absolute value of the perceived stimuli.

Furthermore, such associations generalize to similar stimuli in much the way postulated by Spence. At least this much, then, of that original formulation appears to be an essential ingredient of any contemporary theory of discrimination learning.

REFERENCES

Bower, G. H. Choice-point behavior. In R. R. Bush & W. K. Estes (Eds.), *Studies in mathematical learning theory*. Stanford: Stanford University Press, 1959.

Hull, C. L. *Principles of behavior*. New York: Appleton-Century, 1943.

Kohler, W. *The mentality of apes*. London: Routledge & Kegan Paul, 1925.

Krechevsky, I. "Hypotheses" in rats. *Psychological Review*, 1932, *52*, 516–532.

Lashley, K. S. *Brain mechanisms and intelligence*. Chicago: University of Chicago Press, 1929.

Lawrence, D. H. The applicability of generalization gradients to the transfer of a discrimination. *Journal of General Psychology*, 1952, *52*, 37–48. (a)

Lawrence, D. H. The transfer of a discrimination along a continuum. *Journal of Comparative and Physiological Psychology*, 1952, *45*, 511–516. (b)

Lawrence, D. H. The nature of a stimulus: Some relationships between learning and perception. In S. Koch (Ed.), *Psychology: A study of a science*. Vol. 5. New York: McGraw-Hill, 1963. Pp. 179–212.

Logan, F. A. Specificity of discrimination learning to the original context. *Science*, 1961, *133*, 1355–1356.

Logan, F. A. Decision making by rats. *Journal of Comparative and Physiological Psychology*, 1965, *59*, 1–12.

Logan, F. A. Transfer of discrimination. *Journal of Experimental Psychology*, 1966, *71*, 616–618.

Logan, F. A., & Ferraro, D. P. From free responding to discrete trials. In W. N. Schoenfeld (Ed.), *Theory of schedules of reinforcement*. New York: Appleton-Century-Crofts, 1969. Pp. 111–138.

Logan, F. A., Padilla, A. M., & Boice, R. Contextual variability and transfer of discrimination. *Journal of Experimental Psychology*, 1968, *76*, 673–674.

Mackintosh, N. J. Selective attention in animal discrimination learning. *Psychological Bulletin*, 1965, *64*, 124–150.

North, A. J. Discrimination reversal learning in a runway situation. *Journal of Comparative and Physiological Psychology*, 1962, *55*, 550–554.

Pavlov, I. P. *Conditioned reflexes*. (Translated by G. V. Anrep.) London: Oxford University Press, 1927.

Spence, K. W. The nature of discrimination learning in animals. *Psychological Review*, 1936, *43*, 427–449.

Spence, K. W. Analysis of the formation of visual discrimination habits in chimpanzees. *Journal of Comparative Psychology*, 1937, *23*, 77–100. (a)

Spence, K. W. The differential response in animals to stimuli varying within a single dimension. *Psychological Review*, 1937, *44*, 430–444. (b)

Spence, K. W. Gradual vs. sudden solution of discrimination problems by chimpanzees. *Journal of Comparative Psychology*, 1938, *25*, 213–224.

Spence, K. W. Observational learning of discrimination problems by chimpanzees. *Journal of Comparative Psychology*, 1939, *27*, 133–147.

Spence, K. W. Continuous vs. noncontinuous interpretations of discrimination learning. *Psychological Review*, 1940, *47*, 271–288.

Spence, K. W. The basis of solution by chimpanzees of the intermediate size problem. *Journal of Experimental Psychology*, 1942, *31*, 257–271.

Spence, K. W. *Behavior theory and conditioning*. New Haven: Yale University Press, 1956.

Spence, K. W. *Behavior theory and learning*. Englewood Cliffs, N.J.: Prentice-Hall, 1960.

Sutherland, N. S. Stimulus analysing mechanisms. In *Proceedings of a symposium on the mechanization of thought processes*. Vol. 2. London: Her Majesty's Stationery Office, 1959. Pp. 575–609.

Thorndike, E. L. *Animal intelligence*. New York: Macmillan, 1911.

Tolman, E. C. *Purposive behavior in animals and men*. New York: Century, 1932.

Wagner, A. R., Logan, F. A., Haberlandt, K., & Price, T. Stimulus selection in animal discrimination learning. *Journal of Experimental Psychology*, 1968, *76*, 171–180.

MOTIVATION

A Threshold Model for Drive

G. ROBERT GRICE

INTRODUCTION

The theory which states that associative and motivational processes combine in a multiplicative fashion to produce behavior is one of the most brilliant generalizations and simplifying assumptions of modern behavior theory. Spence, in particular, has explored the theoretical leads of this hypothesis and experimentally investigated a variety of its many implications. This work of Spence and of those stimulated by him constitutes a major segment of the modern literature concerning the relation of learning and motivation. The multiplicative theory has in general achieved considerable success, although there have been some difficulties in dealing with certain aspects of empirical data. The theory has gained fairly wide acceptance, and the writer has little serious doubt that at least some similar hypothesis will be a necessary component of behavior theory.

The purpose of the present paper is to explore in a preliminary way an alternative to the multiplicative theory: the view that it is the reaction threshold which varies when motivational variables are manipulated. Hull and Spence also utilized a reaction threshold in their theories, but did not treat it, in any systematic way, as a dynamic concept. Probability of response is regarded as a function of the amount by which reaction potential exceeds the threshold. Now, it is obvious that variations in this magnitude may be regarded as being produced by variation in the strength of reaction potential or by variation in the location of the threshold. It is the view that drive has the latter of these effects which is to be considered here. This theory

This work was supported by P.H.S. Research Grant No. MH 16400 from the National Institute of Mental Health.

appears to have very little history. A similar view was proposed by Campbell and Sheffield (1953) and by Ausubel (1956), but little has been done to explore its implications. The writer (Grice, 1968) has made some use of the approach in an analysis of stimulus intensity effects. When one does examine the mathematical implications of the threshold theory, it turns out that they are similar but not identical to those of the multiplicative theory. In combination with this hypothesis there will be included the previously stated assumption (Grice, 1968) that behavioral variability is attributable to random fluctuation of the threshold rather than to the separately introduced oscillation function of Hull and Spence. For purposes of the present discussion, this threshold oscillation will be assumed to be normally distributed. Data to be analyzed are from human eyelid conditioning.

Analysis of the Taylor experiment

The first set of data analyzed was selected arbitrarily as an important early example of a study conceived in the context of the multiplicative theory of habit and drive. This is the now classic experiment of Taylor (1951), in which she discovered the relation between eyelid conditioning and Manifest Anxiety. Taylor obtained clearly separated conditioning curves for two groups selected on the basis of her test and which were described as Anxious and Non-Anxious. The curves analyzed here are in terms of percent of conditioned responses and are from Taylor's Figure 1. Two subgroups involving a clearly ineffective instructional variable have been combined. The actual data points are presented here in Figures 5 and 8 to be discussed later.

The starting point of the present analysis is with the plot of the data from Taylor's conditioning curves presented in Figure 1. Here the proportions of CRs for each group have been converted to the corresponding normal deviates (z values). This corresponds to conversion to excitatory potential units (E) in the Hull-Spence system. Each point represents one block of trials, the z values for the Anxious group being plotted as a function of the corresponding z values for the Non-Anxious group. This figure clearly resembles a Receiver Operating Characteristic (ROC) as employed in the theory of signal detection (TSD), plotted on normal-normal coordinates, and is the same as similar figures used by the writer in an analysis of conditioned stimulus intensity effects (Grice, 1968). Since ROC is not descriptive of the present use of these functions, they will be referred to as Response Evocation Characteristics (RECs).

There are two psychologically meaningful dimensions in this REC. The dimension parallel to the minor diagonal is the effect upon response of the anxiety variable. The line through the points is drawn with a slope of unity, the best-fitting line differing from this only by a negligible amount. The implication of this is that the anxiety effect is constant over conditioning trials. This is contrary to the implications of the multiplicative theory, which

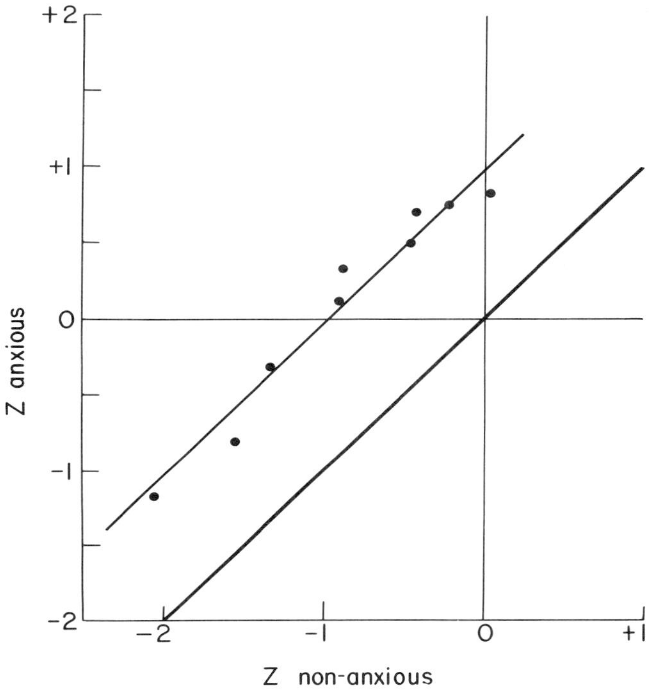

FIGURE 1. REC function from Taylor's (1951) conditioning curves.

predicts an increasing anxiety effect and, hence, an REC slope greater than one. The other dimension is the one parallel to the major diagonal. In TSD applications, there is ordinarily no primary quantitative interest in this dimension other than that its presence makes possible the plotting of an ROC. Such is not the case in the present application. As was previously pointed out (Grice, 1968) this dimension may be regarded as degree of responsiveness. Here, since the points represent successive trial blocks, this is the increase in responsiveness attributable to conditioning, in other words, the growth of habit strength. The points along the REC line from lower left to upper right represent the successive trial blocks, in this instance, with no inversion of order. The coordinates of the projections of these points on the line is a joint estimate of a habit-growth function common to both anxiety conditions.

As in a previous application (Grice, 1968), some clarification of the model and the computations is gained by a 45° counterclockwise rotation of the axes of the REC. In such a plot, the psychologically meaningful dimensions become the axes, the coordinates becoming:

$$A = .707\ (Z_A - Z_{NA})$$
$$H = .707\ (Z_A + Z_{NA})$$

In addition, the scales have been transformed by dividing both by .707 (the sine or cosine of 45°), and then dividing the new horizontal scale by 2. This form of the REC is presented in Figure 2.

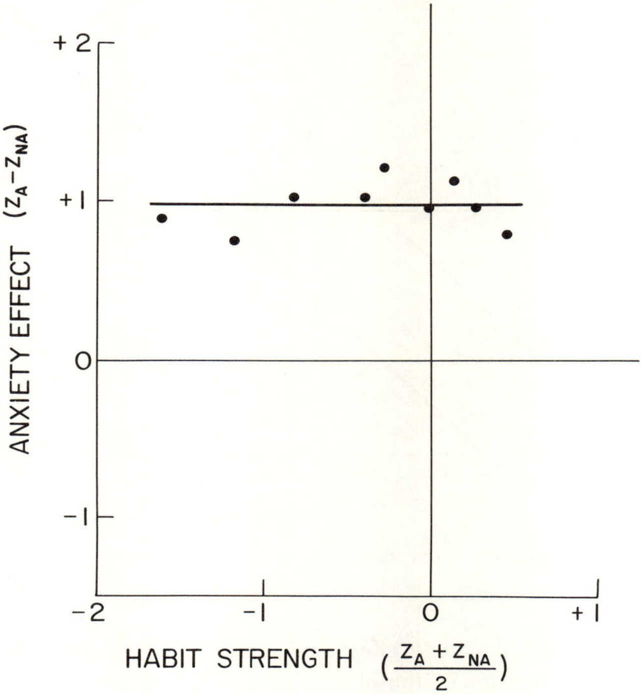

FIGURE 2. REC function from Taylor's data with 45° counterclockwise rotation of axes and linear transformation of scales.

The ordinate is now the difference between the scaled values for the A and NA groups and indicates the size of the anxiety effect. The slope of zero indicates its essential invariance with respect to amount of conditioning. The intercept is the scaled distance value *d′*. Points along the abscissa are the means of the A and NA *z* values for each block of conditioning trials. The increasing function formed by these points is the same as that formed by the coordinates of the projections on the ROC function, but with a different zero point. The zero point here lies halfway between the means of the A and NA conditions and is used as the reference zero in the subsequent analysis.

The next step in the analysis is to obtain an estimate of the form of the habit-growth function common to both the A and NA conditions. This of course involves the assumption that the associative factor is unaffected by the anxiety variable. It is the abscissa (Habit) values of Figure 2 which provide this estimate. In Figure 3, these values are plotted as a function of

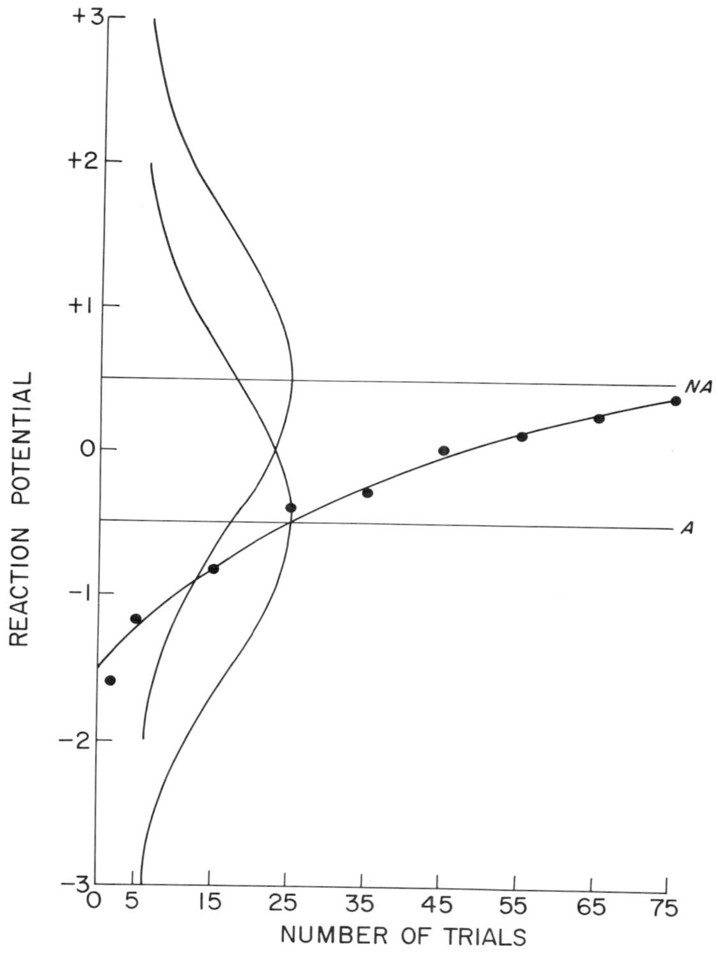

FIGURE 3. Fitted habit curve for Taylor's data. Horizontal lines indicate mean threshold locations and the normal curves indicate threshold variability.

number of trials. It may be seen that they form a rather smooth, negatively accelerated, increasing function. The smooth curve has been fitted to these points and is of the form used by Hull and Spence for the growth of habit. Its equation is:

$$H = .780 - 2.296\ (10)^{-.0102N} \quad (1)$$

where N is the midpoint of the trial block. Calculated values from this equation are used in the derivation of the separate conditioning curves.

Our hypothesis states that the effect of the motivational variable, anxiety, is upon the location of the reaction threshold. The distance between the thresholds is the scaled distance between the A and NA groups. In TSD language, this is the value *d′* which is the NA intercept of the REC or the H-intercept of the rotated REC of Figure 2. This value for the present data is .98. This and the three constants of the habit function are the only parameters estimated from the data. In Figure 3, the mean values of the thresholds for the NA and A groups are located at 0 ± ½ *d′*. Since we are assuming that variability is associated with the threshold, normal curves have been included to indicate the probability density of the location of each threshold. Normality is implied by the linearity of the REC, and equal SDs by its 45° slope. All information needed for the derivation of Taylor's two conditioning curves is included in Figure 3. For any point on the habit curve, the expected probability of a CR is the proportion of area of the appropriate threshold distribution below that value. In other words, for a CR to occur on a given trial the reaction threshold must be less than the amount of habit strength which has been accumulated.

The basic decision axis of the model is presented in Figure 4. Following a previous suggestion of the writer (Grice, 1968), it is based upon a hypothesis which is in effect the reverse of the TSD model. Here, variability is assumed to be associated with the threshold which corresponds to the

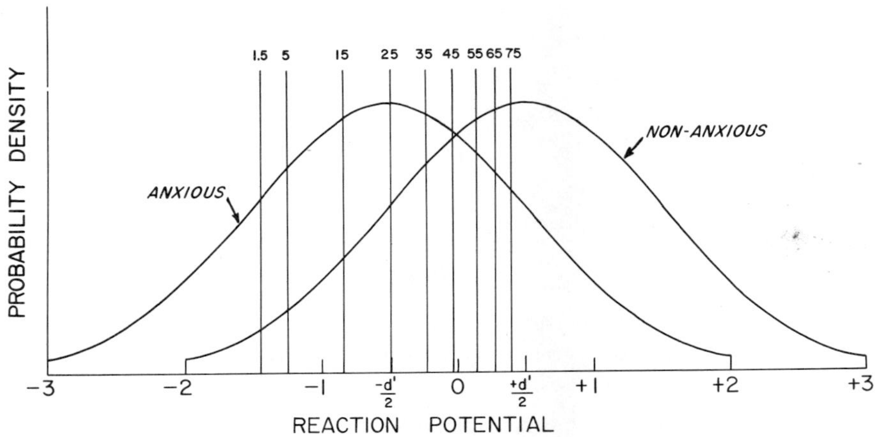

FIGURE 4. Theoretical decision axis for Taylor's data. Distributions indicate threshold locations, and vertical lines indicate habit strength for varying numbers of trials.

criterion of TSD. In TSD any particular criterion location is treated as constant.* In Figure 4 the means of the threshold distribution are separated by the distance d'. The vertical lines indicate the amount of habit strength accumulated by each successive block of trials. Their positions are determined by values calculated from the fitted habit-growth function. Probability of response is estimated by areas of the threshold distribution below (to the left of) the habit-strength values. Thus, the 18 data points of Taylor's conditioning curves are estimated by the areas of two distributions lying below the nine habit-strength values indicated.

The fit of the model to Taylor's data points is illustrated in Figure 5.

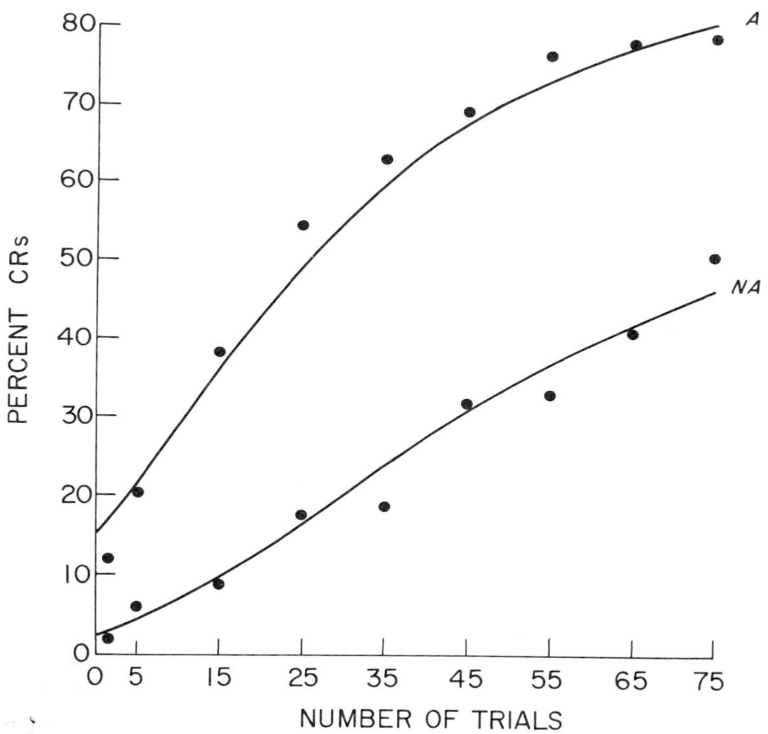

FIGURE 5. Fit of the threshold model to Taylor's conditioning curves.

The smooth curves were computed from the fitted habit function and d' by the preceding logic. This, of course, involves finding the distance in z units from points on the habit curve to the mean of each threshold distribution, and obtaining the areas below the H values. The fit is clearly an excellent

* As previously pointed out (Grice, 1968), the criterion of TSD and the reaction threshold of Hull-Spence theory may be regarded, mathematically, as the same concept.

one, accounting for 99.5 percent of the variance of the points. There remain 14 degrees of freedom after the estimation of the four parameters from the data.

It is appropriate that a similar analysis should be performed for the multiplicative theory in order to compare the relative success of the two theories. It appears that no such analysis has been made in the context of the Hull-Spence approach. However, the possibility of estimating the common habit-growth function from the conditioning dimension of the REC now makes it possible. It turns out that the same habit function used for the preceding analysis is also appropriate here. The demonstration of this is straightforward.

The growth of excitatory potential (E) for the A and NA groups is equal to the common H function multiplied by two factors representing the difference in drive level (D). Following Spence (1956), the normal deviate corresponding to proportion of responses is the suprathreshold reaction potential. Therefore according to the multiplicative theory:

$$E_A = H\ D_A + L \tag{2}$$

and

$$E_{NA} = H\ D_{NA} + L \tag{3}$$

where L is the reaction threshold. However, since the E values are measured from the threshold, L is at zero in this scale.

$$E_A + E_{NA} = H\ (D_A + D_{NA}) \tag{4}$$

$$\frac{E_A + E_{NA}}{2} = H \left(\frac{D_A + D_{NA}}{2} \right) \tag{5}$$

Thus, we see that the equation we have derived previously is the H of equations (2) and (3) multiplied by a constant. The two growth functions of excitatory potential (E_A and E_{NA}) are multiplicative functions of this habit function, the two factors being determined by the scaling constant of H and the values of D_A and D_{NA}. Estimation of these two factors from the data will permit a fit of the model. Following the practice of Spence (1956), an arbitrary constant, 2.5, has been added to the values of E in order to eliminate negative values.* This now locates the threshold at 2.5, and adds the constant to the H function. For convenience in these calculations, we shall regard the mean of the oscillation function (0) to be at E rather than at E − 2.5 as Hull and Spence have done.

* The location of the E-scale has always been arbitrary in any case, since no one has ever solved the problem of satisfactorily defining an absolute zero for the reaction potential. This poses an obvious difficulty for the application of the multiplicative theory. However, the present relation is still multiplicative, though not by the hypothetical "true" D values themselves.

The procedures involved in fitting the multiplicative theory to Taylor's data are best understood with reference to Figure 6.

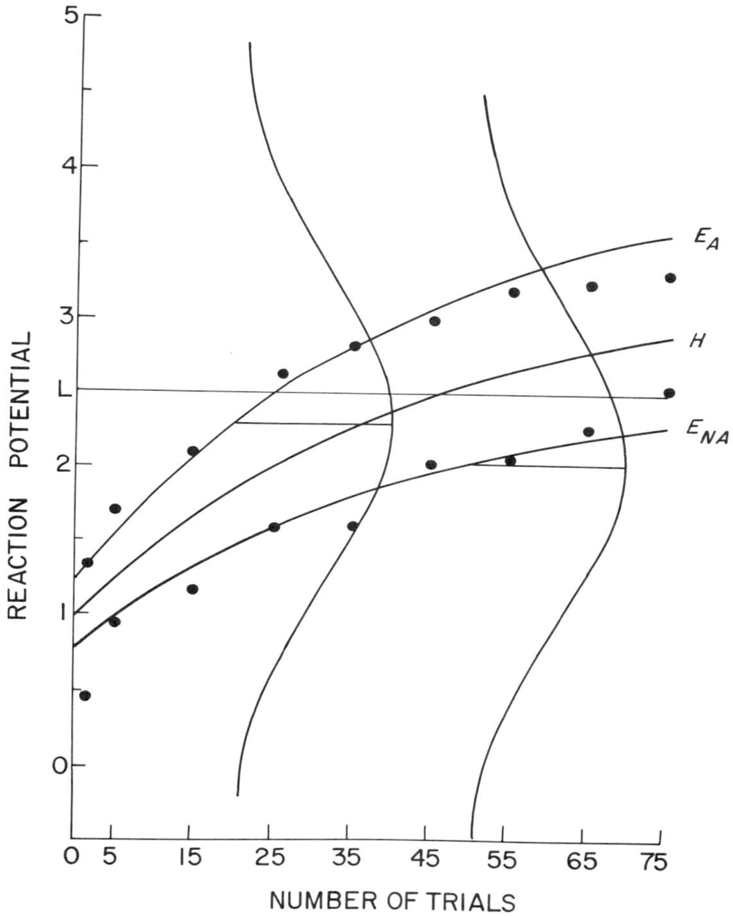

FIGURE 6. Habit curve and estimated curves indicating the growth of reaction potential under the multiplicative hypothesis. Plotted points are z values for Taylor's conditioning curves.

The plotted points are the z transformations (E values) of the original response percentages. The middle of the three smooth curves is the previously derived habit-growth function. The theory implies that the data points should be fitted by multiplying the habit function by two factors—one for each anxiety level. These factors must be estimated from the data. To do this, the ratio of each point to the corresponding point on the H curve was obtained. For each anxiety level, the median of these values was taken as the estimate of the factor. The values were 1.24 and .79. (The median was used simply because it gave a little better fit than the mean.) The smooth curves for the two E functions were obtained by multiplying the habit function by these estimates. While the fits are not unreasonable, it will be noted that predicted functions diverge somewhat more than the transformed data points. For one point on each E function, a normal distribution function is included to indicate the operation of oscillation. Probability of response is estimated by the proportion of the distribution above the threshold (L).

The "decision axis" of the Hull-Spence theory is presented in Figure 7.

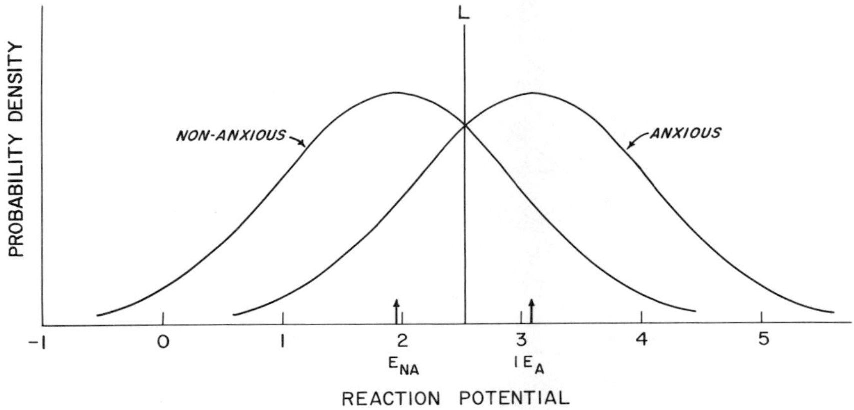

FIGURE 7. Decision axis of the Hull-Spence theory indicating distributions of reaction potential as of Trial 45, and location of the reaction threshold.

This figure presents the theoretical state of affairs as of Trial 45. The means of the two distributions of reaction potential are from the two E functions at that trial. Probability of response is predicted from the areas of these distributions above the threshold. Of course, the positions of these distributions vary with stage of conditioning, and according to the multiplicative hypothesis the distance, $d = E_A - E_{NA}$, increases monotonically with H until asymptote has been achieved. This figure is presented in part to indicate the striking similarity to the model of TSD. That Spence, at least, understood the theory in just this way is clear from his discussion in his Silliman Lectures (Spence, 1956), especially in Appendix A and in his Figure 79. Figures 4 and 7 also indicate the contrast between the multiplicative theory and the variable threshold model presented here.

The fit of the multiplicative theory to the Taylor data is presented in Figure 8. It is, by ordinary standards, a reasonably good fit. It accounts for 99.0 percent of the variance in the points. However, the curves derived from

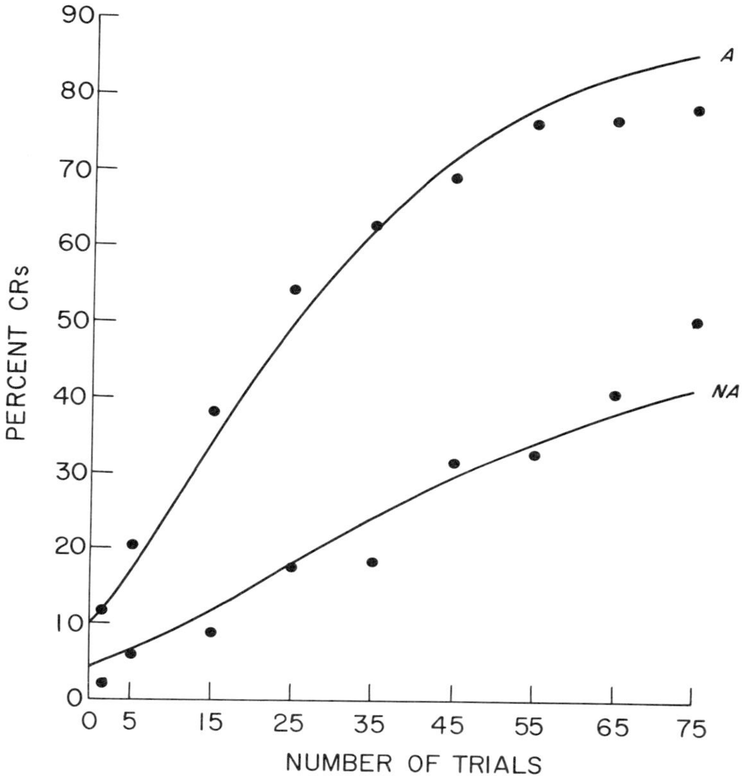

FIGURE 8. Fit of the multiplicative theory to Taylor's conditioning curves.

the theory do systematically diverge more than the data. This was in fact predictable from the fact that the slope of the REC did not exceed unity. The fit based on the variable threshold model shows no such systematic divergence. The sum of the squared residuals for the multiplicative model is twice as great as for the threshold model. One more parameter was estimated from the data, as there were two multiplicative factors as opposed to a single value of d'.

Cases of unequal variability

The next set of data analyzed was selected because it appeared to support the implication of the multiplicative theory. This was pointed out by Prokasy (1967), and the experiment is by Spence and Haggard, reported by Spence (1958). The data, analyzed first, include two levels of anxiety as in the Taylor study, conditioned with an airpuff UCS of 1.5 psi. The REC based on the conditioning curves for this experiment is presented in Figure 9. This func-

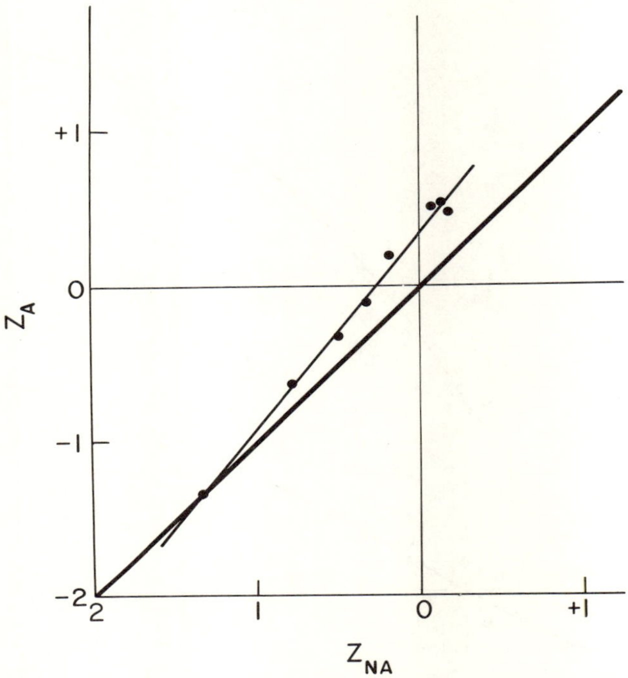

FIGURE 9. REC function for Spence and Haggard's conditioning curves for 1.5-psi airpuff UCS.

tion is precisely of the kind predicted by the multiplicative theory—linearity indicating normality and the slope greater than 45° indicating an increasing anxiety effect. A rotated REC with transformed coordinates, similar to Figure 2, has a slope of +.23 which is the rate of change of $d = E_A - E_{NA}$ with increasing H. As before, the next step was to fit a habit-growth function to the means of the Anxious and Non-Anxious E values. Again, this produced a good fit with an exponential function with the equation:

$$H = 3.0 - 2.32\ (10)^{-.0149N} \tag{6}$$

The multiplicative values, estimated as before, were 1.06 for Anxious and .95 for Non-Anxious. The habit function, the two E curves, and the *z* transformation of the percent CR points are presented in Figure 10. Here the two derived E functions show no systematic divergence from the data as in the fit of the multiplicative model to the Taylor data. The final fit of the model to the empirical percentage of response conditioning curves is presented in Figure 11. Here again the fit is quite reasonable, there being at least no

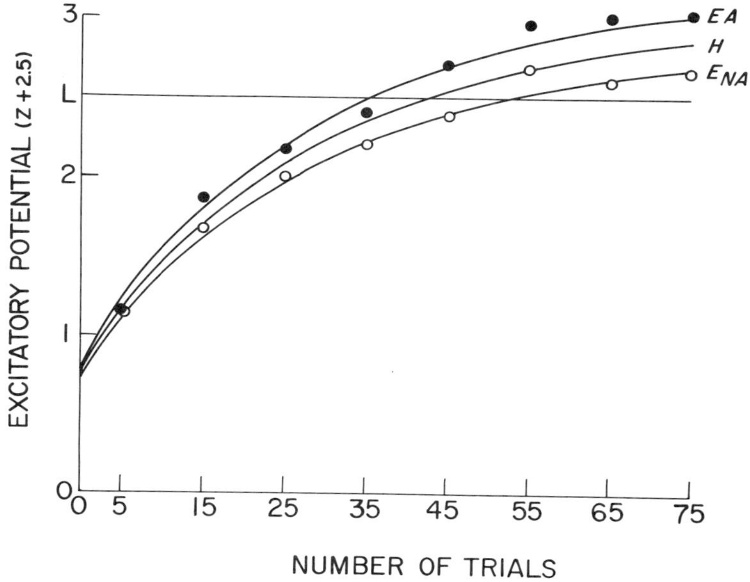

FIGURE 10. Habit and excitatory potential curves for Spence and Haggard data under the multiplicative hypothesis.

serious systematic discrepancies. In other words, the multiplicative model quite adequately describes the results of this experiment.

Application of the threshold-drive model to the Spence and Haggard data makes it necessary to introduce an additional consideration. This is the possibility that variability may be unequal for the two threshold distributions. The threshold model applied to these data with the equal SD assumption, in the same manner as to the Taylor data, does not yield an equally good fit. As is predictable from the REC, the predicted conditioning curves diverge less than the data. When an REC or ROC plotted on normal-normal coordinates is linear, but departs from a 45° slope, this is subject to two alternative interpretations. One of these is that the value of *d'* changes systematically with the degree of responsiveness. This is the interpretation implied by the multiplicative theory. The other alternative is that *d'* is constant but that the standard deviations of the two distributions are unequal. This is the assumption usually made in applications of the TSD, and is also appropriate for the present threshold model. The slope is an estimate of the ratio of the standard deviations. In TSD terms, Slope $= \sigma_N/\sigma_{SN}$, and in the present context Slope $= \sigma_{NA}/\sigma_A$. For those not used to thinking in these terms, perhaps it is clarifying to suggest that if the units of the REC axes are unequal, the slope is the ratio between these units. The availability of this

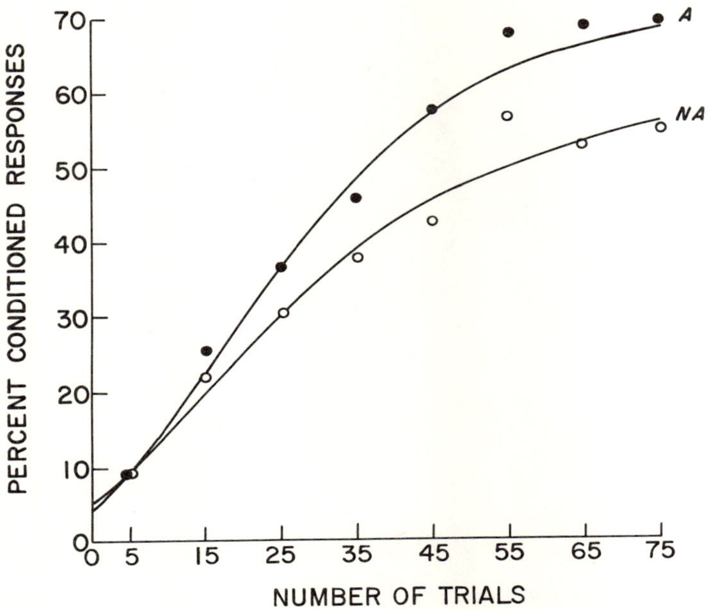

FIGURE 11. Fit of the multiplicative model to the Spence and Haggard conditioning curves.

estimate of the ratio of the SDs suggests the possibility of a solution not based on the equal-variability assumption. The writer, at least, has not seen such a solution in TSD applications, although there would appear to be clear advantages. For example, values of *d′* could be compared between experimental sessions, experimental conditions, or observers in theoretically equal units.

The procedure used here is similar to that used in a Thurstone scaling application by Saffir (1937), also discussed by Torgerson (1958). The first step is simply to convert the A and NA *z* values to a common scale. The slope of the best-fitting mutual regression line was 1.26.* In this instance the A values were converted to units of the NA distribution by dividing each by 1.26. This rotates the REC around its A intercept to a slope of 45°. The NA intercept is now *d′* in NA units and equals 0.27. The habit function

* An adequate method of fitting a line to these functions for present purposes is to use a mutual regression line (Grice, 1966) which is the principle component of a plot of the points in units of their SDs. The slope is merely the ratio of the SDs of the two sets of *z* values. The intercept is determined by passing the line through the centroid. More sophisticated methods and a discussion of additional considerations are presented by Kendall and Stuart (1967, Ch. 29).

estimated for the fit of the multiplicative theory is not appropriate for the unequal SD solution, since the A and NA points must be in equal units before averaging. The habit function fitted to the data expressed in NA units is presented in Figure 12, and had the equation:

$$H = .40 - 1.93\ (10)^{-.0158N} \tag{7}$$

The nature of the solution is also indicated by the inclusion in Figure 12 of the two threshold distributions with unequal standard deviations. The figure indicates how the growth of response probability with conditioning

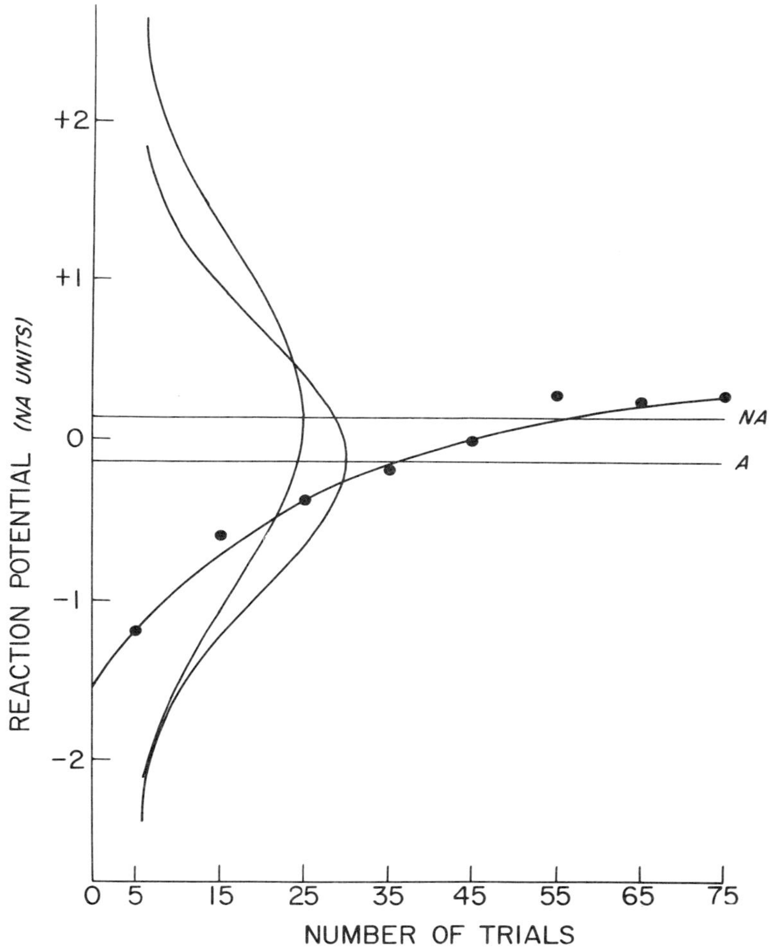

FIGURE 12. Habit function and threshold locations for application of the threshold model to Spence and Haggard 1.5-psi data. Distributions indicate unequal variability for the two groups.

depends not only on the rate of habit growth and the mean location of the threshold, but also its variability. The estimation of percentage response values is carried out in the same manner as before. After obtaining distances from the habit function to the threshold in NA units, the A distribution must be returned to its original units to obtain the appropriate p values. The predicted curves and the original data points are presented in Figure 13. It

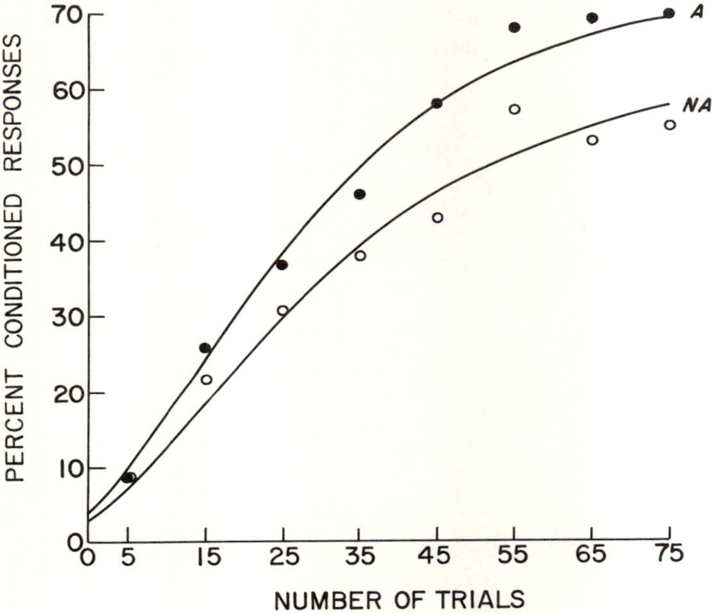

FIGURE 13. Fit of the threshold model to Spence and Haggard conditioning curves.

may be seen that the fit is approximately the same as for the multiplicative model. The number of estimated parameters is now the same (five) for both theories with the addition of the use of the REC slope as the scaling ratio. Thus, for the Spence and Haggard experiment, the multiplicative theory and the threshold theory are equally capable of accounting for the data.

The next set of data was originally selected merely because of the forms of the conditioning curves, but is presented here because it illustrates an additional point. This is an experiment by Spence (1958) in which *S*s were conditioned with or without threat of strong electric shock. When the UCS was a weak airpuff the Threat group showed a negatively accelerated curve, while the No Threat group showed an exaggerated phase of positive acceleration. Note also in the REC of Figure 14 a slope less than one, .72, something of a problem for the multiplicative theory. In terms of the

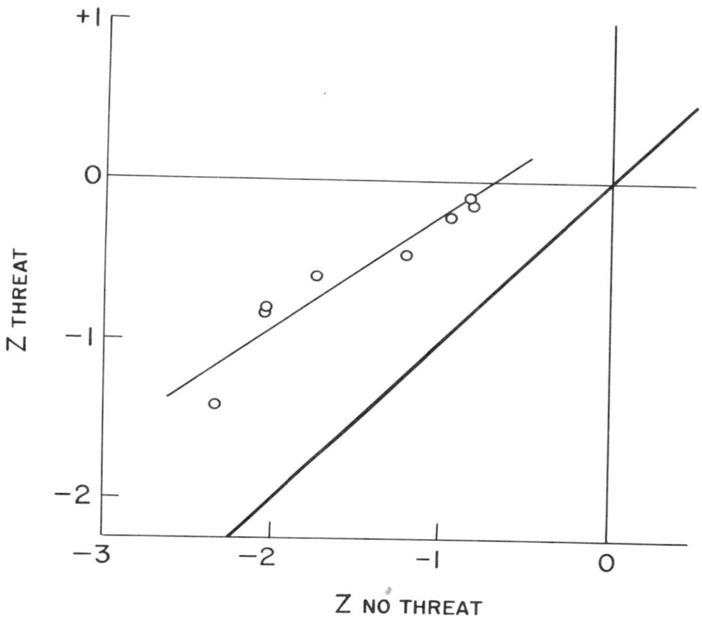

FIGURE 14. REC function from conditioning curves of Spence Threat experiment (.25-psi UCS).

threshold model, the implication is that the Threat condition produced greater variability than the No Threat condition. In any case, a common habit curve estimated from the data, and the heterogeneous variance solution produce, at least, a reasonable fit to the data. The fitted smooth functions of Figure 15 certainly yield fair approximations of the data. The data themselves are based on only 10 *S*s per condition.

EFFECTS OF UCS INTENSITY

Probably the most impressive feature of these applications of the threshold model is that the separate conditioning curves are not fitted individually, but on the basis of a common habit-growth function plus the estimate of the distance between them and the ratio of their standard deviations. The method also generalizes to the simultaneous fitting of larger numbers of conditioning curves involving a common habit function. This feature of the model makes possible an additional level of theoretical analysis. For example, if different curves based upon the manipulation of some experimental variable

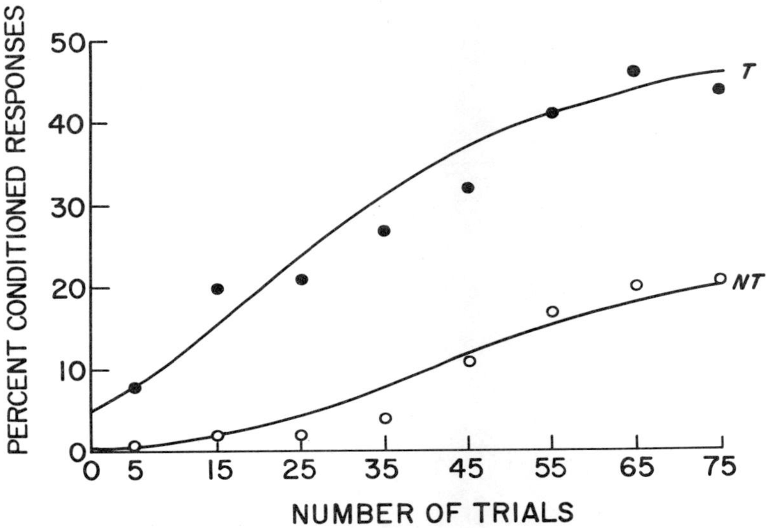

FIGURE 15. Fit of threshold model to conditioning curves of Spence Threat experiment.

can be fitted with a common habit curve, the implication might be drawn that the variable does not affect habit growth. On the other hand, if such a fit could not be obtained, it should be possible to evaluate differences in habit growth. Such an analysis has been made of the effect of UCS intensity in eyelid conditioning.

The Spence and Haggard experiment, previously analyzed, was also replicated at two UCS airpuff intensities, 1.5 and .25 psi, at each level of anxiety. Likewise, the Spence experiment was replicated at these same two UCS intensities at each level of threat. Thus, there were four conditioning curves for each experiment. Combined analyses have been made of these experiments. The Spence and Haggard experiment is presented first. Since the equal SD condition does not apply, the first step was to convert the data for the four conditions into the same units. This was done by constructing three REC functions relating the NA,.25 group to each of the remaining three conditions. The slopes of these RECs were 1.19 for A,.25, 1.54 for NA,1.5, and 1.95 for A,1.5. These values were then used to transform all data to units of the NA,.25 SD. Distance values, *d'*, were then obtained in these units, expressing the distance of each condition from the NA,.25 condition. These values were .52, .65, and .83 in the order given above. A common estimate of the underlying habit-growth function was obtained by computing the means of the four conditions for each block of 10 trials. These

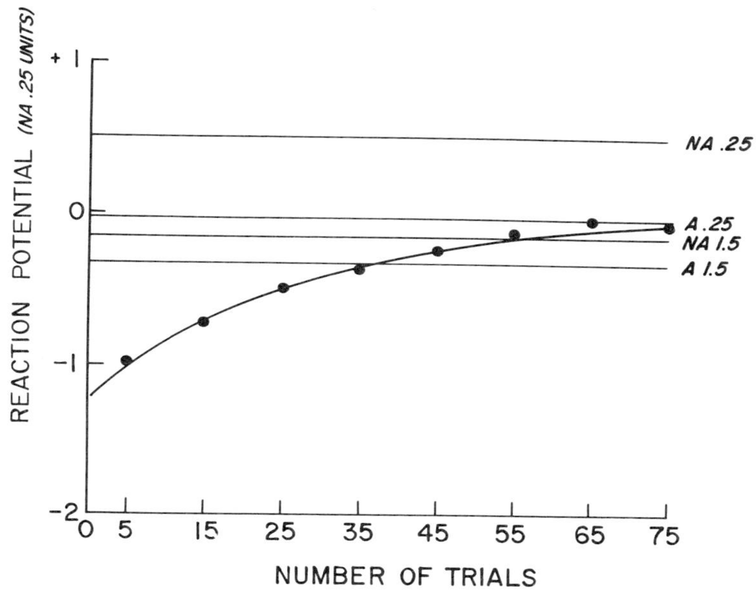

FIGURE 16. Habit function and threshold locations for the four groups of Spence and Haggard data involving two levels of anxiety and two levels of UCS intensity.

values are plotted in Figure 16, where it may be seen that they form a smooth, negatively accelerated function, well fitted with the equation:

$$H = .02 - 1.23\ (10)^{-.0156N} \tag{8}$$

The zero point of Figure 16 is at the general mean of the groups. The threshold values are located with respect to their deviations of the groups from the general mean. Also, the distance from the threshold for NA,.25 to the remaining three are the three values of *d′*. Threshold distributions are not indicated on the figure, but the SD for NA,.25 is one and the other three have the values of their estimated ratios to it. The solution from this point is the same as in the previous examples. Distances, in NA,.25 units, were obtained from points on the fitted habit function to each of the four threshold values. These were then converted back to units of the original distributions and the *p* values were obtained from normal distribution tables. Converted to predicted percentages of CRs, these *p* values form the smooth curves presented in Figure 17.

Considering the irregularities in the data, it is apparent that the model fits the points about as well as any conceivable set of smooth functions. It is par-

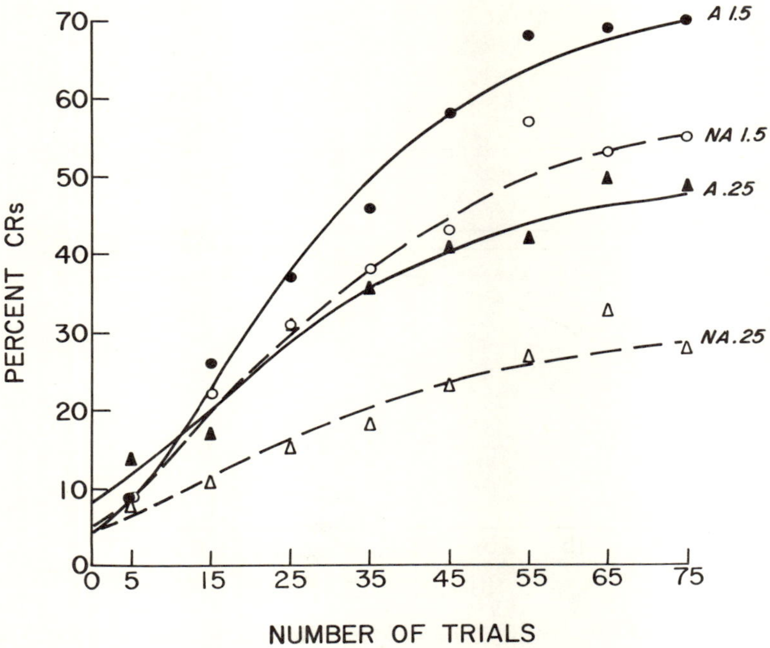

FIGURE 17. Fit of the threshold model to the four conditioning curves of Spence and Haggard experiment, based on a single habit-growth function.

ticularly interesting to note that the crossing, at about 20 trials, of the NA,1.5 and A,.25 curves is successfully predicted. Since nine parameters were estimated from the data, 23 degrees of freedom remain after the fit.

In applying the model to Spence's experiment on the effect of threat, a significant variation was introduced. It is an interesting possibility that the habit-growth curve may have considerable generality, applying not only to a single experiment, but to an entire class of similar conditioning experiments. For this reason, it was decided to attempt to fit the model to the Threat experiment using the habit function which was fitted in the analysis of the Anxiety experiment. In order to do this it is necessary to convert the function into the units employed in the analysis. In this instance, all data were converted into units of the NT,.25 SD. Estimates of the ratios of the other SDs to that of this group were 1.01 for T,1.5; 1.14 for NT,1.5; and .72 for T,.25. Values of d' in NT,.25 units were 1.54, 1.07, and .70, respectively. The habit function of Equation 8 is in units of the NA,.25 group. In order to convert it to the appropriate units, the REC relating Group NA,.25 to group NT,.25 was used. This had a slope of .505. To convert to NT,.25 units, the values of Equation 8 were divided by .505. The zero point was appropriately adjusted by subtracting .01 to compensate for the slight difference in overall responsiveness (mean threshold level) in the two experiments. From this point, the remainder of the solution was the same as in the preceding analysis. The resulting fit of the model is presented in Figure 18. The data for this experiment are rather un-

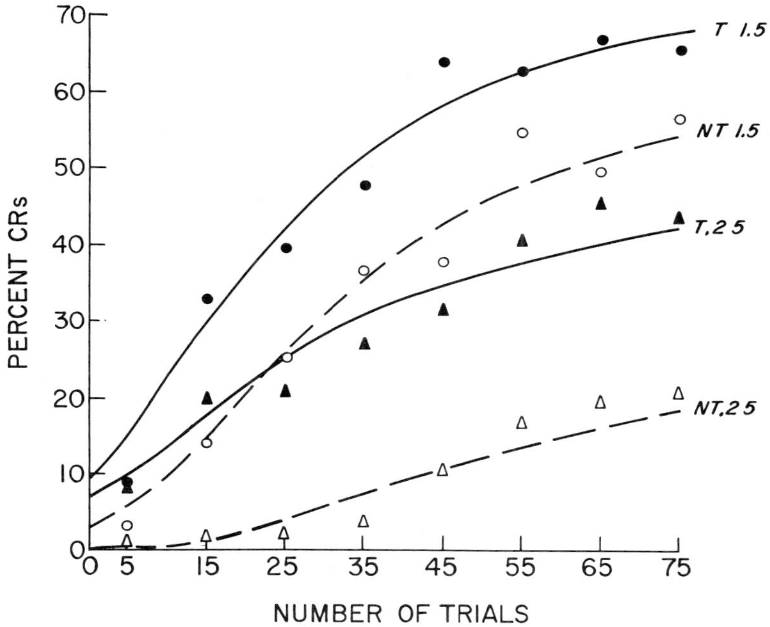

FIGURE 18. Fit of the threshold model to the four conditioning curves of the Spence Threat experiment. The single underlying habit-growth function is the one estimated from the Spence and Haggard data.

reliable, being based on only 10 *S*s per group, and involving a number of very low *p* values which yield notoriously unreliable *z* values. In spite of this, however, the overall fit is quite successful. Again, the crossing of two curves is successfully predicted in the case of NT,1.5 and T,.25.

The net result of these two analyses is that eight conditioning curves, involving two levels of UCS intensity, two levels of anxiety, and two levels of threat, have been quite impressively described on the basis of a single underlying habit-growth curve plus the appropriate estimates of variability ratios and distances. In order to accomplish this, it was necessary to estimate 17 parameters from the data, but there still remain 47 degrees of freedom. The data are consistent with the interpretation that UCS intensity does not affect habit strength, but has a purely motivational effect on the reaction threshold. This is quite contrary to Spence's view, which was that UCS intensity has associative as well as motivational effects. Actually, his conclusion that this variable affects habit was well founded on what the writer has always regarded as an extraordinarily brilliant series of experiments (Spence, 1953; Spence, Haggard, & Ross, 1958a; Spence, Haggard, & Ross, 1958b; Spence & Runquist, 1958; Trapold & Spence, 1960). Generally, the findings were that manipulation of UCS intensity produced relatively permanent and stimulus-specific effects. However, in view of the present findings, it appears that some rethinking of the problem is in order. One possibility to consider is that there are threshold changes of some persistence and which may be stimulus-specific. Perhaps there are two kinds of threshold manipulations—one general, and one in which *S* is alerted to particular stimuli. One rather revolutionary suggestion, from the Hull-Spence point of view, is to consider the possibility that it is a motivational and not an associative process which grows in an orderly fashion with trials.

SOURCES AND EFFECTS OF VARIABILITY

It should be kept clearly in mind that the conditioning curves to which the threshold model has been applied here are functions based upon groups of *S*s and are not the curves of individual *S*s. In other words, the hypothetical threshold distributions are based on between-subjects variability plus within-individuals variations. Such an analysis is appropriate, because of the assumption (Grice, 1968) that differences in threshold are the chief source of individual differences. It is our clear intent, however, that the model should apply to the individual *S*, with distributions based entirely on within-individual variability of the threshold. Application of the model to individual *S* data poses obvious difficulties, but must ultimately be accomplished. One starting point would be to assume that all *S*s share a common habit-growth function, but differ in mean threshold level (responsiveness) and variability. In principle, the methods used here could be used to estimate these parameters for each *S*.

The simple assumption of normality has applied surprisingly well in these analyses. Perhaps, since the percentages were based on frequencies summed over blocks of 10 trials and averaged over groups of *S*s, this may have been influenced to some degree by the operation of the central limit theorem. It will be interesting to see if normality also applies to the distributions of individual *S*s. Based on Spence's (1956) analyses of groups of homogeneous *S*s, the prospect is hopeful.

From the foregoing analyses it is quite clear that differences in variability have a profound effect on the form of conditioning curves. While it has been widely recognized that variability is a major determinate of group-learning curves, the present approach provides additional conceptualization of the problem and methods for analyzing it. It also emphasizes the less widely recognized point, that *within-individual* variability will have similar and equally important effects upon the form of *individual* learning functions. Similar effects are to be expected upon the forms of other kinds of functions, such as extinction curves, retention curves, and generalization gradients.

It is instructive to examine the effects of differences in variability alone with other parameters constant, as well as the effects of interactions of variability with other parameters. An example of the implications of the model is presented in the hypothetical curves of Figure 19. These curves were calculated

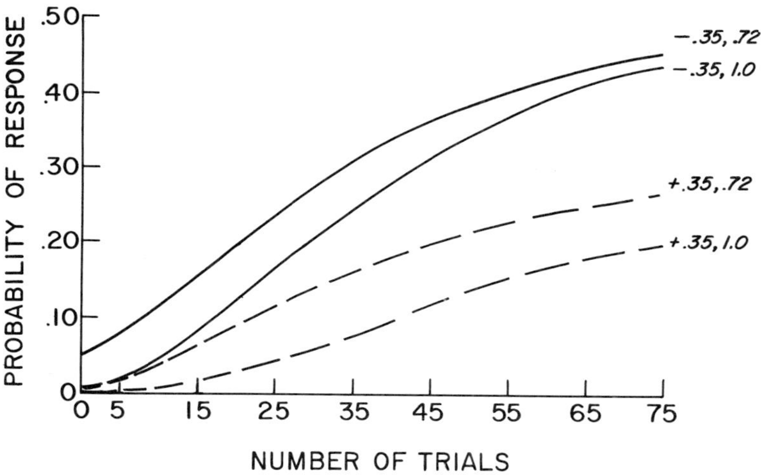

FIGURE 19. Hypothetical conditioning curves for groups differing in threshold and variability, but involving a common habit-growth function. The first number given for each curve is the value of the threshold and the second is the SD. Units are those of the analysis in Figures 14 and 15.

by rearranging the parameters obtained in the analysis of Figures 14 and 15. All four of the curves are based on the same function of habit growth. The two more responsive upper curves have equal, relatively low, mean threshold values, but differ in variability. It will be noted that the functions rise at different rates, but tend to converge. The two lower curves have equal, relatively high, thresholds but differ in variability exactly as the two upper curves. These two functions not only rise at different rates, but also approach quite different terminal levels. Traditionally, inspection of these curves would lead to a conclusion of either different rates of habit growth or different drive levels. Neither of these conclusions would be justified. The model implies that both between- and within-subject variability should be taken into consideration in the interpretation of both the form and level of empirical-learning curves. The general principles are that low variability leads to more rapid improvement, and, for high thresholds, to higher asymptotic performance.

There are two quite different empirical-conditioning curves among those previously analyzed, where the difference can be interpreted as due to difference in variability. The NA,.25 group of the Spence and Haggard experiment, and the NT,.25 group of the Spence Threat experiment were groups of similar *S*s apparently conditioned under the same conditions. A test has been made to determine if the two different curves can be interpreted as due to differing variability. First, an REC was plotted to determine the ratio of their SDs. The line was arbitrarily passed through the origin to conform to the assumption of equal mean thresholds (i.e. $d' = 0$). The slope was determined by also passing the line through the point consisting of the two general means. Actually, the fit was almost as good as that of the best-fitting line. The estimate of the ratio of the SDs was .574. The suprathreshold z values for group NT,.25 had previously been obtained in the solution of Figure 15. These were then simply multiplied by .574 to transform them into units of the NA,.25 SD. The corresponding p values form the upper curve of Figure 20, and the data

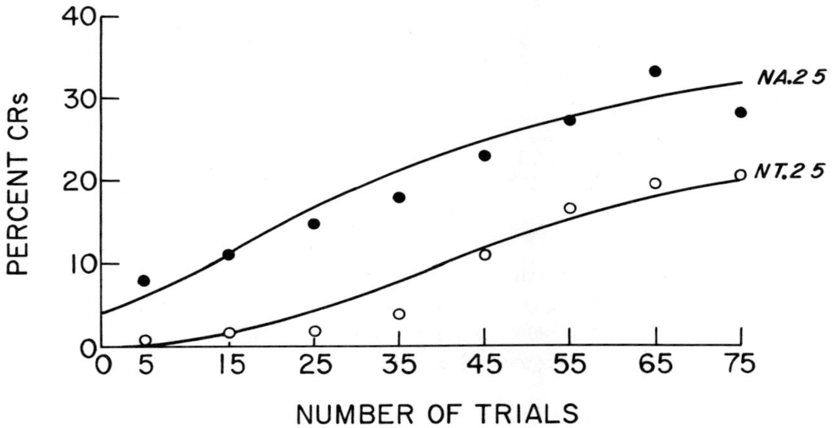

FIGURE 20. Fit of the threshold model to conditioning curves of Group NA,.25 from the Spence and Haggard experiment and Group NT,.25 from the Spence Threat experiment, based on the assumption that the groups differ only in variability.

points are those of Group NA,.25. The curve for NT,.25 is the same as in Figure 15. It is interesting that only one additional parameter need be estimated to fit the NA,.25 data. The result is consistent with the interpretation that the groups have the same habit curve and equal mean thresholds, but differ in variability.

When an analysis suggests the presence of a relation between experimental variables and variability, this may or may not be readily interpretable. In any case, it should frequently lead to further research hypotheses, or to a recognition of the need for improved design. In the Spence and Haggard experiment, the analysis suggested that the NA groups were more variable than the A groups. This may simply have been a function of the psychometric instrument used to identify the groups. For example, one hypothesis is that the A groups consisted of anxious *S*s, while the NA groups consisted of nonanxious *S*s and anxious liars. Of course, this simple-minded explanation may not be the correct one, but, if true, the model implies that it would almost inevitably produce the result. On the other hand, the analysis implies that the Threat groups were more variable than the No Threat groups. This result would be expected if *S*s differed markedly in their susceptibility to threat, or if individuals from time to time were to forget the state of threat.

CONCLUSIONS

This model, based on the assumption that motivational states influence the reaction threshold, has been proposed as an alternative to the multiplicative theory of habit and drive. The success of the model in these limited applications suggests that it is capable of dealing with the kind of data the multiplicative theory was designed to explain, but that it also applies to results where the multiplicative theory has difficulty. Primarily, because of its relation to Thurstone scaling procedures and to TSD, the model also carries with it analytical methods of considerable power. Much remains to be done before the ultimate viability of the approach can be assessed. To use, affectionately, one of Professor Spence's characteristic double negatives, the beginning is not unpromising.

REFERENCES

Ausubel, D. P. Introduction to a threshold concept of primary drives. *Journal of General Psychology*, 1956, *54*, 209–229.

Campbell, B. A., & Sheffield, F. D. Relation of random activity to food deprivation. *Journal of Comparative and Physiological Psychology*, 1953, *46*, 320–322.

Grice, G. R. Dependence of empirical laws upon the source of experimental variation. *Psychological Bulletin*, 1966, *66*, 488–498.

Grice, G. R. Stimulus intensity and response evocation. *Psychological Review*, 1968, *75*, 359–373.

Kendall, M. G., & Stuart, A. *The advanced theory of statistics*. Vol. 2. (2nd ed.) New York: Hafner, 1967.

Prokasy, W. F. Do *D* and *H* multiply to determine performance in human conditioning? *Psychological Bulletin*, 1967, *67*, 368–377.

Saffir, M. A comparative study of scales constructed by three psychophysical methods. *Psychometrika*, 1937, *2*, 179–198.

Spence, K. W. Learning and performance in eyelid conditioning as a function of intensity of the UCS. *Journal of Experimental Psychology*, 1953, *45*, 57–63.

Spence, K. W. *Behavior theory and conditioning*. New Haven: Yale University Press, 1956.

Spence, K. W. A theory of emotionally based drive (*D*) and its relation to performance in simple learning situations. *American Psychologist*, 1958, *13*, 131–141.

Spence, K. W., Haggard, D. F., & Ross, L. E. USC intensity and the associative (habit) strength of the eyelid CR. *Journal of Experimental Psychology*, 1958, *55*, 404–411. (a)

Spence, K. W., Haggard, D. F., & Ross, L. E. Intrasubject conditioning as a function of the intensity of the unconditioned stimulus. *Science*, 1958, *128*, 774–775. (b)

Spence, K. W., & Runquist, W. N. Temporal effects of conditioned fear on the eyelid reflex. *Journal of Experimental Psychology*, 1958, *55*, 613–616.

Taylor, J. A. The relationship of anxiety to the conditioned eyelid response. *Journal of Experimental Psychology*, 1951, *41*, 81–92.

Torgerson, W. S. *Theory and methods of scaling*. New York: Wiley, 1958.

Trapold, M. A., & Spence, K. W. Performance changes in eyelid conditioning as related to the motivational and reinforcing properties of the UCS. *Journal of Experimental Psychology*, 1960, *59*, 209–213.

MEMORY

Recognition Memory

BENTON J. UNDERWOOD

THE PROBLEM

When an event is experienced it usually leaves some relatively permanent representation. This representation is called a memory. To say that memories constitute the raw materials of the intellect, or to say that thousands of past events have a contemporaneity because of memory, may produce awe, but not understanding. It is in seeking this understanding that psychologists have for decades engaged in laboratory experiments on memory. The fundamental approach has been to discover variables which influence some quantitative measures of behavior that are said to be reflecting memory, and then to suggest theoretical notions which will encompass the effects of the variables. Since 1932, when McGeoch planted the concept of interference squarely in the center of explanatory attempts, most empirical and theoretical approaches have in one way or another been directed toward a more and more detailed characterization of the mechanisms believed involved in interference. Thus, the study of memory has been largely a study of interference-produced forgetting.

That interference can markedly influence performance said to be measuring memory does not seem to be in doubt. However, as pointed out many times, the fact that a performance test shows a loss of memory for an event (or events) does not necessarily mean that a memory for the event no longer exists. It means only that the subject did not perform at the moment in such a way as to exhibit a memory. Other types of tests might produce evidence indicating that some aspect of the memory remains. One of the most widely quoted generalizations in the area of memory is that recognition scores will frequently give evidence of the existence of a memory when recall scores will not do so. At a common-sense level, the difference in recall and recognition scores may seem so reasonable that further elaboration is not required. In recall, *S* must produce a word, a nonsense syllable, or a sentence. In recognition, production is not formally required; rather, *S* must merely discriminate between or among events, usually identifying certain events as "old," others as "new." But to say that recognition only requires a discrimination is to lead to an important question: upon what is the discrimination based? The question may be posed more explicitly. The *S* is presented with 20 common words at a fairly rapid rate under appropriate learning instructions. After the presentation, these 20 old words are mixed with 20 additional common words, and *S* is asked to check the old ones. His success will be high; perhaps 90 percent of the old words will be checked, and only a small percent of the new ones. How is this series of discriminations made?

It does not seem sufficient to say that *S* matches each word with his memory for the 20 old words and if there is a "fit" he checks the word. Nor does it seem satisfactory to say that each old word as presented on the test makes contact with its trace from the original presentation. These statements are perhaps useful ways to pose the question, but they do not tell what it is that makes a "fit" or what the nature of the trace contact must be before a word is checked. Suppose that instead of asking *S* to check only the 20 words shown him a few minutes earlier, we ask him to check any of the words which he had seen at any previous time. Since these were all common words, *S* would undoubtedly check all 40 if he could tolerate such an absurd request. The "fit" would be perfect for all; all 40 traces would be contacted. A theory of recognition must state some basis (or bases) by which *S* makes the discrimination between old and new words when old and new represent a momentary distinction within the laboratory.

The present essay records some observations and notions which lead toward a theory of recognition memory. As will be seen, the emphasis will be upon one particular discriminative mechanism. As will also be seen, there are certain recognized inadequacies in the formulation. But the writer joins others who believe that an understanding of recognition learning has become a critical need, and this need perhaps may justify the tentativeness of the present formulation. It will be necessary first to present an overall conception of memory and then show how recognition memory fits into this conception.

THE COMPOSITION OF MEMORY

In a previous paper memory was viewed as consisting of a collection or ensemble of attributes (Underwood, 1969b). These attributes represent various kinds of information which are stored when learning occurs, and the ensemble of attributes *is* the memory. The way *S* processes events determines the nature of the ensemble, such processing often being called encoding. With the young adult *S*, so frequently studied in memory experiments, some encoding appears to occur spontaneously (without intent to learn), although the nature of the ensemble may differ somewhat following incidental vs. intentional instructional conditions.

The attributes

Some of the attributes which may become a part of a memory will be identified. Whenever an event is experienced it is experienced at a given point in time and, by its association with contiguous events, may carry a *temporal* attribute. Certain memories may include a *spatial* attribute. Since all events occur at least once, the memory may involve *frequency* information as another attribute. There is evidence that some memories are associated with one sensory *modality* more than with another.

When attention is turned to memories for verbal units, a number of additional attributes may be identified, although this does not mean that memories for other classes of events could not include some of these. A word has a limited number of letters arranged in a given sequence; these features may be called the *orthographic* attributes. When pronounced, a word has a certain sound spectrum or an *acoustic* attribute. A word may produce an *image;* it may produce an *affective* response. When a word occurs in a learning task other *verbal associates* are likely to be elicited, and these associates are attributes of the memory for the word. Finally, the term *class attributes* indicates that a memory must carry information concerning the class of events involved, perhaps identified on several dimensions.

The attributes and performance measures of memory

A memory consists of a collection of some of the attributes identified above. When memory tests are given, the attributes function in two ways. First, they serve as retrieval mechanisms whereby a given target (such as a word) is produced in a recall sense. Second, they serve as discriminative mechanisms to distinguish one target memory from another. Or, in terms of the materials used in most of the experiments, the attributes distinguish one word from another. The discrimination among words represents the essence of recognition memory, and much of the subsequent discussion will deal with the relationship between procedures for studying recognition and a particular attribute which is believed heavily involved in the discrimination. This attribute, the frequency attribute, seems to become an integral part of most (if not all) memories and serves a fundamental role in discriminating among memories. Before this attribute is examined more thoroughly, one further assumption must be stated.

It seems likely that *S* learns that attributes vary in their validity (for correct responding) depending upon the type of the memory test that is involved. Consequently, there is a hierarchy of attributes which may change as the nature of the memory test changes. In a manner of speaking, in any given test *S* starts at the top of the hierarchy and works down until some "decision" is made. In a recall test, retrieval attributes must stand at the top of the hierarchy; in recognition tests, discriminative attributes are preëminent. It is not possible to separate attributes into two neat categories, retrieval and discriminative attributes; it seems probable that some serve both functions. However, in the case of the frequency attribute the assumption is made that it is primarily (if not exclusively) a discriminative attribute and that it is dominant in the hierarchy in recognition tests of memory.

SENSITIVITY TO EVENT FREQUENCY

In this section the intent is to summarize evidence showing that *S* is extremely sensitive to event frequency, hence to differences in event frequency. Since the overall interest is in the retention of verbal materials, the discussion will be limited to evidence using verbal units. At the end of the section, certain unsolved problems with regard to the assimilation of event frequency will be discussed.

Assimilation of background frequency

By background frequency is meant the frequency information which *S* has assimilated throughout the course of his life and which he brings to the experimental situation. There is considerable evidence to show that frequency of occurrence of verbal units has been assimilated with appreciable integrity. Attneave (1953) demonstrated that judgments of the frequency of occurrence of individual letters correlated 0.79 with true frequency. For the judgments of the relative frequency with which words have been experienced, a number of investigators have shown a high positive relationship between judged frequency and true frequency (e.g., Shapiro, 1969).

Words may be considered natural units in that their boundaries are clearly defined. Fragments of words consisting of two or more letters do not have such natural boundaries unless they form a syllabic unit. It is not clear, therefore, whether such word fragments would carry frequency information. In a previous publication (Underwood & Schulz, 1960) evidence was presented on frequency judgments of word fragments (bigrams and trigrams). The *S* made such judgments with some validity, but the relationship was not as clear as those found with letters and words. Furthermore, it was possible that the judgments were mediated, not by the fragment as a whole, but by a "summing" of individual letter frequencies. By the nature of orthography, such summing would produce more appropriate than inappropriate frequency judgments for word fragments. For reasons which will become apparent later, it seemed important to determine whether valid frequency judgments of word fragments could be made when individual letter frequency was not a confounding factor. Data from such a study will now be reported.

The *S* was presented with a series of bigram pairs and for each pair he was to choose the bigram which he believed to occur with greatest frequency in words. The first letter of each pair of bigrams was identical, the two bigrams being differentiated only by the second letter. Second-letter frequency was controlled in the following manner. Two pairs had an identical bigram, which may be called the key bigram. The other two bigrams had the same first letter as the key bigram but different second letters. In one of these bigrams the second letter had a frequency that was one step higher than the second letter of the key bigram, a step being the adjacent letter in the ranking of the frequency of all 26 letters. The other bigram had a second letter whose frequency was one step lower than the second letter of the key bigram. Thus, within this set of two pairs, individual letter frequency could not be a confounding factor. To illustrate: if a key bigram was GB, *S* judged the relative frequency of GB vs. GP, and at another point in the series, GB vs. GV. The frequencies of P and V bracket the frequency of B in a ranking of the 26 letters on frequency. There were 56 key bigrams, hence 112 pairs. A total of 192 *S*s made the judgments. For each bigram pair the percentage of *S*s encircling the bigram having the highest true frequency was determined and used as a percentage correct measure. The 112 bigram pairs were ordered according to the lowest base frequency, defined as the frequency of the least frequent bigram in each pair. The 56 pairs having the lowest base frequency were then used for one set of determinations, and the 56 pairs with the highest base frequency were used for another set. The 56 bigrams within each set were ordered according to the magnitude of the frequency difference in each pair. Four successive subgroups of 14 pairs each were then used as relatively homogeneous subgroups, and the mean percentage of correct judgments was determined for each of the eight subgroups of 14 pairs each. These judgments can be related to the base frequency and to the frequency difference. To facilitate plotting, the frequency differences were transformed to a log scale and the mean log frequency difference determined for each subgroup of 14 pairs. The resulting data are plotted in Figure 1.

Two facts are apparent from Figure 1. First, the percentage of correct judgments increases as the magnitude of the frequency difference increases. Second, something akin to Weber's Law appears to hold; the lower the base frequency the higher the percentage correct for any given frequency difference. It is concluded that *S* has assimilated some frequency information about two-letter fragments of words.

Two general observations may be made about the assimilation of event frequency. First, the frequency information has accrued incidentally; the *S*s

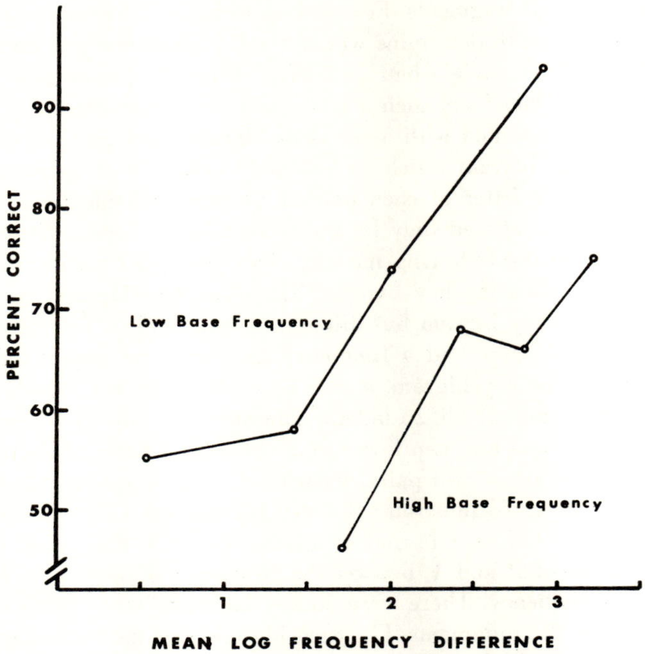

FIGURE 1. Judgment of differences in bigram frequency as a function of the magnitude of the difference and base frequency.

have not spent their lives intentionally making counts of words or letters or bigrams. Second, the frequency knowledge has been abstracted from a larger context. Individual letters are not experienced in isolation with a frequency that corresponds to their frequency within words, and bigrams are rarely experienced in isolation. Words are most commonly seen or heard within the larger context of a phrase or sentence. If evidence as to the true frequency of various phrases were available it seems likely that *S* could make appropriate frequency judgments, and phrase frequency is abstracted from the larger context of sentences. That larger units such as sentences could be recognized as occurring with differential frequency seems beyond doubt; whenever a sentence or a group of words expressing an idea is labeled a cliché the frequency judgment is made explicit.

Assimilation of situational frequency

A number of studies have reported results on the assimilation of word frequency when frequency has been varied in the laboratory (e.g., Hintzman, 1969b; Underwood, 1969a). These studies show that as frequency increases, absolute frequency judgments increase; and as frequency differences between two words increase, the probability of selecting the most frequent word increases. Weber's Law applies to these judgments. Judgments appear to be uninfluenced if *S* is not told ahead of time that frequency judgments will be required. So far as is known there have been no laboratory studies directly concerned with the study of abstracted frequency; that is, studies in which *S* is unexpectedly asked to make judgments about the frequency of occurrence of elements which had appeared in larger presentation units.

The fact that laboratory studies demonstrate that the mean frequency judgments show a close relationship with true presentation frequency does not mean that there is no variance associated with particular words. Such variance is present and the implication will be considered more fully at a later point.

When the assimilation of situational frequency for words is studied, the background frequency appears to have little if any effect on the judgments. In unpublished work done in the Northwestern laboratory, *S*s were asked to judge the situational frequency of words having low and high background frequency. When two words having equal situational frequency but widely different background frequency were paired for a comparative judgment, decisions were about equally split between the two words. Thus, it appears that at least on a short-term basis, situational frequency remains distinct from background frequency.

Unresolved problems

Thus far the evidence seems to show clearly that *S* assimilates event frequency with considerable fidelity. One problem which remains unresolved is the nature or characteristic of the frequency unit which, so to speak, goes on to the frequency counter. Previous writings have assumed that the act of perceiving a word is a representational response (RR), and it is this RR which is the frequency unit. Does the RR represent, or does it overlap with, any of the memory attributes listed earlier? Is it orthographic in nature? Or acoustic? Is it possible that a more primitive perceptual response than implied by these other attributes is the basic unit of frequency? It is assumed that the RR for words is devoid of semantic content, but whether it is less than or different from other nonassociative attributes is not known. The discussion will assume that the RR is the basic frequency unit, recognizing that the failure to identify it precisely, or distinguish it clearly from memory attributes, represents an ambiguity.

With some verbal units, such as a consonant syllable, the frequency unit may not be the syllable as a whole. The *S* may attend only to one letter, or perhaps two, of the syllable so that the RR is not the total syllable. Further, *S* may not produce the same RR to a syllable on two successive presentations so that there is a frequency unit for each RR (they do not sum). This is a part of a more general problem of the size of the category which will receive a so-called repeated event. (Strictly speaking, no event ever repeats itself in detail.) The *S*s are, however, inevitable categorizers and may tolerate considerable variation in the RRs and still route them to the same counter. With common words we assume a stable RR, but there may be times when the same word enters different counters. Does the word *port* in "port of entry" and in "port wine" get recorded on the same counter? As noted above, it has been assumed that the RR is not a semantic unit, but this assumption my be in error.

There is another unresolved set of problems revolving around the frequency unit. Does a frequency unit vary in size? If two words are presented equally often but at different rates will the frequency judgments differ for them? Will the frequency judgment for a word spoken to *S* at a 75 *db* level differ from one spoken at a 30 *db* level? The RRs to words may differ in latency; does this influence the magnitude of the frequency unit? Most of these issues can be empirically resolved but they have not yet been. The implication is that a theory of recognition memory based on frequency as the dominant attribute can at best be only a very rough approximation at the present time.

THE FREQUENCY ATTRIBUTE AND THE RECOGNITION TEST

The evidence presented indicates that *S* possesses a well-developed skill which allows him to detect differences in frequency. If a learning task is such that the detection of frequency differences will allow acquisition, it seems reasonable to assume that learning may occur by applying the skill. Such was the thinking which led to a theory of verbal-discrimination (VD) learning, a theory which assumes that *S* chooses alternatives by discriminating differences in situational frequency (Ekstrand, Wallace, & Underwood, 1966). The use of the frequency attribute in explaining VD learning serves as the background for its application to the more classical recognition situation.

Verbal-discrimination learning and the frequency attribute

In the simplest case of VD learning, *S* is presented a series of pairs of words, one word in each pair having been arbitrarily designated as the correct word. Assume that the pairs are presented for anticipation learning in which the pair is shown briefly, say for 2 sec., and then the correct word is shown alone for 2 sec. When the pair is presented together it is assumed that each word produces an RR, hence each gains a frequency unit. When the correct word is shown alone an additional frequency unit is added so that the frequency difference is two-to-one in favor of the correct word. If this is a sufficient difference in frequency to allow a discrimination, *S* should correctly anticipate the correct word on the following trial. Additional frequency units will accrue to the correct word when a correct anticipation is made; if an incorrect anticipation is made, the incorrect word gains a unit and the discrimination based on a frequency difference is retarded. Some additional frequency units may be gained by the correct word as a consequence of covert rehearsal responses.

The theory leads to a number of predictions, and many of these have been confirmed. It is probably fair to say that it has been a reasonably successful theory, but it seems now too restrictive in that it allows only for a frequency differential to be the basis for the discrimination—no other attributes are involved. Situations have been produced in which it would be impossible for *S* to perform on the basis of a frequency discrimination, and yet performance was far above chance (e.g., Underwood & Freund, 1970a). It seems necessary therefore to take the previously outlined position that the frequency attribute is dominant in the VD situation, but that other attributes will replace frequency when the frequency discrimination is inadequate. This position is also taken to account for classical recognition-memory results.

Recognition learning and the frequency attribute

A VD task is a recognition task only slightly removed in detail from the classical recognition procedures. In VD learning all units involved are given frequency inputs prior to a test; in recognition learning the test is made by *S* comparing units which have received one or more frequency inputs with units which have not received any inputs until a test for recognition learning is made. Thus, in the minimal case, at the time of the test the correct word has had one frequency input, the incorrect word a zero frequency input. The frequency inputs referred to are of course situational in nature. If a difference of zero vs. one frequency unit is discriminable by the *S*, performance on the recognition task should be perfect after a single presentation of the units. But as will be seen, performance is rarely perfect in such circumstances. Likewise, Hintzman (1969b) has shown that when *S* is asked to choose the most frequent word in a pair, the choice is correct about 80 percent of the time when the situational frequencies are zero and one.

The initial and basic test for a theory is the degree of correspondence between its predictions and the effects of major independent variables on behavior for which the theory is held relevant. The remainder of this essay is devoted primarily to an examination of this correspondence, but it is not a comprehensive review of the literature. In the process of the examination, the scope of the theory will be expanded.

Direct tests of the frequency hypothesis which at the same time rule out alternative interpretations are not available. In dealing with the effects of independent variables, therefore, the interest will be in the appropriateness of the frequency theory, not in comparing it with other possible explanations.

VARIABLES IN RECOGNITION PERFORMANCE

Testing effects

Testing effects are changes in behavior, usually decremental in nature, which occur during the act of testing recognition memory. It is the intent to show that these effects represent interference resulting from a breakdown in frequency discriminations. Once again therefore, a study of interference becomes a vehicle for evaluating a theory of memory.

It is necessary to make a distinction between poorly and well-integrated verbal units. By illustration, RZL would be a poorly integrated unit; CAT a well-integrated unit. Illustrations do not afford the precision desired, nor is it possible to bring the needed precision to this matter by other means. An integrated unit can be said to be one in which *S* responds to the unit as a whole and responds on different occasions with the same RR. In fact, it is rarely known when such consistency is achieved in the learning situation. It is known from stimulus-selection studies that *S* often does not respond to all of the elements of what was called above a poorly integrated unit; he may respond to the first letter only. But again, in any particular situation for a given *S* we cannot specify the exact nature of the RR to a poorly integrated unit. Therefore, some ambiguity must remain concerning the continuum defined at one end as poorly or nonintegrated and at the other as well-integrated. This ambiguity is allowed to remain because at the gross level such differences seem apparent and because a point must be made about recognition performance as a function of these gross differences.

Poorly integrated units. In a study by Peixotto (1947), the *S* was shown 30 nonsense syllables for an average of 2 sec. each. On the recognition test, 90 additional syllables were included as new syllables. The 120 syllables were arranged in five columns of 24 each, and there were six correct syllables in each column (although *S* was not told this). The *S* checked the syllables which he thought were old and he did this *in order* across the five columns. It was possible therefore for Peixotto to examine recognition performance as a function of the stage of testing (five successive columns). Actually, each *S* went through the above procedure for five sessions (held on different days). The interest here is in the results for the first session. Across the five columns the number of correct (old) syllables identified constituted 85 percent, 70 percent, 62 percent, 64 percent and 49 percent of the number possible. The number of incorrect items checked (as being correct) constituted 19 percent,

24 percent, 16 percent, 13 percent, and 15 percent of the number possible. Obviously the total number of items checked decreased across columns (from 8.45 in the first column to 5.76 in the fifth). The critical finding is the deterioration across columns in the identification of old syllables. After 85 percent correct on the first column, performance fell so that by the fifth column, *S* was checking only half the correct items. Furthermore, Peixotto noted that there was a small decrement within columns.

What causes this severe decline in performance during the process of testing? Of course, the retention interval is a little longer for the fifth column than for the first, but there is no reason to believe that this accounts for more than a small amount of the decrement. Peixotto interprets the results as due to the effect of the new or distractor syllables. This seems quite appropriate. With nonintegrated units, as the *S* views each successive syllable during the testing there is an increase in the frequency with which various single letters and two-letter combinations are experienced. If the memory for a syllable consists of less than the total of three letters, the pyramiding of the single letter and bigram frequencies during testing could lead to an inability to distinguish on the basis of a frequency differential between the old and new items.

It is highly unlikely that the Peixotto results are intrinsic to nonsense syllables. The results could probably be duplicated by using sets of three three-letter words in the learning list (e.g., LAW-COW-BAR) and then permuting the orders of the words into orders not used in learning and employing these orders as new items on the recognition task.

Other investigators have noted that recognition memory may be based on less than the total unit presented (e.g., McNulty, 1965) when the unit is poorly integrated. Still others have noted that the interference which occurs during testing has certain implications for method (e.g., Dale & Baddeley, 1966; Field & Lachman, 1966). For example, one of the rather consistent findings is that recognition performance decreases as number of alternatives in a multiple-choice type test increases. An experiment may be designed so that as a test of recognition learning there are two, four, or six alternative choices for each correct or old unit. If these three conditions are given to different groups of *S*s, or to the same *S*s at different times, it is clear that the testing effect must be greater the greater the number of alternative choices. This must follow: as *S* goes through the successive sets the probability of building up interference by a buildup of the frequencies of the components of the units increases as the number of alternatives increase. Thus, poorer performance is largely due to a between-sets effect, not to the number of alternatives within any particular set. It appears that to manipulate this variable properly a mixed-testing condition is required (Postman, 1950), so that during the test procedure *S* would be exposed to some items with two alternatives, some with four, some with six, and so on, all intermingled. The retention interval would be equal for all types of items. Of course, such a procedure would not remove the testing effect; it would simply spread it equally over all conditions.

With an appropriate design the effect of number of alternatives is small in magnitude. Postman (1950) used two, four, seven, and ten alternatives and found that recognition scores did not differ for the first three conditions but all were superior to the condition in which there were ten alternatives. Strictly interpreted, frequency theory would predict that number of alternatives would not influence recognition performance for either integrated or nonintegrated units. However, because there appears to be considerable variability in apparent frequency as a function of a constant input frequency (Underwood & Freund, 1970a), a small effect of number of alternatives may be observed. The greater the number of alternatives the greater the likelihood that the apparent frequency of one of the alternatives would overlap the apparent frequency of the old or correct word. In any event, the theory can tolerate a small effect as number of alternatives is varied.

Integrated units. It is assumed that the situational-frequency counting mechanism to words involves the word as a whole. A small testing effect may be observed because of variability in apparent frequency with situational frequency constant (as noted above), or it may occur under special circumstances where certain associative relationships exist among the words (a matter to be covered later). Most evidence indicates that the testing effect is of very small magnitude when words are used in the recognition task. The contrast between integrated and nonintegrated units is shown in a comparison of results reported by Shepard and Teghtsoonian (1961) with those reported by Hintzman (1969a).

Shepard and Teghtsoonian developed a procedure which may be called running recognition. Essentially, the study and test phase are not separated. Three-digit numbers were used, with a certain proportion of the numbers occurring twice. From the beginning of the series *S* was to classify each successive three-digit number as old (it occurred before in the series) or new (it had not occurred before). The results for these nonintegrated units show a heavy decrement associated with the number of units falling between the two occurrences of a given number. That is, the longer it had been since *S* had seen a particular number, the greater the likelihood that he would fail to identify it as an old number.

Hintzman (1969a) used this technique with three-letter nouns as the units and found no decrement as a function of number of intervening words, although latency of responding was directly related to the number of intervening words. At all points in the testing decisions were approximately 96 percent correct.

Results of three studies using words may now be reported (Underwood & Freund, 1970c). These studies were designed to test a deduction from frequency theory, but their nature allows determination of a testing effect. The *S* was initially shown a large number of words of low frequency, one at a time for 5 sec. each. Recognition memory was tested by pairing each old word with a new word, and the *S* was to identify the correct word. The test was unpaced.

In the first experiment *S* was presented with 200 different words, each once, for study. Of these, 100 were tested by pairing each with a new word, these being scattered throughout the testing period (the remaining 100 words were used for other purposes to be discussed later). During the first half of the testing period 82 percent of the first 50 words were correctly recognized, and 79 percent of the last 50 words, for a testing effect of 3 percent. In a second experiment, with 10 words tested in both the first and second halves, the values (correct) were 96 percent in the first half and 92 percent in the second, for a 4 percent decrement. In a third experiment with the same number of items, the values were 90 percent and 88 percent for a 2 percent decrement. It is quite apparent from such results that the testing effect with low-frequency words is very small.

There are some data in discord with the above generalization. Norman and Waugh (1968) were also concerned about the testing effect and the misleading nature of the results when it is not taken into consideration. Their data show an appreciable testing effect across only 20 words on the test, from 81 percent on the first word tested to 54 percent on the last (20th). Their methods were quite different from those described above. The *S* was shown 30 words in succession for 1 sec. each. Immediately after the presentation of the last word the test started. The test consisted of 20 words, one-third old and one-third new (on the average), and *S* had 2 sec. to decide whether the word was old or new. Further, each *S* had 45 such tests during a single session. The differences in procedure between this study and the others described are marked. However, an examination of the Norman-Waugh data indicates that most (but not all) of the testing effect was produced by the position of the tests for the last five words on the presentation lists. When these last five words were tested in the initial positions performance was very accurate, in some cases 100 percent. However, when they were tested near the end of the test list, performance was only slightly better than chance. Words which appeared in the first eight positions of the presentation showed very little decrement as a function of test position. It is highly probable that, as with the results for free recall, had a short interval followed the presentation and the test, the recency effect would not have been present and the testing effects would have been much reduced. This is not to deny that an explanatory problem exists, but it does suggest that the problem is tied to the recency phenomenon, and the present paper is not prepared to cope with this.

A test of the frequency theory by a test effect. It was noted above that three experiments using words had shown only very minor testing effects

(Underwood & Freund, 1970c). These experiments were designed to produce certain testing effects which were predicted from frequency theory. Assume that three words, A, B, and C, are shown (along with many others) for a single learning trial. The recognition test consists of pairing each word with a new word (X, Y, or Z), and *S* makes a choice for each pair, a choice between the old and new. The slight testing effects noted earlier were determined by the choices A-X, B-Y, and C-Z, such pairs being distributed evenly throughout the testing period. Consider the implications, however, when each of the old words is paired with the same new or wrong word, A-X, B-X, C-X, and they are tested in that order. The frequency theory assumes that for the first pair, A-X, *S* chooses A because it has a frequency of one while X has a frequency of zero. However, if on the test of A-X, *S* makes an RR to X in the act of making his choice, X will now have a frequency of one. Therefore, when B-X occurs, both B and X have a frequency of one (B having received its unit during presentation, X when tested with A), and performance should be at a chance level. During the B-X test, X gains another frequency unit and when C-X occurs on the test, X should be chosen since it has a higher frequency level than C. Of course, in the testing sequence, the three pairs were separated by many other pairs.

Three different experiments tested this deduction. In the first the values for the three tests were, respectively, 81 percent, 69 percent, and 70 percent correct. In a second, very similar experiment, the values were 86 percent, 67 percent, and 68 percent. In a third experiment, where five successive tests were given (A-X, B-X, C-X, D-X, E-X), the correct choices were 83 percent, 66 percent, 57 percent, 59 percent, and 56 percent. It is apparent that the results do not conform to a pure frequency interpretation. In the first two experiments the initial drop occurred (although it did not fall to 50 percent), but there was no further decline between the second and third tests. A greater fall was observed in the third experiment (for reasons which need not be of concern here) but, strictly according to frequency theory, the drop should reach to zero correct.

How is the frequency theory as applied to recognition learning to be evaluated in the light of the above results? It will be remembered that the overall conception of memory for a word stated that the memory consisted of a collection of attributes. When *S* makes decisions on a recognition test it is assumed that the frequency attribute was the dominant but not the exclusive attribute available. If, as is presumed by the theory, the frequency of B and X is equivalent following the A-X pairing, the decision must be made on the basis of secondary attributes. These secondary attributes have not been identified in this experiment. The failure of performance to fall on the third test (C-X) in two of the experiments is troublesome for the theory. At this test the frequency difference should have favored X, the erroneous alternative, and if *S* responded on the basis of frequency, X should have been chosen. It is possible, of course, that the frequency difference is not discriminable and that secondary attributes again determined the decision. It has been assumed that the frequency unit produced by a 5-sec. exposure during the study trial is equivalent to the frequency unit produced during the test procedure whenever a word appeared on the test sheet. This may be an improper assumption. Another possibility is that *S* remembers particular words as having been called incorrect earlier in the test, and this determines his decision.

In two of the above experiments, additional tests of the theory were included. These tests should have resulted in an improvement in performance during the testing phase. An old word (correct word) was tested several times, but each time with a different wrong word (i.e., A-X, A-Y, A-Z). With each test the frequency of A should have increased and the frequency discrimination between it and each successive wrong word should have become easier. In one experiment the values were 87 percent, 92 percent, and 94 percent for the three tests in order. In the other experiment there were five such tests and the values were 84 percent, 91 percent, 93 percent, 94 percent, and 92 percent. In both experiments the increases are highly significant statistically, and it can be shown that the increases are almost as great as would be expected by presenting the word an equivalent number of trials during the study phase. The general conclusion is that these experiments have given some support to the idea that frequency is a major discriminative attribute in recognition memory.

Similarity of correct and incorrect units

Nonintegrated units. The evidence indicates that with nonsense syllables or longer strings of letters not forming a word, recognition performance is inversely related to the degree of formal similarity (letter overlap) between the units presented for learning and the distractors added for the test (e.g., Postman, 1951; McNulty, 1965). Insofar as the memory for such units involves less than the total letters presented, the high-similarity distractors may include exactly the same letters as stored for a correct unit. The lower the similarity, the less likely this is to happen. Further, insofar as the acoustic attribute is a part of the memory for such nonsense units, the higher the formal similarity, the higher the acoustic similarity. As discussed earlier, it is possible that the acoustic attribute for nonintegrated units also represents the frequency-counting mechanism. Unless an acoustic attribute is highly precise for a stored unit, a distractor unit having much the same acoustic properties may be indistinguishable from it, which is to say they would normally be categorized together. These matters are by no means clear, however, and the necessity for some correlation between orthographic attributes and acoustic attributes is a further impediment to analysis.

Integrated units. The nature of the attribute reflecting similarity between study and distractor words changes markedly. With the young adult, acoustic similarity is usually found to have little effect on recognition (e.g., Davis, 1967; Underwood & Freund, 1968), although the findings are not completely consistent (e.g., Buschke & Lenon, 1969). Young children are influenced by acoustic similarity between the study and distractor words (Bach & Underwood, 1970), but *S*s between the ages of 70 and 85 years are not (Hartley & Marshall, 1967).

The attributes which are most critical in influencing recognition performance when words are used are the associative attributes, and these attributes cannot be appropriately described by any particular similarity dimension. The processes by which the associative attributes are assumed to influence recognition tie directly into frequency theory. Therefore, the influence of some additional variables can best be discussed following the presentation of the extension of the theory.

Associative attributes and frequency

When a word is presented for learning, certain implicit associative responses (IARs) are assumed to occur. As a rough index of these IARs, word-association tables are normally used. The IAR occurs to the RR of the word presented, and when the IAR is a single word, it may be assumed to have a frequency of one in that situation. One may proceed to predictions concerning recognition performance by treating the IAR as if it were a word actually presented to *S*. Because not all *S*s make the same IAR to a given word, and because the data in word-association tables may not represent the frequencies of IARs which occur in any particular learning situation, the predictions must be of a gross nature.

If IARs occur as assumed, it should be possible to detect this by having *S* make frequency judgments. Judgments of situational frequency for words assumed to have occurred as IARs, but not actually presented, ought to be higher than judgments for words not presented and which were not IARs to any of the words presented. Leicht (1968) varied the number of words in a list which were presumed to produce the same IAR, there being one, three, and five such elicitors. The words representing these IARs were then given to *S* for frequency judgments along with control words. The results show that rated frequency increased directly as number of IAR elicitors increased. The increase was not great, and the absolute level of the judgments was far below that of words actually presented for varying frequencies. Nevertheless, the results are consonant with the notion that IARs occur and that they have properties similar to words actually presented.

There is another type of experiment which in a sense requires a frequency judgment from *S*. This is the running-recognition procedure described earlier. The *S* is presented with a long series of words, one at a time, and he must make a judgment for each word as to whether it had or had not occurred earlier in the series. If at some point in the series a word is presented which is assumed to have occurred earlier as an IAR, *S* should be more likely to say "yes" for this word than for a neutral word. A number of studies show that this is exactly what happens (e.g., Anisfeld & Knapp, 1968). Certain quantitative expectations have also been confirmed. If a low-frequency associate is chosen from word-association tables and assumed to be an IAR to its stimulus which comes earlier in the running-recognition series, the proportion of "yes" responses to it should be less than if it were a high-frequency associate. Data confirm this expectation (Marshall, Rouse, & Tarpy, 1969). It would also be expected that as number of different words presumed to elicit the same IAR increases, the likelihood of a "yes" error should increase. It does (Moates & Koplin, 1967).

It must be noted that the IAR can be a word which is a synonym of the word producing it. Some investigators have not found synonyms to be error-producing distractors on recognition tests (e.g., Mandler, Pearlstone, & Koopmans, 1969). According to the present formulation, a synonym should not be a source of error unless it occurred as an IAR to the word with which it is tested, or unless *S* uses secondary attributes in making decisions.

Interitem associations. When a word which is an IAR to a word presented for study is included in the recognition test (by any method), it is error-producing. However, assume that both a word and its IAR are included in the learning list. For example, suppose the words are HIGH and LOW, two words with strong bidirectional associative relationships. When HIGH is presented for study the IAR LOW should occur; when LOW is presented, HIGH should occur as the IAR. In effect, therefore, the frequency for both words is two and recognition based on a frequency discrimination should be better than for two words not associatively related. To the writer's knowledge, an experiment of this exact nature has not been done, but one by Rosenberg (1968) is a close approximation. He presented *S*s with either a passage in which there were strong associations among several words in the sentence or a passage in which such associations were weak. The critical words were then removed from the passage context, mixed with distractors, and a recognition test given. Recognition for the strongly associated words was better than recognition for the weakly associated ones.

Word frequency. Some studies have shown that recognition performance is poorer with high-frequency words than with low (e.g., Gorman, 1961). However, analytical data are not available to allow a determination of the locus of the effect. In terms of the present theory, the initial point of departure would be the fact that interitem associations are more frequent among a group of randomly chosen high-frequency words than among a group of randomly chosen low-frequency words. Therefore, probability of an IAR being another word in the list is greater for high-frequency words than for low.

As noted above, associations among the words presented for learning should facilitate recognition; associations among words presented for learning and words used as distractors should inhibit recognition performance. The appropriate analysis, therefore, appears to require a fourfold table in which distractor-word frequency is orthogonal to study-word frequency. According to the present formulation, the highest recognition scores should occur when high-frequency study words are tested with low-frequency distractors, and poorest recognition should occur under the high-high condition. For low-frequency study words, the frequency of the distractors is of little consequence. These expectations have been confirmed (Underwood & Freund, 1970d).

Incidental learning. Although there is not unanimous agreement among the number of studies available, the consensus is that recognition performance is uninfluenced by instructions associated with intentional and incidental learning. With regard to the present formulation, two matters are relevant. First, as noted earlier, storage of frequency information appears to be independent of intent to store. This obviously leads to the expectation that recognition should not be influenced by intent to learn if a frequency discrimination is fundamental in recognition learning. The second issue concerns IARs. It would not seem unreasonable to assume that one of the effects of instructions to learn would be the activation of associative attributes; thus, intentional learning may involve more IARs than incidental learning. If this is true, incidental and intentional recognition performance would be predicted by examining the effect of IARs in the particular situation employed for recognition, as discussed earlier. For example, if an IAR to a word presented for study is included as a distractor word on the test, more errors should be made to this word following intentional than following incidental instructions. There is some support for this expectation (Eagle & Leiter, 1964). However, there is some evidence against the idea that IAR production differs for intentional and incidental *S*s (Wallace, 1968), so expectations based on IAR differences may not be supported. In any event, based only on RR frequency as the dominant discriminative mechanism in recognition, no differences in recognition should be observed following intentional and incidental instructions provided that the incidental instructions lead to the production of the RRs.

Other variables. There are certain variables influencing recognition performance for which the frequency theory as thus far developed is not applicable. For example, recognition performance is better with concrete than with abstract words (e.g., Gorman, 1961), and pictures will yield higher scores than will words naming the pictures (e.g., Jenkins, Neale, & Deno, 1967). These effects may be in some way mediated by imagery differences (Paivio, 1969), which support (as secondary attributes) the frequency discrimination. It is possible that apparent frequency, with constant situational frequency, differs for concrete and abstract words, but no evidence is available concerning this possibility. In the case of a picture it is difficult to specify the RR which occurs and which could serve as the basis for the frequency discrimination, although recognition performance is very high for pictures (e.g., Shepard, 1967). Moreover, Bahrick and Boucher (1968) show that the relationship between the visual and verbal attributes of pictures has a certain degree of independence which is not easily interpreted. The ability to recall the name of a picture was unrelated to recognition performance on pictures of the object. Such facts do suggest, however, that the attributes of memory may be "arranged" differently for recognition and recall, and that conforms to the general thesis of this paper.

FORGETTING

Recognition scores will show decreases over time, which is to say that recognition memory shows long-term forgetting. If a frequency discrimination is dominant in recognition memory, such forgetting must mean there is a loss of the apparent frequency difference which produced the discrimination originally. There is some evidence that with the passage of time there is a gradual assimilation of situational frequency to background frequency (Underwood & Freund, 1970b). If this is true, it would account for certain facts in the forgetting of a discrimination. Low-frequency letter sequences should be forgotten more rapidly than high-frequency letter sequences (Turnage & Anderson, 1965). The background frequency gradually replaces situational frequency as a basis for responding, and such a tendency would influence low-frequency letter sequences more than high-frequency sequences. However, correlated evidence is needed concerning changes in apparent frequency with the passage of time and such evidence is not available. Nevertheless, it seems almost axiomatic that background frequency represents an accumulation of a great many situational frequencies which have lost their situational identities. The mechanism by which these are lost is unclear.

That interference paradigms will influence recognition of nonintegrated units has been demonstrated (e.g., Postman, 1952), and these results may be interpreted in the manner in which the testing effects were interpreted earlier in this paper. But, the evidence for interference paradigms does not allow a conclusion that a discrimination, such as represented in VD learning or recognition learning, follows the same laws of forgetting as represented in associative learning where recall is used to measure memory. Indeed, there is evidence that some fundamentally different mechanisms may be involved (e.g., Bower & Bostrom, 1968; Underwood & Freund, 1970b). The frequency attribute is believed to be one of these mechanisms.

FINAL COMMENTS AND CONCLUSIONS

A number of investigators have reported that in paired-associate learning the recognition of the stimulus as an appropriate list stimulus is propaedeutic to the recall of the response term (Asch, 1969; Martin, 1967; Rock, Lasker, & Simon, 1969). None of the evidence rules out the possibility that the stimulus-recognition response is based in part at least upon an associative attribute, namely, the association between the stimulus and response term. However, since it is easy to show that *S* can recognize the stimulus term without being able to produce the response, it is evident that recognition is not dependent upon the associative attribute. This is to say that there is no reason to believe that the recognition of the stimulus term is not dominated by the frequency attribute as discussed in this paper.

Perhaps a more critical question concerns the role of recognition in associative formation and the production of the response in paired-associate learning. Retrieval or production per se is, according to the present thinking, due to attributes other than frequency, attributes which take more trials to acquire than does the frequency discrimination. But, as others have pointed out, recognition may be involved in the selection of the response to be given. Two or more response terms may be retrieved in the presence of a given stimulus and *S* must choose the correct one from among the alternatives. Recognition memory may be involved in this choice, and if it is based on frequency, it is a contingent frequency—the situational frequency with which this particular response term has been paired with this particular stimulus term. Is such a mechanism reasonable? When mediators are not involved in associative formation it may be. Such a mechanism would seem to be particularly likely to be involved in the incidental learning of so-called associations in a VD task (e.g., Spear, Ekstrand, & Underwood, 1964). What has been called associative learning by contiguity may represent a contingent frequency discrimination.

A number of studies have examined the influence of recall on subsequent recognition. The studies are not in agreement, but the most typical finding is that recall produces a small decrement in subsequent recognition. This is a difficult situation for predicting a particular outcome by frequency theory in spite of the fact that the theory is clear concerning the factors involved. First, the theory must state that items which are recalled correctly will be recognized correctly more frequently than those not recalled. This follows from the fact that recalling an item adds at least one further frequency unit to it. The theory would also state that intrusions in recall would be sources of error in recognition if the intrusion is a distractor on the recognition test. There are two other sources of errors, but their likelihood is not known and therefore there is a lack of definitiveness in predictions. If during attempted recall *S* thinks of a word which was not in the list but does not give it in his protocol, it has situational frequency and, like an overt intrusion, may be a source of error if it occurs as a distractor on the recognition test. This possibility has been pointed out by Brown and Packham (1967). A further source of error would stem from IARs to the words recalled. If the IAR occurred both during the study trial and during recall, its situational frequency is higher with recall than without it and again, if it occurs as a distractor word, would have an increased probability of being selected.

It is apparent, therefore, that by the present theory the major negative effect of recall results from increased likelihood that certain distractors will be more error-producing on recognition following recall than without recall. The characteristics of the distractors become critical, and it seems probable that sets of distractors could be devised so that recall will facilitate subsequent recognition and other sets could be devised which will inhibit subsequent recognition. The available studies show both outcomes.

In summary, this essay has noted the sensitivity of the human organism to event frequency. Lower animals may be equally influenced, but the implications of this possibility have not been examined. It does not seem reasonable that the human sensitivity to event frequency should be irrelevant to learning and memory as studied in the laboratory. Therefore, this attribute of memory was put to work as an explanatory mechanism for recognition learning. It is to be hoped that it has not been overworked.

REFERENCES

Anisfeld, M., & Knapp, M. Association, synonymity, and directionality in false recognition. *Journal of Experimental Psychology*, 1968, *77*, 171–179.

Asch, S. E. A reformulation of the problems of associations. *American Psychologist*, 1969, *24*, 92–102.

Attneave, F. Psychological probability as a function of experienced frequency. *Journal of Experimental Psychology*, 1953, *46*, 81–86.

Bach, M. J., & Underwood, B. J. Developmental changes in memory attributes. *Journal of Educational Psychology*, 1970, *61*, 292–296.

Bahrick, H. P., & Boucher, B. Retention of visual and verbal codes of the same stimuli. *Journal of Experimental Psychology*, 1968, *78*, 417–422.

Bower, G. H., & Bostrom, A. Absence of within-list PI and RI in short-term recognition memory. *Psychonomic Science*, 1968, *10*, 211–212.

Brown, J., & Packham, D. W. The effect of prior recall on multiple response recognition. *Quarterly Journal of Experimental Psychology*, 1967, *19*, 356–361.

Buschke, H., & Lenon, R. Encoding homophones and synonyms for verbal discrimination and recognition. *Psychonomic Science*, 1969, *14*, 269–270.

Dale, H. C. A., & Baddeley, A. D. Remembering a list of two-digit numbers. *Quarterly Journal of Experimental Psychology*, 1966, *18*, 212–219.

Davis, G. A. Recognition memory for visually presented homophones. *Psychological Reports,* 1967, *20,* 227–233.

Eagle, M., & Leiter, E. Recall and recognition in intentional and incidental learning. *Journal of Experimental Psychology,* 1964, *68,* 58–63.

Ekstrand, B. R., Wallace, W. P., & Underwood, B. J. A frequency theory of verbal-discrimination learning. *Psychological Review,* 1966, *73,* 566–578.

Field, W. H., & Lachman, R. Information transmission (I) in recognition and recall as a function of alternatives (k). *Journal of Experimental Psychology,* 1966, *72,* 785–791.

Gorman, A. M. Recognition memory for nouns as a function of abstractness and frequency. *Journal of Experimental Psychology,* 1961, *61,* 23–29.

Hartley, J., & Marshall, I. S. Aging, recognition, and partial learning. *Psychonomic Science,* 1967, *9,* 215–216.

Hintzman, D. L. Recognition time: Effects of recency, frequency, and the spacing of repetitions. *Journal of Experimental Psychology,* 1969, *79,* 192–194. (a)

Hintzman, D. L. Apparent frequency as a function of frequency and the spacing of repetitions. *Journal of Experimental Psychology,* 1969, *80,* 139–145. (b)

Jenkins, J. R., Neale, D. C., & Deno, S. L. Differential memory for picture and word stimuli. *Journal of Educational Psychology,* 1967, *58,* 303–307.

Leicht, K. L. Recall and judged frequency of implicitly occurring words. *Journal of Verbal Learning and Verbal Behavior,* 1968, *7,* 918–923.

Mandler, G., Pearlstone, Z., & Koopmans, H. S. Effects of organization and semantic similarity on recall and recognition. *Journal of Verbal Learning and Verbal Behavior,* 1969, *8,* 410–423.

Marshall, J. F., Rouse, R. O. Jr., & Tarpy, R. M. Acoustic versus associative models of short-term memory coding. *Psychonomic Science,* 1969, *14,* 54–55.

Martin, E. Relation between stimulus recognition and paired-associate learning. *Journal of Experimental Psychology,* 1967, *74,* 500–505.

McGeoch, J. A. Forgetting and the law of disuse. *Psychological Review,* 1932, *39,* 352–370.

McNulty, J. A. Short-term retention as a function of method of measurement, recording time, and meaningfulness of the material. *Canadian Journal of Psychology,* 1965, *19,* 188–196.

Moates, D. R., & Koplin, J. H. Convergent associations in mediated generalization. *American Journal of Psychology,* 1967, *80,* 81–87.

Norman, D. A., & Waugh, N. C. Stimulus and response interference in recognition-memory experiments. *Journal of Experimental Psychology,* 1968, *78,* 551–559.

Paivio, A. Mental imagery in associative learning and memory. *Psychological Review,* 1969, *76,* 241–263.

Peixotto, H. E. Proactive inhibition in the recognition of nonsense syllables. *Journal of Experimental Psychology,* 1947, *37,* 81–91.

Postman, L. Choice behavior and the process of recognition. *American Journal of Psychology,* 1950, *63,* 576–583.

Postman, L. The generalization gradient in recognition memory. *Journal of Experimental Psychology,* 1951, *42,* 231–235.

Postman, L. Retroactive inhibition in recall and recognition. *Journal of Experimental Psychology,* 1952, *44,* 165–169.

Rock, I., Lasker, A., & Simon, J. Stimulus "generalization" as a process of recognition. *American Journal of Psychology*, 1969, *82*, 1–22.

Rosenberg, S. Associative facilitation in the recall and recognition of nouns embedded in connected discourse. *Journal of Experimental Psychology*, 1968, *78*, 254–260.

Shapiro, B. J. The subjective estimate of relative word frequency. *Journal of Verbal Learning and Verbal Behavior*, 1969, *8*, 248–251.

Shepard, R. N. Recognition memory for words, sentences, and pictures. *Journal of Verbal Learning and Verbal Behavior*, 1967, *6*, 156–163.

Shepard, R. N., & Teghtsoonian, M. Retention of information under conditions approaching a steady state. *Journal of Experimental Psychology*, 1961, *62*, 302–309.

Spear, N. S., Ekstrand, B. R., & Underwood, B. J. Association by contiguity. *Journal of Experimental Psychology*, 1964, *67*, 151–161.

Turnage, T. W., & Anderson, N. S. Letter-frequency and associative probability as determinants of learning and retention. *Journal of Verbal Learning and Verbal Behavior*, 1965, *4*, 463–468.

Underwood, B. J. Some correlates of item repetition in free-recall learning. *Journal of Verbal Learning and Verbal Behavior*, 1969, *8*, 83–94. (a)

Underwood, B. J. Attributes of memory. *Psychological Review*, 1969, *76*, 559–573. (b)

Underwood, B. J., & Freund, J. S. Errors in recognition learning and retention. *Journal of Experimental Psychology*, 1968, *78*, 55–63.

Underwood, B. J., & Freund, J. S. Relative frequency judgments and verbal-discrimination learning. *Journal of Experimental Psychology*, 1970, *83*, 279–285. (a)

Underwood, B. J., & Freund, J. S. The retention of a verbal discrimination. *Journal of Experimental Psychology*, 1970, *84*, 1–14. (b)

Underwood, B. J., & Freund, J. S. Testing effects in the recognition of words. *Journal of Verbal Learning and Verbal Behavior*, 1970, *9*, 117–125. (c)

Underwood, B. J., & Freund, J. S. Word frequency and short-term recognition memory. *American Journal of Psychology*, 1970, *83*, 343–351. (d)

Underwood, B. J., & Schulz, R. W. *Meaningfulness and verbal learning*. Philadelphia: Lippincott, 1960.

Wallace, W. P. Incidental learning: The influence of associative similarity and formal similarity in producing false recognitions. *Journal of Verbal Learning and Verbal Behavior*, 1968, *7*, 50–54.

Name Index

Numbers in italics denote entries in chapter reference sections.

Subject Index